Clinical Management of Alzheimer's Disease

Contributors

Deborah Berkley
Father Roger J. Brady
June Brown
Kathy J. Fabiszewski
Mary Glennon
Melody J. Hobbins
Phyllis Innis
Judith A. Jones
Josephine Karner
Donald C. Kern
John P. Larkin

Kathryn E. Lasch
Paula C. Lyon
Linda C. Niessen
Yvette L. Rheaume
Mary Ellen Riley
Anthony B. Sandoe
T.D. Sellers
Benjamin Seltzer
Rita A. Shapiro
Susan Shea
Ladislav Volicer
Mario C. Zocchi

Clinical Management of Alzheimer's Disease

Edited by

Ladislav Volicer, MD, PhD
Deputy Director
Geriatric Research Education Clinical Center

Kathy J. Fabiszewski, RN, MS
Gerontological Nurse Practitioner
Dementia Study Unit, Nursing Service, and Geriatric Research Education Clinical Center

Yvette L. Rheaume, RN, BSN
Nursing Unit Administrator
Dementia Study Unit, Nursing Service, and Geriatric Research Education Clinical Center

Kathryn E. Lasch, MSW, PhD
Medical Sociologist
Geriatric Research Education Clinical Center

Edith Nourse Rogers Memorial Veterans Hospital
Bedford, Massachusetts

AN ASPEN PUBLICATION®
Aspen Publishers, Inc.
1988
Rockville, Maryland
Royal Tunbridge Wells

Library of Congress Cataloging-in-Publication Data

Clinical Management of Alzheimer's disease.

"An Aspen publication."
Includes bibliographies and index.
1. Alzheimer's disease—Patients—Care.
2. Alzheimer's disease—Social aspects. I. Volicer,
Ladislav. [DNLM: 1. Alzheimer's Disease.
WM 220 C6415]
RC523.C57   1988   618.97'683   87-27549
ISBN: 0-87189-899-3

Copyright © 1988 by Aspen Publishers, Inc.
All rights reserved.

Aspen Publishers, Inc. grants permission for photocopying for personal or internal use, or for the personal or internal use of specific clients registered with the Copyright Clearance Center (CCC). This consent is given on the condition that the copier pay a $1.00 fee plus $.12 per page for each photocopy through the CCC for photocopying beyond that permitted by the U.S. Copyright Law. The fee should be paid directly to the CCC, 21 Congress St., Salem, Massachusetts 01970.
0-87189-899-3/88 $1.00 + .12.

This consent does not extend to other kinds of copying, such as copying for general distribution, for advertising or promotional purposes, for creating new collective works, or for resale. For information, address Aspen Publishers, Inc., 1600 Research Boulevard, Rockville, Maryland 20850.

Editorial Services: Ruth Bloom

Library of Congress Catalog Card Number: 87-27549
ISBN: 0-87189-899-3

Printed in the United States of America

2 3 4 5

To Phyllis Innis, R.N.

*A true nursing pioneer in the care of
Alzheimer's disease patients*

Table of Contents

Contributors	xi
Foreword	xiii
Preface	xv
Chapter 1—Epidemiology and Prevention of Alzheimer's Disease *Donald C. Kern*	1
Definitions	2
Epidemiology of Alzheimer's Disease	3
Prevention of Alzheimer's Disease	5
Ethics of Prevention of Alzheimer's Disease	10
Conclusions	11
Chapter 2—Management of the Outpatient with Alzheimer's Disease: An Interdisciplinary Team Approach *Benjamin Seltzer, John P. Larkin, and Kathy J. Fabiszewski*	13
Initial Evaluation	14
Follow-up Evaluation and Care	20
Conclusions	27
Chapter 3—Caring for the Family Caregivers *June Brown, Paula C. Lyon, and T.D. Sellers*	29
Caregiver Evaluation and Education	31
Problems and Intervention Strategies	32
Caregiver Counseling	36
Sexuality and Maternal Pathologic Bonding	37
Institutional Care	38
Impact of Death on Caregivers	40

Chapter 4—Economic Considerations in Alzheimer's Dementia............... 43
Kathryn E. Lasch

    Personal and Societal Costs of Alzheimer Dementia............... 43
    Current Financing Mechanisms for Care of Alzheimer Patients..... 45
    Home and Community Based Resources......................... 47
    Current Proposals to Fund Care for Alzheimer Dementia.......... 49
    Managing the Personal Costs of Alzheimer Dementia............. 50

Chapter 5—Legal Considerations in Alzheimer's Disease..................... 53
Anthony B. Sandoe

    Management of Property Interests................................. 54
    Preservation and Conservation of Property Interests.............. 62
    Clinical Management... 70
    Conclusions... 73

Chapter 6—Institution-Based Respite Care................................. 75
Yvette L. Rheaume, John P. Larkin, and Benjamin Seltzer

    Description of a Specific Inpatient Respite Program............... 76
    Family Attitudes about Respite Care.............................. 77
    Comprehensive Plan of Care..................................... 78

Chapter 7—Management of Advanced Alzheimer Dementia................... 87
*Kathy J. Fabiszewski, Mary Ellen Riley, Deborah Berkley,
  Josephine Karner, and Susan Shea*

    Overview of the Stages of the Disease Process.................... 88
    The Decision To Institutionalize.................................. 90
    Interdisciplinary Teamwork...................................... 90
    Philosophy of Care.. 91
    Treatment Goals... 92
    Management Issues.. 93
    Promoting Quality of Life.. 106
    Issues of Institutional Care....................................... 108
    Conclusions... 108

Chapter 8—Oral Health Care for Patients with Alzheimer's Disease......... 111
Judith A. Jones, Linda C. Niessen, Melody J. Hobbins, and Mario C. Zocchi

    Oral Problems and Their Risk Factors............................ 111
    Preventive Care... 115
    Personal Oral Hygiene... 116
    Professional Dental Care... 120
    Conclusions... 123
    Appendix 8-A: Fluoride and Saliva Substitutes................... 125

**Chapter 9—Management of Intercurrent Illnesses in Institutionalized
  Patients with Alzheimer's Dementia**......................... 127
Kathy J. Fabiszewski, Rita A. Shapiro, and Donald C. Kern

    Interdisciplinary Teamwork...................................... 128
    Determining the Extent of Appropriate Medical Care............. 130

The Therapeutic Plan...	131
Major Areas of Clinical Concern.................................	132
Appendix 9-A: Management Guidelines..........................	144

Chapter 10—Ethical Issues in the Treatment of Advanced Alzheimer Dementia: Hospice Approach.................................. 167
Ladislav Volicer, Yvette L. Rheaume, June Brown, Kathy J. Fabiszewski, and Roger J. Brady

Alzheimer's Disease As a Terminal Illness.......................	167
Decisions To Limit the Scope of Medical Care...................	168
Description of a Formal Hospice Approach Program.............	169
Appendix 10-A: Hospice Care Plan..............................	183

Chapter 11—Drugs Used in the Treatment of Alzheimer Dementia.......... 185
Ladislav Volicer

Drugs Used in the Early Stage of Alzheimer Dementia...........	185
Drugs Used in the Middle Stage of Alzheimer Dementia.........	192
Drugs Used in the Late Stage of Alzheimer Dementia............	196
Drugs Used in the Terminal Stage of Alzheimer Dementia........	198

Chapter 12—Education and Training of Interdisciplinary Team Members Caring for Alzheimer Patients............................... 201
Yvette L. Rheaume, Kathy J. Fabiszewski, June Brown, Phyllis Innis, Mary Glennon, Deborah Berkley, Susan Shea, and Ladislav Volicer

Need for a Specialty Care Unit.................................	203
Criteria for Staff Selection......................................	204
Orientation and Training..	205
Ongoing Staff Education..	208
Staff Support..	210
Retention Incentives...	213
Team Approach to Care of Alzheimer Patients...................	213
Program Implications for Therapeutic Recreation................	216
Therapeutic Recreation Goals and Objectives....................	217
Program Implications for Occupational Therapy.................	218
Maintaining Patient Dignity.....................................	220
Interdisciplinary Management of Challenging Behaviors..........	220
Facilitating Communication.....................................	221
Educating Additional Support Personnel........................	221
Appendix 12-A: Curriculum for Orientation of Professional Nurses to Alzheimer Dementia Caregiving in the Long-Term Care Facility..	223

Glossary...	225
Index...	239
About the Editors...	251

Contributors

Deborah Berkley, BSE
Therapeutic Recreation Specialist
Recreation Service and GRECC
E.N. Rogers Memorial Veterans Hospital
Bedford, Massachusetts

Father Roger J. Brady, M Div
Chief, Chaplain Service
E.N. Rogers Memorial Veterans Hospital
Bedford, Massachusetts

June Brown, LCSW
Family Studies Unit
Social Work Service and GRECC
E.N. Rogers Memorial Veterans Hospital
Bedford, Massachusetts

Kathy J. Fabiszewski, RN, MS
Gerontological Nurse Practitioner
Dementia Study Unit, Nursing Service, and GRECC
E.N. Rogers Memorial Veterans Hospital
Bedford, Massachusetts
Adjunct Clinical Faculty and Instructor
University of Lowell, College of Health Professions
Lowell, Massachusetts

Mary Glennon, RN
Nursing Unit Administrator
Dementia Study Unit, Nursing Service and GRECC
E.N. Rogers Memorial Veterans Hospital
Bedford, Massachusetts

Melody J. Hobbins, DMD
Director, Geriatric Dental Program
Veterans Administration Medical Center
Durham, North Carolina
Assistant Professor, University of North Carolina,
  School of Dentistry
Chapel Hill, North Carolina

Phyllis Innis, RN
Nursing Unit Administrator
Dementia Study Unit, Nursing Service, and
  GRECC
E.N. Rogers Memorial Veterans Hospital
Bedford, Massachusetts

Judith A. Jones, DDS
Director
Dental Geriatric Fellowship Program
E.N. Rogers Memorial Veterans Hospital
Bedford, Massachusetts
Assistant Professor, Harvard School of Dental
  Medicine
Boston, Massachusetts

Josephine Karner, RN
Nursing Unit Administrator
Dementia Study Unit, Nursing Service
  and GRECC
E.N. Rogers Memorial Veterans Hospital
Bedford, Massachusetts

Donald C. Kern, MD, MPH
Associate Director for Program
  Evaluation/Education, GRECC
E.N. Rogers Memorial Veterans Hospital
Bedford, Massachusetts
Assistant Professor, Boston University School of
  Medicine, and Boston University School of
  Public Health
Boston, Massachusetts

John P. Larkin, MSW
Social Work Service and GRECC
E.N. Rogers Memorial Veterans Hospital
Bedford, Massachusetts

Kathryn E. Lasch, MSW, PhD
Medical Sociologist, GRECC
E.N. Rogers Memorial Veterans Hospital
Bedford, Massachusetts
Research Associate, University Professors Program
Boston, University
Boston, Massachusetts

Paula C. Lyon, EdM
Psychologist
Family Studies Unit, GRECC
E.N. Rogers Memorial Veterans Hospital
Bedford, Massachusetts

Linda C. Niessen, DMD, MPH
Director
Geriatric Dental Program
Veterans Administration Medical Center
Perry Point, Maryland
Clinical Assistant Professor
University of Maryland, School of Dentistry
Baltimore, Maryland

Yvette L. Rheaume, RN, BSN
Nursing Unit Administrator
Dementia Study Unit, Nursing Service and GRECC
E.N. Rogers Memorial Veterans Hospital
Bedford, Massachusetts

Mary Ellen Riley, RD
Dietitian
Dementia Study Unit, Dietetic Service and GRECC
E.N. Rogers Memorial Veterans Hospital
Bedford, Massachusetts

Anthony B. Sandoe, JD
Professor of Law and Associate Director
Center for Continuing Professional Development
Suffolk University Law School
Boston, Massachusetts

T.D. Sellers, MD
Director
Family Study Unit, GRECC
E.N. Rogers Memorial Veterans Hospital
Bedford, Massachusetts
Assistant Professor of Psychiatry, Boston University
  School of Medicine
Director, Psychopharmacology Clinical
  Study Unit
Boston University Medical Center,
  Boston, Massachusetts

Benjamin Seltzer, MD
Associate Clinical Director
GRECC
E.N. Rogers Memorial Veterans Hospital
Bedford, Massachusetts
Associate Professor of Neurology and
  Psychiatry
Boston University School of Medicine,
  Lecturer in Neurology, Harvard Medical
  School
Boston, Massachusetts

Rita Shapiro, DO
Section Chief
Neurology Service
Hines Memorial Veterans Hospital
Chicago, Illinois

Susan Shea, OTR
Occupational Therapist
Hampton, New Hampshire

Ladislav Volicer, MD, PhD
Deputy Director
GRECC
E.N. Rogers Memorial Veterans Hospital
Bedford, Massachusetts
Professor of Pharmacology and Psychiatry
Assistant Professor of Medicine
Boston University School of Medicine
Boston, Massachusetts

Mario Zocchi, DDS
Assistant Chief
Dental Service
E.N. Rogers Memorial Veterans Hospital
Bedford, Massachusetts
Clinical Instructor
Harvard School of Dental Medicine
Boston, Massachusetts

Foreword

Almost at once, Alzheimer's disease seems to have become everybody's business. It is therefore mine as well as yours and I should be neither bemused nor surprised at the editors' request of me for this foreword. After all, mastery of the subject based on our present knowledge does not take long to acquire and personal experience with the disease is difficult to avoid in current medical practice. But my most authentic credentials are similar to those of other senior academic physicians of this century who have experienced task force operations by the medical community to combat a devastating disease. The exhortation and support of the public to do so is now ringing in our ears with the same importunate note that characterized the outcry against rheumatic fever, poliomyelitis, tuberculosis, and other scourges of the youth of our population.

Having all but conquered many of these medical disasters, the strange current twist of medical fate is the blighting of the promise of a healthy life that can extend with increasing frequency into the 70s, 80s, and even 90s by a condition that robs us of our very personhood in old age, just when we should be enjoying its full glory.

The best response of medical professionals to the challenge of Alzheimer's disease is epitomized in this timely volume. While searching feverishly for an explanation of the cause of this mysterious disease of the brain with the aid of all of our research disciplines, the immediate burden of care of the victims of Alzheimer's disease falls on the least developed resources of our health care system—home care and nursing home care for the demented. Such care requires the support not only of an interdisciplinary team but also of health care professionals of unusual empathy, maturity, and dedication. When such team members are also well equipped to study and teach optimal strategies for care that stem from their extensive experience, their advice and counsel can be invaluable to afflicted patients, families, and professional colleagues.

All aspects of care, including caring for the family caregivers and the social, economic, and political priorities of public care, are addressed in this book. In addition, the role of hospice care is evaluated and the agonizing ethical and legal dilemmas that confront us at the end of life when the quality of the person is gone are discussed realistically.

It is fair to say, then, that this book is a lesson in medical care in its most poignant and challenging form. Alzheimer's disease is the paradigm, and, like other human tragedies, it is capable of bringing out the best in us.

Gene H. Stollerman, M.D.
Distinguished Physician
Veterans Administration
Professor of Medicine
Boston University School of Medicine
Editor, *Journal of the
American Geriatric Society*

Preface

This book originates from 10 years of experience in caring for patients suffering from dementia of the Alzheimer type at the Geriatric Research Education Clinical Center (GRECC) of the E.N. Rogers Memorial Veterans Hospital in Bedford, Massachusetts. GRECC is one of several centers established by the Veterans Administration to perform basic and clinical research on various aspects of aging. From its inception, the primary emphasis of our GRECC has been the investigation of Alzheimer dementia. Through this work we have come to recognize the needs of Alzheimer victims and their families and have developed the program that forms the foundation of this book.

Many people have participated in the development of this program. In addition to the contributors to this book, we would like to acknowledge contributions of former GRECC Directors Ira Sherwin, MD and Michael Malone, MD; former GRECC Staff Members Thomas Walshe, III, MD, Howard Hermann, MD, and Mary Howell, MD, PhD; former GRECC Nurse Coordinator Donna Campbell, RN; former Geriatric Fellows Thomas Moorehead, MD, Edward Kaye, MD, Harold Schiff, MD, Elliott Hurwitz, MD, Kirk Nelson, MD, Judith Wohlgethan, MD, Adam Sulkowski, MD, Gerald Indorf, MD, Rogelio Alarcon, MD, Larry Herz, MD, Konrad Mark, MD, and Frederick Moolten, MD; former GRECC Clinical Unit Social Worker Shelton Hogan; and all staff members from Nursing, Rehabilitation Medicine, Recreation, Dietetic, and Chaplain Services who cared for our patients. We would also like to thank Chief of Staff Edgar Cathcart, MD, DSc, Chief of Medicine Robert Freeburn, MD, and Director of GRECC Richard Fine, PhD for their support of our program and Elaine Ratute, Priscilla Johnson, and Karen Anderson for their administrative support.

We would like to dedicate this book to all those who are touched by the tragedy of Alzheimer's disease. We hope that it may help them to cope with their daily stresses and to realize the importance of their work. Caring for the Alzheimer victim is often a thankless task, because the victim is unable to express his or her appreciation and the society does not reward and recognize the contribution of caregivers. Therefore, the interdisciplinary team approach is important not only for the patients but also for the caregivers because it establishes a support network for everybody involved. We believe that interdisciplinary teams provide superior care for Alzheimer victims and increase the job satisfaction of caregivers. This approach might help us to cope with the increased number of Alzheimer victims until the disease can be cured or prevented.

Ladislav Volicer
Kathy J. Fabiszewski
Yvette L. Rheaume
Kathryn E. Lasch
February 1988

CHAPTER 1

Epidemiology and Prevention of Alzheimer's Disease

Donald C. Kern

Alzheimer's disease was first described in 1906 by the German physician Alois Alzheimer. The clinical features of the disease have a gradual but relentless onset and include impairment of recent memory, disorientation, confabulations, and retrogressive loss of remote memories.[1] Over time, reasoning ability, concentration, speech, and handwriting degenerate. In the late stages patients can deteriorate to a vegetative state.

No specific diagnostic test exists for Alzheimer's disease. During life, the diagnosis is clinical, to be confirmed only in retrospect by postmortem examination. Thus, acceptance of the clinical diagnosis should occur only after careful and, in some cases, repeated exclusion of other possible causes of Alzheimer's signs and symptoms. Even then, diagnosis by experts is still only 80% accurate.[2]

Professionals in the fields of preventive medicine and public health have had difficulty dealing with Alzheimer's disease. For example, in the *Monthly Vital Statistics Report* published by the National Center for Health Statistics, dementia is not considered to be an independent, reportable cause of death, at least in the same sense as cancer, cardiovascular disease, and infectious diseases. Yet dementia is estimated by workers in the field to be the underlying cause of death in 70,000 to 100,000 U.S. residents per year, which would make dementia the fourth or fifth highest cause of death in the United States.[3]

Since the etiology of Alzheimer's disease remains unknown, the identification of risk factors has been very difficult. A discussion of studies of possible risk factors is presented in this chapter. First, however, it is important to define dementia as it relates to Alzheimer's disease and to present other definitions needed for an understanding of epidemiology and prevention. The current state of epidemiologic knowledge about Alzheimer's disease is then reviewed, along with a detailed discussion of several recent findings. The latter part of the chapter is a discussion of the precepts of preventive medicine as they relate to Alzheimer's disease, to show that there are indeed many aspects of this condition that can be positively influenced by the health care system.

Definitions

The word *dementia* refers to any state of decreased mental ability. Years ago, dementia was thought to be a natural consequence of aging. Because of this, different names were applied to dementias based on patient age at disease onset (presenile vs. senile). If a dementia of unexplained etiology had a clinical onset before the age of 65, it was labeled Alzheimer's disease. If a dementia of unexplained etiology occurred after the age of 65, it was labeled senile dementia and considered a consequence of age-induced "hardening of the arteries."

In recent years research has revealed that pathologic findings are similar in patients who were classified as having Alzheimer's disease because dementia started before they reached the age of 65 and in patients who were classified as having senile dementia because they became demented after the age of 65. To reflect this similarity, the term *dementia of the Alzheimer type* is often used. Some authors even differentiate between a presenile and a senile form of this disease.[4] However, the term *Alzheimer's disease* is commonly used as a diagnosis regardless of the age at onset of dementia. In this book the terms *Alzheimer's disease*, *Alzheimer dementia*, and *dementia of the Alzheimer type* will be used interchangeably to describe patients suffering from dementia of the Alzheimer type regardless of the age at onset.

Primary degenerative dementia is a more global term used in the third edition of the *Diagnostic and Statistical Manual of Mental Disorders (DSM-III)* to refer to a dementia for which no specific cause can be found. Since Alzheimer's disease comprises the vast majority of primary degenerative dementia, the term *primary degenerative dementia* also will be assumed to refer to Alzheimer's disease. For purposes of this book, then, an *Alzheimer patient* will refer to any person who is diagnosed as having Alzheimer's disease, dementia of the Alzheimer type, or primary degenerative dementia.

Other forms of dementia include multi-infarct dementia (patchy deterioration with evidence of cerebral and/or systemic vascular disease), mixed forms of primary degenerative and multi-infarct dementia, and secondary dementias (e.g., multiple sclerosis), some of which may be reversible (e.g., pernicious anemia). These forms of dementia need to be differentiated from Alzheimer's disease.

Epidemiology is the science concerned with studying the distribution and determinants of disease in populations. Distribution is affected by factors that influence why one person becomes diseased while another remains healthy. Examples of factors include age, gender, and occupation. Epidemiologists tend to apply their science to a limited number of factors involving a large population, rather than to an exhaustive analysis of a few individuals.

Preventive medicine is concerned with activities that help avoid the development or exacerbation of physical, mental, or emotional disease or injury. As such, there are three levels of prevention: primary, secondary, and tertiary. *Primary prevention* focuses on not permitting a disease process to start. Examples are immunizations against infectious diseases and the wearing of seat belts in automobiles. *Secondary prevention* comprises the early detection of a disease process with intervention to either block or at least retard the development of clinical features. Examples are screening programs such as screening for cervical cancer using the Papanicolaou smear technique. *Tertiary prevention* implies the avoidance of complications and premature deterioration in an established disease condition. Examples include proper bladder care in patients with spinal cord injuries and cardiac rehabilitation programs for patients who have had myocardial infarctions.

Risk factors are those determinants of disease that are associated with a statistically increased likelihood of acquiring or exacerbating disease. Risk factors can be physical (e.g., toxins), social (e.g., loss of a job), behavioral (e.g., smoking), or inherited (e.g., hemoglobinopathies). Although associated with a disease, risk factors are not necessarily causative agents of the disease. For example, a risk factor for diarrhea may be eating unwashed fruit, while the cause of the diarrhea is a bacterial pathogen.

The effect of exposure to risk factors can be reported in two ways, as *attributable risk* and as *relative risk*. Attributable risk is the numerical difference between the amount of risk faced by an exposed person and by an unexposed person. Relative risk is the ratio of these same two factors. Suppose for a hypothetical condition, five people per million in the general population contract a disease, but ten people per million in a population exposed to a risk factor contract the disease. The attributable risk of that risk factor would be five per million, while the relative risk would be two.

Risk estimates are typically presented as relative risk alone, but attributable risk is also important. An exposure leading to a rare form of dementia may have a high relative risk but a low attributable risk. This means that while that exposure has a powerful influence on one person, controlling it will not have much effect on the overall incidence of dementia in the population. By contrast, an exposure leading to a common form of dementia may have a low relative risk but a high attributable risk. In this case, while the exposure is not as powerful, controlling it will have greater impact on the population.

Epidemiology of Alzheimer's Disease

Population estimates for the United States project a great increase in the group most likely to develop Alzheimer's disease. In 1978, 24.1 million Americans were 65 years old or older, while 2.5 million were 85 years old or older. By the year 2000, this last group may be as large as 6.7 million.[5] Since the prevalence of Alzheimer's disease increases with age, this general population trend implies a marked increase in the number of people with Alzheimer dementia over the next decade.

The best estimate of the prevalence of Alzheimer's disease in a population has been reported in a study from Finland, in which a stratified cluster sample of 8,000 Finnish citizens was selected to yield an age- and gender-proportional cross-section of the population.[6] Carried out from November 1977 to August 1980, the study consisted of a health interview by a public health nurse and a health examination by a physician. Since the diagnosis of dementia might be questioned, the accuracy of classification was confirmed by further review of a subsample by a neurologist and psychologist as well as by additional diagnostic tests as indicated.

The prevalence of all forms of dementia was 1.8% in the population over age 30. This rose to 6.7% for the group aged 65 or over and 17.3% for the group aged 85 or over. Focusing specifically on primary degenerative dementia, the prevalence for the population over age 30 was 0.9%, rising to 3.6% for the population over age 65 and 14.8% for the population aged 85 or more. Primary degenerative dementia represented 50% of all dementia found, with multi-infarct and combined dementia adding another 39%. Only 11% of the dementia was secondary, and much of this was not readily reversible (i.e., post-traumatic encephalopathy, sequelae of encephalitis, and multiple sclerosis). The pattern of types of dementia also varied by age. In the group aged 30 to 64, only 12% of dementia was of the primary degenerative type. This compares with 40% in the group aged 65 to 74, 59% in the group aged 75 to 84, and 86% in the group aged 85 or over. Gender differences were also noted. For all dementia in people 65 years of age or older, the prevalence was 6.2% in men and 6.9% in women. In those aged 85 and over, this increased to 11.6% in men and 20% in women. The gender differences are even more striking in relation to primary degenerative dementia. While in the group aged 65 to 74 the prevalence was 1.8% for men and 1.6% for women, for the group aged 75 to 84 the prevalence for men and women was 4.5% and 7.3%, respectively, and for the group aged 85 and older, the prevalence was 7.7% and 18.2%, respectively. Almost three fourths of all primary degenerative dementia was found in women.

An alternative to conducting a relatively small sample of a large population is to do a complete survey of a small population. Such a prevalence study was conducted on the population of a city in Finland.[7] In this study the entire city was canvassed to identify people possibly having dementia. All suspect patients were examined by a neurologist to confirm the diagnosis. Since patients with unrecognized dementia were not examined, the prevalence estimate may be biased toward a lower value than is true. For primary degenerative dementia, Molsa and colleagues[7] found a prevalence of 2.0% for the population over age 65 and of 6.3% for the population over age 85. A preponderance of identified cases in women was also noted.

Maule and colleagues[8] conducted a random sample of the population over age 65 in northern Edinburgh, Scotland. They found a prevalence of dementia of 3%. More recently, Folstein and colleagues[9] surveyed a random sample of adults residing in eastern Baltimore. Like Molsa, they found a prevalence of Alzheimer's disease of 2.0% in people aged 65 and older. Unfortunately, they did not report gender-specific rates. In other, older studies in the literature, prevalence estimates of dementia in people over age 65 have ranged from 1.0% to 6.2%.[7]

Recently Pfeffer and colleagues[10] reported on a white, middle class, southern California retirement community. Surveying 817 randomly selected individuals, they found an overall prevalence of dementia of 15.3% for the population over age 65, and a prevalence of 35.8% for the population over age 80. Further, they found a higher prevalence of Alzheimer's disease in men (19.1%) than women (13.1%). However, these values include a very large proportion of subjects classified as "questionable" or with "mild dementia." If case finding is limited only to those individuals with "moderate" or worse dementia, the prevalence estimate falls to 2.2% overall.

The authors speculate that their case-finding methods may have been more sensitive than others, and their highly educated population may be more likely to exhibit recognizable signs of early disease. Unfortunately, although some patients were re-examined almost four years later, no data were reported on whether questionable or mild cases advanced in severity and thus changed prevalence figures for more severe disease. The authors urge appropriate caution in any extrapolation from their data to other populations.

Incidence, the rate at which new dementia occurs, is less often reported because its calculation requires repeated examinations of the same population. By conducting a 5-year follow-up examination on the same sample population, Maule and colleagues[8] found an annual incidence of 0.4% in men and 1.4% in women over age 65. Nilsson and co-workers,[11] looking at people in their seventh decade, found incidences of senile Alzheimer dementia of 0.4% in men and 0.3% in women aged 70 to 75, and 1.8% in men and 1.1% in women aged 75 to 79. Secondary dementias were identified in 16% of the population with dementia, but Nilsson and co-workers did not report if any were potentially reversible. There were no statistical differences as to any gender relationship, but a suggestion was reported that men may become demented and die at an earlier age than women.

The variety of findings cited previously are caused by many factors, which have been excellently summarized by Gruenberg.[12] For example, age composition and population characteristics affected by migration must be considered as reasons for finding different results in different populations. Consistent diagnostic criteria need to be employed among studies to ensure comparability. Variations in the intensity of case-finding may have a major effect on measured rates. Rates may be relatively unstable when the investigator has a fairly large number of diagnostic categories so that the total number of subjects in any one category is small. By categorizing some cognitive impairment as "normal with age," rather than being recognized as of disease, age-specific rates may be inappropriately reduced as age increases. Finally, comparing studies from different eras will be difficult, since over time diagnoses are made earlier in the natural history of the disease and people with the diagnosis survive longer, both factors that may lead to increasing prevalence rates.

Prevention of Alzheimer's Disease

Primary Prevention

Primary prevention is that form of prevention that attempts to intervene before a disease process begins. In order to accomplish this, practitioners usually need to understand the cause of a disease process. In the absence of understanding of causation, a practitioner may also rely on risk factors, which are associated in some unproven but highly suggestive causal way with the disease. Thus, to practice primary prevention in Alzheimer's disease, one needs to first identify causes and risk factors that can be influenced in some positive way.

As noted from the studies already cited, the primary risk factor for Alzheimer's disease is age. As age increases, especially over age 75, the prevalence and incidence of Alzheimer's disease greatly increases. Since the most rapidly growing segment of the U.S. population is the group over age 85, this risk factor will play an important and growing role in this population segment. Another major risk factor is gender, with most studies showing a preponderance of women with Alzheimer's disease. However, there are more elderly women than men, elderly women are more likely to live alone, and women are more likely to see a physician who may make the diagnosis, so that the magnitude of the gender difference may be subject to more error than the risk factor of age.

Genetics has been associated with Alzheimer's disease in that Down's syndrome is a clear risk factor for development of the condition.[2] Sporadic cases of families with Alzheimer's disease inherited in an autosomal dominant pattern have also been documented, but it is not clear how either of these special cases of genetic risk relates to the general population.

Schweber[13] and Delabar and associates[14] have reported finding a triploid sequence of DNA on chromosome 21 that appears to be related to Alzheimer's disease. Schweber found this triplication in all of 15 Alzheimer patients studied, including 4 with post-mortem confirmation of Alzheimer's disease by neuropathologic examination. By contrast, all of 12 control subjects (10 adults lacking any signs of Alzheimer's disease and 2 with age-matched normal brains) did not show this triplication. Delabar and associates found the same results comparing 11 normal subjects with 3 Alzheimer patients. These exciting early results still require confirmation, especially to determine to what extent the presence of the DNA triplication in healthy people is a risk factor for the development of Alzheimer's disease and are disputed by other investigators.[15-17] Testing for the triploid genetic material may become an important screening test for Alzheimer's disease. Such a screening test might permit meaningful genetic counseling as well as identifying populations at risk with whom innovative primary preventive strategies might be employed.

Another area of suggested risk is that of geographic location. However, this potential risk factor has been poorly studied. Certain isolated groups, such as the Chamorro people of Guam,[18] have a dementia that resembles Alzheimer's disease but with very high prevalence rates. Differences based on geography may be attributable to varying exposure to environmental influences that are in some way geographically limited. Possibilities that have been raised, for example, are levels of dietary intake of elements such as calcium and aluminum. No geographic factors that affect larger and less isolated population groups have been reported.

Race may also be a mild risk factor. Schoenberg and colleagues[19] surveyed an entire rural county in Mississippi. Case finding was limited to severe dementia in people over age 40. Half of the dementia found was classified as Alzheimer's disease. Controlling for age and gender, these investigators found a higher prevalence rate of Alzheimer's disease for blacks than whites. For all women studied, the prevalence was 0.52% in whites and 0.74% in blacks; for men, the values were 0.26% and 0.41%, respectively. The greatest difference for all types of dementia occurred in the age group 70 to 79. In these septuagenarians, white women had a prevalence of dementia of 1.4% compared with 2.5% for black women. For men, the respective values were 1.3% and 2.1%. Statistical significance was not reported. The most important aspect of this study, while suggesting a risk factor, is in confirming that Alzheimer's disease is not limited to northern Europeans.

The one risk factor that may be approached in a program of prevention is that of antecedent head trauma. French and co-workers[20] reported on a case-control study conducted in a Veterans Administration hospital. Although no occupational exposure or allergic conditions showed any statistical association, patients were more likely to have experienced head trauma prior to developing dementia of the Alzheimer type than controls. This finding was also noted in a different case-control study by Heyman and co-workers.[21] The head trauma reported by these authors is different from the trauma leading to dementia pugilistica.

Several other conditions have been suggested as risk factors but have not been well supported in the literature. Maternal age has been suggested as a risk factor for Alzheimer's disease.[22] This idea is reasonable given the relationship between maternal age and Down's syndrome, and between Down's syndrome and Alzheimer's disease. However, a case-control study of Alzheimer patients with spouses of Alzheimer and Parkinson patients serving as controls did not demonstrate any association between maternal age and Alzheimer's disease.[23] No consistent pattern among cases as maternal age increased was noted either.

Aluminum exposure has received much publicity as a possible risk factor for Alzheimer's disease. Certainly, dialysis dementia has been associated with the aluminum content of the dialysis water supply[24] and aluminum in higher concentration is found in neurofibrillary tangles in patients with Alzheimer's disease. However, no studies have been able to establish any causal link. Indeed, studies among people with a high occupational exposure to aluminum have not shown increased incidence of Alzheimer dementia.[5] Thus, aluminum exposure is not considered a risk factor for Alzheimer's disease at the present time.

Lower socioeconomic status has been proposed as yet another risk factor for Alzheimer dementia.[5] However, studies that have reported this often rely on questionnaires that bias against people of lower socioeconomic status. In the Mississippi study,[19] blacks and whites in a rural county were of equivalent socioeconomic status, although blacks had higher rates of dementia. In the Veterans Administration study,[20] patients actually had statistically significantly more years of education than hospital controls and no difference in socioeconomic status with neighborhood controls.

Antecedent thyroid disease has also been suggested as a risk factor.[21] This risk was found in a group of relatively young (average age of 61) women. However, the same finding could not be confirmed in the Veterans Administration study.[20] One possible explanation is that antecedent thyroid disease is a gender-specific risk factor. Further work is needed to either confirm or refute this hypothesis.

The previous discussion shows that more research is needed to identify risk factors for Alzheimer's disease that can be influenced by primary prevention programs. Certainly, the reduction of occupational and recreational head trauma may have some effect on Alzheimer's disease rates, but the immediate gains of those programs will probably have much greater impact than any long-term effect on the incidence of dementia. It is hoped that data from ongoing longitudinal studies and multicenter case-control studies will shed some badly needed light in this area.

Secondary Prevention

Secondary prevention assumes that the disease process has already begun but has not as yet been diagnosed. Therefore, a correct diagnosis must be made at the earliest opportunity in order to more effectively treat, if not cure, the disease. In a program of secondary prevention, early treatment is assumed to have a positive effect on the disease process.

When a disease process first begins, it is often undetectable by any diagnostic test and any symptoms that would make a patient aware of it are lacking. Furthermore, in the course of the disease, there may be a period when the patient is asymptomatic but the disease could now be diagnosed if a screening test were used. If not diagnosed, the disease continues to progress until symptoms appear. Some time after this the patient comes to medical attention and the disease is finally diagnosed.

Secondary prevention involves making the diagnosis at some time before the diagnosis would be made in the natural course of events. The period between the preventive diagnosis and the usual diagnosis is referred to as the lead time. The primary desire to practice secondary prevention is to maximize this lead time so that effective therapeutic intervention may be implemented.

However, as is discussed in Chapter 2, no curative regimen exists for the treatment of Alzheimer dementia once the diagnosis has been made. The underlying disease process will progress over time despite all presently available interventions. Thus, there is no current therapeutic benefit in making a presymptomatic diagnosis of Alzheimer's disease. Since the genetics of Alzheimer's disease are still being elucidated, there is no advantage to early diagnosis in familial forms of the disease, since meaningful genetic counseling cannot yet be done.

The philosophy of secondary prevention can nevertheless be applied to Alzheimer's disease in a limited form. Once symptoms have appeared, accurate diagnosis, especially in an attempt to find reversible causes of dementia, becomes the goal of secondary prevention. If a reversible dementing process has become symptomatic, uncritical acceptance of a diagnosis of Alzheimer's disease may delay and sometimes stop entirely the chance of clinical improvement. Thus, secondary prevention, by trying to identify treatable causes of dementia, remains of great importance in Alzheimer's disease.

Numerous authors have detailed diagnostic strategies for patients presenting with dementia, including a task force of the National Institute on Aging.[25] A detailed review of the diagnosis of dementia is outside the scope of this chapter. Several comments on reversible dementia are useful in the context of secondary prevention, however.

The prevalence of reversible dementia in the general population is not clear. The prevalence studies cited earlier seem to indicate that the vast majority of dementia is either Alzheimer or multi-infarct dementia and so not reversible. Of course, recognized reversible dementia should be treated and so might not be found in a cross-sectional prevalence study. Only unrecognized reversible dementia would be catalogued, and so prevalence estimates might imply an underestimate of the true incidence of reversible dementia. A major consideration for the likelihood of finding reversible dementia is the age of the patient. Although Beck and colleagues[26] claim that up to 20% of patients may have reversible illness, Barker[27] points out that most of these cases occur in groups with an average age of 58 to 66. In older people in whom the prevalence of Alzheimer's disease is greater, the prevalence of reversible dementia is probably 10% or less.

In practicing secondary prevention, four diagnoses of potentially reversible dementia are most common to find and certainly should not be missed: (1) drug effects, (2) hypothyroidism and other metabolic abnormalities, (3) mass lesions of the central nervous system, and (4) depression.[28] The ingestion of drugs should be considered both based on their reported effects on cognition as well as on their ubiquity. Thus, cimetidine and sedative hypnotic drugs are suspect specifically because of their side-effect profile. However, although effects on mentation are less common in their drug profile, antihypertensives, because of their widespread use in the elderly, also may be responsible for a significant proportion of drug-induced cognitive problems.

Hypoglycemia, hyponatremia, hypothyroidism, and hyperparathyroidism are all easy to screen for and not rare in the elderly. Mass lesions, especially subdural hematoma in patients on anticoagulation, should be sought in a diagnostic evaluation. Depression affecting cognition but without any other form of dementia may occur in up to 8% of patients being evaluated for cognitive problems. Although the previously mentioned four diagnoses are most likely to be found, other reversible causes of dementia also exist. Thus, careful, systematic, and, in the event of a negative first evaluation, repetitive diagnostic examinations are certainly warranted in the practice of secondary prevention of Alzheimer's disease.

Tertiary Prevention

Taking actions that ameliorate an incurable condition or delay the clinical progression of a disease process in a compassionate fashion is the hallmark of tertiary prevention. What is being prevented is the premature expression of a clinical disease process that will eventually occur. Also involved in tertiary prevention is the primary and secondary prevention of concomitant diseases that may exacerbate the original disease process. Tertiary prevention, in sum, comprises much of the practice of chronic care medicine.

Some conditions, although bothersome, do not have any effect on life expectancy. This is probably not the case with dementia. In an interesting study, Vitaliano and colleagues[3] performed logistic regression to test whether certain factors were predictive of mortality. They used data from patients in New York City and repeated the analysis using data from patients in Tokyo. Controlling for gender, age, and functional status, they found that the presence of chronic dementia was an independent predictor of mortality. Over a 4-year period, women with dementia had an 81% greater chance of dying than women without dementia, while the corresponding figure for men was 43%. Gender was the most powerful predictor, explaining the greatest amount of difference in mortality, followed by age and then dementia. Functional status was not an independent predictor of mortality. In addition, Seltzer and Sherwin[4] have shown a shortening of relative survival time the earlier in life that Alzheimer's disease becomes evident.

Given that Alzheimer dementia itself shortens life expectancy, tertiary prevention encourages the recognition and control of other conditions that may affect the quality of these fewer remaining years. Since the majority of Alzheimer patients are elderly, it is reasonable to assume that other chronic illnesses may be present. Indeed, in one series by Larson and associates,[29] fully half of the patients presenting for a dementia evaluation were found to have other undiagnosed chronic and acute medical illnesses that were believed to contribute in an important manner to the patient's cognitive dysfunction.

It is vitally important to remember that while the pathology of Alzheimer's disease may progress in a systematic manner, the clinical picture is quite varied and that functional ability can be maintained on a very even level even if the pathologic process is advancing. Clinicians caring for Alzheimer's patients should remain active in giving care and not prematurely surrender responsibility. Gruenberg[12] has stated the following:

> Neither loss in cognitive functioning nor decline in the activities of daily living progresses inexorably regardless of treatment. Loss of brain substance and the associated decline in testable cognitive functioning will become more manifest if anemia is permitted to develop, if nutrition is neglected, and if fecal impactions are missed. While in the end the patient with senile dementia will die, the same is true of the clinician. The object of care is not only to influence when the patient will die, but mainly to preserve comfort, a sense of dignity, and a maximum level of functioning for as long as possible.

This precept is especially important during the early stages of the disease.

In caring for Alzheimer patients, Blass[2] cites four major areas of concern: (1) medical, (2) pharmacologic, (3) behavioral, and (4) social. Medical care involves the treatment of other chronic and acute illnesses to which the Alzheimer patient is still susceptible. Pharmacologic treatment focuses on psychotropic medications. Drugs to treat anxiety, depression, sleep disturbances, and wandering may all have their place. Other drugs may be found to have beneficial effects on the underlying disease process. As in all pharmacologic interventions in the elderly, caution in the choice of therapeutic agent and in determining an optimum dosage should be exercised.

Behavioral supports should not be neglected. These extend from identification bracelets and list making to supports for urinary and fecal continence, proper personal hygiene, and adequate nutrition. An emphasis on ambulatory and home-based medical care should be made, and hospitalization avoided as much as possible. Social supports also are a mainstay of care in Alzheimer's disease. As noted by Eisdorfer, "When the primary caretaker gives out, the care system gives out."[2]

Thus, tertiary prevention plays a major role in the care of Alzheimer patients. As in most other diseases of the elderly, Alzheimer dementia requires the health care practitioner to emphasize both the art and the science of medicine. Caring for an Alzheimer patient is not a hopeless task as long as the goals of care are in agreement with the realities of the disease. When this is true, tertiary prevention can be a major benefit both to the patient and to the patient's family.

Ethics of Prevention of Alzheimer's Disease

Questions of ethical behavior occur frequently in caring for the patient with Alzheimer's disease. Clearly, the health care professional is expected to perform primary and secondary prevention of Alzheimer's disease. The major ethical decisions arise in the application of tertiary prevention, especially to patients who may be incompetent to make certain kinds of decisions.

Craig[30] makes a cogent argument for the continuing need to practice primary and secondary prevention for patients who are institutionalized, which can include Alzheimer patients. Examples of preventive measures that could be offered to Alzheimer patients include immunization against influenza, control of hypertension (especially if multi-infarct dementia is also suspected), and avoidance of immobilization. Craig[30] believes that performing primary preventive measures for institutionalized patients "might be seen as an ethical and, perhaps, legal responsibility rather than merely a laudable luxury dependent upon the physician's motivation."

The burden of ethical decision making in Alzheimer's disease is great. Questions of patient competence, advance directives, and determining the patient's best interests abound. Dealings with ethics committees, facility administrators, opposing family members, and the judicial system can try even the most dedicated professional's patience. Considerations of pain and suffering, quality of life, institutionalization, and life-sustaining therapies, to mention a few, may become overwhelming. A natural response might be to avoid these issues because of their difficulty rather than confronting them. However, the ethics of preventive care that apply to other disease states do not gain an exception when applied to Alzheimer's disease. Immunizing and preventing a pneumonia that would take a premature toll of precious remaining cognitive function is a valuable goal. No ethical constraints exist that would bar the consideration of preventive medical practice in Alzheimer's disease. These issues are further explored in Chapter 10.

Conclusions

Strategies to assess the prevalence and incidence of Alzheimer's disease are still being developed. Epidemiology in the best of circumstances is far from an exact science, and its application to Alzheimer's disease is especially difficult. Unlike the studies of cardiovascular disease or cigarette smoking, the data needed to answer many of the questions about prevention in Alzheimer's disease are not yet known. Longitudinal studies are underway that in time may provide the answers.

Although as yet there is no way to prevent the onset of Alzheimer's disease (primary), there are many ways to prevent the misdiagnosis of dementia (secondary) and to prevent premature deterioration of patients with Alzheimer's disease (tertiary). Secondary prevention involves searching both for reversible causes of dementia, when improvement in cognition can be achieved, as well as for otherwise treatable causes of dementia, when at least the cognitive decline can be arrested. Tertiary prevention is presently the mainstay for preventive practice in Alzheimer's disease and is especially important in the frail elderly population.

REFERENCES

1. Glenner GG: Alzheimer's disease (senile dementia): A research update and critique with recommendations. *J Am Geriatr Soc* 1982;30:59-62.

2. Blass JP: Alzheimer's disease. *DM* 1985;31:1-69.

3. Vitaliano PP, Peck A, Johnson DA, et al: Dementia and other competing risks for mortality in the institutionalized aged. *J Am Geriatr Soc* 1981;29:513-519.

4. Seltzer B, Sherwin I: A comparison of clinical features in early- and late-onset primary degenerative dementia. *Arch Neurol* 1983;40:143-146.

5. Brody JA: An epidemiologist views senile dementia—facts and fragments. *Am J Epidemiol* 1982;115:155-162.

6. Sulkava R, Wikstrom J, Aromaa A, et al: Prevalence of severe dementia in Finland. *Neurology* 1985;35:1025-1029.

7. Molsa PK, Marttila RJ, Rinne UK: Epidemiology of dementia in a Finnish population. *Acta Neurol Scand* 1982;65:541-552.

8. Maule MM, Milne JS, Williamson J: Mental illness and physical health in older people. *Age Ageing* 1984;13:349-356.

9. Folstein M, Anthony JC, Parhad I, et al: The meaning of cognitive impairment in the elderly. *J Am Geriatr Soc* 1985;33:228-235.

10. Pfeffer RI, Afifi AA, Chance JM: Prevalence of Alzheimer's disease in a retirement community. *Am J Epidemiol* 1987;125(3):420-436.

11. Nilsson LV: Incidence of severe dementia in an urban sample followed from 70 to 79 years of age. *Acta Psychiatr Scand* 1984;70:478-486.

12. Gruenberg EM: Epidemiology of senile dementia, in Schoenberg BS (ed): *Advances in Neurology*. New York, Raven Press, 1978, vol 19, pp 437-457.

13. Schweber M: Down syndrome and the measurement of chromosome 21 DNA amounts in Alzheimer's disease, in Blass J, Mower G, Mower L, et al (eds): *Familial Alzheimer's Disease: Molecular Genetics, Chemical Aspects and Societal Issues*. New York. Marcel Dekker, in press.

14. Delabar JM, Goldgaber D, Lamour Y, et al: β-Amyloid gene duplication in Alzheimer's disease and karyotypically normal Down syndrome. *Science* 1987;235:1390-1392.

15. St George-Hyslop PH, Tanzi RE, Polinsky RJ, et al: Absence of duplication of chromosome 21 genes in familial and sporadic Alzheimer's disease. *Science* 1987; 238:664-666.

16. Tanzi RE, Bird ED, Latt SA, et al: The amyloid beta-protein gene is not duplicated in brains from patients with Alzheimer's disease. *Science* 1987; 238:666-669.

17. Podlisny MB, Lee G, Selkoe DJ: Gene dosage of the amyloid beta precursor protein in Alzheimer's disease. *Science* 1987; 238:669-671.

18. Gajdusek DC: Foci of motor neuron disease in high incidence in isolated populations of East Asia and the Western Pacific, in Rowland LP (ed): *Human Motor Neuron Diseases*. New York, Raven Press, 1982, pp 363-393.

19. Schoenberg BS, Anderson DW, Haerer AF: Severe dementia: Prevalence and clinical features in a biracial U.S. population. *Arch Neurol* 1985;42:740-743.

20. French LR, Schuman LM, Mortimer JA, et al: A case-control study of dementia of the Alzheimer type. *Am J Epidemiol* 1985;121:414-421.

21. Heyman A, Wilkinson WE, Stafford JA, et al: Alzheimer's disease: A study of epidemiological aspects. *Ann Neurol* 1984;15:335-341.

22. Cohen D, Eisdorfer C, Leverenz J: Alzheimer's disease and maternal age. *J Am Geriatr Soc* 1982;30:656-659.

23. English D, Cohen D: A case-control study of maternal age in Alzheimer's disease. *J Am Geriatr Soc* 1985;33:167-169.

24. Davison AM, Oli H, Walker GS, et al: Water supply aluminum concentration, dialysis dementia, and effect of reverse-osmosis water treatment. *Lancet* 1982;785-787.

25. National Institute on Aging Task Force: Senility reconsidered: Treatment possibilities for mental impairment in the elderly. *JAMA* 1980;244:259-263.

26. Beck JC, Benson DF, Scheibel AB, et al: Dementia in the elderly: The silent epidemic. *Ann Intern Med* 1982;97:231-241.

27. Barker WH: Curable dementia. *Ann Intern Med* 1983;98:411.

28. Larson EB, Lo B, Williams ME: Evaluation and care of elderly patients with dementia. *J Gen Intern Med* 1986;1:116-126.

29. Larson EB, Reifler BV, Sumi SM, et al: Diagnostic evaluation of 200 elderly outpatients with suspected dementia. *J Gerontol* 1985;40:536-543.

30. Craig TJ: Ethical aspects of primary preventive measures among the institutionalized elderly. *J Am Geriatr Soc* 1982;30:475-476.

CHAPTER 2

Management of the Outpatient with Alzheimer's Disease: An Interdisciplinary Team Approach

Benjamin Seltzer, John P. Larkin, and Kathy J. Fabiszewski

Most patients with Alzheimer's disease spend the major part, if not the entire course, of their illness residing in the community. In the early stages, symptoms are mild and some degree of independent living is usually possible. Even in the late stages, many patients continue to remain at home. Outpatient management is thus a major component of any comprehensive program for the care and treatment of these patients.[1,2]

Alzheimer's disease has certain features that influence strategies for management. Since it is a progressive disorder whose signs and symptoms change with time, different clinical problems come to the fore at different stages of the disease. This means that management must be flexible and frequently adjusted to meet the patient's changing needs. Second, Alzheimer's disease erodes a person's ability for self-care. As a result, relatives and friends find themselves increasingly involved in supervision and care, a role that can entail considerable stress. The education, support, and encouragement of family members therefore assume major importance in the overall management process. Finally, Alzheimer's disease is a multifaceted disorder that touches nearly every aspect of a person's life. Professionals from many health disciplines need to be involved in the patient's care and treatment. Few illnesses require such a concerted interdisciplinary effort.

In this chapter an interdisciplinary approach to the management of outpatients with Alzheimer's disease and their family members is presented. It is based on the program at the Geriatric Research Education and Clinical Center, Veterans Hospital, Bedford, Massachusetts, but is applicable to other hospital-based specialty clinics and community health programs as well. The model is that of the "primary health care team,"[3] in which a group of health care professionals provide comprehensive diagnostic and evaluative services and continuing care to a discrete population of patients. The core members of this team are the physician (preferably, neurologist, or other practitioner with expertise in dementia), nurse practitioner, and clinical social worker, but representatives from other fields, such as neuropsychology and occupational therapy, may also play important roles. While the family physician might also serve as a member, in most cases the team acts as a consultant to the family practitioner for the special problem of dementia. Continuity in the composition of the team is important. The provision of services to patients with Alzheimer's disease and their families is too often fragmented. Patients and caregivers experience multiple, one-time contacts with different health care providers. The continuity of care by the core interdisciplinary team, by contrast, fosters the development of a therapeutic relationship with a relatively small, but consistent, group of professionals.

The model that is being presented is an interdisciplinary one. Each team member first applies his or her special skills and training to an evaluation of the patient and family. The physician generally focuses on the neurologic diagnosis, co-existing medical conditions, and the use of medication. The nurse practitioner concentrates on assessing the patient's physical limitations and the capacity of the caregiver to compensate for them. The social worker attempts to define the social, psychological, and situational stressors that impact on the patient and the family. Following these individual assessments, however, the members of the team meet to share their findings and prepare an integrated management plan. Individual members then proceed to carry out specific interventions, appropriate to their specialties, but the overall product is a coordinated effort. Then, at periodic intervals, the evaluation process is repeated, and the team meets again to revise the treatment plan according to the current situation.

In this chapter, a distinction is made between the initial and the follow-up phase of outpatient management. The initial phase will be described as involving the medical diagnosis, a baseline assessment in several functional areas, and the establishment of a therapeutic relationship with the patient and family. In discussing the follow-up phase, some common problems are described and specific interventions to deal with them presented. This distinction between initial and follow-up phases is not, however, meant to be inflexible. For example, therapeutic interventions may begin at the very first contact with the patient and family and reassessment of functional status and the diagnosis should continue at all subsequent follow-up visits.

Initial Evaluation

The initial evaluation of the patient suspected of having Alzheimer's disease has three main objectives: (1) confirmation of the diagnosis; (2) determination of "baseline" levels in a number of functional spheres; and (3) establishment of a therapeutic alliance with the patient and family that will continue through subsequent phases of the management process.

It is obvious that the diagnosis must be as accurate as possible. Because Alzheimer's disease implies progressive deterioration, for which no satisfactory therapy is currently available, all other potentially treatable causes for the patient's dementia must be carefully excluded. Indeed, the principal reason for conducting what has been termed a *dementia workup* is to look for some other reason for dementia. The details of this examination procedure, and the differential diagnosis of dementia, have been discussed by a number of authors.[4,5]

There exists no specific biologic marker that can conclusively predict in life that a patient has the neuropathologic features associated with Alzheimer's disease. The diagnosis remains purely clinical, based on the recognition of a constellation of signs and symptoms and on the exclusion of other potential causes of dementia by appropriate laboratory tests. Although studies show that this procedure has a reasonably high degree of diagnostic accuracy,[6] there is always the possibility of error. In addition, some patients with Alzheimer's disease have coexisting medical conditions contributing to dementia that may be potentially treatable. For these reasons, the physician must keep an open mind about the diagnosis and be willing to reevaluate it.

Alzheimer's disease is a progressive disorder. Signs and symptoms change as the patient passes from one phase of the illness to another. Some authors have developed elaborate schemas to describe the different stages of Alzheimer's disease,[7-9] and nearly all writers discuss at least early, middle, and late (or advanced) stages, to which might be added a fourth, or terminal, stage (Table 2-1). Most of these schemas are based on cross-sectional analyses of groups of patients with Alzheimer dementia, however, and little strictly longitudinal data are available. It is unclear then whether all patients with Alzheimer's disease do in fact pass through a specific sequence of deterioration and whether the "staging" of a patient at initial evaluation has any prognostic implications in terms of speed of decline. Nevertheless, there is considerable practical utility in developing some

Table 2-1 Stages of Alzheimer's Disease

Stages	Signs and Symptoms
Early Stage	Forgetfulness Mild objective memory deficit Difficulty with novel or complex tasks Apathy and social withdrawal
Middle Stage	Moderate to severe objective memory deficit Disorientation to time and place Language disturbance Visuoconstructive difficulty Apraxia Personality and behavioral changes Cannot survive without supervision
Late Stage	Intellectual functions virtually untestable Verbal communication severely limited Incapable of self-care Incontinence of bladder and bowel
Terminal Stage	Unaware of environment Mute Bedridden Joint contractures Pathological reflexes Myoclonus

Table 2-2 Assessment of the Outpatient with Alzheimer's Disease

Functional Area	Clinical Evaluation	Standardized Instruments (Selected)
Cognitive	Mental status examination	*Mini-Mental State Examination*[10] *Information-Memory-Concentration Test*[11] *Brief Cognitive Rating Scale*[12] *Alzheimer's Disease Assessment Scale*[13]
Noncognitive	Psychiatric examination Interview with family members	*Performance of Daily Activities Test*[11] *Alzheimer's Disease Assessment Scale*[13] *Sandoz Clinical Assessment—Geriatric Scale*[14]
Neurologic	Neurologic examination	
Activities of Daily Living	Interview with family members	*Katz Index of ADL*[15] *Performance of Daily Activities Test*[11] *Instrumental Activities of Daily Living Scale*[16]
Needs for Assistance	Interview with family members	Same as above
Psychosocial	Psychosocial history	*Burden Scale*[17]

formulation of the patient's current functional status since this directly influences decisions for management.

For the present purpose, six different, although overlapping, functional spheres that are affected by Alzheimer's disease can be identified (Table 2-2). Each should be assessed in evaluating the patient. The initial assessment gives baseline data; assessments at subsequent visits show where, and to what extent, deterioration has occurred. As will be seen, this information can usually be obtained by direct questioning of the patient and the family or by traditional examination techniques. In some situations, these routine procedures can be supplemented by certain standardized tests or scales that provide quantitative measures of the function in question.

Cognitive Functions

Cognitive, or intellectual, disturbance is the clinical hallmark of Alzheimer dementia. This includes such well-recognized symptoms as memory impairment, language disorder, apraxia, visuoconstructive difficulty, and problems with abstract thinking. Other common symptoms such as getting lost, failure to recognize familiar faces, and certain types of hallucinations are also manifestations of cognitive disturbance. Intellectual function is usually assessed by the traditional neurologically oriented mental status examination.[18] In addition, a number of well-known test instruments are sensitive to this aspect of Alzheimer's disease. Among these are the *Mini-Mental State Examination*,[10] the *Information-Memory-Concentration* component of the test of Blessed and co-workers,[11] the *Brief Cognitive Rating Scale*,[12] and *Alzheimer's Disease Assessment Scale*.[13] One must also, however, ask the family directly about the patient's ability to work, drive a motor vehicle, handle finances, and do household chores. Some patients score within the normal range on standardized test measures and yet have significant difficulties in the natural setting of their daily lives.

Noncognitive Functions

Another important functional domain to assess is the noncognitive. Changes in affect, personality, and behavior are extremely common, if not invariable, findings, in Alzheimer's disease, but this aspect of the syndrome is often downplayed in discussions of the illness. Few standardized scales or formal tests tap this facet of dementia, although some items of the *Performance of Everyday Activities* component of the test of Blessed and co-workers,[11] the *Sandoz Clinical Assessment—Geriatric Scale*,[14] and *Alzheimer's Disease Assessment Scale*[13] do deal with certain of these features, such as irritability, apathy, hyperactivity, and bothersomeness. Depression, anxiety, and delusions may be apparent on psychiatric examination of the patient, but some noncognitive symptoms of Alzheimer's disease occur sporadically and do not necessarily coincide with the time of the examination. For example, a patient who is prone to become agitated under special circumstances at home (e.g., dressing, bathing) may be quiet in the physician's examining room. One must therefore supplement the examination with close questioning of the family to elicit this information. Since some of the behavioral symptoms of Alzheimer dementia are unpleasant, many family members are hesitant to mention them. It is sometimes easier for the relative to discuss behavioral problems if the examiner takes the initiative and systematically asks about each of these symptoms. This should be done in a sympathetic and nonjudgmental manner. Personality and behavioral changes are frequently the most distressing symptoms of Alzheimer's disease. One does a disservice to the patient and to family members by avoiding these issues. Furthermore, many noncognitive symptoms can be controlled by appropriate medications and nonpharmacologic interventions.

Neurologic Functions

Neurologic function is usually preserved through the early and middle stages of Alzheimer's disease, although seizures, gait disorder, and tremors may occur at any time. In the late stages of the disease, neurologic signs such as flexion contractures and primitive reflexes are prominent features. One probes this domain by questioning the family and by performing a neurologic examination.

Activities of Daily Living

Cognitive, noncognitive, and elementary neurologic changes all impact on a person's activities of daily living. Although not a single group of physiologic functions, this is another important functional domain to explore in assessing the status of the patient with Alzheimer dementia. At first limitations may primarily involve instrumental activities such as shopping, preparing meals, and performing other household chores, but later elementary physical dysfunctions, such as incontinence, ataxia, dysphagia, and contractures, also supervene. In surveying this domain, it is helpful to keep in mind a systematic typology, similar, for example, to that of Gordon,[19] and include bathing, grooming, dressing, toileting, feeding, nutritional status, physical mobility, communication, sleep pattern, and sexuality. Certain standardized inventories of activities of daily living such as the scales of Katz and colleagues,[15] Lawton,[16] Kane and Kane,[20] and the *Performance of Everyday Activities* test of Blessed and co-workers[11] provide an objective measure of these functions. Although many of these scales were developed primarily for patients with physical handicaps, they are also useful in assessing functional status in a patient with Alzheimer's disease.

Needs for Assistance

As a patient gradually loses the ability to perform many of the activities of daily living, there is a corresponding increase in his or her need for assistance. Indeed the physical symptoms require special nursing attention from the caregiver if the patient is to remain in the community. In addition to determining the availability of family members to assist with personal care, one must also probe the caregiver's understanding of the patient's deficits and his or her physical and emotional capacity to deal satisfactorily with them. This latter assessment forms the basis for developing a caregiver educational and training program (see Chapter 3).

Psychosocial Functions

All diseases occur in a psychosocial context, but this aspect assumes special importance in Alzheimer's disease. Dementia interferes with a person's ability to interact socially as much as it disrupts intellectual functioning. Not only the patient, but other people as well, are affected by Alzheimer's disease. For the primary caregiver the involvement can be considerable. Therefore, in dealing with Alzheimer's disease, the entire social network must be considered, with the caregiver and other family members sometimes assuming the role of "co-patient."

To ensure the accuracy and inclusiveness of the data, the social history must obviously be obtained from a family member or some other responsible person. The initial interview should primarily be a structured information-gathering process in which relevant baseline data are obtained. Minimal data include basic sociodemographic information on the patient, principal caregiver, and other household members. A genogram provides an easy-to-examine pictorial representation of the family system. Obtaining information on the patient's work history and personal habits helps define a patient's premorbid accomplishments and lifestyle. Because of issues of patient competency, specific questions also need to be asked concerning whether the patient still retains control of financial resources. Finally, the extent of the primary caregiver's personal, informal, and formal support systems must be defined, as well as his or her personal resources, skills, and stressors. Several interviews may be needed to expand on this data base. At subsequent visits, as the respondent grows more comfortable with the interviewer, open-ended questions concerning patient and family feelings and beliefs can also be asked. A home visit is often helpful because it gives the social worker an opportunity to see the patient in his or her natural environment. Several instruments have been designed specifically to measure burden and physical and emotional symptomatology in the caregivers of demented patients.[17,21] Although designed principally for research purposes, they may also have some clinical use in providing an objective measure of this variable.

The psychosocial evaluation summarized above provides objective data on the patient's social circumstances, as well as an impression of the patient's family: its structure, sociocultural beliefs, attitudes to health and disease, myths, patterns of communication, and degree of psychopathology, if any. One can then identify the situational and psychosocial stressors that impact on the patient and family and define the coping strategies that they use to meet them, including their ability to seek out appropriate community resources.

Discussion of the Diagnosis and Formation of a Rapport with the Family

Two remaining issues relating to the initial evaluation deserve mention. These are discussing the diagnosis and prognosis and laying the foundation for a long-term therapeutic relationship. It is best to be frank in discussing the diagnosis with the patient's family. Alzheimer's disease has attracted considerable media attention, and many people have had previous experiences with dementia in other relatives, friends, or acquaintances. It is probable that most members of the general public know something about Alzheimer's disease even if they continue to hold many misconceptions about it. Also, since dementia begins insidiously, relatives may have suspected the diagnosis long before consulting the physician. To cloak the diagnosis in euphemistic terms, or to be vague, serves no useful purpose and may actually be counterproductive in establishing the rapport necessary to form an alliance with family members in the long-term management of the patient. Furthermore, because of the implications of the diagnosis for patient safety, employability, and financial and legal competence, the multidisciplinary team is obliged to inform some responsible person of the diagnosis. On the other hand, if there is some legitimate question about the diagnosis, or if there are unusual clinical features, this uncertainty should be conveyed to the family, who should then be kept up to date regarding the current status of the provisional diagnosis. Whether one should discuss the diagnosis with the patient is a separate question. Few patients have enough insight to understand the full significance of the diagnosis even if they can register and retain this information. Nevertheless, there are occasional patients who, in the early stages, do retain insight and in whom learning the diagnosis might precipitate considerable depression and anxiety. In these cases, one should first try to obtain some idea of how much the patient wants to know and then discuss the diagnosis in general terms only.

At the time of diagnosis, family members frequently inquire about the prognosis in terms of rate of decline and expected duration of the illness. As mentioned previously, there is little objective basis for making such a determination at the present time. Although relatives should be informed that Alzheimer dementia is an irreversible process and that further decline is to be expected, there is little gained by a graphic description of the stages of decline and an enumeration of all the problems they may eventually have to face. Rather, one should adopt a "one step at a time" approach and limit one's focus to current and immediately expected problems.

No matter how well prepared a family may be to accept the diagnosis of Alzheimer's disease, and no matter how compassionately this information may be transmitted to them, the time of the initial diagnosis is always one of great stress and a sense of being overwhelmed. Unfortunately, this is often precisely the point at which patients and families also feel abandoned by the medical community because of poorly organized, or nonexistent, follow-up services. The most helpful thing health care professionals can do at this point is to convey to patients and their families a firm intention to stay with them throughout the subsequent course of the illness and to help them cope with problems as they unfold. Not only does this lift morale, but it helps the professionals enlist the family in a joint effort to care for the patient. Indeed it is only with the full participation of a family member or other responsible person that a moderately or severely demented patient can safely remain an outpatient. The absence of such a support system is an indication for admission to a long-term care facility.

Follow-Up Evaluation and Care

At follow-up visits, each of the six functional areas should be surveyed again. This makes possible the charting of the patient's course and the identification of current problems. Based on this information, the interdisciplinary team can then plan appropriate therapies and interventions. Follow-up visits also serve as an opportunity to reassess the diagnosis and to provide education and encouragement to family members in their caregiving role. A well-organized system of regularly scheduled follow-up visits is the most important service that can be offered to the patient and the family since it helps avoid many potential crises. Some common problems encountered in outpatients with Alzheimer's disease are discussed in this section, followed by suggestions for management. As in the earlier section, these issues will be grouped according to the six functional areas.

Cognitive Functions

Cognitive symptoms form the core of the dementing process, and an effective treatment of these symptoms would amount to a definitive treatment for Alzheimer's disease. Unfortunately, this is not available at the present time. In the past, a wide variety of therapies have been tried, including vasodilators, vitamins, hyperbaric oxygen, cholinergic drugs, neuropeptides, naloxone, and certain ergot alkaloids.[22-24] Although slight degrees of transient improvement on certain measures of cognitive function have occasionally been reported in some subgroups of patients with some of these therapies, no clinically significant improvement has been reported up to now. For this reason, their routine use in Alzheimer's disease is not justified. One important exception to this policy of therapeutic nihilism is the situation in which a patient and the family may wish to participate in a well-designed clinical trial of a particular drug or other therapy. Provided that the treatment is a safe one and that unreasonable expectations for improvement are not held, participation should be encouraged, since this will at least contribute scientifically sound data on the potential efficacy of a particular therapy for Alzheimer dementia.

Noncognitive Functions

Unlike cognitive symptoms, the noncognitive features of Alzheimer's disease can often be influenced in a favorable way by pharmacologic and other therapeutic modalities. For this discussion, noncognitive symptoms will be divided into disorders of mood, personality, and behavior.

Mood

Depression is the most common disturbance of mood encountered in patients with Alzheimer's disease; manic symptoms are distinctly less common. Different studies have reported that from 20% to 30% of demented patients have significant symptoms of depression.[25-27] In a retrospective study, 23% of outpatients attending the Geriatric Research Education and Clinical Center's dementia clinic had symptoms suggesting significant depression at some point during the course of the illness. Whether depression in Alzheimer's disease is a psychological reaction to the underlying dementia or a more intrinsic part of the disorder is not clear. In this study, as well as in others, the patient's depression tended to occur relatively early in the course of the disease and became less prominent as dementia advanced. This suggests that it is, at least in part, a psychological response to cognitive deficits. On the other hand, with increasingly severe dementia, depressive symptoms are more difficult to evaluate, and it is possible that the manifestations of depression change as the disease enters a new phase. In the absence of definite evidence of dysphoric mood, symptoms such as agitation, sleep disturbance, and lack of appetite, which are commonly found in patients with Alzheimer's disease, cannot by themselves be considered evidence of depression. For this reason, the use of antidepressant medications should be reserved for those patients who clearly manifest feelings of sadness and hopelessness. In these cases medication is often quite helpful in treating the target symptom, and some patients' cognitive functions seem to show a transient improvement, possibly as a kind of "halo effect." Many different agents (e.g., amitriptyline, nortriptyline, imipramine) may be used. Maprotiline (Ludiomil), which has minimal anticholinergic side effects, is least likely to cause confusion and urinary retention. A further discussion of antidepressant therapy is presented in Chapter 11.

Personality

Personality change almost invariably accompanies Alzheimer's disease. This can take the form either of an accentuation or a marked alteration of a person's previous lifelong character traits. The neural substrates underlying personality change in Alzheimer's disease are not understood. On purely empiric grounds, an attempt has been made to delineate two contrasting patterns. One is marked by apathy, lack of spontaneity, and passivity. The other involves growing irritability, irascibility, self-preoccupation, and intolerance of and lack of concern for others. The first pattern, which involves an emotional distancing between the patient and others, often leads to a sharp decrease in sexual activity, whereas the second pattern sometimes results in increased demand for sexual activity on the part of the patient.

Behavior

Personality disorders, whether on an organic or functional basis, are notoriously difficult to treat. Since the withdrawn, but docile, patient does not exhibit bothersome behavior, treatment is not usually required. In fact, this kind of personality change may actually facilitate the family's ability to care for the patient. The second pattern of personality change, however, is much more troublesome, particularly since it is frequently associated with behavioral changes of restlessness, agitation, verbal abusiveness, and, sometimes, physical assaultiveness. In most patients, agitated behaviors occur only sporadically, and in response to some obvious stress, such as the patient realizing he or she is in unfamiliar surroundings or having to be disturbed by the caregiver to perform some activity of daily living such as dressing or bathing. Other patients, however, seem to exhibit a more or less continuous state of restlessness, manifested by pacing back and forth and other forms of compulsive, repetitive behaviors.

To some extent, these undesirable behaviors can be reduced by environmental manipulation. If they occur in obvious relation to a particular stressful circumstance, then eliminating the stress, or finding some alternative way of accomplishing a stressful activity, may help reduce the response. For example, a gentle, soothing, unhurried approach on the part of the caregiver may make dressing and bathing less disturbing experiences. Family members and friends invariably react negatively to a patient's agitated and belligerent behavior, but their own anger and anxiety, when conveyed to the patient, only increase agitation. If the family understands the basis of the patient's changed behavior and learns to withhold the instinct to react angrily, then some of these problems may be avoided. Often, however, these measures are ineffective, and one must have recourse to some form of pharmacotherapy.

Two broad classes of drugs—the sedatives and antipsychotics—are the chief agents used to control behavioral symptoms in Alzheimer's disease.[28-30] Theoretically, the first class should be used for anxiety and hyperactivity; the second should be targeted for irrational, disruptive behaviors and hallucinations. In practice, however, it is often impossible to distinguish between these two types of symptoms, and both are found frequently together in the same patient. Considerable variability also exists among patients in how they respond to these agents. Since no study convincingly shows the superiority of one class of drug over the other, it is the personal preference of the physician, and concerns about side effects, that dictate the eventual choice of medication.

Sedatives pose a problem of causing excessive sleepiness, although this may sometimes be a desired side effect. The benzodiazepines have the additional potential of provoking a paradoxical agitated response in elderly, demented patients. Because of this, diphenhydramine (Benadryl) is sometimes the first drug of choice if one chooses to use a sedative. Among the benzodiazepines, oxazepam (Serax) has the advantage of a relatively short time of action. Antipsychotics, the other major class of drugs used for behavioral symptoms, can cause drowsiness, confusion, and various extrapyramidal side effects. Two particular antipsychotics have been favored in the treatment of patients with Alzheimer's disease: haloperidol (Haldol), because it has less anticholinergic effect than other drugs in this category, and thioridazine (Mellaril), because of its comparatively low risk for causing extrapyramidal side effects. Finally, if both sedatives and antipsychotics prove ineffective in controlling behavioral symptoms, one may occasionally use an antidepressant, although their chief value may lie in the treatment of dysphoric mood. The drug treatment of noncognitive symptoms in Alzheimer's disease is further discussed in Chapter 11.

Since elderly patients are often exceptionally sensitive to the effects of medication, one should begin with a low dose of whatever agent has been chosen and then gradually raise the dose until there is either a therapeutic response or an undesirable side effect. Unfortunately, patients are often prematurely switched from one drug to another before having been given a sufficient dose of the first agent. Or, not enough time is allowed to elapse to evaluate response to the medication. Although these drugs may have immediate effects, the variability of the target symptoms makes a relatively long period of observation necessary to determine whether they are significantly influencing the patient's symptoms. Although it is always preferable to rely on a single medication, use of multiple drugs is sometimes indicated. The dose schedule must be adjusted to the temporal pattern of the patient's symptoms. Since many patients become increasingly agitated as the day wears on, giving most or all of the daily dose in the late afternoon is often a useful strategy. An evening or bedtime dose may also help in promoting sleep.

Sleep disturbance is common in Alzheimer dementia and is particularly stressful to family members. Hypnotics, such as diphenhydramine (Benadryl), chloral hydrate, and the benzodiazepines, may therefore be necessary. Since patients who are awake at night tend to doze during the day, this tendency to daytime napping further compounds the problem of nocturnal insomnia. Family members must be counseled to keep the patient up during the day and keep him or her from falling asleep early in the evening. On the other hand, in the case of patients who nap during the day and yet sleep well at night there is no need to impose any specific sleep schedule.

Family members are often hesitant to use medications to treat behavioral symptoms in Alzheimer's disease. In addition to fears about possible side effects, they are concerned that medication is being prescribed primarily for their own convenience rather than for the benefit of the patient. The interdisciplinary team must bring relatives to see that their own welfare is a legitimate concern, particularly since they bear such a large proportion of the burden of caregiving. Moreover, it should be pointed out to family members that patients themselves seem troubled by anxiety, agitation, and restlessness and that these medications relieve them of some of these unpleasant symptoms.

Neurologic Functions

Elementary neurologic symptoms of Alzheimer's disease include seizures, myoclonic jerks, difficulty walking, and abnormal movements. For the most part, these are late manifestations of the disease. Seizures can generally be controlled without difficulty with conventional anticonvulsants (e.g., phenytoin [Dilantin], phenobarbital) in usual therapeutic doses. Serum levels should be monitored on a regular basis. Myoclonus, on the other hand, has no satisfactory treatment, although treatment with diazepam (Valium) may reduce the violence of the jerky movements.

Most patients in the early and middle stages of Alzheimer's disease have no difficulty with ambulation, but with advancing dementia many become ataxic. For some patients, a "walker" may be helpful; for all such patients, supervision and assistance in ambulation are needed to avoid the danger of falls. Ataxia, bradykinesia, and tremor in the demented patient sometimes suggest the coexistence of Parkinson's disease, but only a small percentage of patients with Alzheimer's disease have both conditions.[31] Treatment with a combination of carbidopa and levodopa (Sinemet) should be restricted to that small subgroup with the additional clinical diagnosis of Parkinson's disease.

Activities of Daily Living

The multiple cognitive, noncognitive, and neurologic deficits of Alzheimer's disease limit a person's ability to perform activities of daily living. At the highest level is occupational performance. If the patient with Alzheimer's disease holds a responsible position, declining intellectual abilities and poor judgment may lead to errors that adversely affect others. On the other hand, if supervisors and coworkers do not understand that poor work performance is the consequence of a medical condition, they may unfairly subject the patient to demotions and ridicule. The multidisciplinary team must counsel the patient and family concerning preparation for retirement, disability pensions, and other benefits. Similar actions need to be taken with regard to the patient's ability to handle legal and financial affairs. Referral to a lawyer and financial consultant may be necessary. Driving a motor vehicle poses another problem, particularly since many patients are reluctant to stop driving. The team must, however, ensure that the patient is not engaged in any hazardous activity. If persuasion is ineffective, the family may need to have the patient's driver's license revoked. In some instances it may be necessary to hide the car keys or mechanically immobilize the car.

With mild degrees of dementia, many patients are able to remain at home by themselves during the day; later, this becomes more problematical. The team must assess the patient's requirements for supervision and must discuss with the family such options as asking a neighbor to look in on the patient, hiring a part-time attendant, sending the patient to a day care facility, or having a family member remain at home. Wandering is one of the hazards of inadequate supervision. Aside from having someone constantly monitoring the patient's whereabouts, special locks and alarm systems also help prevent the patient from leaving the premises.

Incontinence of bladder and bowel are almost inevitable physical consequences of Alzheimer's disease, although these symptoms may not occur until relatively late in the clinical course. Various features of the dementia (e.g., amnesia, visual agnosia, failure to monitor internal sensations) either singly or in combination contribute to incontinence. Coexisting physical causes, such as obstructive uropathy and urinary tract infections, which are common in the elderly, may also play a role. Pharmacologic agents are another factor. They contribute to incontinence either by further clouding a patient's sensorium and causing a delirium or through specific anticholinergic effects.

If the incontinence is due, as least in part, to an underlying correctable cause, then an appropriate physical treatment is indicated. If this is not the case, other strategies need to be employed. Urinating in inappropriate places can be controlled by carefully noting the patient's voiding pattern and then taking him or her to the toilet at appropriate intervals. Once brought into the bathroom, many patients void appropriately, although some may need further reminding and gentle assistance.

For nocturnal incontinence, other strategies may be effective. Limiting the amount of fluid consumed after the evening meal, toileting the patient just prior to bed, and taking the patient to the bathroom on awakening during the night should reduce or eliminate nocturia. Some caregivers may, however, elect to clothe the patient in a disposable adult diaper. For men, use of an external condom catheter, attached to a drainage bag, eliminates contact of urine with the skin. With advancing dementia, diapers and catheters may be required during the day as well.

The psychosocial implications of incontinence cannot be ignored. This is a major source of emotional stress, as well as a considerable physical burden, to caregivers. Indeed, this symptom often precipitates a family into the active pursuit of long-term placement. The interdisciplinary team must gauge the family's ability to cope with the problem of incontinence. Frequent contacts with them, for educational purposes and for support, are needed if they are to deal effectively with incontinence on an outpatient basis.

Eating is another problem area for the patient with Alzheimer dementia. As patients lose their social abilities, table manners deteriorate. Apraxia and other cognitive difficulties also contribute to a loss of the ability to handle utensils properly. This can make dining in public an embarrassing experience for family members. Although patients' nutritional needs are basically similar to those of normal adults, those who pace, or show other evidence of motor hyperactivity, need an increased caloric intake to balance their expenditure of energy.[32] Some patients have a tendency to hoard food in their mouths without actually swallowing it, while others swallow too rapidly or fail to chew their food sufficiently before attempting to swallow. These symptoms obviously put them at risk for aspiration and asphyxiation. In these cases, family members must pay special attention to the texture of the food and must also monitor the patient closely at mealtimes. Finally, some patients with advanced dementia show certain features of the Kluver-Bucy syndrome[33] and put inedible objects into their mouths. This is presumably because they fail to recognize them as nonfood items. These patients need close supervision.

Medications should never be left in sight of the patient, nor should the person retain the responsibility for self-administration of medications. Many patients are unwilling to take prescribed drugs. Some have difficulty swallowing pills. Others refuse because of paranoid ideas or a lack of understanding. For these patients, it may be necessary to use liquid forms of the medication or to grind up tablets and mix them with soft foods to disguise their presence.

Caregiver Education and Training

Since most of the interventions that have been mentioned depend on the cooperation of a family member, special attention must be directed toward the education and training of the family caregiver. It is often helpful to have caregivers verbalize their understanding of what they have been taught. Other approaches that help reinforce instruction include providing detailed, but simple, written instructions; following up educational sessions with a telephone call; and home visits.

Psychosocial Functions

Many studies show that the family caregivers of patients with Alzheimer's disease suffer from stress, physical fatigue, and depression.[20,21,34,35] Aside from causing much suffering, these symptoms interfere with the caregiver's ability to manage the patient properly. An essential component of psychosocial interventions in Alzheimer dementia therefore involves attention to the problems of the family caregiver. Many of these problems are discussed in detail in Chapter 3.

As care demands increase, caregivers become emotionally and physically fatigued. They feel "constantly tired" and "exhausted" and experience sleep disturbances, somatic symptoms, and a sense of having lost control of their own lives. Poor work performance, difficulty in making decisions, and alcohol and other substance abuse may also occur. As a result, some caregivers become incapable of understanding simple instructions and following through on recommendations for treatment of their demented relative. Moreover, just as the patient experiences a "loss of self,"[36] the caregiver experiences depressive symptoms because of the loss of a close relationship. A protracted period of grieving, which has been called an "ongoing funeral,"[37] then ensues. And, as the patient requires increased supervision, the caregiver must devote more time to the task, frequently giving up work and withdrawing from other outside activities. This social isolation further worsens the person's depression.

Caregivers must be regularly assessed for changing levels of depression, including possible suicidal ideation and behavior. The possibility of patient neglect and abuse must also be evaluated. Referral to a psychiatrist or protective services may be urgently needed under certain circumstances. Even in less extreme situations, psychotherapy is important. Indeed, all primary caregivers of patients with Alzheimer's disease should consider some kind of psychological counseling during their caregiving career. This can take many different forms and is discussed in detail in Chapter 3. Finally, it is important to point out that other family members as well as friends also experience feelings of loss, anger, and guilt because of the patient's illness. Children and siblings of patients have the additional concern that Alzheimer's disease may have a genetic basis. These people also require counseling.

With optimal medical management, favorable social circumstances, and effective family caregivers, patients with Alzheimer's disease may remain at home for many years. Some patients never require placement in a long-term care facility. For others, however, this becomes inevitable. A variety of factors contribute to the need for placement in an institution. The chief patient-related factors are the presence of agitated behavior, sleep disturbance, and incontinence. Caregiver factors include depression, poor psychological coping skills, and physical inability to meet the demands of caregiving. Finally, practical considerations such as whether there is an available primary family caregiver, the economic status of the patient, and the availability of inpatient beds also contribute to the decision to seek long-term care. The interdisciplinary team must periodically assess whether such care is indicated. If this is deemed necessary, assistance must be provided to the family so that they can make suitable arrangements. The decision to institutionalize a patient invariably increases or reactivates the family's emotional turmoil. The interdisciplinary team needs to use all of its skills to mediate the decision-making process and help the family adjust psychologically to the new circumstances. Even after the patient is placed in a nursing home or chronic disease hospital, and their relationship with the patient enters a new phase, family members often continue to need psychological counseling.

Conclusions

A comprehensive approach to the outpatient with Alzheimer's disease includes the need for a thorough initial evaluation and for regular follow-up assessments covering a broad range of areas by an interdisciplinary professional team. Special emphasis should also be placed on meeting the needs of the family caregiver.

Many physicians and health workers are reluctant to deal with Alzheimer's disease. Since there is no specific treatment, they tend to ignore patients and their families. These people suffer considerably, however, and clearly deserve the same professional attention unhesitatingly offered to those with other medical conditions. Moreover, as more people reach advanced age and become vulnerable to the development of dementia, these services will be demanded by ever-growing numbers.

Interventions *can* make life more bearable for the Alzheimer's disease patient and his or her family. Most of the interventions described are not technological. Rather, they consist primarily in the establishment of a supportive and educational relationship with the patient's family. This relationship is then used to help individuals develop appropriate coping strategies to deal with the problems that they face. Interacting with patients and families, at this interpersonal level, can offer much gratification. Helping people deal effectively with major problems of daily life can be an immensely satisfying experience for the health care professional.

REFERENCES

1. Bergman K, Foster EM, Justice AW, et al: Management of the demented elderly patient in the community. *Br J Psychiatry* 1978;132:441-449.

2. Seltzer B, Fabiszewski K, Brown J, et al: A multidisciplinary team approach to the outpatient with Alzheimer's disease. *Gerontologist* 1985;25:115.

3. Reifler BV, Larson EB: Alzheimer's disease and long-term care: The assessment of the patient. *J Geriatr Psychiatry* 1985;18:9-26.

4. Cummings JL, Benson DF: *Dementia: A Clinical Approach*. Boston, Butterworth, 1983.

5. Seltzer B: Organic mental disorders, in Nicholi AM (ed): *The New Harvard Guide to Modern Psychiatry*. Cambridge, Mass, Harvard University Press, 1988.

6. Sulkawa R, Haltia M, Paetau A, et al: Accuracy of clinical diagnosis in primary degenerative dementia: Correlation with neuropathological findings. *J Neurol Neurosurg Psychiatry* 1983;46:9-13.

7. Botwinick J, Storandt M, Berg L: A longitudinal, behavioral study of senile dementia of the Alzheimer type. *Arch Neurol* 1986;43:1124-1128.

8. Hughes CP, Berg L, Danziger W, et al: A new clinical scale for the staging of dementia. *Br J Psychiatry* 1982;140:566-572.

9. Reisberg B, Ferris S, DeLeon MJ, et al: The Global Deterioration Scale (GDS): An instrument for the assessment of primary degenerative dementia (PDD). *Am J Psychiatry* 1982;139:1136-1138.

10. Folstein MF, Folstein S, McHugh PR: "Mini-mental state": A practical method for grading the cognitive state of patients for the clinician. *J Psychiatr Res* 1975;12:189-198.

11. Blessed G, Tomlinson BE, Roth M: The association between quantitative measures of dementia and of senile changes in the cerebral grey matter of elderly patients. *Br J Psychiatry* 1968;114:797-911.

12. Reisberg B, Schneck MK, Ferris SH: The Brief Cognitive Rating Scale (BCRS): Findings in primary degenerative dementia. *Psychopharmacol Bull* 1983;19:47-50.

13. Rosen WG, Mohs RC, Davis KL: A new rating scale for Alzheimer's disease. *Am J Psychiatry* 1984;141:1256-1364.

14. Shader RL, Harmatz JS, Salzman C: A new scale for clinical assessment in geriatric populations: Sandoz Clinical Assessment—Geriatric (SCAG). *J Am Geriatr Soc* 1974;12:107-113.

15. Katz S, Moskovitz AB, Jackson BA, et al: Studies of illness in the aged, the index of ADL: A standardized measure of biological and psychological functions. *JAMA* 1962;185:914-919.

16. Lawton MP: Assessment of older people: Self-maintaining and instrumental activities of daily living. *Gerontologist* 1969;9:179-186.

17. Zarit SH, Reever KE, Bach-Peterson J: Relatives of the impaired elderly: Correlates of feelings of burden. *Gerontologist* 1980;20:649-655.

18. Strub RL, Black FW: *The Mental Status Examination in Clinical Neurology*, ed 2. Philadelphia, F.A. Davis, 1985.

19. Gordon M: *Manual of Nursing Diagnosis*. New York, McGraw-Hill, 1982.

20. Kane R, Kane RL: *Assessing the Elderly*. Lexington, Mass, Lexington Books, 1981.

21. O'Quinn JA, McGraw KO: The burdened caregiver, in Hutton JT, Kenny AD (eds): *Senile Dementia of the Alzheimer Type*. New York, Alan R. Liss, 1985, pp 65-75.

22. Hollander E, Mohs RC, Davis KL: Cholinergic approaches to the treatment of Alzheimer's disease. *Br Med Bull* 1986;42:97-100.

23. Kopelman MD, Lishman WA: Pharmacological treatments of dementia (non-cholinergic). *Br Med Bull* 1986;42:101-105.

24. Volicer L, Herz LR: Pharmacologic management of Alzheimer-type dementia. *Am J Fam Practice* 1985;32:123-128.

25. Reifler BV, Larson E, Hanley R: Coexistence of cognitive impairment and depression in geriatric outpatients. *Am J Psychiatry* 1982;139:623-626.

26. Reifler BV, Larson E, Teri L, et al: Dementia of the Alzheimer's type and depression. *J Am Geriatr Soc* 1986;34:855-859.

27. Ron MA, Toone BK, Garralda ME, et al: Diagnostic accuracy in presenile dementia. *Br J Psychiatry* 1979;134:161-168.

28. Barnes R, Veith R, Okimoto J, et al: Efficacy of antipsychotic medications in behaviorally disturbed dementia patients. *Am J Psychiatry* 1982;129:1170-1174.

29. Maletta GJ: Medications to modify at-home behavior of Alzheimer's patients. *Geriatrics* 1985;40:31-42.

30. Risse SC, Barnes R: Pharmacologic treatment of agitation associated with dementia. *J Am Geriatr Soc* 1986;34:368-376.

31. Boller F, Mizutani T, Roessman U, et al: Parkinson's disease, dementia, and Alzheimer's disease: Clinicopathological correlations. *Ann Neurol* 1980;7:329-335.

32. Rheaume YL, Riley ME, Volicer L: Nutritional risk associated with constant walking in Alzheimer's disease. *J Nutr Elderly* (in press).

33. Lilly R, Cummings JL, Benson DF, et al: The human Kluver-Bucy syndrome. *Neurology* 1983;33:1141-1145.

34. Fengler AP, Goodrich N: Wives of elderly disabled men: The hidden patients. *Gerontologist* 1979;19:175-183.

35. Rabins PV, Mace NL, Lucas MJ: The impact of dementia on the family. *JAMA* 1982;249:333-335.

36. Cohen D, Eisdorfer C: *The Loss of Self*. New York, W.W. Norton, 1986.

37. Kapust LR. Living with dementia: The ongoing funeral. *Soc Work Health Care* 1982;7:79-91.

CHAPTER 3

Caring for the Family Caregivers

June Brown, Paula C. Lyon, and T. D. Sellers

The insidious course of Alzheimer's disease creates significant disruption in the lives of the Alzheimer's victim and his or her family. The chaos of early stage disease is followed by the turmoil resulting from the ever-increasing decline in all levels of patient function—the loss of the very essence of self. As these losses mount within the victim, the family caregivers find less and less time to acknowledge their own needs as they are caught in accelerating caregiving responsibilities.

Dementia of the Alzheimer type has unique characteristics that lead to special problems for the families: the early loss of the patient's ability to communicate; the slow progression of the disease resulting in a mourning period that extends over many years; and the childlike state of the Alzheimer patient that leads to the formation of a unique bond between the patient and family members or other caregivers. The neurologic disintegration of the patient with Alzheimer's disease is reflected in the psychological and social disintegration of the family unit.

A treatment program for the Alzheimer patient should include professional counseling and support for the family. Sympathetic recognition of the difficulties that families encounter and a humane and practical approach to management of this most destructive illness may avert caregiver "burnout" and premature institutionalization of the patient.

The early symptoms are subtle, often occurring during those years when families have established expectations of relative life stability. At first the patient's memory lapses seem to be merely inconsiderate behavior, emotional withdrawal, or as not quite "being there." This is often attributed to and excused as the normal stress and strain of daily life. Observers, such as friends and extended family, see little need for concern and, indeed, may see no problem at all. A kind of social facade is maintained at this very early stage by family members, but they do begin to worry. The patient in the early stage of dementia begins to worry and activates defenses, with denial being one of the chief mechanisms used.[1] Irritability, confusion, and disruption develop in the normal course of daily life. This is often viewed as a temporary problem, but it is not. As time passes and symptoms intensify, family members may seek the advice of a member of the clergy or a family physician, but they do not define a real problem, describing only absentmindedness or thoughtlessness. These problems are dismissed as the normal difficulties of growing older, with the frequent prescription to stop worrying. There is seldom any real understanding of the very early stages of the disease; yet these are the beginning throes of what is to be a catastrophic life event.

Finally the spouse or the adult children become so concerned that they force the patient to see a physician. However, even at this time the family may not really be certain who has the problem or which spouse is overreacting to the other. The victim may by now be depressed, often with a clinical depression. The person is aware of losing function, that there is something wrong; but he or she does not know what it is and uses denial if questioned directly. The family physician at this point may make a first diagnosis of depression and a course of treatment may ensue.

When a diagnosis of Alzheimer's disease is made the family enters into the heart of the crisis and becomes dispirited and demoralized. For years the family has been living with a massive amount of disruption, anger, guilt, and sorrow. Now the spouse or children feel they should not be angry at the victim because the illness is not his or her fault or choice. Who is to blame? Generally at this point a spouse may accept the blame, turning the anger and sorrow inward and often developing a clinical depression.

Especially difficult for the family is the perplexing phenomenon of sporadic bursts of appropriate responses by the patient in the middle of the usual chaos of garbled speech and bizarre behavior. A victim of Alzheimer's disease making nonsensical statements will suddenly become appropriate and ask, "Have you paid the taxes?" These episodes of normalcy confuse the caregiver, who wonders if the victim is getting better. This response in the caregiver may be allied with what Kubler-Ross[2] has described as the bargaining phase of grief. Then as the patient drops back into the usual patterns of dementia, the caregiver wonders which is the "real" loved one. Questions develop around establishing what is reality; who is the sick one becomes problematic for the well caregiver. Reality testing seems difficult and assessments are shaky.

The effect of a patient's inconsistent behavior causes family members added stress as they balance between hope and hopelessness in the struggle for equilibrium. The caregiver may suspect that the entire sequence of symptoms has been an ugly practical joke, that the patient has been "faking it." When the patient's behavior swings from "normal" back to the symptoms of the illness, the caregiver is left with yet more guilt, that he or she doubted the legitimacy of the illness and became angry with the patient. This guilt is more fuel to propel the family member into an overkill of caregiving. This creates another source of isolation for the caregiver, one that contributes to the sense of unreality about what is happening. As the relative becomes entangled in the minutia of caregiving that absorbs all his or her time and energy,[3] he or she seems to enter a kind of limbo. Time seems to stop for the relative who feels caught in the endless existence of life with a victim of Alzheimer dementia, while the life of those outside seems to speed by.

Life for the families is a chronicle of sorrow, rejection, and frustration. It is helpful to encourage family members to acknowledge not only their grief but also those "forbidden" feelings of shame, anger, embarrassment, and the wish to flee from the problems. The admission that it is embarrassing or frustrating to take one's spouse to a favorite restaurant can result in a more comfortable acceptance of the feelings and then a conscious decision about the value of the action. The family is trying to cope with the loss of the loved one *who is still there*. The victim walks and talks but is dying by degree. His or her personality is dying, and it is a devastating process. The victim and the family become more and more vulnerable to the stress of the disease that is now the center of their lives.

Another important aspect of the family's experience is isolation from the medical profession. After the diagnosis is made, physicians often have the helpless reaction to an incurable and virtually untreatable disease that causes them to take a kind of "hands off" attitude. To see a patient suffering from Alzheimer's disease is to see a person regress from a robust life, backward through childlike stages, to become what some describe as "the walking dead," and finally to become locked into a vegetative fetal state. Families describe physicians who do not pursue active workup or diagnosis, perhaps as an avoidance of the reality they would rather not confirm. The medical profession pulls back, as do extended family and friends. The caregiver is left with little support, all of the decisions, and very little certainty about what to do and how to manage.

Caregiver Evaluation and Education

A team composed of physician (neurologist), nurse practitioner, social worker, and psychologist begin treatment with an assessment of both patient and caregiver levels of function. The determinations of such an interdisciplinary team should aim to provide education, support, and intervention strategies.

Caught in the complexity of living with a victim of dementia, the caregivers seldom seek help for themselves. Thus, the clinic appointment for the patient should also be designed as an opportunity for the caregiver to receive assistance. Tests used to measure the patient's capacity to function aid the team in identifying the problems in caregiver coping. Unless these problems are addressed, the overstressed caregivers may mismanage the patient's treatment. Too often the caregiver, who is confused and filled with a sense of failure and shame (Wexler, personal communication, April 1985) in controlling the course of the illness, develops a pattern of self-defeating behaviors, often exacerbating the patient's symptoms. For example, if a caregiver measures his or her measure of devotion and quality of care by how well groomed the patient appears, but the patient is resistive to this care, is incontinent, or denuditive, then the caregiver needs assistance in lowering the standard of "good care" to a more achievable goal. Growing a beard may be a solution for the patient who forgets how to shave but resists having someone else do it. Clothing the patient in sweatshirts and pants often eases the tension of dressing and mastering buttons, zippers, etc. When the caregiver's insistence on giving "good care" results in added tension within the patient who is unable to be cooperative, both caregiver and patient are subject to increased stress.

The treatment team must be prepared to give repetitive instructions for patient care. The stressed caregiver dealing with a confused patient whose behavior may fluctuate from hour to hour is not always able to hear or remember instructions for caregiving. Therefore, the treatment team must be prepared to repeat instructions for care ("if he's refusing to get in the bathtub, wait an hour, or a day") as frequently as needed, despite the fact time may have previously been spent explaining the same issue. The patient's continuing decline in function requires the caregiver to frequently readjust his or her perceptions of the patient, which often is a difficult task. For that reason a strong support plan should be included in the treatment program, including regular clinic appointments at three-month intervals with the interdisciplinary team and a measure of team outreach intervention. A willingness on the part of the treatment team to telephone or occasionally visit the patient and caregiver is to reaffirm interest in their welfare. A reminder to an overburdened and lonely caregiver that a team member is always available through a telephone hot line may lessen the caregiver's sense of isolation, which is so frequently a by-product of Alzheimer's disease. The affirmation of the caregiver's right to question may also aid in restoring a level of self-confidence.

With the philosophy that Alzheimer's disease has a catastrophic effect on the family as well, the treatment team must espouse the concept that nurturing the caregiver is an integral part of treatment for the patient.

Families struggling with the impact of Alzheimer's disease benefit from a liaison to information, medical treatment, interpretation, and understanding. Today there is access to education through several fine books, a continual flow of newspaper and popular journal articles, and support groups.

Each of these may be highly useful or may be the source of increased anxiety. A comprehensive book may serve as a resource, an encyclopedia of sound advice. However, if it is used in isolation it may overwhelm the caregiver with the enormity of potential problems. The treatment team must provide the caregiver with adjuncts to the educational material through teaching and counseling based on his or her ability to cope. It may be necessary to reassure the caregiver that not all he or she has heard or read about Alzheimer's disease is certain to happen. This expectation may be so frightening that it lessens the caregiver's capacity to function.

Problems and Intervention Strategies

Assessment of the feasibility of continued patient care at home should reveal the need for the intervention of home health aides, visiting nurses, or respite care for the caregiver. Included should be an assessment of aids and safety measures within the home. Day care for the patient may be a highly successful form of respite. Community resources and respite care are discussed in Chapters 4 and 6.

Home Assistance

Early in the disease process the patient and the family are able to participate jointly in the management of problems. The team can encourage the transfer of responsibility. For example, an ill husband can assist with the housekeeping and his wife can then manage the financial affairs, in which the patient's "little memory problem" may cause him frustration and the family costly financial errors. If there is resistance to this role adjustment, the team can support a position of change, perhaps suggesting to the patient that it is the other spouse's "turn" to do this chore. Often neither patient nor spouse is ready or able to deal with the fact that the change in roles is permanent. To emphasize the permanence is not always helpful at this time, and could add to the stress. Time alone will reinforce this reality of change. With encouragement, many couples can enjoy the aspect of themselves in some role reversals. This is a healthy coping response to the trauma of change, enabling a gradual transition to the losses incurred in Alzheimer's disease. However, there is a danger that minimizing the immediate problems can increase the shock of subsequent decline. Thus the team should monitor and correct unrealistic expectations, taking care that they do not overwhelm the caregiver with fear of the future.

There is a time when memory aids are useful for the patient. An appointment book can be maintained for the patient, and notes on the stove and refrigerator tell when and what to eat, serving as reminders to someone who otherwise might forget meals. The patient may also benefit from carrying an address book and wearing an identification bracelet. Some men who resist wearing the bracelet find it more acceptable if their wife also wears one. Gentle reminders and memory aids can bridge the patient's ever-increasing deficits.

As the disease symptoms increase, there is a corresponding increase in the levels of stress within the caregiver. Changes in the patient are often reflected in the caregiver as feelings of helplessness sometimes verging on panic. For example, when the patient forgets where he or she left the car, a new crisis has arisen, with serious implications for the future.

Driving

The decision not to permit the patient to drive may be a very difficult one. Families need assistance with this because they regard taking away this privilege as removing one of the few remaining pleasures left to the patient. The patient may manage the mechanics of driving in a seemingly acceptable fashion, but in reality judgment and reaction time may be grossly impaired. If the spouse does not drive, and also depends on the patient for shopping, physician's appointments, and social excursions, the spouse may enter into an unconscious conspiracy to allow driving to continue. In American society where getting behind the wheel symbolizes independence and power, the driver impaired by Alzheimer's disease is already programmed to resist any efforts to dissuade him or her from driving.

A spouse who is convinced the patient should not drive may feel helpless to prevent it, fearing and receiving verbal and sometimes physical abuse when attempting to keep the patient from behind the wheel. It is the responsibility of the treatment team to assist with the problem, with firm instructions to the patient and encouragement to the family, supporting whatever ruses might help (disabling the car if necessary), and in the final instance taking action to have the driver's license removed when less drastic action has failed. The danger to the patient, family, and other innocent drivers must not be ignored when the patient demonstrates markedly impaired judgment.

Violence

If the Alzheimer patient is subject to outbursts of aggressive or violent behavior, both the patient and the caregiver need immediate help. A formerly gentle person who becomes assaultive, shouts and curses, and breaks things is frightening and dangerous. So, too, is the patient who has always displayed episodic violence but becomes markedly more uncontrollable. Unfortunately, violent behavior may serve to make the abused feel guilty and ashamed and therefore reluctant to ask for help. The treatment team can prepare the caregiver for the possibility of violence and provide counsel that such behavior may be unavoidable. Strategies for managing uncontrollable behavior can be suggested (see Chapter 7). Patients and caregivers alike need protection from unacceptable behavior. Medication control (see Chapter 11) may be necessary[4] for severe agitation or assaultive behavior. Persistent actions, such as use of dangerous tools or machinery, walking in dangerous traffic areas, or wandering, are other issues of concern. Where these hazards exist, the patient's comfort and safety are at risk, and both patient and caregiver need protection. Above all, caregivers need to know that they need not jeopardize their own safety by failing to protect themselves. Leaving the room, or the premises, when in danger is a perfectly acceptable response, as is seeking assistance of neighbors, family, police, ambulance, or fire department.

Legal Implications

If liaison to medical treatment, education, and understanding are first lines of intervention, what follows is equally important. A sound assessment often indicates the need for legal advice to safeguard assets and protect the family from catastrophic mistakes, and to clarify questions pertaining to guardianship, financial, and legal issues (see Chapter 5).

The judgmentally impaired patient may continue to wield the power of the checkbook. As in driving, strong issues of control are at work here and deferring to the well partner is not always a simple logical decision, especially when the illness has damaged logical thought processes. When the patient has the power to make important financial decisions, he or she has the potential for making serious errors, such as becoming a victim to his or her own mistakes in arithmetic or flagrantly dishonest "get-rich-quick" scams. Again family members must be advised of the serious danger to their economic equilibrium if the patient manages the finances and properties. The process of gaining control and the kind of legal action necessary does vary from state to state. Referral for legal advice is vital. Often the local chapter of the Alzheimer's Disease and Related Disorders Association (ADRDA) can supply names of sympathetic and knowledgeable lawyers to properly advise a course of action.

Therapeutic Lying

Telling the truth is not always a measure of love and respect for the patient with Alzheimer's disease. It may be necessary to lie to an Alzheimer victim. A caring spouse or other family members may agonize over how much to tell a patient about the illness and are torn between the desire to protect the patient from the horrible knowledge of the future course of the disease and the feeling that it is unfair of them to be deceptive. The treatment team can assist with these decisions by helping the family better understand the patient's capacity to comprehend and to mourn his or her losses. Forcing an understanding of the reality of Alzheimer's disease on the victim may indeed be a needless cruelty, or an impossible task. Some families embark on programs to educate and retrain the patient when he or she no longer is able to fully understand or to learn. This effort by caring families can be exhausting and ultimately fails after a high expenditure of time and patience.

Families can be helped to learn that a lie is sometimes a useful tool when it works in the patient's best interest. For example, a patient who insists on visiting a mother who died 25 years previously may respond with anger and disbelief to a spouse who recites a lengthy history of the mother's death and patiently repeats it with each request, but he or she may turn away satisfied when the response is "We'll go after dinner." This kind of simple lie is helpful at times to protect the patient from emotional confrontations and the family from repetitious exercises in futility.

Although no one can determine exactly how much information the patient can process, it is a kindness not to overburden him or her with stimuli. If the caregiver is helped to observe what best keeps the patient calm and relaxed, the burden of truth may be lightened. Educating caring family members to this concept may be met with anger and resistance because of their ambivalence created as the victim of the disease declines. It is the caregiver who needs and deserves the patient repetition of methods of management of the victim and orientation to changing concepts of loyalty and devotion.

Communication

As the disease progresses the patient's behavior must be interpreted to the family as a reflection of disease symptoms, not as willful actions. This is a difficult concept for family members to grasp, and they need help in understanding behaviors and responses as virtually uncontrollable by the patient. Families need frequent reassurance and explanations of symptoms that are distressing. A patient who laughs when his or her spouse is sad does so because of the inability to understand what has happened. A barrage of profanity from the patient may be interpreted as intense criticism by the caregiver when in reality it is a symptom of brain damage, as are assaultive or resistive actions. With this knowledge family members can be released from some of the feelings of anger and shame engendered by the patient's confusing and troublesome words and actions.

The members of the treatment team must be aware that their vocabulary can be misunderstood. A caregiver hearing that a patient is "resistive" may feel this is an indication that the patient is deliberately causing problems for those trying to help. The resulting action in the caregiver is likely to be an attempt to persuade the patient to be more cooperative, causing him or her to be more confused and "resistive." The possibility that resistance may be a reflex response may never occur to the family.

The treatment team should monitor the usage of words that cause distress for the caregiver and to the variable definitions applicable in different stages of the illness. The patient may also use inaccurate language. Hearing a patient state that he or she is "bored" leads the family to seek elaborate methods to provide activities. The greater kindness to everyone might be to recognize that the patient may be expressing an inability to keep up with what is going on in his or her environment and needs encouragement to take time "to do nothing," a useful rest from the strain of living in confusion.

Families observing a patient with a severe startle reflex should be reassured this is not an indication that the person is frightened. A patient who is "anxious," "agitated," "restless," or "assaultive" may be exhibiting symptoms of confusion that may be misinterpreted by the caregiver as his or her failure to provide needed stimulus for the patient.

Another aspect of communication is nonverbal language. The family can be helped to learn that tone of voice is often more important than words, that a low soothing voice may accomplish far more than a firm voice of authority. Body language often communicates the tension or anxieties of the caregiver, resulting in undesirable behaviors in the patient. Slow movement and gentle touch are reassuring and tranquilizing messages to the patient who cannot be reached through direct conversation. As caregivers learn the power of nonverbal communication, they may also be cautioned against the use of another method of communication that may have been practiced prior to the onset of Alzheimer's disease, that of "mind reading" (Carter, personal communication, November 1984). Through the years family members develop methods of knowing what each other is thinking or feeling, a process that is perfected by verbal exchanges and repetitive practice. Interpreting the Alzheimer victim's thoughts is counterproductive because the dementing process skews his or her thinking and reactions to people and events. The seeds of guilt are often sown by a caregiver who interprets present negative responses by reading the mind that can no longer signal accurately.

Although careful assessment of the patient and attention to his or her needs is paramount, so, too, is the use of a careful vocabulary, both verbal and nonverbal, that does not inflict unnecessary pain on the families.

Caregiver Counseling

Professional counseling and support for family members should be available, on a continuing basis, from first contact through the death of the patient. If the treatment facility or team does not provide counseling services, they can recommend that the family contact the local ADRDA chapter. Some communities may provide counseling through their Visiting Nurse Association (VNA) or the agency directing issues of elderly affairs. Often a family doctor may refer the family for psychiatric consultation. The clergy is another source of comfort and support. Such counseling should be directed by a counselor, experienced with issues of death and dying, toward management of stress and grief.[5] Counseling is a powerful source of comfort and guidance, but unless directed by professional or skilled counselors the danger exists that the complexity of problems and feelings can be mismanaged. The skilled counselor works toward the interruption of destructive coping patterns such as self-imposed isolation, the displacement and projection of painful feelings, excessive denial, and guilt. Greater self-awareness and growth are developed through the therapeutic process using support and positive transference as instruments to renew alliances and to form new ones.

Family members should be evaluated prior to being referred for individual, family, or group therapy. Assessment of communication skills, ego strengths, past life adjustment, and the capacity to relate to others is useful in determining the appropriate counseling modality. Group members must contract to abide by defined purpose and commitment: sharing experiences in coping with the patient's illness and giving and receiving support from other members.

To varying degrees Alzheimer's disease has an impact on all family members. With the goal of strengthening family unity, counseling is useful for all family members of caregivers. Spouses and adult children of Alzheimer's patients need to be assisted with priority setting so that the sense of duty to the patient does not seriously weaken commitment to careers, other family members, personal health, and social ties so important to the future. The counselor can also be helpful in clarifying the patient's capacity to interact at the various stages of his or her disease so that the family can be freed from expenditure of time and energy if the patient does not require or appreciably benefit from it. The family is helped to develop a better understanding of the most functional way to deal with a relationship with the demented patient, present as it were, in body only. Families are encouraged to learn to trust again, to share, to mourn for one not yet dead, and to begin rebuilding their lives. The recognition that they are not bad people who caused their family member's disease enables the families to begin to see themselves as worthwhile. They have the opportunity to accept, gain insight, and use new methods of dealing with this catastrophic life event.

Coping devices for dealing with loss and grief and preparation for future loss are ongoing foci of the therapy. A lack of understanding of the illness after several years of conflicting diagnoses and bewildering experiences has left families with a residue of confusion. Many sessions of therapy deal with factual data and a sorting out of past information and misinformation. The counseling process may serve as a guide toward more stable living and as a means of expressing conflicting and sorrowful feelings within this seemingly unending mourning process. An orderly grieving period is an unrealistic goal in the adjustment to the loss of a close relative with Alzheimer's disease.[6,7]

The family members exhibit similar but varying degrees of anxiety, depression, and alienation resulting not only from the effects of illness on the family structure but also from society's reaction to the disease. There is an almost universal avoidance of the real horror of Alzheimer's disease's destructive process.

Sexuality and Maternal Pathologic Bonding

The progression of Alzheimer's disease, with the relentless destruction of brain cells, usually includes a phase of increased motor activity accompanied by a growing social disinhibition. This combination of symptoms often results in an increase of sexual activity.[8] For the spouse, accustomed to the pattern of sexual expression evolved throughout the marriage, the sexual act with one who no longer recognizes the meaning of intimacy becomes a parody of lovemaking.

Although symptoms of the Kluver-Bucy syndrome, such as hyperorality, emotional blunting, and hypersexuality have been described as occurring late in the course of Alzheimer's disease,[9] families have reported fragments of these symptoms occurring much earlier.

The patient, responding to the vicissitudes of the illness, may feel a sexual urgency: the male patient may or may not achieve an erection; the female patient may become seductive and immediately rejecting. The sex act is performed without real foreplay and can be over abruptly without tenderness and without either emotional or physical satisfaction. It is a mindless act that leaves the well spouse with feelings of rejection and repugnance. This is made more disturbing by a marked increase in frequency. Spouses do not know how to react. They are repulsed, but ashamed of this reaction, and they find this difficult to talk about.

Together with these increased sexual demands, the spouse is assuming more and more responsibility for the caregiving of the patient. The childlike needs of the patient activates a kind of maternal bonding within the spouse. Many aspects of becoming parent to the Alzheimer patient/child are fostered as the decline of higher functions causes the victim to become more infantile, further authenticating a parent-child relationship. Attempts by the spouse to retreat from the intensity of such a relationship seems to trap him or her in an almost instinctive taboo against child abandonment. The mix of this maternal bonding and the patient's hypersexuality creates new kinds of internal conflicts for the spouse. As many have told us, "It's like having sex with my child." This culturally forbidden act serves as a further source of pathologic bonding. This bond is seemingly more intense and more problematic with Alzheimer patients than with other chronic debilitating illnesses.

The premorbidly compromised marital relationship complicates the bond. Mounting responsibilities for patient care intensify resentments over unresolved conflicts,[10] particularly when the caregiver has the prior sense of being overburdened in the marital role.

This pathologic bond affects the way the spouse feels about himself or herself, and the way he or she relates to people outside of the marriage relationship. Typically, the defense against his or her own sexual feelings, which, at best, become confused, is an almost slavelike devotion to the patient. This increases isolation, as does the suppression of feelings that develop around participation in sexual activities that frustrate, humiliate, and repulse while serving as a cruel reminder of what was once an expression of mutual love and respect.

The treatment team may find this pathologic bonding firmly entrenched and difficult for the spouse to acknowledge. Special care must be taken to educate the spouse to the disease process at work in this entangled bond.

A spouse should be taught how to gently dissuade or distract the sexually persistent patient, using medications when advisable. It is also necessary to teach the spouse that rejecting a patient's behavior is not a renunciation of love or marital duty. In short, the spouse needs to know that it is all right to reject bondage to practices initiated by a dementia victim. If the spouse is assisted in recognizing disease symptoms, he or she can learn that expressions of love need not involve responses that diminish self-esteem.

Institutional Care

Institutionalization is almost inevitable for the Alzheimer's patient. The family both dreads and welcomes it and needs help with this ambivalence (see Chapter

7).[11] If institutionalization is achieved, the caregiver is often criticized for abandoning caregiving responsibilities. For the most part, family and friends take an accusatory, judgmental attitude toward the caregiver, indicating either subtly or openly that hospitalization for the patient is a result of the caregiver's failure to cope. This affirms the caregiver's deepest fears and doubts about his or her role in the illness.[12] Nursing staff and physicians, with their innate goal of health restoration, may exert pressure on the caregiver to try again to maintain the patient at home. These efforts may unwillingly serve to reactivate the despair and continue the destructive pattern of the illness on the caregiver.

The treatment team participates in family education. A social worker serving as liaison between staff and family may heighten understanding and tolerance. By helping families deal with their grief, the displacement of these painful feelings onto the staff and each other may be lessened. An informed staff who fully understands the impact on the family of institutionalizing a loved one is able to bring comfort, not blame, and is able to support the necessary separation and anticipation of death.

This is a period of accelerated mourning and increased depression for caregivers and their needs should be monitored. This is also the period when family members enter into a sense of rivalry with the staff caregivers and may become critical and demanding. Families need education about the patient's behavior within the institution and support for the emotions aroused when the patient's care is transferred to others. This period may also mark for the family the beginning of their re-engagement and re-socialization apart from the patient.

During the period of institutionalization comes a series of crises with each infection and feeding problem—each a "little death" in the ongoing process of dying from Alzheimer's disease. An important aspect of family support is acknowledgement that the wish for the victim's death may be an ultimate expression of love as well as a wish for relief from the pain of observing its process. Families must be helped to anticipate death and learn to live with the mixture of joy and rage at the prolongation of the dying process. Grief and mourning seem never ending.

Usually a visit to a hospitalized patient is a gesture of concern. In contrast, the Alzheimer's patient may not even recognize the visitor. This is awkward for friends and heart breaking for families. A patient who calls his wife "mother" or does not acknowledge his son can cause them to feel intense rejection. On the other hand, a labile patient who weeps and clings to visiting family renews their guilt and uncertainty about abandonment. A visiting spouse will pace the corridors with the patient, straining to find a point of contact, waiting hopefully for a flicker of the past relationship. If the patient, who has long since lost the concept of time, says to a visitor, "I haven't seen you in a long time," that visitor is likely to make greater efforts to spend time with the patient, who does not know whether he or she was visited this morning or last year.

Educating the family and friends to a realistic visiting schedule is an important aspect of responsibility of the treatment team. Although some families need to be relieved of the burden of too frequent visits that tax their physical state and debilitate their already shattered emotional equilibrium, others seek staff acceptance of their need to visit with greater frequency. Visitors need to know that a "proper" visit need not be an extended one. Indeed, the patient might better enjoy a visit that is not prolonged beyond the capacity to participate, and the visitor may feel greater satisfaction if the visit has not been unduly stressful. As a general rule, the visit should be for the benefit of the visitor, not the patient.

Impact of Death on Caregivers

There is intense emotional impact on both the family and the nursing staff who care for the Alzheimer patient in the final days, hours, and moments of death. The patients, who have been described by families as "the walking dead" much earlier in the course of the disease, have, at best, only remnants remaining of the unique beings they once were.

The myriad of basic human emotions that are activated in the presence of death are responded to in a variety of ways, from emotional or physical flight to an intensification of involvement in final care. There is a strong impulse, for those who remain with the patient, to comfort him or her, ease the passage, and to make contact. There is an urgency to let the patient know he or she is not alone. To achieve this with the Alzheimer's patient necessitates a kind of re-engagement. How does one establish a deep personal contact with one already lost and mourn the dying of the dead? If this hoped for sense of contact does not come, the nursing staff may feel inadequate and the family feel more cheated, more guilty, and more bereaved. In addition, there exists a macabre quality to the event. The dying patient, contracted, emaciated, and grotesque, seems to amplify the caregiver's primordial fear of death.

At present, while the struggle is to better understand and cope with the disease process, little attention has been given to helping the caregivers. Unfortunately, the failure to support the family during the dying process may be a prologue to future emotional stress for the survivors.

With death comes the final intervention. Even in death, the family of an Alzheimer victim may remain alone. Although families are usually ambivalent, final bereavement work is important. Perhaps the reasons are best stated by a widow of an Alzheimer's patient: "They don't allow you to mourn. Everyone tells me he had a chronic disease so I've got to be happy his suffering is over." Team efforts should be made after the patient's death to continue the relationship with the caregiver in order to provide emotional support in a still critical period in the course of Alzheimer's disease.[13]

This illness, which wastes the lives of its victims and their families, may continue its course of destruction unless those survivors are helped to alleviate the sense of failure and guilt and to retrieve what was positive in their lives before the Alzheimer's disease affected a loved one.[14] Death may leave a residue of bitterness and continuing sorrow. If the living can be helped to recall warm memories and loving feelings, while acknowledging their devastating losses, they will be better equipped to rebuild their lives.

Families who are helped to express their anguish and despair, and who are treated as ones deserving help, concern, and respect, can learn again to trust a world that seemed to have abandoned them. They can recover a sense of self-respect and pride in their accomplishments, both in the care of the Alzheimer victim and their own survival of this catastrophic event.

REFERENCES

1. Katzman R: Alzheimer's disease. *N Engl J Med* 1986;314:965.

2. Kubler-Ross E: *On Death and Dying*. New York, Macmillan, 1970.

3. Mace NL, Rabins PV: *The 36-Hour Day: A Family Guide to Caring for Persons with Alzheimer's Disease, Related Dementing Illnesses, and Memory Loss in Later Life*. Baltimore, Johns Hopkins University Press, 1981.

4. Volicer L, Herz LR: Pharmacologic management of Alzheimer-type dementia. *Am Fam Physician* 1985;32:123-128.

5. Wason M: Support groups for family caregivers of patients with Alzheimer's Disease. *Soc Work* 1986;March/April:93-97.

6. Kapust LR: Living with dementia. *Soc Work Health Care* 1982;Summer:79-91.

7. Levine NB, Gendron CE, Dastoon DP, et al: Existential issues in the management of the demented elderly patient. *Am J Psychother* 1984;38:217.

8. Lezak M: Living with the characterologically altered brain injured patient. *J Clin Psychiatry* 1978;39:592-598.

9. Cummings JL, Duchen LW: Kluver-Bucy syndrome in Pick disease: Clinical and pathologic correlations. *Neurology* 1981;31:1415-1422.

10. Gilleard CJ, Belford H, Gilleard E, et al: Emotional distress amongst the supporters of the elderly mentally infirm. *Br J Psychiatry* 1984;145:172-177.

11. Cath SH: Orchestration of disengagement. *Int J Aging Hum Dev* 1975;6:207.

12. Scharlach A, Frenzel C: An evaluation of institution based respite care. *Gerontologist* 1986;26:81.

13. Vaillant GE: Attachment, loss, and rediscovery. *Psychiatr Times* 1986;3:1.

14. Goin MK: Timeless attachment to a dead relative. *Am J Psychiatry* 1979;136:988-989.

CHAPTER 4

Economic Considerations in Alzheimer Dementia

Kathryn E. Lasch

The economic issues involved in Alzheimer dementia are complex. Just as a definitive diagnosis for Alzheimer dementia remains elusive, so do the solutions to the present and potential personal and societal economic problems posed by this disease. The financial issues that arise for Alzheimer dementia victims occur within a labyrinth of tax laws; federal, state, and local health and mental health policies and resources; personal resources; and health insurance schemes and the incentives for various kinds of care these schemes provide. The purpose of this chapter is to describe the personal and societal costs involved in Alzheimer dementia, to sort out from this labyrinth what services and resources are actually currently available to patients and their families, to point out where gaps remain, and to discuss new programs and proposals that have been designed to fill unmet needs.

Personal and Societal Costs of Alzheimer Dementia

Alzheimer dementia exacts a significant cost from patients, caregivers, and society in general. It is estimated that Alzheimer's disease afflicts 1.2 to 4 million people in the United States today.[1] Each one of these patients requires care ranging from minimal supervision, some assistance with instrumental activities of daily living such as balancing checkbooks, some help with activities of daily living such as bathing and dressing, to total care. Diagnosis and medical treatment of Alzheimer patients is in general a costly process. Many Alzheimer patients in addition require medical care for secondary illnesses (see Chapter 9). The cost of this medical and personal care is high.

Estimates of the personal and societal costs of Alzheimer dementia suggest a rather bleak picture of the economic context of the disease. Using epidemiological projections of the prevalence and incidence, and survival time estimates of victims of Alzheimer dementia, Hay and Ernst[2] were able to estimate the expected (or average) net direct and indirect costs associated with the disease. They estimated that on the average personal costs per patient were about $18,000 per year:

the total costs of the disease per patient in 1983 ranged from approximately $48,000 to $495,000 per year, and total national costs for all persons first diagnosed with Alzheimer dementia in 1983 were about $28 billion to $31 billion.

Direct costs of Alzheimer dementia stem from diagnosis, medical treatment, day care and respite services where available, and formal and informal long-term care. The cost of diagnosis varies with the number of times a patient is seen before a diagnosis is made, the number and training of professionals a patient sees, local medical costs, and whether the evaluation is conducted on an inpatient or an outpatient basis. It has been estimated that outpatient diagnosis, which can entail physician charges, laboratory tests, neuropsychological testing, brain imaging studies, and ancillary services can range from $1,000 to $2,000; costs of laboratory tests alone can range from $150 to over $1,000 per patient.[3] Hay and Ernst estimate the expected cost of a diagnosis of Alzheimer dementia to be $874 per patient.[2] Inpatient diagnosis would cost substantially more. Most diagnoses at this time, however, are made on an outpatient basis.

Medical management of patients with dementia may require continued visits to physicians, drug treatment of behavioral symptoms and other medical problems, mental health services, and intermittent hospital care for secondary illnesses. The costs of what is called informal care delivered to patients in their homes, at senior citizen centers, and in adult day care centers is difficult to estimate. In-home care may include respite care, home health care, and volunteer services. Most informal care is delivered by spouses and the adult children of patients.

In addition to these direct costs of care, indirect costs of care need to be added when the cost of Alzheimer dementia is calculated. Loss of opportunity to earn money by patients who have to terminate employment because of their impairment represents significant psychological and economic costs. Similarly, caregivers who have to terminate employment or reduce hours to provide care forgo the economic and psychological benefits of employment. Many caregivers, including those of retirement age, have expressed their dissatisfaction with their inability to seek employment due to their caregiving responsibilities and the impact a part-time salary would have on other benefits they may be receiving.

Personal costs to families also include those incurred because the patient has not paid bills, has overdrawn on his or her checking account, has abused credit cards, or in other ways has mismanaged finances unbeknown to the family. The psychological costs, and at times medical costs, exacted from families owing to the stress of caregiving and the forgone opportunities for leisure and recreation have not been estimated. Personal costs also include the lost value of assets that are depleted when families "spend down" to be eligible for Medicaid.

Significant expenditures have been made to further biomedical research into the etiology of Alzheimer's disease and other dementias. The motive behind this research is to ameliorate or prevent future medical and social problems associated with Alzheimer dementia by finding an effective drug or surgical treatment that could reduce symptoms or arrest this disease process. It is projected that federal agencies supporting biomedical research on dementia will spend approximately $67 million in 1987.[3] One to two million dollars will be spent on health services research on dementia. This research includes questions on patient assessment, epidemiology, service needs, cost of and access to care, and quality of care.[3]

The most consuming of the costs of Alzheimer's disease, however, is the cost of formal long-term care. Those with dementia constitute the largest definable population group requiring long-term care. There are approximately 1.2 million residents of nursing homes in the United States, and it is estimated that more than 50% of these residents are cognitively impaired. Alzheimer's disease is estimated to account for 40% of the dementias in the elderly. In 1980, federal funds for long-term care were $12 billion ($10.4 billion from Medicaid, $0.4 billion from Medicare, and $1.1 billion from the Veterans Administration).[1] Using 1982 data, the Health Care Financing Administration estimated that the government spends over $6 billion annually in nursing home costs alone for Alzheimer patients.[1]

Most authorities assume that institutional long-term care is much more costly than in-home care. At present more is spent on institutional care, and it has been suggested that quality accessible community care may be more costly than institutional care.[4] One small pilot study tried to compare the costs incurred annually in caring for a senile demented elderly patient in the home with nursing home care. This study found that, on the average, home care per patient per year costs $11,735 and nursing home care costs $22,458.[5] Nursing home care is by far the largest cost component of long-term care, with costs ranging from $750 to over $3,000 per month.[3] Health economists have estimated that while out-of-pocket costs (those paid by the patient) were approximately 5.2% of inpatient services and 10.3% of outpatient services in 1986, 49% of nursing home care was paid for out-of-pocket.[3]

Current Financing Mechanisms for Care of Alzheimer Patients

Direct federal government involvement in the financing of medical care delivery is a relatively recent phenomenon in the United States. There is no constitutionally defined role for the federal government in health.[6] To date its approach has been categorical, providing care only to certain segments of the population. Unlike the state-subsidized and regulated European public medical care delivery systems, the United States has encouraged the development of a voluntary system—a vast, complex mechanism of medical care financing involving primarily private health insurance and federally subsidized medical care programs.

The 1965 amendments to the Social Security Act, Medicare (Title 18) and Medicaid (Title 19) broadened the scope of federal financing of health care. The Kerr Mills Act, the 1960 Social Security Amendments, established, among other programs, a program of medical assistance for the medically indigent aged (medically needy elderly not receiving public assistance). Medicare and Medicaid remain the basic mechanisms by which the federal government subsidizes the health care of the elderly.

Several federal and state programs currently provide funds for the health care and income of disabled people: Medicaid, Medicare, the Nursing Home Cap Program, Supplemental Security Income (SSI), and Social Security Disability. However, for those suffering from dementia coverage is incomplete owing to wording and exclusion criteria in statutes that provide for these benefits and complicated formulas to determine eligibility and benefits.

Medicare Part A, the hospital insurance program, protects those aged 65 and older against the major costs of hospital and related care. Eligibility is determined by reaching the age of 65 and having been employed at some point in one's life. It is administered by the Social Security Administration and monthly premiums are deducted from the Social Security check. It is financed through the Hospital Trust Fund based on tax contributions from the working population and as such is called a social insurance scheme. It is uniformly administered in all states.

The wording of the Social Security Act that established Medicare, which excludes for reimbursement those charges that are "not reasonable and necessary" for treatment of disease or provides "custodial care", places Alzheimer patients at a disadvantage and assures that the kind of care they need will not be reimbursed.[1] The Medicare program does provide short-term skilled nursing or "rehabilitative" care in skilled nursing facilities, home health care, and hospice care. But because of its emphasis on rehabilitation, Alzheimer patients do not meet the definitional requirements to receive these benefits.

The 1982 Tax Equity and Fiscal Responsibility Act and 1983 Social Security Act Amendments created fundamental restructuring of the Medicare hospital payment system. Hospitals were no longer to be reimbursed retrospectively on a fee-for-service basis, but prospectively, based on a predetermined fixed payment rate for each case determined by the diagnosis-related group (DRG) into which the case fell. The DRG system imposed a cost control mechanism by providing incentives to limit costs per Medicare recipient admission. The hope was that non-hospital services (skilled nursing home services and home health services) would substitute for costly inpatient care.

Many of the services mentioned above may be particularly useful in delaying or avoiding long-term institutional care. However, to be eligible for any Medicare benefits, the patient's disease must be "medically determinable." The difficulty in diagnosing Alzheimer dementia renders dementia victims ineligible. Once again Alzheimer victims are penalized by the characteristics of their own disease. In addition, Alzheimer dementia is not among the "listing of impairments" meeting severity and duration requirements for Medicare disability benefits.

Medicaid eligibility is determined by income and financial assets, including bank accounts, stocks and bonds, and real estate. It is therefore a welfare program with a strict means test. It is administered by welfare offices of the states. Benefits and eligibility criteria vary widely by state. Most federal spending for long-term care is through the Medicaid program. Medicaid is the major payer for nursing home care in the United States, paying an estimated $10.4 billion for this type of care in 1984.[7]

Eligibility requirements for Medicaid are extremely complicated and often confusing. One factor creating this complexity is that eligibility for Medicaid is tied to eligibility to two welfare programs, Aid to Families with Dependent Children (AFDC) and Supplemental Security Income (SSI), an adult welfare program. The overall effect of this linkage is to ensure that dementia victims seeking Medicaid coverage will have to become impoverished before they qualify for benefits.

Applicants for SSI are required to meet strict income and resources criteria. On January 1, 1987, a single SSI recipient could own $1,500 in nonexcludable resources and couples could own $2,250. An applicant must have a net monthly income under $336. Those who have pensions and similar outside income are generally ineligible because of SSI's low income standards.

There are two programs available for those dementia patients who cannot meet SSI and Social Security Disability requirements: The Nursing Home Cap Program and the medically needy option. The Nursing Home Cap Program is based on a fixed income test in which a nursing home resident in 1986 is eligible for coverage of the costs of nursing home care and other medical services while residing in the home if the resident's income is less than $1,009.[3]

Thirty-nine jurisdictions have elected the medically needy option, by which those who are ineligible for AFDC and SSI in terms of income or resources but have unusually high medical bills that would impoverish them without assistance qualify for Medicaid. Medical expenses are deducted from their net income and are incurred beyond that point by the state.

The Veterans Administration (VA) provides health and social services to eligible populations either directly or under contract to other providers. Eligibility for VA benefits goes first to those who have service-connected disabilities. Services are next provided on a space-available basis. Twelve VA medical centers have developed special programs for dementia patients and their families. However, long-term care is not guaranteed. In fiscal year 1983, VA hospitals and nursing homes treated over 20,000 veterans with a diagnosis of dementia.[3] The Office of Technology Assessment (OTA) survey found that 45% of the caregivers interviewed who had applied for extended-care services were refused services.[3] The VA remains, however, the largest single provider of long-term care services in the country.

The VA also provides some community services. Home care is provided through 30 of the 172 VA medical centers. Adult day care is provided at 5 VA medical centers, and 12 provide respite care. The VA's present strategy regarding extended care is to provide a mix of extended care services and facilities. Its objectives include increasing the number of VA hospital-based home care programs from 30 to 76 by 1990 and the number of adult day health care programs from 5 to 40.[3]

Home and Community Based Resources

In 1981, federal funding became available through Medicaid for the costs of community services for individuals who would otherwise require long-term institutional care. Under the Omnibus Budget Reconciliation Act, case management services, homemaker, home health aide, personal care, adult day health, habilitation and respite care services were to be provided for Medicaid eligibles. However, according to a recent OTA report,[3] delivery of these services has been largely unrealized. The OTA suggests that this is because states wishing to add them to their Medicaid benefit package have been unable to show that these services would cost less than nursing home services, an assurance required by the Health Care Financing Administration and the Office of Management and Budget.

Medicaid will only reimburse for medical day care and personal care services if provided through what is called a medical model of service delivery. For adult day care, a medical model requires that the agency's staff include a registered nurse who will provide nursing assessment of patients. The agency will ensure that a patient has had a recent physical exam and will keep the patient's physician informed as to the patient's progress at the day care center. The nurse will dispense medication and provide training in medication management. Through contact with a visiting nurse association the agency will provide home care to educate families and, where possible, patients about medical problems.

For those who are ineligible for Medicaid, however, day care and personal care services are costly. Home health care nationally costs about $8-$9 per hour.[8] Generally a three hour minimum is imposed which means that care of this type may be as much as $27 per day. Overnight aides who provide personal care and ensure a patient's safety cost approximately $90-$105 daily.[8] This service can be especially important for families of Alzheimer patients where the patient still lives alone or to familial caregivers who are stressed due to the patient's sleep problems and night wandering. Live-in helpers who assist five days a week may cost about $74 to $83 per day. Day care centers may cost as much as $40 per day.[9] These costs are direct costs to clients and not administrative costs of these various programs.

Familial caregivers surveyed about the desirability of these services overwhelmingly agreed that these services were essential, very important, or important.[3] Medicare, which is the major provider of home care, spends only about 3% of its budget on this type of care.[3] Neither the number of individuals receiving federally funded home health care, nor the proportion of recipients who are demented is known.

Adult day care centers and respite programs have primarily been a private and/or state initiative. Some adult day health programs accept Alzheimer patients. However, mixing Alzheimer patients with those who are not cognitively impaired presents problems for both patients and staff. Some day care centers will not accept Alzheimer patients. Some states are starting to establish day care programs specifically designed for Alzheimer patients. Within the state of Massachusetts, for example, there are four adult day care centers for Alzheimer dementia patients. Recipients pay for this service privately, with Medicaid funds, or in part through funds provided through the Office of Elder Affairs. An Alzheimer's day care program is part of Maine's initiative to establish a 30-bed boarding and respite-care facility.[10]

New York City was the first municipality to sponsor a comprehensive resource center for Alzheimer dementia patients and their families. The organization put out a handbook on resources for Alzheimer patients in which it indicates that, in New York, area agencies on aging sponsor programs providing cost-free legal services for the elderly.[11] Referrals to lawyers specializing in the legal and financial complications of diseases such as Alzheimer dementia can be obtained through local chapters of the Alzheimer's Disease and Related Disorders Association. There is a growing number of Alzheimer day care centers in the state of New York.

Many support groups have sprung up nationwide for Alzheimer victims and their families. These groups are generally free of charge. Occasionally dollar donations are suggested but not required. Many are led by family members who have experienced having a dementia patient in the family. Some are sponsored by local chapters of the Alzheimer's Disease and Related Disorders Association. Others are sponsored by hospitals, senior citizens centers, and other agencies.

Current Proposals To Fund Care for Alzheimer's Dementia

Since 1984 many states have established task forces to develop recommendations for the adequate care and support of Alzheimer patients and their families. The motivation behind these task forces, in part, is to develop systems of care which could potentially postpone or avoid placement in a nursing home. The fear is that, with the aging of our population, service utilization and the need for chronic care will escalate, overwhelming existing resources. The OTA report[3] mentioned previously was requested by seven congressional committees to comprehensively examine the cost and care issues in Alzheimer's disease. It provided a comprehensive synthesis of the costs of Alzheimer dementia, the resources available to Alzheimer victims and their families, and the complex financing mechanisms that fund Alzheimer care.

The unmet needs identified by these state task forces, the OTA, and other agencies and groups are a result of the fragmented, uncoordinated, and costly system of care presently available to patients with Alzheimer dementia and their families. The recommendations of these fact-finding endeavors and the programs implemented in the last three and one-half years attempt to address these problems. Most proposals and programs suggest joint public and private sector responsibility for the long-term care required by Alzheimer patients.

Support groups are proliferating. Many, although not all, states are attempting to put in place or expand respite options such as homemaker services, personal care, companions, home health aides, and adult day health. However, at present most of these services are small scale and part of demonstration programs.

Educational programs to train professional and familial caregivers in the care of Alzheimer patients are being proposed and in some states implemented through demonstration projects. Families are being advised through newsletters of associations such as visiting nurses associations and the Alzheimer's Disease and Related Disorders Association to plan financially and to start early in the disease process.

Current legislative proposals and enacted legislation address the broad range of cost issues involved in Alzheimer dementia such as the funding of Alzheimer biomedical and health services research, financing mechanisms for the delivery of services, and the education and training of personnel to work with Alzheimer patients and their families. For example, the House of Representatives recently approved HR-1451, the reauthorization of the Older Americans Act, which if successfully enacted will expand nonmedical services to frail elderly individuals, including Alzheimer victims. In-home services are presently a part of this bill, but a separate authorization may be necessary to expand existing services and to develop new in-home services. California, Washington, and Michigan recently passed legislation that allows elderly couples to divide their assets, so that only the resources of the impaired partner are expended for medical and personal care.

There have been proposals put forward to encourage private initiative to finance long-term care, to subsidize individual efforts to meet long-term care needs privately, to expand the long-term care services to Alzheimer veterans, to modify Medicare and Medicaid by changing eligibility requirements and expanding benefit packages to more closely fit the needs of the Alzheimer population, and to support comprehensive reform of long-term care financing.[3] Congressional attention has been turned towards Alzheimer's disease, but the mix of service delivery options and financing mechanisms for its care is yet to be hammered out.

Funding to conduct research on this disease which may affect as many as 3.5 million people in the U.S. today has been made available through the private and public sector. In 1984, Congress appropriated $3.5 million to establish five Alzheimer's Disease Research Centers. Since 1984, Congress has funded an additional five centers. Each center provides shared resources for work on basic, clinical, and behavioral studies of Alzheimer's disease and related disorders.[3] In 1987, the federal government will spend approximately $32 million on research on Alzheimer's disease and related disorders.[3] The federal outlay for health services research in 1987 will be about $2 million. This seems insufficient in light of the many questions that remain about the quality of care and the appropriateness and effectiveness of actual and proposed services for Alzheimer's patients.

Several states have put through legislation that allocates funds for the operation of Alzheimer day care centers or proposes demonstration projects of the same.[12] Many states have set up task forces and committees to examine the feasibility of covering home health services, regardless of prior hospitalization, respite care services, day care services, long-term care insurance, and health insurance packages. The suggestion has been made to offer an income tax credit for Alzheimer caregivers.

Managing the Personal Costs of Alzheimer Dementia

This discussion of financial issues indicates that to many Alzheimer dementia patients and their families, this disease means heavy caregiving requirements, an uncoordinated and often inaccessible formal care system, high costs, and inadequate resources or funds to provide the comprehensive, humane, and continuous model of care presented in this book. In addition to coping with the deterioration of their afflicted relative and the lack of a specialized system of formal care, families and patients are faced with complicated financial and legal issues that arise in caring for patients with Alzheimer dementia. (See Chapter 5 for further discussion of some of these issues.)

Knowledge of and competence with financial issues vary widely by families. Many caregivers are confused or uninformed about them. Some families have not thought about financial issues at all even though their relative's cognitive functioning may be grossly impaired. For example, some still allow their relatives to carry money even though they no longer are able to handle finances. Other families, however, set a conservatorship in place or through legal means change ownership of the patient's home or other assets very early in the disease process.

Often families are given conflicting advice from the many institutions they contact as they secure a diagnosis and seek treatment for their diseased relative. Consequently, decisions are often made or are put off that jeopardize the financial situation of the family needlessly.

Money issues within families can be troublesome in general; with Alzheimer dementia the sensitivity concerning them is often heightened. The question of who in the family should assume responsibility arises. If the patient is married, the spouse may be the most appropriate party. However, many spouses are wives who have not handled financial and legal issues in the past. If both spouses happen to be incapacitated, the family needs to decide the often tension-fraught question concerning responsibility for financial and legal decisions.

Some families are hesitant to take steps regarding financial issues. They may not believe or accept the relentless course of the disease. When queried whether they have considered talking to a lawyer or financial advisor, a common response is that their relative is still able to sign checks even though it is a frustrating and lengthy experience.

For those who are aware of the financial issues, the fears of financial loss and the high costs of long-term care may be overwhelming. It has been suggested that many of the elderly may omit prescribed medications, put off needed hospitalization, and refuse to hire extra help in their homes due to the anxiety associated with impending financial insecurity.[8]

In communities where some services such as respite or day care are provided, families will often ration these services to keep within provider agencies' funding caps per year. The result is that the utilization of these services may be based on a certain reimbursement schedule rather than actual need.

Families are often confused about the benefits they are entitled to through pensions, Medicare, and Medicaid, and how to process the paper work to claim their entitlement. Families are often unaware of community resources such as home health aid, homemakers, day care centers, and respite care services. Service providers are often frustrated because they feel that many of these services and benefits are somewhat mythical for the Alzheimer dementia patient. Service providers who have contact with patients and their families may not be aware of the resources or benefits that are available. Agencies may not conduct sufficient outreach to inform potential clients of the services they provide and the funding available for these services. Potential clients often do not avail themselves of available services for reasons which are unclear at this time.

Practitioners can be of use to patients and their families regarding these financial issues. The following are suggestions which may help to ameliorate some of the problematic economic issues:

1. Practitioners should become as knowledgeable about financing mechanisms and benefits as possible. Familiarizing themselves with publications such as *Little Max: Creating Maximum Benefits for Children, Elderly, Poor, and Disabled People* may be particularly useful.[13]
2. Legal education to train lawyers in dealing with the financial problems involved in Alzheimer dementia should be available. In some states such as New York, Minnesota, and California a growing number of attorneys are skilled in dealing with the problems of the disabled. A publication, *Beyond the Safety Net: Maximizing the Resources and Medicaid Benefits for the Elderly Disabled Patient*,[14] presents the legal/financial issues involved in long-term care.
3. Families should be alerted to financial issues. If families desire counseling or guidance in this area it should be provided or they should be referred to sources which could do so.
4. Cost free legal services for elders unable to pay for such services should be made available.

5. Practitioners should alert families to the array of services available in their communities and the cost of these services.
6. Research on the cost-effectiveness of interventions for families and patients should be conducted.
7. Families and other interested parties should be made aware of organizations such as the Alzheimer's Disease and Related Disorders Association, which serves as a referral source and advocate for services for Alzheimer's patients.
8. Agencies providing services for Alzheimer patients should be encouraged to publish newsletters keeping families aware of changes in available benefits and services.

REFERENCES

1. Office of Technology Assessment: *Technology and Aging in America*, OTA-BA-264. Washington, D.C., U.S. Government Printing Office, 1985.

2. Hay JW, Ernst RE: The economic costs of Alzheimer's disease. *Am J Public Health* 1987; 77:1169-1175.

3. Office of Technology Assessment: *Losing a Million Minds: Confronting the Tragedy of Alzheimer's Disease and other Dementias*, OTA-BA-323. Washington, D.C., U.S. Government Printing Office, 1987.

4. Brody E, Lawton MP, Liebowitz B: Senile dementia: Public policy and adequate institutional care. *Am J Public Health* 1984;74:1381-1383.

5. Hu T, Huang L, Cartwright W: Evaluation of the costs of caring for the senile demented elderly: A pilot study. *Gerontologist* 1986;26:158-163.

6. Wilson F, Newhauser D: *Health Services in the United States*. Cambridge, Mass, Ballinger, 1974.

7. United States General Accounting Office: *Post-Hospital Care: Efforts to Evaluate Medicare Prospective Payment Effects Are Insufficient*, GAO-PEMD-86-10. Washington D.C., U.S. Government Printing Office, 1986.

8. Hooyman NR, Lustbader W: *Taking Care Supporting Older People and Their Families*. New York, The Free Press, 1986.

9. Personal communication with director of local day care center, May 13, 1987.

10. Faunce IB, Brunette MG: The Alzheimer's project of Tennessee Valley—A national model. *Am J Alzheimer Care Rel Dis*, Fall 1986.

11. Tanner F, Shaw S: *Caring: A Family Guide to Managing the Alzheimer's [sic] at Home*. New York, New York City Alzheimer's Resource Center, 1985.

12. State and federal legislation. *Am J Alzheimer Care Rel Dis* 1986;1:8-11.

13. Maged G, Stage ME (eds): *Little Max: Creating Maximum Benefits for Children, Elderly, Poor, and Disabled People*. Boston, Massachusetts Poverty Center, 1984.

14. Massachusetts Continuing Legal Education Center. *Beyond the Safety Net: Maximizing the Resources and Medical Benefits for the Elderly Disabled Patient*, Publication No. 87-202, 1984.

CHAPTER 5

Legal Considerations in Alzheimer's Disease

Anthony B. Sandoe

Legal considerations in the management of the patient with Alzheimer's disease affect two principal areas: property management and clinical management. Early in the course of Alzheimer's disease, patients begin to experience a gradually diminished capacity to manage their personal and business affairs and it becomes increasingly apparent that they will need help in this regard. Accordingly, the patient's family must identify the patient's assets and sources of income that will require management. The questions of the form of ownership in which these assets are held, the forms of management that may eventually be employed, and who will make these decisions will need to be addressed.

The degenerative nature of Alzheimer's disease, however, necessitates more than mere management of the patient's assets. The prospects of confinement ultimately in a long-term health care facility, perhaps for a significant period, combined with the extraordinary attendant costs will force a consideration of how patient and family resources can be marshaled to meet such expenses. Custodial expenses are potentially devastating to the family with inadequate resources, financial and otherwise, to meet them. The family must, therefore, examine whether their resources are adequate to care for the patient and in addition to care for the continuing needs of the patient's spouse as well as others who are economically dependent on the patient. As the disease progresses, further and more difficult issues begin to emerge. The family must now decide the nature and type of care that will be required at each successive stage of the patient's deterioration as well as the issue of who will have the authority to make such decisions.

NOTE: The author wishes to acknowledge the invaluable assistance of Julia O. Gregory, Esq. of Cambridge, Massachusetts in the research and preparation of this chapter. In addition, Ms. Gregory wrote portions of the section on Clinical Management.

Copyright © 1987 Anthony B. Sandoe. All rights reserved.

Management of Property Interests

Management Issues

During the early stages of Alzheimer's disease, frequently prior to diagnosis, there usually are small, barely noticeable lapses of memory and capacity. As the disease progresses, however, and memory problems increase, it becomes gradually more difficult for patients to perform once-routine daily tasks. Although patients may become more forgetful, especially of recent events, they can, nevertheless, still cope with daily management matters with slight behavioral modifications and can still live effectively with such modifications for extended periods. It has been suggested that a unique characteristic of Alzheimer's disease is that a patient's ability to think logically is far superior to recent memory capacity, although this too diminishes over time. These characteristics coupled with the probability that Alzheimer's disease is not yet suspected often enables loss of memory and other cognitive functions to remain undetected by family and friends for a long period during which time there may be no particularly serious consequences regarding property.

Critical problems and issues, however, may occur and require solution when the patient's memory loss and diminished intellectual capacity begin to intrude on the daily management of a person's business and personal financial affairs in a more serious fashion. It is at this later stage of the disease that the undiagnosed patient may begin to forget appointments or fail to meet important deadlines. Symptomatically, for example, cash may be misplaced, deposits and withdrawals forgotten, and a checking account inadvertently overdrawn. Insurance policies may be allowed to lapse, investments may be allowed to mature untended, and recurring bills and other obligations may be neglected. Because of continual mistakes such as these, undiagnosed patients have lost both valuable and sentimental personal possessions, cash and other property, their credit standing, and even worse, in the absence of other apparent symptoms to their employers, their jobs. Creating a conscious or even unconscious confidence crisis in the patient, such continued, seemingly unexplainable lapses together with the attendant frustration may often provoke defensiveness, irrational outbursts, and other uncharacteristic behavior. When confronted by understandably mystified family members and friends, it is not unusual for a patient in exasperation and denial to discount the problem. In an apparent effort to compensate for such lapses, individuals may modify lifelong behavior patterns. Cash may be hidden away in unusual locations, household items may disappear and reappear without explanation, and reminder notes may proliferate. Health care professionals, however, understand the symptoms and can advise family and friends of their importance.

It eventually becomes apparent to family and friends, however, that there is indeed a problem. This awareness may be gradual or sudden, yet once the problem is recognized and understood, the fact that the patient's deteriorating mental condition has placed his or her personal financial affairs at considerable risk can be acknowledged and appropriate measures taken to remedy the situation and to reduce in so far as possible the vulnerability of the patient and his or her property.

It may be sufficient, initially, for someone simply to assist the patient in the daily management of personal affairs. Eventually, however, it will become necessary for someone to assume complete control of these affairs. Although there will be other, far more difficult problems later, for now, there are assets to manage, income to collect, and recurring liabilities to discharge—the constant financial management responsibilities that the patient is barely able to discharge, if at all.

Identification of Assets and Liabilities

The initial issues confronting the family will be the location and identification of the patient's various assets, sources of income, and liabilities. Although no two people or family situations are identical, the patient will in all probability have an interest in a variety of assets. Typically, these might include the following:

- *Real estate*—the family home, condominium, or apartment and perhaps even investment properties such as a multifamily dwelling, commercial buildings, or undeveloped land
- *Securities*—stocks, bonds, and notes of publicly traded companies and of governmental units, held individually or in common in mutual fund form
- *Cash and equivalents*—demand and term deposit accounts and fund investments in a variety of financial institutions
- *Life insurance*—policies issued on the life of the patient and perhaps on the life of others. These policies, depending on the owner's objectives, may simply provide for insurance (term life) or may, in addition, contain a savings/investment component (whole life)
- *Business interests*—a family or other closely held business entity held in corporate, partnership, or sole proprietorship form
- *Tangible personal property*—art, antiques, precious metals, a stamp or coin collection held for investment or for heuristic value, as well as automobiles, furniture, furnishings, and other household possessions held principally for use and consumption.

Complementing these assets may be sources of income requiring similar attention. Typically, these might include the following:

- *Entitlements*—Social Security, Veterans Administration, or other forms of entitlement income, depending on age, service, and physical condition
- *Retirement*—pension, profit sharing, deferred compensation or salary reduction plans, individual retirement accounts (IRAs), or Keogh accounts depending on current or former status of employment
- *Beneficial*—various forms of insurance, annuity, or trust income that might be coupled with a power to appoint underlying assets during lifetime or at death by will depending on the existence and generosity of a relative or friend.

As a result of a person's lifelong financial habits or of the behavior modifications incidental to Alzheimer's disease, the task of simply locating these assets and sources of income may prove to be a formidable challenge.

As the family members begin to focus on these issues of asset, income, and liability identification, they must also consider the related issues of the identity of a manager, the legal form of the management, and objectives of the administration of the patient's property. Who will assume the necessary control? What form will that control take? The significant issue to be considered should be the immediate and long-term objectives of the asset management. What, optimally, should be accomplished by the placement of the patient's assets under the management of another? There are several objectives: some are immediate, and others are of more long-term impact.

Of most immediate concern, clearly, is the physical security of the patient's property. The initial objective then should be for the manager to take possession and assume control of all of the patient's property to preserve and protect its integrity. Unique and valuable tangible personal property, such as jewelry, as well as valuable intangible personal property such as cash, stocks, bonds, and notes together with important documents of ownership such as deeds and insurance policies should be placed in safekeeping to prevent their loss or imprudent sale. Attention may then be turned to matters of their daily management: the maintenance of real property; the collection of rents, dividends, interest, Social Security and other retirement income (which might be directly deposited to the patient's bank account); and the payment of recurring bills, including mortgages and insurance premiums. Because of the patient's recent mental lapses, these matters may be in a state of disarray.

Once the assets and sources of income are secure and their proper daily management restored, consideration may be given to other, more long-range matters, such as investment management. The state of the patient's present investments requires review both in the context of the patient's present investment objectives as well as in relation to the constantly changing market conditions. The investment objectives of a younger patient with children still in school, for instance, will be significantly different from those of one nearing retirement age whose children have completed their education or from those of one who has previously retired. Such differences in objectives should be carefully considered in determining investment strategies.

In this context investment portfolios require review and decisions must be made with respect to continued ownership of certain stocks and bonds. Interest rates require daily review, and as term certificates mature, decisions must be made to "roll over" the investment or to seek alternatives. The objectives of an insurance plan also require review and decisions must be made as to the continued propriety of particular forms of insurance (term vs. whole life) as well as to the extent of present coverage.

Business and employment issues should also be addressed. These will include decisions regarding the continued participation of the patient in a closely held business, or, if the patient is an employee, decisions as to the terms of the termination of employment and the payment of any retirement income or benefits.

In addition to a review of the patient's current investments in light of present investment objectives the increasing prospects of confinement ultimately in a long-term health care facility, potentially for a significant period, at extraordinary expense requires a reassessment of the investment objectives of the patient as well as those of the patient's family. The family must, therefore, anticipate whether the patient's present investments adequately meet such expenses and, in addition, adequately care for the continuing needs of the patient's spouse as well as others who are economically dependent on the patient. This latter consideration requires an analysis of the entire family as an economic unit—its circumstances and objectives, as well as those of the patient. Within this framework, each of the types of assets, their current form of ownership, as well as the various sources of income will present its own set of issues and problems that must be satisfactorily resolved.

There are a variety of legal management devices available to the Alzheimer patient and the patient's family. Principally, these include guardianship, conservatorship, power of attorney, intervivos trusts, joint ownership, and transfers with or without retained interests. Each of these management forms possess unique advantages as well as limitations. They vary considerably in terms of flexibility and sophistication. Although all of these forms are not appropriate for every patient, each of them or perhaps some combination may be used for the care, maintenance, and preservation of assets and income during the remainder of the patient's life. Accordingly, each patient's particular financial circumstances and objectives require careful analysis and the selection of the appropriate form or combination of them by a skilled professional.

Although a person's circumstances, objectives, assets, and income are clearly important factors in the selection of the appropriate form, they are by no means the only considerations. The mental capacity of the patient may well be the most significant factor involved. The law recognizes different degrees of mental capacity. A person may, for example, be perfectly competent to execute a simple will yet lack the necessary capacity to enter into a complex contract. The standards for determining degrees of capacity vary somewhat among the states, but because some degree of capacity is a necessary prerequisite to the application of many of these forms of management, the relative mental capacity of the patient at the time of the analysis will be a critical and sometimes determinative factor in their selection. Moreover, while the objectives of the management, the nature of the assets, and the capacity of the patient may help determine and in certain circumstances dictate the choice of management form, the form or forms themselves may in some respects help determine the identity of the manager. Although a clear and probably desirable choice of manager will often be one or more family members, the management form together with the relative sophistication of the assets and of the management objectives may prompt a search outside the family for a professional or corporate manager. In certain circumstances a bank, trust company, lawyer, accountant, or financial advisor, serving alone or together with a family member, may be a desirable alternative.

Property Management Devices

Guardianship/Conservatorship

A guardian or a conservator, referred to as a committee in some states, is a person or institution appointed by the court having jurisdiction over such matters (i.e., a probate or surrogate's court) and who is judicially charged with the duty of caring for the property and/or the person of one who is judged incapable.

These forms of management are traditionally used when a person lacks required capacity and are imposed on the incompetent person by judicial decree, a characteristic that distinguishes them from other management forms. Although the terminology and the precise form vary somewhat among the various states, a formal court proceeding is generally required and the appointment is based on a finding by the court that a requisite degree of capacity is absent. Such findings are supported by the necessary testimony of the person's family, friends, and, usually, a physician or other professional skilled in the diagnosis of mental deterioration. In either case, there is normally a requirement that the guardian or conservator render an account of their activities to the court on some periodic basis (customarily annually). A close family member such as a spouse or adult child of the patient is normally appointed by the court, but few state legislatures actually establish a statutory preference, leaving such matters of choice to the courts in the exercise of judicial discretion with the expectation that such appointment will be made in the best interests of the patient. As previously mentioned, most states distinguish among degrees of mental capacity. Many states, for example, draw a distinction between a person's capacity to care for his or her assets and the capacity to care for himself or herself. It is possible, therefore, for a court to appoint a person or an institution to manage the financial affairs of the patient while the patient retains the capacity and freedom to make decisions with respect to physical needs. In some states, therefore, a conservator will be vested with limited authority for the care of the incompetent person and will have custody of assets only. A guardian, on the other hand, will have custody of both the assets as well as the person and will be charged with the complete responsibility of making decisions with respect to that person, much as a parent acts on behalf of a minor child. This form may be used exclusively for asset management and, under appropriate circumstances, may also be used for management of the patient's person. As an asset manager, the conservator or guardian may be authorized by the court to conduct, subject to varying degrees of judicial supervision, all of the patient's business and personal affairs for the rest of the patient's life.

The law is very specific about these responsibilities as they relate to a person's assets. The guardian/conservator is charged by the court to identify these assets, take physical possession of them, and submit an inventory of them to the court. The guardian/conservator is then responsible to the court for the management and conservation of these assets as well as for their expenditure. The guardian/conservator must always act in the best interests of the patient and not permit personal interests to stand in conflict with such duties.

The death of the patient will serve to terminate the office as well as the management responsibilities of the guardian/conservator. The patient's assets must then be transferred to the duly appointed representative of the patient's estate (i.e., the executor or administrator).

Power of Attorney

A power of attorney is an agreement in which the patient appoints another person as his or her agent for purposes of transacting a variety of matters. Depending on the nature of these matters, the patient may give the agent possession of certain property for whatever purposes are desired. Although the creation of such a relationship requires no formal transfer of title and no court authority, it does require a requisite degree of mental capacity. Although in practice a family member is often appointed, there are usually few restrictions with respect to such appointment. With a few exceptions limited to specific situations, anyone who is of full age and capacity may be granted a power of attorney regardless of their relationship to the patient. A professional advisor, close friend, or a corporate entity such as a bank could, therefore, be designated as an agent.

The design of these agreements may be expansive or limited. The patient could, for example, grant authority to the agent to accomplish only one specific act, such as the sale of a particular security or the leasing of an apartment.

Alternatively, the patient could confer on the agent a general power granting broad and extensive authority to transact any and all matters on the patient's behalf. The creation and use of these powers may become quite sophisticated, particularly when combined with other devices. Yet as an asset management vehicle, the power of attorney permits the appointed agent to conduct within designated limits all of the patient's business and personal affairs for the rest of the patient's life, or until the earlier revocation of this authority by the patient.

Just as this authority may be granted, so may it be revoked. In its traditional form, the death of the patient or his or her earlier mental incapacity automatically revokes the power of attorney, rendering it useless in incompetency situations. However, many states have authorized a so-called durable power of attorney that survives the incompetence of the patient. Unlike the traditional form, however, there is a requirement in some states that the holder of a durable power of attorney have a particular family relationship to the one granting the power. As an asset management vehicle for the Alzheimer patient, the durable power of attorney presents clear advantages to the traditional form, provided such authority is accepted. It should be noted, however, that as a practical matter a power of attorney is only effective if third parties are willing to accept it. Because the agreement is between the patient and the agent, third parties are not required to accept or honor them.

Although usually a power of attorney, whether traditional or durable, is intended to take effect immediately to accomplish whatever current purposes are desired, the durable power of attorney can be made to become effective only on the event of a disability. Because a determination of incapacity must be made before such power of attorney takes effect, it may be more difficult to use this type of document without challenge from some source (probably the third party who is requested to accept its validity and authority). Although this form of a durable power of attorney is not yet available in all states, it is available in an increasing number of jurisdictions. Either form of power, however, is terminated by the patient's death, and all of the patient's assets previously managed by the agent will be administered by the duly appointed representative of the patient's estate.

Intervivos Trusts

A trust created during the lifetime of the patient (intervivos) is an agreement in which the patient formally transfers assets/property to a trustee who agrees to hold and manage the property for the patient (and sometimes for the patient's beneficiaries) for a specific period of time. In the case of the Alzheimer patient, this management would most probably extend for the rest of the patient's life.

A trust is a fiduciary relationship in which the trustee holds the legal title to the property subject to an obligation to use the property for the benefit of the beneficiary. The creation of an intervivos trust relationship requires no court authority. It does, however, necessitate a requisite degree of mental capacity. Although a close family member is often selected for the office, there are few restrictions in this regard. Usually anyone of full age and capacity who is capable of managing the transferred assets may be appointed as a trustee regardless of the relationship to the patient. The trustee may be a professional advisor, close friend, or corporate entity such as a bank or trust company. When assets are extensive or complex and objectives are sophisticated, a professional or corporate entity could be a desirable choice, serving alone or together with a family member.

In its simplest form, the trust can be compared in some ways with the power of attorney. As a legal concept, however, it is more complex and capable of far greater sophistication. In the hands of a skilled and imaginative lawyer a trust is capable of accomplishing an almost limitless array of objectives far beyond the capacity of a power of attorney. Trust agreements may, therefore, be as expansive or as limited as the person creating them desires.

As an asset management instrument, the trust may permit the trustee to manage all of the patient's assets for the rest of the patient's life. Although the patient may revoke the trust under certain circumstances, the patient's death will not necessarily serve to automatically revoke the arrangement. Unlike conservatorships, guardianships, and powers of attorney, the life of the trust may be designed to extend beyond the death of the patient and may provide an instrument through which the trustee may continue to manage the deceased patient's assets for the benefit of those who survive. The fact that a trust may survive the patient and provide continuity of property management presents significant asset transfer and estate planning advantages.

Joint Tenancies

Joint tenancies are forms of joint ownership established, for example, when one person places funds in a deposit-type account or purchases other types of assets such as securities or real property in his or her name and that of another person. This form of transaction technically requires a requisite degree of mental capacity. Joint tenancy relationships may continue for the lifetime of the depositor/purchaser, or they may be terminated at an earlier time through complete withdrawal of the account or the sale of the security or real property. Depending on the creator's intent, such joint tenancies may have survivorship attributes, such as entitling the surviving joint tenant to the entire balance or asset on the patient's death, or thus may not, such as entitling the patient's executor/administrator to administer the entire balance or asset at the patient's death. This survivorship attribute presents obvious asset transfer and estate planning benefits to the patient and family.

A close family member is usually "placed on the account" or added to the security certificate or deed together with the patient. As an asset management instrument the joint arrangement permits a spouse or caregiver to manage these assets while the patient retains mental capacity and to continue to manage them after the patient loses such capacity. Although this legal form is easily created, it requires management on an asset-by-asset basis, which can be cumbersome when there is a significant amount of assets to be managed. In addition, there are certain limitations on this form of management imposed by the nature of the assets themselves or by the requirements of their transfer. These limitations further serve to make joint tenancies somewhat less useful as management vehicles for some assets, particularly after the patient loses mental capacity. Dividends and interest generated by stocks and bonds, for instance, may be readily endorsed and deposited to a bank account by one joint tenant. The sale or other transfer of such security, however, generally requires the signature of both joint tenants, a requirement that presumes competency of both signers. Similarly, while rents may be collected and expenses paid by one of two joint owners with respect to jointly owned real estate, a sale or other transfer would likewise require the signature and presumed competence of both. Funds on deposit in a bank account, on the other hand, may be freely withdrawn on a single signature if the agreement with the bank so provides. Because of their simplicity and ease of creation, forms of joint ownership, with or without rights of survivorship, are a frequently sought and commonly used form of management for the assets of one beginning to lose competence because they require neither court action nor the services of an attorney. Accordingly, the families often resort to their use prior to seeking formal legal advice and counsel. However, owing to their inherent limitations, their use is often limited to the type of asset most readily managed by one of two co-tenants (i.e., the joint bank account relationship).

Transfers with Retained Interest

A transfer with a retained interest involves the legal transfer of an asset by the patient to another while reserving certain legal rights to enjoy that property for some period of time, most commonly for the rest of the patient's life. The transfer is accomplished by the execution of a deed of transfer and by the concurrent execution of a contract that presumes a requisite degree of capacity. For example, a patient could transfer the family home to a spouse or child while legally reserving the right to live there for life. During that period of time, the responsibilities of management may be shifted to the designated person by contractual agreement, while the patient enjoys residence. This transaction may involve near-complete loss of legal control of the asset by the patient except for the privilege of residing in the property. As a management vehicle, however, the transfer with a retained interest successfully shifts the responsibility of management to another. Death will terminate the rights and interests of the patient, at which time title will vest completely in the designated person, a result that presents certain advantages with respect to asset transfer and estate planning. Because certain legal difficulties may arise during the period when no one person possesses the entire title, this legal device is used infrequently in favor of the far more flexible trust instrument, which may accomplish the same results.

Outright and Complete Transfer

As its designation implies, an outright and complete transfer involves the legal transfer of an asset by the patient to another person. Unlike the transfer with the retained interest described previously, this transfer involves no retained legal rights. The transfer is done simply by the execution of a deed of transfer, an action that presumes a requisite degree of capacity.

Usually assets such as real estate, securities, and cash are transferred to a close family member with the expectation that these assets will be managed and used for the patient's benefit as the need arises. Although legal title is formally held by the family member, there is an understanding that the patient will have access to the assets for life or until earlier relinquishment. It should be understood, however, that in this form ownership as a legal matter—and accordingly management—is irrevocably transferred, and the right to any continued use by the patient, such as living in the house or receipt of dividends or interest, would be only with permission of the family member. Thus, although there may exist a moral obligation, there is no legal one. This transaction involves a complete loss of legal control by the patient, a result that may produce a certain amount of anxiety. Yet, as a management vehicle, this transfer successfully shifts management responsibilities to another and can be effective, provided the family member honors the moral obligation. Death of the patient, while terminating the moral obligation of the family member, is legally irrelevant to the interest and the title, a situation that presents certain advantages with respect to asset conservation and preservation as well as to asset transfer and estate planning.

Additional Considerations

In addition to these principal management vehicles, a relatively simple form of income management of Social Security benefits is provided by the Social Security Administration in which a family member or friend may become a "representative payee" of the benefits on behalf of the patient.

It should be emphasized that these forms of asset management are not mutually exclusive. They are frequently used in tandem as circumstances require. Using some combination of these forms will, in fact, often overcome the inherent limitations of one particular form.

Prior to using any of these asset management forms, proper consideration should be given to the integrity of the assets once they are transferred. As a practical matter, there are possibilities that the manager could voluntarily convert the assets and income to personal use with any of these forms. In some of these forms, the possibilities are greater than others. Although legal remedies exist in varying degrees of effectiveness provided someone other than the incompetent patient is available to enforce the duties of the manager, personal trust is a necessary prerequisite to the establishment of any of these relationships.

There also exists the possibility that assets held in some of these relationships could be legally attached and taken to satisfy the personal debts and obligations of the manager. Again, while legal remedies do exist in varying degrees of effectiveness, the personal circumstances of the manager, both financial and domestic, should be carefully considered prior to the establishment of either relationship, particularly joint tenancies and outright transfers.

Preservation and Conservation of Property Interests

Preservation and Conservation Issues

As the patient's condition deteriorates the family will eventually seek medical assistance and a diagnosis will be made. At that time, the patient's prognosis will become clear. Since there is no cure for Alzheimer's disease, there will be no recovery. The family's attention must now begin to focus on considerations of estate planning—what will happen to the patient's assets and sources of income prior to the patient's death and thereafter.

In any estate planning context there should be two principal components: (1) a so-called lifetime estate or financial plan that involves the creation of an estate, its maintenance and conservation, together with its use to provide support and security for the family, a process that reflects in a number of significant ways the current popular trend in financial planning, and (2) the traditional estate plan, a so-called postmortem estate plan, which provides for the distribution of the estate thus created, used, and preserved.

The lifetime, or intervivos, planning aspect of an estate plan for an Alzheimer patient should have at least two primary objectives: (1) current asset management for the benefit of the patient (considered in the previous section) and (2) future asset conservation and preservation for the needs of the patient, the patient's spouse, and others for whom the patient may be financially responsible, as well as for the benefit of the patient's heirs.

At this time, however, the family's principal concern is the preservation and conservation of those assets and sources of income presently available to the patient and family as well as those that may become available. Given the nature of the disease, it is unlikely that in most cases there will be an opportunity for further estate creation. How, therefore, can existing patient and family resources be most effectively used for the benefit of the patient and the patient's spouse and family during the remainder of the patient's life and also be available to be passed on to the survivors on the patient's death?

In addition, there should be traditional postmortem estate planning objectives common in any estate planning context, including the orderly transfer of the patient's property to those who will receive it, the subsequent management of assets for those who will receive them, minimization of taxes, and the avoidance of costly and time-consuming probate entanglements. All of these essentially death-oriented issues are outside the scope of this presentation and will not be considered here.

In the accomplishment of all of these objectives, both intervivos as well as postmortem estate planning for the Alzheimer patient is not entirely dissimilar to estate planning for anyone else. There are, however, two potentially troublesome issues that set the estate plan for a patient with Alzheimer's disease apart: the possibility of long-term custodial care and the loss of mental capacity.

The expenses of the extended type of custodial care generally required by a patient with advanced Alzheimer's disease are not covered by Medicare or by private insurance contracts. Moreover, Medicaid benefits are available only to those who qualify under severely restrictive financial qualification tests permitting minimally available assets and income (see Chapter 4). Thus the patient and the patient's family, whose personal financial resources are inadequate to afford such costs, are confronted with potential impoverishment. In the absence of proper lifetime estate planning, a healthy spouse could be left with inadequate financial resources for support, dependent children could be deprived of an anticipated education, and subsequent generations could be unintentionally but unavoidably disinherited.

In anticipation of such potentially devastating custodial expenses, the estate plan of the patient with Alzheimer's disease who has limited personal financial resources should, therefore, be designed to respond to this potential problem. Such a plan might include two specific measures: (1) the removal of those assets and other resources necessary for support of the patient's spouse and other financial dependents from the pool of resources available for such expenses and (2) the availability of public financial resources to support the patient's medical and physical care requirements. The first measure involves a restructuring of the patient's assets to avoid their eventual depletion. This requires their transfer into other forms of ownership. The second measure involves the qualification of the patient for public medical assistance within the framework of the public welfare laws and regulations.

Unfortunately, often by the time the nature and extent of the problem is finally appreciated and the family eventually seeks legal advice, the requisite degree of mental capacity required of a patient to create a well-designed estate plan may be rapidly diminishing or absent. The estate planner may, therefore, have severely limited options. This loss of capacity and, therefore, of planning options, increases the importance of developing a comprehensive plan as early as possible.

Lifetime Financial Planning Considerations

Health Care Issues

Some families of Alzheimer patients may be financially able to absorb the extraordinary costs of extended health care while still adequately providing for the financial requirements of a spouse and others who are economically dependent on the family unit. Although the specific costs of such care will obviously vary, it is fair to state that minimal estimates in the range of $20,000 to $25,000 annually are common, and in many locations the annual costs are considerably higher. Not all patients will require similar degrees of care for similar periods of time nor are their financial and personal resources similar. However, all families should develop a financial plan to preempt the crisis and to deal with it as effectively as possible.

When confronted with the probability of extended custodial health care for a member, each family should analyze its requirements and its available resources. Any such analysis would seem to have at least two primary components: (1) an analysis of the present and future physical management needs of the patient together with an estimate of their cost and (2) an analysis of the family resources, financial and personal, that can be assembled to meet these needs. Depending on the outcome of these analyses, consideration should be given to the availability of public resources to either supplement or supersede the family's own resources.

Physical Management Requirements. Because of the nature of Alzheimer's disease, a family may well anticipate that a patient will ultimately live in a dependent status for some period of time requiring 24-hour custodial care. As the disease progresses, however, there will be numerous stages of care through which the patient will pass before reaching such an advanced stage. Initially, the present physical needs of the patient must be assessed and met. Thereafter, the family should consult with the medical practitioner to ascertain what medical and corresponding behavioral changes may be expected over the course of the disease and the time frame within which such changes might be anticipated. Since the course of the disease is erratic, definitive answers and precise projections are not possible. Even tentative answers to these questions depend on many variables, such as the age and physical condition of the patient at the onset of the disease. However, even the most speculative of timetables together with an understanding of symptomatic conditions will be extremely useful for planning purposes. Prepared with this information, the family can begin to project the patient's future physical needs and their attendant costs. Periodic updated examinations and reviews of prognosis help to confirm the rate of the disease's advance.

Once an appreciation for the progressive physical needs and requirements of the patient is developed, a corresponding set of caregiver needs may be formulated. This includes the kind of care required at each stage of the disease and the physical and personal resources of the family and the community available to meet these projected needs. The capacity of the family to provide total home care will probably be exceeded by the ultimate demands of the patient. At the very least, the patient will eventually require skilled 24-hour nursing care within the home or within a long-term care facility. In the short term, however, the patient may simply need homemaker care, later perhaps a companion to provide respite for the family caregivers, and still later the services of a primary day care center. The availability within the patient's community of each successive anticipated caregiver should be examined as well as the costs. Although available information will probably be restricted to current cost levels, anticipated inflationary increases must be factored into the equation. Medical insurance policies may cover "some" of the costs for a "limited" period of time; therefore, families should review the extent of policy coverage with their insurance carriers. In addition, some states and local communities now have special programs to assist families with home nursing and homemaker needs. Programs for the elderly are excellent repositories of information on the availability of such care resources within a particular area.

Resource Availability. A systematic inventory of family assets together with present and future sources of income is a prerequisite to any orderly estate planning process. Families with substantial financial resources may already have this information readily available through records held by an attorney, accountant, security broker, or financial planner. Families who have previously engaged in this process through the creation of an estate or financial plan may also have ready access to such information. On the other hand, the patient's family may have difficulty locating a patient's resources as a result of the person's lifelong financial habits or of the behavior modifications incidental to Alzheimer's disease. In the absence of the patient's capacity to be of personal assistance in this compilation, however, the patient's income tax returns generally prove to be an excellent source of information because of the variety of data required to be included on completed returns.

The family should also prepare an inventory of "personal," or perhaps more accurately "personnel," resources. Within the immediate or extended family are there persons available to provide varying degrees of care to the patient on a regular basis during any given stage of the degenerative process? Because of age, occupation, inclination, or family status, there may be members of the family who are willing to devote valuable time to the care and management of the patient, thereby conserving precious financial resources.

Once the inventory of family resources has been completed, a similarly comprehensive and highly detailed inventory of family liabilities should be prepared that includes every aspect of the family's current living expenses. Not only current expenses and obligations but also those that are anticipated in the future should be listed.

When completed and compared, these two inventories should provide a reasonably clear picture of the family's current net worth and estimated annual gross and net income, as well as that of the patient. Moreover, there should be an equally clear picture of the changes in asset and income levels that may be anticipated as a result of retirements, bequests, and other future events. That picture, then, may be compared with the anticipated financial requirements of the Alzheimer patient. If the family resources fall short, as may well be expected, or even if they marginally exceed projected patient needs, it would seem prudent for the family to give serious consideration to the availability of public financial assistance at this time.

Public Welfare Availability. Any consideration of the availability of public financial assistance must begin with an understanding of the pattern of Medicaid and Medicare (see also Chapter 4).

Medicare, the federal health insurance program, is designed to assist those who are receiving Social Security retirement benefits as well as those who are receiving Social Security disability benefits for a required period of time. Medicare pays for necessary physicians' services and for inpatient hospital care. Generally, however, coverage is extremely limited for inpatient skilled nursing home care and for home health agency care in a patient's home. In particular, Medicare provides no coverage for the kind of total care required by the patient with Alzheimer's disease.

Medicaid is the medical assistance program administered by the various states with federal aid. It is designed to assist only those with extremely limited financial resources. Although Medicaid pays for a broad range of medical and medically related services, including extended nursing home care, a person must qualify under a variety of tests and special rules in order to be eligible to receive such assistance.

In general, to qualify for Medicaid benefits a patient must be both categorically and financially eligible. To be categorically eligible a patient must be over the age of 65, blind, or disabled as defined by Social Security Administration regulations. To be financially eligible, a patient must qualify under an asset test as well as an income test, both of which establish maximum acceptable levels. Currently, to qualify for Medicaid benefits a person may not receive income in excess of approximately $450 a month and with certain exceptions may not own assets in excess of $2,000. Certain assets are considered exempt from this asset test such as a home, certain personal property, certain life insurance, and certain assets specifically designated for burial. If a patient's income or assets exceed these minimal levels, the patient must "spend the difference" on medical expenses in order to qualify.

This is an extremely general overview of the Medicaid framework as if relates to qualification for medical assistance. Within this framework, there exists a wide latitude for interpretation and among the various states there is a broad diversity of approach to these matters. Depending on a particular state's attitude toward welfare assistance in general, the public policy of the various jurisdictions spans the spectrum from the very liberal to the ultra conservative. The practical application of the laws and regulations among the states reflects this diversity. However, one fact is unavoidably and undeniably clear—to qualify for public assistance, within the broad design of the Medicaid program, one must be impoverished or become so.

The conclusion to be drawn would seem to be that a patient must either have sufficient personal and family financial resources to support annual nursing home expenses while still adequately providing for a spouse and other dependents or lose whatever financial resources are available for the family unit. Clearly, the vast majority of families cannot sustain such a financial burden for any length of time. Since a patient's assets and sources of income are generally "available" for the payment of such expenses, those families who cannot sustain these expenses face potential financial ruin. Fortunately, however, these are not the only alternatives. With foresight, an understanding of available estate planning opportunities, and timely action, there are other available options.

Financial Planning Strategies. The solution to this problem can be achieved by the removal of the patient's assets and other sources of income from the categories of financial resources that are considered by the Medicaid statutes and regulations as "available" for such expenses and therefore "available" for determining a patient's eligibility for benefits. This asset and resource "removal" may be accomplished in a number of different ways. The most obvious and straightforward, however, is simple asset transfer.

An applicant should consider the advisability of a transfer of both individually owned and jointly held assets to a spouse, child, or other beneficiary. Such a transfer could assume the form of an outright transfer, a transfer with a retained interest, or a transfer in trust depending on the overall objectives of the transfer. Such assets would, of course, no longer be available to discharge the patient's personal expenses. Moreover, subject to certain specific limitations, assets thus transferred would not be counted in determining Medicaid eligibility. Medicaid regulations, for example, currently deny eligibility to applicants who transfer assets within a certain period of application (generally 24 months) but only if such transfer is motivated with the intent and purpose of qualifying for medical assistance.

Although such transfers may achieve the immediate desired result of removing the patient's property from "harm's way," they are not without potential problems. Principally among these would be the problems in transfers to the patient's spouse, the psychological impact of transfer on the patient, and the impact of such transfers on admission to a health care facility.

Because of the immediacy and magnitude of the Alzheimer disease patient's estate planning problems, it is easy to become completely immersed in them and to overlook and neglect the corresponding estate planning problems of the patient's spouse. Transfer of the patient's assets to the patient's spouse may be the appropriate solution to the asset preservation issue and other objectives, but in spite of all expectations to the contrary it is conceivable that the patient's spouse may not survive the patient. If there is no appropriate estate plan, the transferred assets could be returned to the patient together with the deceased spouse's own assets. This situation can be avoided simply by ensuring that the spouse also has an adequate estate plan that appropriately disposes of the transferred assets as well as any personal assets.

In all probability the spouse may indeed survive the Alzheimer patient, thus avoiding such difficulties. Nevertheless, the survivor, regardless of future health concerns, will undoubtedly encounter some of the same management issues in advanced age as an Alzheimer patient. It would, therefore, seem prudent to plan for such matters on behalf of the patient's spouse, or at the very least to give them a measure of consideration.

The issue of unintentional inheritance is not simply limited to the patient's spouse. Although the spouse is the most likely source of an unintended inheritance, other individuals within, and even without, the immediate family may be a potential source of inheritance to the patient. Therefore, the estate planning instruments of all family members should be carefully analyzed to ensure that assets will not be inadvertently conferred on the patient.

All of the transfers considered here involve the relinquishment of some degree of control by the patient over the assets transferred. Outright transfer, of course, involves the complete loss of control. As might well be anticipated, this aspect of transfer may produce a degree of anxiety. Not unreasonably, patients may fear not only for the integrity of the assets themselves but also for the continued use of the assets on their behalf.

When it becomes necessary to place the patient in a health care facility, locating a "suitable" one and securing admission may prove to be a formidable task, not simply because of the availability of space but also because of financial considerations. It is advisable, therefore, that potential health care facilities be visited in advance of need and that financial arrangements be discussed.

Although Medicaid law prohibits discrimination by participating health care facilities against Medicaid recipients, the existence of widespread de facto discrimination in certain locations is acknowledged and difficult to overcome. Although legal remedies are available, the immediate concern obviously is expedient admission. Considerations should be given to the patient's retaining "sufficient" assets to effectively "buy" admission to a facility in a timely fashion, however repugnant the concept.

Asset transfer is not the only measure available to the family to accomplish such a removal of the patient's assets from "availability." Other specific measures include severance of jointly owned assets, segregation of income between spouses, and purchase of so-called exempt assets. The specifics of these measures and their application are somewhat technical and therefore beyond the scope of this chapter.

Mental Capacity Issues

Overshadowing all aspects of a comprehensive patient plan is the mental capacity of the Alzheimer patient, which is usually in a state of continual deterioration throughout the planning process.

Virtually all of the planning objectives for the Alzheimer patient, intervivos or postmortem, involve a transfer of property or the provision for a future transfer, regardless of the extent of the estate.

It is widely understood that a certain degree of mental capacity is required for the execution of a valid will. In the absence of such capacity, the will cannot effectively provide for property transfer at death. What may not be so widely understood is that a requisite degree of mental capacity is also needed for all intervivos transfers whether outright, in trust, or with a retained interest. If the required degree of capacity is absent at the time of the transfer, a patient will be deemed legally incompetent to effect a transfer and any transfers made by such patient will lack full legal force and effect. Therefore, if a patient is to effect immediate property transfers for asset management and preservation purposes, or to provide for their future transfer by will at death, it is critical that such transfers or arrangements be accomplished while sufficient mental capacity remains.

Not all patients are equally disposed to begin immediate transfers for a variety of reasons. Nonetheless, timing is crucial. If Alzheimer's disease is diagnosed sufficiently early, while the patient still retains the necessary mental capacity to make decisions regarding his or her assets, as an alternative to effecting the transfers at that time the patient may, through the use of the previously considered durable power of attorney, empower another person to make such decisions and to effect such transfers on his or her behalf at such later time as he or she becomes incapable of managing his or her assets.

If, however, Alzheimer's disease is diagnosed late in its course, planning options become severely circumscribed. There is virtually no action that the patient can take legally with respect to the transfer of his or her own assets. Furthermore, depending on the relative level of incapacity, the execution of any kind of estate planning documents, such as a will, may well be beyond the capacity of the patient. The only remaining option in most states may be the establishment of a conservatorship or guardianship to effect such transfers.

Once appointed by the court, a guardian/conservator must accomplish any further financial arrangements, such as asset transfer, with the advice and consent of the court. Although courts generally permit use of those assets not specifically required for the patient's own personal maintenance to be "used" for the "support" of the spouse and other dependents, any "divestiture" of the patient's property for "preservation" purposes, however small, would probably not be approved.

Some states, however, recognize that such an inflexible approach to the management of the assets of a person deemed incompetent is both unrealistic and unnecessary. As a result, several states provide statutory authority for the creation of an estate plan for the benefit of an incompetent person by that person's guardian/conservator. Such statutory authority may in addition specifically provide for gifts of the patient's property in certain circumstances as part of the estate plan. These gifts may include the intervivos transfer of those assets not required for adequate support of the patient to those individuals likely to receive them at the patient's death. It is extremely unlikely that a court would permit the complete or nearly complete divestiture of assets for purposes of Medicaid eligibility, but the court might permit assets in excess of need to be given away.

The disadvantages of guardianships and conservatorships are numerous and perhaps obvious. Inherently cumbersome and inflexible in administration, they are expensive to maintain because of the substantial amount of professional time necessary to comply with extensive statutory requirements. Moreover, any action requiring judicial authorization, including the initial appointment, is subject to the conventional and unanticipated delays of any court proceeding.

Clinical Management

Management Issues

As Alzheimer's disease continues to run its course, and the attendant mental deterioration increases, patients gradually begin to experience increasingly serious difficulties in making appropriate decisions and judgments regarding their own personal physical care. It may become physically dangerous for the patient to function without some supervision. Moreover, the patient's irrational behavior, previously confined to relatively harmless matters, may now begin to manifest itself in a far more serious and potentially dangerous manner, such as in a refusal to relinquish the automobile keys when driving has become a hazard; in a refusal to seek appropriate medical assistance and treatment when such is required; and in a refusal to consider alternative living arrangements when the current living accommodations are no longer appropriate. The patient's potential to harm himself or herself or others and the potential of legal liability both to the patient and to the patient's family become of significant concern to the physician and the patient's family. The physician, knowledgeable of the symptoms and of their implications, can be most helpful to the family in identifying the risks. Once these risks have been acknowledged, appropriate measures must be immediately taken to remedy the situation and to reduce the exposure of the patient.

When it is time for critical decisions to be made concerning a patient's physical care and management, someone will have to make those decisions on behalf of the patient without the patient's consent. The family and physician must then consider who will undertake to make those personal management decisions and what form, legal or otherwise, that management will take. There are generally three sources of decision-making authority: (1) judicial determination, (2) personal grant, and (3) de facto management.

Patient Management Devices

Judicial Determination—Guardianship

If the diagnosis of Alzheimer's disease was made sufficiently early, the family can institute a conservatorship so that someone appointed by the court can manage the patient's assets. Early in the course of the disease, while still possessed of sufficient mental capacity, the patient could personally institute such a proceeding. By the time the patient is unable to physically care for himself or herself, however, the conservatorship is no longer an appropriate legal vehicle and guardianship is generally the only legal alternative available in most states for the patient's care and management. If such a conservatorship was established earlier as a form of asset management, such form may readily be "upgraded" to that of a guardianship by judicial decree when the requisite degree of mental deterioration has been reached and custody and control of the patient is then an issue.

A guardian will have physical custody of both the assets as well as the person and will be charged with the complete responsibility of making decisions with respect to that person, much as a parent acts on behalf of a minor child. When an adult patient becomes a ward, he or she is reduced to the legal status of a child. The ward no longer controls property and can no longer drive a car, manage money, write checks, or consent to or refuse medical treatment. The guardian determines where the ward lives and every other significant aspect of his or her life.

Alzheimer's disease is not recognized legally as a category under which guardianship is granted. Therefore, those seeking guardianship for the Alzheimer patient must "fit" the patient into another category, which typically is that of the mentally ill. It may be extremely difficult for the family or friends of the Alzheimer patient to consider their loved one as "mentally ill" and to petition the courts on that basis. There is, however, a national movement to establish a neurologic category for guardianship determination.

The responsibilities of a guardian encompass a broad spectrum from care and management of the ward's assets to care and management of the ward's person. The law is very specific about these responsibilities as they relate to the ward's assets, but it is not unusual to discover that state law is less specific about a guardian's responsibilities toward the person than it is toward the person's assets. Historically, it was assumed that the guardian had the best interests of the ward in mind and, unless served with a court order, the guardian was under no obligation to report to the court on the physical or personal status of the ward.

There has been a recent trend, however, for the courts to appoint a special guardian to review the significant decisions of the regular guardian with respect to the ward's physical status and condition, particularly with regard to the giving or withholding of medical treatment.

Although not usually prescribed by the court, the guardian may expect to be involved with the physician and caregiver in day-to-day patient management. The guardian may be responsible for locating and investigating day care programs, nursing homes, physicians, and facilities. The guardian may also be involved together with the physician in the coordination of care activities, particularly for those Alzheimer patients who do not require 24-hour institutional care. For example, while day care programs may be available, the hours may not correspond to the work schedules of the primary caregiver with whom the patient lives. Arrangements for care and transportation may have to be made to cover the "gap" at the beginning and/or end of the day.

Beyond this, the guardian may be the person who has to make the decision to place the ward in a nursing home. Although considerations of cost may appear to be a paramount concern, the quality and type of care are also highly significant and extremely sensitive issues. Alzheimer patients often need a physical environment that allows them to wander without harm to themselves or to other patients. Therefore, it may be difficult to find nursing homes equipped to meet the needs of patients who are not yet bedridden or heavily medicated, and the guardian may anticipate spending a great deal of time working with a physician to arrange for the physical care of the Alzheimer patient, whether at home or in a health care facility setting.

Although guardians can make routine decisions about medical treatment, sometimes medical care institutions and the courts require special authorization to administer certain drugs in nonemergency situations. In certain stages of the disease, for example, the patient may experience severe agitation and the physician may wish to use antipsychotic medication. In addition, guardians will need to seek judicial permission when decisions need to be made about the withholding or giving of extraordinary medical treatment.

Personal Grant of Decision-Making Authority—Power of Attorney

The use of the previously considered special form of agency agreement known as the durable power of attorney may be an informal alternative to the formality of the judicially determined guardianship. Customarily, powers of attorney (both traditional and durable) have been used for asset management purposes as well as for financial or estate planning. Such powers, however, have been used far less frequently for management of the patient's person. Although patients may specifically designate their conservators/guardians in their powers of attorney, such designations are nonetheless generally accorded the judicial status of nominations (mere expressions of intent and preference), which must nevertheless be judicially confirmed. Unless there is good and sufficient reason not to appoint the nominee and thereby honor the request of the patient (e.g., a conflict of interest), such nominations routinely receive judicial confirmation.

There is, however, an increasing awareness nationwide of the need for medical powers to be included within the scope of agency powers. In recognition of this, one enlightened jurisdiction, California, has legislated a durable power specifically for health care. Provided the power is executed in accordance with statutory requirements, the agent is empowered to make health care decisions for the patient, including the power to give or withhold medical treatment, as would a court-appointed guardian. Given the pressing need for such an alternative, it is anticipated that such a form of management may soon become more widely available.

De Facto Management

Guardianships and durable powers of attorney may not always prove to be absolutely necessary for the personal management of the Alzheimer patient. Many nursing homes do not require that there be a guardian to authorize the admission of patients or to approve routine care and treatment, although more and more private institutions do require it. As a purely practical matter, medical practitioners and caregivers may simply accept the judgment of the immediate family with respect to ordinary care and treatment, particularly if there is agreement among family members and when the patient is cooperative. Such acceptance would obviously save the considerable expenditure of time, emotional energy, and financial resources necessary to obtain a judicially appointed guardian.

Sometimes, however, there is no choice but to seek a judicial determination. The Alzheimer patient, for example, may insist on a course of action that would jeopardize his or her safety and the safety of others, the family members may not be in accord on a particular course of action, or the health care provider may require authority. It would perhaps be fair to state that the proliferation of lawsuits in recent years has resulted in a cautionary approach by the medical and health care communities with respect to such decisions. Without proper authority, it is unlikely that any medical or care facility will authorize a treatment program that may be subject to question, criticism, and ultimately to litigation.

It would seem that before seeking the formal guardianship approach to patient management, it would make sense to inquire of the particular health care facility as to its practices and procedures. It may well be that a little foresight and planning among family members, physicians, and the facility may alleviate the necessity of the "legal" alternative and permit the patient and family to seek and successfully employ the simple pragmatic solutions to the issues of health care and management.

Conclusions

Each of the various strategies, options, and legal forms considered here possesses unique advantages as well as inherent limitations. Not all are necessarily appropriate for every patient or family situation. Each patient's particular financial and family circumstances and objectives require careful analysis. Selection of the appropriate measures or combination of them should be by one skilled in their use. Moreover, although the various legal forms and options were often considered and analyzed separately, they are by no means mutually exclusive.

The day when a person's estate consisted solely of real and personal property managed individually and transferred by will has largely disappeared. The nature and types of property interests held by individuals have increased dramatically, as have the measures for their management and transfer. Sophisticated asset management as well as financial and estate planning will use a variety of legal devices, both testamentary and intervivos, and an array of strategies to accomplish the various lifetime and postmortem objectives of the owner. When properly integrated, the combination of devices and strategies used will often overcome the inherent limitations of any one of them and ideally should result in a substantial savings of time, expenses, and taxes, as well as the critical preservation of the assets themselves.

It should be emphasized that state laws do vary, sometimes significantly. Moreover, the maze of Medicaid laws, in particular, and the regulations promulgated under them are highly technical and subject to a broad range of interpretation among the various states. Furthermore, given the sensitivity of the area, it is anticipated that there will be periodic changes in the law. Therefore, competent legal counsel should be sought to refine the options and perhaps to expand on them within the permissible context of the current laws and regulations of the particular jurisdiction and to place them appropriately within the perspective of the other concerns of the Alzheimer patient and the family.

The earlier the financial and estate planning is begun, the better. As perhaps in no other planning context imaginable, the problems and issues presented here dramatically emphasize the critical importance of timing to a comprehensive plan that successfully accomplishes the objectives of the family.

CHAPTER 6

Institution-Based Respite Care

Yvette L. Rheaume, John P. Larkin, and Benjamin Seltzer

There is increasing recognition that families who provide care to a relative suffering from progressive dementia experience considerable physical and emotional stress.[1] A variety of respite services have been developed in an effort to help reduce this strain. Thus in this chapter a description is provided of a hospital-based respite program for patients with Alzheimer's disease and their families, including a discussion of its goals, policies, and procedures, as well as other important issues as they impact on patients, family members, and hospital staff.

Respite has been described as "a temporary intermission of labor," "an interval of rest,"[2] and "an emerging family support service, through which a wide range of medical and social services are provided to the frail elderly or chronically ill and their family caregivers.[3] *Respite* is defined here in the broad sense as any formal support service or treatment intervention aimed primarily at providing temporary physical and emotional relief to the family caregiver of a frail elderly or demented person. Support services may range from "at home" assistance programs (e.g., home health care and homemaker services) to external "out-of-home" care programs such as adult day care centers and inhospital respite. In addition to offering relief to caregivers, respite programs represent an alternative approach to maintaining patients in the community and sharing limited medical resources among a wider number of people.

Institution-based respite is one type of respite program in which services are provided in a setting out of the home, such as a day hospital or an adult day care center. Inpatient respite is a subcategory of institutional respite in which a patient is temporarily admitted or "guested" in a nursing home, hospital, supervised living arrangement, or group home. The length of stay can range from overnight to several weeks. Although all forms of institutional respite provide some direct care to the patient, the primary purpose is to provide short-term relief to the family caregiver.

Formal inpatient respite programs date back at least to the early 1960s when a hospital in Oxford, England, developed a "floating-bed system," in which elderly patients were periodically admitted to the hospital to provide their family caregivers with a temporary holiday.[4] Hospital admissions also allowed the medical staff an opportunity to reassess the patients' care and treatment. Variations of this "floating bed" principle were later introduced for more specialized purposes, including the evaluation of geriatric patients with dementia and the support of patients with terminal illnesses.[5]

In the United States, institution-based respite for the elderly has primarily taken the form of day care. The development of inpatient respite programs has tended to lag behind outpatient programs, possibly because of limitations in the allocation of beds by state licensing agencies and cost-reimbursement policies. More recently, however, many facilities have begun to explore inpatient respite as one service within their overall long-term care programs. Some of this renewed interest may be in response to the underutilization of acute care hospital beds.

Several recent studies have focused on inpatient respite. In a large-scale, 18-month demonstration project, the Foundation for Long-Term Care[6] analyzed the admissions of frail elderly patients to respite programs in six long-term care facilities in New York State. Hasselkus and Brown[7] described a respite program situated on an acute care unit of a general hospital while Scharlach and Frenzel[8] surveyed the results of a respite program conducted by a Veterans Administration nursing home. In a retrospective study, Dunn and co-workers[9] reviewed a respite program that was a part of a geriatric assessment unit. All of these programs have dealt with a diagnostically mixed group of patients, however, and there is little information on inpatient respite programs specifically designed for the patient afflicted with Alzheimer's disease. Furthermore, although some of these studies report the sociodemographic characteristics of their patients, with the exception of the study by Scharlach and Frenzel, there has been little attempt to evaluate objectively the effectiveness of these programs.

Description of a Specific Inpatient Respite Program

At the E.N. Rogers Memorial Veterans Hospital in Bedford, Massachusetts, an inpatient respite program focuses on providing physical and emotional relief to the family caregiver of patients suffering from Alzheimer's disease. Institution-based respite is offered as one component of a more general program for the support of caregivers that includes such interventions as educational presentations, an emergency "hot line," as well as individual and group psychotherapy. Although intended primarily to give the caregiver temporary relief, respite is also used as a way of sharing scarce medical resources among a larger number of patients and possibly delay long-term institutional placement.

All patients included in this respite program are diagnosed as having a progressive dementia of the Alzheimer type according to criteria from the third edition of the *Diagnostic and Statistical Manual of Mental Disorders (DSM-III)*, the National Institute of Neurological and Communicative Disorders and Stroke (NINCDS), and the Alzheimer's Disease and Related Disorders Association (ADRDA).[10] Patients are drawn from those individuals who are outpatients of the Geriatric Research, Education and Clinical Center's, Dementia Study Unit. This is a multidisciplinary program for biomedical and psychosocial research in Alzheimer's disease and related disorders, supported by the Veterans Administration. Following initial diagnosis, patients and their families are seen at 3-month intervals for continuing evaluation and care by a team consisting of a physician (neurologist), a social worker, a nurse, and a psychologist. Two types of respite admission can be distinguished:

1. Regular respite—a preplanned 2-week inhospital stay every 3 months to give family caregivers a rest.
2. Crisis respite—respite admission in response to a sudden unexpected change in circumstances such as caregiver illness or loss of community supports needed to safely manage the patient at home. (Use of the respite in a crisis situation does carry considerable risk to the respite program. Crisis admission essentially closes the respite bed to other respite patients in need.)

At the time that a patient is first enrolled in the outpatient program, family members are acquainted with respite admission as one of several special modalities designed to help them cope with the many problems brought on by having a relative with Alzheimer's disease. The request for respite admission is then initiated by the family at some future time. It is left to family members to decide whether they wish to consult with the patient in choosing to take advantage of the program. For some families, respites are timed to coincide with a particular event such as a trip, a wedding, or elective surgery for the primary caregiver. Others take it simply as a temporary rest from the burden of caregiving. Each respite admission is for a period of 2 weeks; a repeat admission is scheduled after an interval of 3 months or more. Prior to admission, the family signifies its understanding that respite is intended solely as a temporary hospital admission and that the patient is expected to return home at the conclusion of the 2-week period to make the bed available to another patient. Respite beds are located on special care units housing 25 long-term patients diagnosed as having Alzheimer's disease. Approximately 50% of these other patients are ambulatory; the remainder are bedfast.

Family Attitudes about Respite Care

Since the disease process is fairly advanced in those patients whose family is "ready" for institutional respite, the ill patient is often unable to participate in decision making about respite use. Families are thus called on to make decisions in the interest of the patient and themselves. Moreover, this is often a time of considerable conflict, both intrapsychic and interpersonal within the family system. Families need an opportunity to examine their decisions thoughtfully and to explore their feelings about respite care participation.

Some caregivers are hesitant to use the respite program. Although most agree that it would provide much needed physical and emotional relief, the suggestion nevertheless elicits considerable anxiety. One concern is that a patient's level of functioning will decrease as a consequence of respite. For example, some families fear that a continent patient will become incontinent and that any relief they experience during the respite admission will be offset following respite by an increase in their caregiving tasks or burden. Second, many families fear that their ill relative will "resent" being placed in a hospital or nursing home for respite care and will "act out" or "hold a grudge" following discharge. In addition, many primary caregivers, particularly spouses who have been married for decades, experience familial and cultural obligations to be the sole care provider. They feel compelled to provide all caregiving within the confines of the family home, for as long as humanly possible, regardless of the physical, emotional, and economic cost. For these people, respite signifies an abandonment (albeit temporary) of their marital duties and obligations and a lapse in their sense of caring, and the thought of, and use of, respite care is likely to evoke strong feelings of guilt.

Family members may also view formal respite as a potential threat to their self-esteem, since they view participation in respite care as bringing into question their own competence as caregivers. Some families unrealistically compare their caregiving skills and experience to those of the professional respite care staff and so perceive themselves as ineffective caregivers. The staff may unintentionally reinforce this view by stressing how well the patient did during the respite. In fact, some patients with Alzheimer's disease do improve behaviorally in the structured institutional environment. Unfortunately family caregivers may interpret this outcome as a personal failure. Finally, respite use is largely influenced by how well a family deals with the problem of separation and gradual loss of a family member. With all of these issues in mind, the social worker and other professional staff can provide the necessary preparatory counseling of families who are prospective users of respite care. Adult children who witness the physical toll of caregiving on a well parent may strongly advocate the use of respite. Families need an opportunity to explore their feelings and wishes prior to making a decision about respite admission. Since the patient is usually unable to be involved in this decision-making process, the family must also address the issue of this nonparticipation.

Another barrier to respite use is cost. Because of the care-intensive demands and operational expenses of a respite program, many nursing homes and hospitals require minimum stays and charge considerable fees. Although public institutions, including Veterans Administration hospitals, can provide respite at nominal cost to the caregiver, these governmental programs usually have stringent eligibility requirements.

To address these many issues, a respite program must establish administration procedures, policies, and counseling services that prepare families for the respite stay of an Alzheimer patient. This is accomplished through an extensive family orientation to respite care services. For example, families are encouraged to visit the ward, meet with staff, and observe patient activities. This usually serves to dispel fears and preconceptions about an Alzheimer unit. Administrative issues are also discussed such as the cost of care, recommendations about visiting, and admission and discharge procedures.

Comprehensive Plan of Care

When a family makes a request for respite, the interdisciplinary staff, consisting of neurologist, attending physician, social worker, geriatric nurse practitioner, and nurse unit administrator, meet to assess the patient's current level of func-

Institution-Based Respite Care

Table 6-1 Respite Care Plan

Nursing Diagnosis	Outcome	Nursing Intervention
Impending impaired home maintenance management	Family will feel secure in taking the patient home.	1. Suggest day care if possible. 2. Encourage respite stays every 3 months. 3. Suggest helpful hints for home maintenance (e.g., locks on closets, cupboards; use of adult disposable diapers).
Anxiety	Patient will adjust to respite experience.	1. Speak slowly and calmly in simple short sentences. 2. Remove patient from source of stimulus when agitation level is on the rise. 3. Medicate for high agitation if necessary. 4. Assess source of anxiety.
Potential for injury	Patient will be injury-free for 2-week stay.	1. Place visible identification stickers on patient's outside clothing to lessen risk of elopement. 2. Ensure patient wears ID bracelet at all times.
Ineffective family coping	Family members will receive rest and replenishment of energies during respite.	1. Encourage family members to stay away during respite. 2. Ensure families that their feelings are normal. 3. Encourage respite every 3 months. 4. Refer families to social worker for group and/or private support.

Source: Courtesy of Patricia Wilbur, RN, AD

tioning and to discuss family coping skills. After a decision is reached to admit the patient to the respite program, an individualized and comprehensive plan of care is designed (Table 6-1). Each patient admitted to respite care is recognized and accepted as having his or her own special needs. As a consequence, the approach to the management of the patient is personalized. Broadly speaking, however, it is possible to conceptualize five main categories of need that pertain to all respite patients:

1. The need for physical security
2. The need for emotional security
3. The need for social interaction and communication
4. The need for personal comfort
5. The need for stabilization of the underlying dementia

Physical Security

The safety of patients is a major concern. Since wandering is such a serious hazard for the patient suffering from Alzheimer's disease, the physical environment of the respite program must be designed to ensure that patients will not get lost or injure themselves. Aside from the obvious need for constant supervision by the nursing staff, all doors to the clinical unit must either be locked or there must be some alternate security system so that patients will not wander from the ward. However, it is good practice to request a recent photograph of the patient for identification in the event that a respite patient is able to escape the confines of the unit. Patients should, however, have access to all public areas of the unit including day room, dining room, and corridors. Patients are generally less agitated, although physically secure, when allowed to walk freely within the boundaries of a protected environment. Of course, with close staff supervision, respite patients may also go for walks outside the ward, and this is an effective way to reduce their feelings of confinement. Repeated reassurance is often necessary for patients who complain about confinement. After a few days of respite care, most patients become acclimated to the new environment and cease to complain about confinement.

Attention to other aspects of the physical environment is also necessary to ensure patient safety. For example, items such as toiletries and cleaning products, which might be hazardous when handled by a patient with Alzheimer's disease, need to be stored in locked cabinets away from patient access. To prevent accidental poisoning, live plants are hazards and should be removed from patient areas and artificial floral arrangements substituted. Thermostats and radiators should be covered with guards to prevent restless patients from inadvertently tampering with them. Television sets and stereo systems should be out of a patient's reach.

The importance of creating a safe physical environment is reinforced by the fact that many patients with Alzheimer's disease have a variety of other medical conditions that affect their mobility and perception. These include osteoarthritis, Parkinson's disease, impaired visual acuity, and visual agnosias. Modifications in the physical environment are necessary to circumvent these additional problems. A highly polished or waxed floor may be misperceived by the patient, thereby resulting in a fall. To prevent glare, overhead lighting should therefore be evenly distributed. Nightlights should be available in every bedroom and in bathrooms and corridors and also help prevent nocturnal confusion ("sundowning"). The use of immovable furniture kept consistently in the same place helps prevent falls and provides a more stable and reassuring environment to the patient. Although the physical appearance of the unit may appear drab to the staff and visitors, this simplification of the physical environment helps patients, not only in terms of safety but also because it is less perplexing to them.

Emotional Security

Emotional security is another important need of the respite patient. Admission to respite represents a marked change in a person's living circumstances. It has previously been reported that elderly[11] and demented[12] patients experience behavioral change when relocated from one environment to another, and many patients do experience some behavioral change (e.g., increased anxiety, confusion, and agitation) for the first few days of a respite admission. This is especially so during the first admission. On the other hand, this is by no means a universal finding and many patients adjust easily and quickly to the new environment. Prior use of antianxiety medications such as oxazepam (Serax) or diphenhydramine (Benadryl) may possibly influence the patient's reaction to respite since it has repeatedly been observed that patients who have required antianxiety medications for home management seem less likely to develop agitation on admission to respite than those who did not need medication at home. With subsequent respite admissions, however, the hospital environment becomes more familiar and less threatening to the patient and such reactions are rare. Furthermore, results from a clinical study on the short-term effects of respite on patient functioning suggest that no persistent objective deficits occur.[13] Overall, these relocation reactions are mild and can be easily managed by interpersonal staff skills. Many patients accept their hospitalization without protest if they receive repeated explanations. Furthermore, the judicious use of low doses of antianxiety medications may also allay these reactions.

The attitudes and behaviors of the nursing staff play a crucial role in establishing a trusting relationship with patients and thereby provide emotional security for the respite patient. Most patients remain acutely sensitive to nurses' facial expressions, sound of voice, and touch, even when dementia is severe. Patients perceive the emotional state of the caregiver nurse and respond appropriately. Nonverbal communication skills such as a pleasant and cheerful facial expression and reassuring the patient with a pat on the shoulder are important aspects of the therapeutic approach. Patients should be spoken to slowly, clearly, and with short words and simple sentences. Even patients with impaired verbal comprehension seem to correctly sense "tone of voice." For example, they readily sense an approving tone of voice as well as intonations of frustration and anger. Other effective communication strategies include getting the patient's attention before speaking. This may be accomplished by beginning all conversations by addressing the person by name. Direct eye contact with the patient should be maintained throughout all verbal interactions.

Need for Social Interactions and Communication

Meaningful communication is one of the most important needs of the respite patient. Regardless of the difficulties a person may have in understanding and interpreting the respite experience, the patient with Alzheimer's disease has the need to be understood by others. Since most patients are disoriented, they repeatedly ask questions such as, "Where am I?" and "When am I going home?" To facilitate orientation, a "written reminder" is given to them answering their questions. If the patient is still able to read, this reminder helps orient the patient. As a consequence, the frequency of repeated questions is reduced and anxiety is relieved. For patients who retain some degree of temporal orientation, a calendar is posted in the room, with the admission and discharge dates circled for emphasis.

Some respite patients are aware of, and disturbed by, the lack of privacy that they experience during respite, especially intrusions by other patients who wander in the corridor and inadvertently into their room. To facilitate privacy for the patient who requires it, a private room is available.

Most social interactions between patients, and between patients and staff, seem to occur in the corridors of the unit, rather than the day room. Patients seem to especially enjoy interacting with staff who take the time to stop and share a few words with them. Alcoves or nooks in the corridor allow the patient to be seated in the hallway, yet out of the way of ambulatory patients. Thus individuals can choose between socializing with others and having time by themselves. In shared living spaces such as the dining room and day room, chairs should be placed in small groupings since it seems that demented patients are better able to cope and interact with small groups of two to four people. Similarly, small group recreational and occupational activities are better tolerated than programs involving large members of individuals. A description of recreational opportunities for patients is provided in Chapters 7 and 12.

Meal times are another opportunity for the respite patient to socialize with others. While food is served in the day room, taped music is played at a low volume. Patients often sing the words of tunes they recognize, and this helps promote relaxation and fosters self-feeding. Forty to 50 minutes are allowed for each meal, and opportunities for social interaction with other patients and the staff are encouraged. The maintenance of such an environment does place certain demands on the professional caregiver. Although self-feeding is encouraged, this activity obviously requires guidance and supervision. Nearly every patient needs some supervision in the handling of utensils and the eating process. Patients are served one food item at a time. For those patients who are too restless to sit still, a Gerichair with secured tabletop can be used. Diet textures and consistency are modified to meet the needs of patients who have difficulty swallowing. Because of the risk of choking, staff members must remain in the dining room throughout the meal.

The Need for Personal Comfort

All respite patients have the need to be comfortable and relaxed during respite stay. Pacing, or constant and compulsive walking, is a common phenomenon in Alzheimer's disease[13] and a potential cause of physical discomfort. Pacing may also be harmful to the nutritional status of the patient. In a clinical study, it was demonstrated that pacing increases energy demand by as much as 1600 kcal/day and is thus an energy-consuming activity that places patients at risk for excessive weight loss.[13] To avoid this, patients who pace should be supplied with a hypercaloric diet designed to meet their nutritional needs (Table 6-2).

Pacing also causes physical exhaustion and injuries to the feet. To avoid these complications, patients should rest in a reclining chair for 30 minutes every 2 hours. During the enforced rest time, the patient's feet are assessed for signs of swelling and blisters. According to physical fitness experts, walker's heel, a painful condition that causes both bone bruises and spurs, may occur whenever a person walks excessively. Wearing ill-fitting shoes also predisposes individuals to Achilles tendonitis, a painful inflammation of the calf muscle. Since the Alzheimer patient may not be able to express discomfort verbally, any change in gait or limp-

Table 6-2 Hypercaloric Alzheimer Diet

Principle: This diet is intended to be used for patients with Alzheimer's disease to meet increased metabolic needs. It includes chopped foods that are easily chewed and provides approximately 3,000 calories per day, including two snacks. Excluded are coffee and condiments.

Breakfast	Approximate Calories
2 Fruit Juice	80
2 Eggs	150
2 Toast	140
2 Margarine	90
2 Cereal (hot)	140
1 Carton Milk	150
2 Pkg. Sugar	40

Lunch and Dinner	
4 oz. Meat (#8 Scoop)*	300
2 #8 Scoops Potato or Substitute*	140
2 #8 Scoops Vegetables	70
2 Bread	140
2 Margarine	90
Geriatric Dessert	200
1 Carton Milk	150
1 Pkg. Sugar	20

2 PM

8 oz. supplement 1.5 calories/ml	355
Pudding or Yogurt	170

8 PM

Sandwich with ground filling	250
1 Carton Milk	150
TOTAL CALORIES	2,825

*Or double serving of Geriatric entree (casserole)

Source: Dietary Service, Edith Nourse Rogers Memorial Veterans Hospital, Bedford, Massachusetts.

ing or favoring of one leg over the other should alert the caregiver to the possibility of blisters or walker's heel. For patients who pace more than 30 minutes a day, quality running shoes that provide support, protection, and cushioning to prevent injuries to the feet can be worn.

Another area of personal comfort concerns bathing, dressing, and grooming functions, which are frequently impaired by Alzheimer's disease. Although some respite patients need only reminders to shave, shower, or brush their teeth, others need greater guidance. Some patients become resistive, and even agitated, with their caregivers during bathing and grooming tasks. To reduce or minimize this behavior, these activities can be initiated early in the morning as soon as patients awake. Bathing the patient in privacy as well as a calm, gentle, and reassuring manner on the part of the caregiver help to reduce anxiety. Occasionally, it may be necessary to administer antianxiety medication prior to bathing. To facilitate dressing, simple clothing, such as jogging outfits with pullover shirts and elasticized waistbands, helps eliminate confusion. Maintaining an attractive and well-groomed appearance is essential to a positive self-image and a sense of individuality.

Attention to bladder and bowel management is also necessary to ensure patient comfort during respite stay. Preventive measures should be initiated to promote continence. Because many patients void or eliminate in inappropriate places the bathroom should be clearly marked with signs or symbols. Patients should be encouraged to use the bathroom on waking, after all meals, and before bed. To reduce nocturnal incontinence, fluids are restricted for at least 4 hours before bed. To reduce the incidence of falls in patients who have an impaired gait or visual problems, a bedside commode is helpful. To promote independence in toileting, modifications are necessary, such as wide bathroom stalls with raised toilet seats and hand grab bars. For those patients who are too confused, agitated or fearful, disposable incontinence products are useful.

Need for Stabilization of Underlying Dementia

There are two main ways to judge the effectiveness of an institution-based respite program. One relies on the subjective reports of patients, families, and professional caregivers. The other involves the objective measurement of change on a particular parameter as a consequence of respite. Ideally, the latter method should also include suitable control data.

Since respite is intended primarily for the benefit of the family caregiver, one way to evaluate it is clearly the influence it has on the patient's condition. If this effect were to be negative, and patients' functional statuses worsened as a result of respite, this might lead ultimately to increased caregiver burden and earlier need for long-term institutional placement. Indeed, there is some evidence that elderly, demented patients tend to show a further decline if relocated from one environment to another,[14,15] although these findings are considered controversial.[12]

A study of the short-term effects of a 2-week inhospital respite stay on a diagnostically homogeneous group of patients with Alzheimer's disease has been completed.[16] At admission, and then on discharge, the cognitive and functional statuses of 37 patients were assessed by the *Mini-Mental State Examination*,[17] test of Blessed and co-workers,[18] and the *MACC Behavioral Adjustment Scale*.[19] The study showed that participation in a 2-week inhospital respite program affects the functional status of a group of patients with Alzheimer's disease differently according to their functional levels on admission. When the initial severity of dementia is taken into account, patients with scores indicating the most severe dementia tended to show improvement on some of the measures after 2 weeks in the hospital. By contrast, patients with higher initial levels of performance, suggesting milder dementia, showed worsening on some of the measures at the conclusion of respite. All of the changes were small, however, and largely restricted to tests that tap activities of daily living. No significant changes in cognitive status were found. These results indicate that patient status must be carefully assessed before recommending respite admission to a family. In some instances, special interventions may be necessary during the admission to present further deterioration. According to pilot data from a subset of 24 patients whose relatives completed the Blessed test two and four weeks after the patient had returned home, the changes weren't sustained in the weeks following discharge. The results of the study indicate, however, that patient status must be carefully assessed before recommending respite admission to a family. For example, it may not be appropriate to place respite patients with comparatively high levels of functioning on wards with severely regressed inpatients. Those patients who retain some degree of insight may need counseling from staff and family members prior to respite so that they do not decompensate emotionally upon admission. In some instances, special interventions may be necessary during the admission to prevent further deterioration. Such interventions might include repeated reality orientation, intensive efforts to maintain patient functioning in spheres where skills are preserved, and constant reassurance to combat any sense of having been abandoned. For all respite patients the management plan must be tailored to meet the unique needs of the patient.

REFERENCES

1. O'Quinn JA, McGraw KO: The burdened caregiver: An overview, in Hutton JT, Kenny AD (eds): *Senile Dementia of the Alzheimer's Type.* New York, Alan R. Liss, 1985.

2. *Webster's International Dictionary,* ed 2. Springfield, Mass, G & C Merriam Co, 1959.

3. Meltzer J: *Respite Care: An Emerging Family Support Service.* Washington, DC, Center for the Study of Social Policy, 1982.

4. Griffiths RA, Cosin LZ: The floating-bed. *Lancet* 1976;1:684-685.

5. Robertson D, Griffiths RA, Cosin LZ: A community-based continuing care program for the elderly disabled: An evaluation of planned intermittent hospital readmission. *J Gerontol* 1977;32:334-339.

6. Foundation for Long-Term Care: *Respite Care for the Frail Elderly: Final Report.* Albany, NY, Center for the Study of Aging, 1982.

7. Hasselkus BR, Brown M: Respite care of community elderly. *Am J Occup Ther* 1983;37:83-88.

8. Scharlach A, Frenzel C: An evaluation of institution-based respite care. *Gerontologist* 1986;26:77-82.

9. Dunn RB, MacBeth L, Robertson D. Respite admissions and the disabled elderly. *J Am Geriatr Soc* 1983;31:319-342.

10. McKhann G, Drachman D, Folstein M, et al: Clinical diagnosis of Alzheimer's disease: Report of the NINCDS-ADRDA Work Group under the auspices of Department of Health and Human Services Task Force on Alzheimer's Disease. *Neurology* 1984;34:939-944.

11. Coffman TL: Relocation and survival of institutionalized aged: A re-examination of the evidence. *Gerontologist* 1981;21:483-500.

12. Horowitz MJ, Schulz R: The relocation controversy: Criticism and commentary on five recent studies. *Gerontologist* 1983;23:229-234.

13. Rheaume YL, Riley ML, Volicer L: Nutritional risk associated with constant walking in Alzheimer's disease. *J Nutr Elderly* 1987;7 (in press).

14. Aldrick CK, Mendkoff E: Relocation of the aged and disabled: A mortality study. *J Am Geriatr Soc* 1963;11:185-194.

15. Borup JH: Relocation mortality research: Assessment, reply, and the need to refocus on the issues. *Gerontologist* 1983;23:235-242.

16. Seltzer B, Rheaume Y, Volicer L, et al: The short-term effects of in-hospital respite on the patient with Alzheimer's disease. *Gerontologist* (in press).

17. Folstein MF, Folstein SE, McHugh PR: Mini-mental State, a practical method for grading the cognitive state of patients for clinicians. *J Psychiatr Res* 1975;12:189-198.

18. Blessed G, Tomlinson BE, Roth M: The association between quantitative measures of dementia and of senile changes in cerebral grey matter of elderly subjects. *Br J Psychiatry* 1968;114:797-811.

19. Ellsworth RE: *The MACC Behavioral Adjustment Scale: Revised 1971 Manual.* Los Angeles, Western Psychological Service, 1971.

CHAPTER 7

Management of Advanced Alzheimer Dementia

Kathy J. Fabiszewski, Mary Ellen Riley, Deborah Berkley, Josephine Karner, and Susan Shea

Approximately 5% of the population at age 65 and up to 20% of the population at age 80 will be affected by Alzheimer dementia, a devastating, debilitating, irreversible, and progressive neurologic disorder that erodes personality, memory, and intellect, resulting, inevitably, in regressive behavior and functional deterioration.[1] An estimated 2 to 4 million middle-aged and elderly Americans are presently afflicted; by the year 2000, the number of victims is expected to double and, because of the rapidly growing number of older people in the population, it will increase fivefold by the year 2040 unless cures or means of prevention are found.[2] Not only is Alzheimer's disease the major cause of institutionalization among the more than 4 million Americans residing in nursing homes, it is the culprit that robs countless, productive members of society, without respect for race, sex, or socioeconomic status, of those very qualities that make one human.

Medical research and technology have yielded substantive advances in the treatment of many age-related illnesses[3]; yet the pace of promising research breakthroughs in Alzheimer dementia has been excruciatingly slow. Since its exact cause remains unknown, there exists no effective therapy or cure to reverse or arrest the disease's progression.[4] Consequently, once an accurate diagnosis is made, treatment efforts are generally care oriented (as opposed to being cure oriented) and managerial strategies are directed at providing symptomatic relief of the physical, emotional, and psychosocial discomforts associated with the advancing illness. Identifying and strategizing to meet the complex needs of a patient with the myriad of compromised intellectual, behavioral, and functional abilities seen in advanced Alzheimer dementia becomes a formidable challenge for the entire health care community.

An overview is presented in this chapter of the stages of the Alzheimer dementia disease process, with emphasis on decrements in function associated with the late or advanced stage of the illness. Emphasis is placed on interdisciplinary teamwork with an inherent philosophy of care and clearly delineated treatment goals for the individual patient. Techniques for the assessment and management of physical, emotional, stimulation, and security needs are discussed, particularly as they pertain to the institutionalized Alzheimer dementia patient. Issues of institutional care as they apply to family members and professional caregivers are also identified.

Overview of the Stages of the Disease Process

The age-related clinical syndrome of Alzheimer's disease is characterized by progressive impairments in a wide spectrum of cognitive, behavioral, and functional abilities. The course of the illness may extend from 1 to 15 years, with the average duration being 7 to 8 years.[5] Clinical features of the illness may vary considerably depending on the age at disease onset.[6] Patients who experience onset of Alzheimer dementia prior to age 65, for example, appear to demonstrate a greater prevalence of language disturbance and a much shorter relative survival time than victims with onset of symptoms after age 65.

The emergence of certain characteristic aberrancies in intellect, behavior, and self-care ability has resulted in "staging" of the disease progression by many clinicians. Unfortunately, the disease does not progress in a sequential, uniform, and organized pattern. This, coupled with the wide degree of symptom heterogeneity often seen,[7] makes it neither possible nor realistic to "assign" patients to a specific illness stage at any given point in the course of the illness. Although lost abilities are seldom regained, impairments characteristic of all or some stages may occasionally exist in a person one day and may erratically disappear the next. Usually this is in response to a fluctuating environmental or social situation or may represent the result of a medication adjustment. In some instances, clinical features of advanced Alzheimer dementia appear prior to some of the characteristics of middle stage disease. Thus, clinicians should be aware that each patient is affected by the illness in a unique manner and, although commonalities often occur from patient to patient, there is no stepwise progression that exists routinely or systematically. This pattern, or lack of pattern, to the illness greatly influences managerial strategies and necessitates that each person be assessed and managed symptomatically on an individualized basis. Thus, staging of the illness serves the primary purpose of providing a guideline for effective care planning and preparation of counter-measures that are possible and necessary in maximizing patient abilities throughout the course of the illness,[8] rather than serving to label patients or predict decrement in function.

Therefore, more generally, as described in Chapter 2, three stages of Alzheimer dementia progression can be distinguished: the early, middle, and late stages.[9,10] For the purpose of this chapter, the illness phases will be further delineated to include a fourth stage, the terminal stage of the illness. It is important, once again, to emphasize that because of the progressive nature of the illness and the intricacy of its underlying pathology, its signs, symptoms, and clinical manifestations in the afflicted person may be continuously changing.

In the early stage of Alzheimer dementia, which often precedes clinical diagnosis, discrete personality changes such as apathy, disinterest in previously enjoyed hobbies, social withdrawal, irritability, and lack of spontaneity may surface. These changes tend to be so insidious that neither the affected person nor his or her family or co-workers are often aware of them initially. The forgetfulness, which is often present in conjunction with transient episodes of disorientation, particularly to time and space, however, may create difficulties in effective employment performance. Inattentiveness, inability to concentrate, and impaired judgment and decision-making ability, particularly in stressful situations, often force a premature retirement. Insight into one's deficits may lead, not only to fear and possibly panic but also to frustration and depression. Denial and attempts to conceal deficits are not uncommon in this stage of the illness. In addition, there may be word-finding difficulty; problems handling sums of money and balancing the checkbook; difficulty in driving an automobile, especially in unfamiliar environments; inability to adapt to change; difficulty with novel or complex tasks; and disinterest in personal appearance with neglect in personal hygiene.

Problems in independent living begin to arise in the middle stage of the disease. As disorientation and confusion increases, the afflicted person may experience feelings of paranoia, suspiciousness or embarrassment as previously assumed responsibilities of everyday life become overwhelming. Consequently, restlessness and varying degrees of anxiety may be present. The frustration associated with progressive memory loss, particularly immediate and recent memory loss, and failure to comprehend simple requests of caregivers or casual remarks made by them may lead to catastrophic behavioral reactions, such as unexpected, unprovoked outbursts of physical or verbal aggression. Motor hyperactivity may become apparent, manifested by aimless wandering (commonly during the night), incessant pacing, and shadowing of caregivers. Loss of coordination and apraxia, in conjunction with visuoconstructive difficulty, may affect independent ambulation and maneuverability around "obstacles" such as home furnishings or doorways or the performance of seemingly simple, overlearned activities of daily living such as feeding oneself with the proper utensils or dressing in the proper sequence. "Sundowning," a syndrome characterized by unexplained restlessness, excitement, hallucinations, and agitation in the late afternoon or early evening, is commonly seen in patients in the middle stage of the disease.[11] Intellectual function declines further to affect verbal communication, reading with comprehension, writing, and calculating. Perseveration may develop in which the individual has a tendency to "get stuck" on one particular activity and not "shift gears." Because of difficulties locating the bathroom or failure to recognize the need to void, urinary incontinence may be seen early in the middle stage of the disease.

As the illness progresses into the late or advanced stage, institutionalization becomes inevitable in the majority of cases. Both expressive and receptive language ability disintegrates further, considerably hampering effective communication. Bowel and bladder incontinence occurs. Physical mobility, with respect to gait and posturing, is compromised and the person is at great risk for the development of flexion contractures as the limbs are used less and less to carry out purposeful movements. Most patients with advanced Alzheimer dementia are unable to ambulate even with major assistance and must resort to a chairfast or totally bedfast existence. Needless to say, the risks for traumatic injuries and falls are greatest during the advanced stage of Alzheimer's disease. Approximately 10% of patients with advanced Alzheimer dementia experience generalized seizures.[6] Dangerous behaviors such as hyperoralia (an apparent need for oral stimulation manifested by chewing or tasting whatever objects are available)[12] may result in the ingestion of inedible objects. Aggression or assaultiveness may occur, seemingly unprovoked, in a patient while being cared for, because the person is unable to understand the need for personal care provision. In most cases, the patient in an advanced stage of dementia is totally dependent on others for all aspects of bathing, grooming, dressing, feeding, and toileting, with the possible exception of performing some basic tasks, such as drinking from a cup. One of the more fortunate aspects of advanced Alzheimer dementia is that these patients have lost all insight into their condition; this, however, may create intense sadness in family members and friends who, then, must come to realize that because recognition is so profoundly impaired, their faces and voices no longer have meaning to the affected person as they once did.

In the terminal phase of the illness, patients are severely physically debilitated and may be unable to swallow, unable to move, and unable to communicate. Seldom is there any meaningful interaction with the environment. This total helplessness makes the person extremely vulnerable to the hazards of prolonged immobility, such as pneumonia, cardiovascular complication, and decubitus ulceration. Death ultimately results from these complications, which represent extensions of the Alzheimer dementia process.

The Decision To Institutionalize

Although socioeconomic constraints necessitate home care of the Alzheimer patient well into the advanced stage of the illness, premature hospitalization should be avoided whenever possible. The intensified personal care needs of the patient, the need for continual health status monitoring, and the need for continuous patient supervision, all of which are physically and emotionally exhausting to family caregivers, ultimately necessitate institutionalization in most cases. The decision to institutionalize a patient in the advanced stage of Alzheimer dementia is seldom made with ease and confidence, particularly if family caregivers possess feelings of helplessness or hopelessness or begin to realize that the death of the person is imminent.[9] Emphasizing that the decision for nursing home or hospital placement is a "medical" decision, made in the mutual best interest of both the patient and the family, minimizes the guilt and despair that family caregivers experience when they realize that they can no longer continue to safely manage their loved one's care in the home setting. Family members, at the time of institutional admission, may benefit from reassurance that the decision to hospitalize the patient will have no untoward effect on the patient, nor will it affect the course of the illness or the patient's longevity.

In addition, assisting family members in understanding that, because of the multitude of physiological, behavioral, psychosocial, and functional deficits that are inherent in advanced Alzheimer dementia, the patient can best be cared for in a setting where an interdisciplinary treatment team is available to assist them in acknowledging the complexity of the illness, its progressive and incurable nature, and the reality of the need for institutional care. Many families may have difficulty grasping the concept that the decision to place their loved one in an institution is actually a very caring decision.

Interdisciplinary Teamwork

Given the complexity of Alzheimer dementia in its advanced stage, the interdisciplinary team approach to care, which stresses the wide range of health care professionals appropriate to the delivery of quality care, enhances holistic health care provision. The formulation of an interdisciplinary treatment plan with input from a variety of medical specialists, nurses and nursing assistants, social workers, recreational therapists, and rehabilitation specialists for each Alzheimer dementia patient and his or her family is instrumental. Formulating realistic short-term and long-term goals for the patient and the family are key components of illness management, particularly in the advanced stage of the disease when its tragedy is often fully realized. Having a team in place to collaborate, consult, communicate, and share in some of the very difficult decisions that confront Alzheimer dementia caregivers, both professional and family, appears to be of great benefit to all in terms of minimizing the burden. Teamwork facilitates and maintains the most nurturing, comfortable, and pleasant atmosphere for the patient, as well as fosters the most caring and supportive environment for the family.[13] The establishment of a long-term, caring, therapeutic relationship between the treatment team and both the patient and the family is of utmost importance. Members of the interdisciplinary treatment team are described in Chapters 2 and 9.

Philosophy of Care

Since institutional care of the patient with advanced Alzheimer dementia constitutes a major portion of the treatment required along the extensive spectrum of the illness, having a philosophy of care that is understood by and acceptable to professional caregivers and family members is imperative. Special care units for Alzheimer patients may have such a "unit philosophy" that serves to guide caregivers in consistent treatment approaches. Although philosophies may vary in their overall goals and approaches, most will have certain elements in common. For example, a philosophy that facilitates palliative, hospice-like, supportive care tends to be welcome and well-accepted by many families of individuals with advanced Alzheimer dementia[4] (see Chapter 10). Shifting the emphasis away from intensive medical technological interventions, such as feeding gastrostomy tubes and respirators, which family members may expect because of the hospital or nursing home setting, to striving for maximal patient comfort, dignity, safety, and quality of life is not only realistic but humane. Emphasizing the use of intact patient abilities, regardless of how primitive or regressed those abilities may be, demonstrates the respect for personhood and the notion of adding quality to life rather than just years to life. The needs of the individual with advanced Alzheimer dementia, by far, exceed what has traditionally been referred to as custodial care. More realistically, given its true nature, it should be referred to as a modified form of intensive care.

Recognition that continuous assessment of continuous change is required in order to implement the most appropriate interventions and evaluate their effectiveness is another essential component of a caring philosophy. It must be recognized and accepted by all members of the treatment team that every Alzheimer dementia victim dependent on others for care has the right to achieve maximal potential for wellness and optimal functional ability. Every Alzheimer dementia patient must be afforded the opportunity to derive as much pleasure and satisfaction from life as possible.

Treatment Goals

Preventing Premature or Excess Disability

Because Alzheimer dementia is incurable at present and characterized by progressive deterioration, it is associated with a variety of decrements in function, that is, disabilities that will increase with time. Although it is self-defeating to attempt to prevent inevitable distressing losses such as that of physical mobility or bladder and bowel continence, efforts should be directed at alleviating premature or excess disability (i.e., disability that is over and above that which is a direct consequence of Alzheimer dementia itself). In other words, while patients with advanced Alzheimer dementia cannot be actively rehabilitated because of their impaired cognition, inability to learn new information, and lack of ability to cooperate and participate actively in their treatment regimens, they can be maintained at existing levels of function for as long as possible. Although the underlying disease pathology is not amenable to therapy, the symptoms of the illness can be altered in a favorable manner by continual willingness on the part of caregivers to alter their approaches and behaviors.

Optimizing Overall Health Status

Despite the patient's lack of awareness of body and self, it is possible to maintain optimal physical and emotional health. With continual assessment of health indicators such as vital signs, activity tolerance, body weight, skin integrity, appetite, and sleep patterns, areas of actual or potential compromise can be identified and deficits compensated for before their impact on health status is insurmountable. Striving to adequately meet basic physical needs such as hygiene, nutrition, hydration, elimination, and rest are important components of overall treatment goals.

Maximizing Patient Safety and Security

The advanced stage of Alzheimer dementia carries with it an increased vulnerability to illness, injury, and emotional stress. Treating episodic and intercurrent illness expeditiously and directing efforts at protecting the afflicted person from physical injury due to falls, choking, or seizure are of paramount importance. Careful, around-the-clock supervision and ongoing environmental modification provide an atmosphere of security and promote feelings of safety, familiarity, and relaxation.

Promoting Normal Adaptive Responses

Providing appropriate levels of social and sensory stimulation is a formidable challenge in caring for the advanced Alzheimer dementia patient. Treatment goals pertinent to patient stimulation should focus on eliciting positive patient responses such as smiling or laughing, minimizing the use of psychotropic medications for behavioral symptomatology that can possibly be managed by environmental manipulation or by an alteration in social or sensory stimuli.

Ensuring Patient Comfort

The physical and emotional comfort of the patient, as evidenced by relaxed posturing, minimal restlessness, and a content-appearing or satisfied facial expression, is the ultimate treatment goal in advanced Alzheimer dementia. Although comfort, itself, is a difficult parameter to measure in a noncommunicative patient, caregivers, by developing, sensitivity to nonverbal cues and behaviors that occur in response to an intervention can objectively estimate degrees of comfort or distress. Ensuring adequate amounts of rest and relaxation, for example, is instrumental to promoting comfort.

Although all patients with advanced Alzheimer dementia will ultimately die of complications of the illness, establishing and reevaluating treatment goals that are realistic and feasible for the profoundly impaired patient requires skill, ingenuity, and a concerted team effort. Respecting the patient's premorbid wishes in establishing treatment goals, if they had at any time been verbalized, is likewise important, as is promoting coping mechanisms of significant others while assisting them in the grieving process.

Management Issues

Continual Assessment

Effective care management of the person with advanced Alzheimer's disease requires continual assessment of capabilities and needs. Because the patient is likely to be only minimally communicative, assessment cannot take place via the traditional interview methodology. Assessment of the patient with advanced Alzheimer dementia requires use of all of the senses: vision, hearing, smell, and touch. It involves having a solid knowledge base on which to compare changes in the patient from one day to the next. And since many individuals with advanced Alzheimer dementia are members of the geriatric population, a detailed understanding of normal changes associated with the human aging process is imperative.

Proper "Diagnosis" of the Problem

After the person is systematically evaluated, identification of the management issue must take place. It becomes highly important to describe objectively and identify what is the real issue in Alzheimer dementia patient care. Compensating, for example, for a deficit such as inability to bathe or incontinence is not a "problem" per se. Rather the problem lies in attempting to bathe or toilet an individual who, because of his or her inability to understand the need for such procedures, is uncooperative, resistive, or even assaultive during personal care provision. Vital to promoting the comfort of the patient with a total self-care deficit is caregiver understanding and acknowledgment of how stressful the bathing and grooming procedures might be to the person who has no control over performance of the procedure, who may feel actual physical discomfort associated with the procedure performance, or who may not understand the rationale for procedure performance. One of the goals in meeting the physical needs of the advanced Alzheimer dementia patient is to minimize the amount of stress, anxiety, and fear that is involuntarily produced. Increased muscle tone (rigidity) in many patients with advanced stage disease may, for example, present as intentional resistiveness to care. Seldom is this "resistiveness" a conscious effort on the part of the patient; rather it is an involuntary reaction to tactile or possibly vocal stimuli that occur during personal care provision. Identifying innovative ways to distract the patient, to prevent sensory overload, to minimize dangerous behaviors that result from fear or anxiety, and at the same time to provide the very best personal care possible becomes more of a true management issue.

Creative Interventions

Interventions that are initiated by a caregiver to manage a specific problem need to be continually reevaluated for both their therapeutic effectiveness and their efficacy in terms of caregiver time and the cost (psychological and economic) of the interventions. A technique that appears to be helpful one week may not be effective the next. Since the pathologic process is always progressing but at a variable rate, the patient's response to a given stimulus or intervention will vary. It can be distressing for caregivers to believe they have reached a plateau or remission in managing symptoms of belligerence or agitation, only to find that the remission was too short lived or brief to provide them, as caregivers, with temporary relief from what sometimes is a relentless struggle. Emphasis should be placed on patterns of behavior and function rather than on isolated occurrences of difficult behaviors or abnormal functional decrements.

Meeting Basic Physical Needs in the Patient with Self-Care Deficit

As Alzheimer dementia progresses into its advanced stage, the affected person will require total personal care in bathing, grooming, dressing, feeding, and toileting. Providing this care is neither problematic nor particularly challenging in the patient who is passive or able to cooperate with personal care provision. Neuroleptic medication, in doses titrated in minute increments to achieve the desired behavioral outcome without thwarting patient spontaneity, is an asset to optimizing patient comfort and relaxation and to facilitating personal care provision.

One major challenge in meeting the basic physical needs of the patient lies in organizing a daily routine that is expedient yet effective in meeting the intensive, total hygienic needs of the patient. Direct caregivers cannot rush or hurry while providing care to the cognitively impaired patient. Any "sense of urgency" on the part of a caregiver is generally contagious to the patient and may result in exacerbation of unacceptable behaviors such as aggression or assaultiveness, which, in the long run, only serve to increase the amount of time required to provide personal care.

Maintaining Skin Integrity

Providing direct personal care affords the opportunity for assessment of many physical parameters of the patient. The condition of the skin of the patient, for example, may be either actually altered or at risk of being impaired owing to pressure, shearing force, nutritional compromise, urinary or fecal incontinence, and/or environmental irritants. Daily evaluation of skin integrity over pressure points is particularly important in immobile patients who are subject to pressure, shearing force, and maceration. Massage and frequent repositioning in bed alleviates impairment of skin integrity in the bedfast patient. Alternating pressure mattresses, egg-crate mattresses, and Clinitron beds supplement the frequent, mandatory turning of the patient. Preventing the development of pressure ulcerations, which ultimately increase patient discomfort and caregiver workload, requires continuous monitoring of skin color, temperature, circulatory supply, texture, and turgor. When a deficiency of the integument is noted, the vigorous skin care interventions already in place for prophylaxis must be intensified. If an actual pressure sore is present, its location, size, color, configuration, and any drainage noted must be documented and the ulceration should be staged and subsequently treated according to the following criteria[14]:

Stage I Skin is unbroken but red.
Stage II Epidermis is broken. Skin is cracked, is blistered, or has superficial ulceration. Surrounding tissue is red and warm. Pain and/or drainage may be present.
Stage III Epidermis, dermis, and subcutaneous tissue are broken. Wound depth is greater than in stage II. There may or may not be drainage, pain, hard eschar, or necrotic tissue.
Stage IV Epidermis, dermis, and subcutaneous tissue are broken. Muscle and bone are exposed. There is drainage and evidence of necrosis. Pain may be present.

The treatment of any decubitus ulceration will depend on its cause, its characteristics, and the overall condition of the patient. Although appropriate management of decubitus ulcerations is of utmost importance, it is not within the scope of this chapter to describe all possible treatment modalities.

Promoting Optimal Nutritional Status

The advanced Alzheimer dementia patient is at substantial risk for nutritional compromise. Thus, individualized nutritional assessment and diets modified in both texture and volume to optimize patient tolerance and satisfy nutritional requirements are required. Apraxia (the inability to carry out purposeful movement), agnosia (the inability to attach meaning to sensation, e.g., the inability to recognize food by sight, smell, or taste), and impaired visuoperceptual abilities impede patient capacity to self-feed. Clinical data from one cross-sectional study indicate that 50% of institutionalized Alzheimer patients lose the ability to feed themselves 8 years after onset of symptoms.[15]

Hyperoralia (an apparent need for oral stimulation manifested by chewing or tasting whatever items are available[12]), may be observed as an isolated phenomenon or as a component of the Kluver-Bucy syndrome, which is also characterized by visual agnosia, emotional diminution, and hypermetamorphosis. When identified, the patient with hyperoralia requires frequent reminders to swallow because a constant chewing motion can be functionally nonproductive.[12]

Unique feeding problems such as food refusal (the active rejection of food by either ceasing to feed oneself or by refusing to open one's mouth when spoon-fed[16]) and uncoordinated swallowing (the inability to properly chew and swallow food placed in the mouth when spoon-fed[16]) lead to potential weight loss, dehydration, malnutrition, and choking with aspiration and possible asphyxiation. These feeding problems not only jeopardize patient safety but also cause the patient considerable distress and discomfort.

In a survey of 90 moderately to severely impaired Alzheimer patients, it was found that feeding difficulties, although present to some degree in the majority of patients, were more pronounced in patients who had to be fed than in patients who remained able to feed themselves on a regular basis (Table 7-1). Two thirds of patients surveyed required coaxing and constant supervision to eat, while more than one half were unable to consume their full serving of food.

Although a lack of information exists about whether sensations of hunger and thirst remain intact in advanced Alzheimer dementia, it is known that these sensations, along with the senses of taste and smell, diminish in acuity with age. Even if hungry or thirsty, it is unlikely that the patient is able to communicate this desire or the need for hydration or nourishment. It cannot be assumed that because of the aforementioned problems the patient is hunger or thirst free.

The nutritional requirements of the Alzheimer patient do not differ significantly from the average, normal, older adult. What does differ is the ability of the Alzheimer patient to ingest amounts and types of quality nutrients adequate for maximizing health status.

The chewing, swallowing, and overall "feedability" of patients with advanced Alzheimer's disease are seldom stable. Food refusal, for instance, is sometimes temporary and resolvable. Patients who hold food or liquid in their mouth without swallowing it or clamp their mouth shut, spit food out, or turn their head away from the feeding spoon one day may capably swallow food or willingly accept it the next. Caregivers must continually assess patient eating patterns because of their variability. The volume, texture, and consistency of foods must be increased or decreased in accordance with the patient's ability to masticate and swallow. Dietary changes may need to be implemented on a daily, weekly, or monthly

Table 7-1 Incidence of Feeding Difficulties in Patients with Advanced Alzheimer Dementia

	Ability to Feed Themselves		
Response to Meal Time	Always (n = 35)	Sometimes/Never (n = 55)	Total (n = 90)
Needs coaxing to eat	18 (51%)	41 (75%)*	59 (66%)
Eats always adequate amounts	23 (66%)	18 (33%)†	41 (45%)

* $p<.05$,
† $p<.005$.

basis to accommodate the patient's spectrum of ability in safely handling various types and textures of foods. Patients must be monitored carefully for any deterioration in the chewing or swallowing process to minimize the risk of choking or aspiration. This includes evaluating recent changes in environmental or pharmacologic regimens that may influence appetite, musculoskeletal coordination, and level of consciousness.

The hydrational status of the patient with advanced Alzheimer dementia warrants particular attention. Clinical indicators of hydrational status such as skin turgor, body temperature, and mucous membrane moisture and integrity may be evaluated daily during the bathing or dressing procedure. Since the majority of these patients are unable to communicate their thirst needs (if they are aware of them at all), ensuring adequate hydration of at least 1500 to 2000 ml/day and meticulous care of the oral mucosa are essential to preventing patient discomfort due to possible dehydration.

Successful nutritional management necessitates frequent collaboration among caregivers, particularly between the dietitian who formulates specific nutritional care plans for the patient and the nursing staff who serve as primary caregivers and who are highly knowledgeable of the patient's functional capabilities. Sharing observations, for instance, about the foods the patient finds most palatable, the meal at which the patient consumes the most food, the degree of truncal elevation at which the patient's intake is optimized, or even the side of the mouth the patient prefers to be spoon-fed to are paramount to preventing nutritional compromise. Some profoundly impaired patients manage finger foods amazingly well, possibly because hand-to-mouth motion is an overlearned task that requires minimal dexterity and coordination. If this ability remains intact, maximal advantage should be taken of it, not only to increase patient pleasure associated with oral intake but also to decrease the nursing staff time required to feed patients.

Feeding the advanced Alzheimer dementia patient can be an extremely time-consuming, emotionally draining task that may raise conflicting emotions in nursing or family caregivers who are usually responsible for feeding the patient. Force feeding a patient, for example, who clearly does not appear to enjoy eating may create feelings of anger at the patient for not "appreciating" caregiver efforts or guilt over inflicting what may be undue suffering. Caregiver anxiety is likewise increased in attempting to feed dysphagic patients who cough violently and choke, even with the most cautious of caregiver efforts. Conversely, patient weight loss may be inadvertently interpreted as inadequate nurturing.

Many ethical issues are encountered in any discussion of the nutritional management of the advanced Alzheimer dementia patient (see Chapter 10). Artificial means of feeding, such as feeding via nasogastric tube, gastrostomy tube, or intravenous line, may be viewed as an acceptable treatment modality by some families; to others, it is considered inappropriate, heroic, and unwarranted and not consistent with established treatment goals, given the terminal, incurable nature of the underlying disease process. It is essential to ascertain the true reason for any decision to initiate artificial feeding. For example, is the feeding initiated in order to benefit the patient's quality of life or is it initiated to relieve caregiver anxiety? Unfortunately, artificial feeding does not improve the patient's underlying condition and merely prevents the person from finishing the dying process.[17] In terms of patient comfort, there are no data to suggest that artificial feeding increases a patient's comfort level. On the contrary, these technological interventions may further increase patient discomfort. Patients without Alzheimer dementia who have had nasogastric tubes in place for surgical procedures often complain about considerable distress from sore throat. Even the newer, pediatric-size, pliable, small-lumen tubes may place the patient at great risk for aspiration because their placement in the stomach or duodenum is difficult to verify without radiographic confirmation. In addition, some patients with tube feedings experience an alteration in bowel elimination (diarrhea) in response to tube feedings that are hyperosmotic enough to deliver adequate numbers of calories. A gastrostomy tube requires surgical intervention and may result in infection at the gastrostomy site with possible impairment of skin integrity. Intravenous hydration predisposes one to the discomfort of needle sticks, possible infiltration, hematoma, and phlebitis. And all of these interventions may undoubtedly require the patient to be either chemically or mechanically restrained to prevent accidental extubation or discontinuance of these modalities by the patient who, again, is made uncomfortable by them and who does not understand the need for them. Restraint, then, places the patient at risk for additional hazards and certainly will increase the emotional discomfort of the patient as well.

Therefore, preventing the use of artificial feeding is an important treatment goal in the care of the Alzheimer patient. Enteral nutrition can be provided in a variety of ways, including with a pureed texture diet, a geriatric texture diet (chopped or ground food), a dental soft diet, or a regular texture diet modified for safety. Most patients with advanced Alzheimer dementia will require either the geriatric texture diet or a pureed diet.

The geriatric diet consists of foods appropriately cut, ground, and diced for minimal mastication. This diet excludes fresh, hard fruit, salads, nuts, all meats with bones such as chicken, hard rolls, and hard cookies. Dry rice may be aspirated by the patient and is recommended only if covered with sauce and gravy or in casseroles. The diet provides ground meat in stews and casseroles and only soft desserts.

The pureed diet requires no chewing. Foods are blenderized to a semiliquid consistency. Pureed foods will contain fewer calories than the same amount of whole foods since liquids, usually water, added in processing dilute and decrease calorie content. For this reason, a special pureed diet was invented to include only low-volume nutrient-dense items.[18] This diet achieves decreased feeding time and reduces the incidence of aspiration.

The nutritional status of the patient with advanced Alzheimer dementia is dependent on an interdisciplinary approach to maximizing nutritional status. Occupational therapy evaluates patients with feeding difficulties for adaptive feeding equipment needs. Nursing staff monitor the patient's individual eating patterns, diet tolerance, and eating idiosyncrasies. In addition, they collaborate with other team members to develop feeding techniques that optimize nutritional status. Dietitians modify diet volume, calories, protein content, and texture. The physician treats depression and iatrogenic dysphagia and monitors the use of medications that may alter mealtime alertness.

The following guidelines can be used to improve the nutritional status of patients with advanced Alzheimer dementia without artificial feeding devices.

1. *Monthly weights*. Monitor patient weights for change, striving to reach ideal weight goals and avoiding excessive weight gain, which leads to patient fatigue and discomfort.
2. *Hydration status*. Maintain adequate hydration with 1.5 to 2 liters of nutritious fluids per day. Aphasic patients are at increased risk for dehydration, particularly if they are prone to pacing. Medication-induced dry mouth (xerostomia) may cause discomfort and possible swallowing difficulty.
3. *Oral intake*. Discuss weekly at the interdisciplinary team conference such parameters as tolerance of diet texture, any chewing or swallowing problems, and the need for calorie counts.
4. *Aspiration/choking risks*. Increase semi-solid foods if possible since they are often easier to control. Liquids flow to the pharyngeal cavity quickly and can result in choking. An increase in liquids in the diet may be necessary if the patient tolerates liquids better. In these cases, the patient should be sitting upright with the head in midline and neck slightly flexed, preferably with a pillow in the small of the back. This position reduces choking since the foods will fall forward out of the mouth rather than backward into the throat.[19] Decrease food or liquid volume to prevent aspiration while increasing the nutrient density.
5. *Monitor milk-based foods*. Patients should be monitored for collecting phlegm and excessive coughing or choking since these foods may produce respiratory mucus.[19]
6. *Vitamin/mineral supplementation*. These supplements are recommended if oral intake is assessed to be only marginal or if drug-induced vitamin or mineral depletion can occur.
7. *Nutritional supplementation*. This should be varied to prevent patient from tiring of the same taste and texture, and extremes in temperature should be avoided.

The primary goal of nutritional management of the advanced Alzheimer dementia patient is to maintain patient comfort while maximizing nutritional status, which will prevent fever and infection, build immunocompetence, and improve the quality of life for the patient.

Providing Oral Hygiene

Providing meticulous oral hygiene for the patient who is unable to perform self-care is a time-consuming task that presents a considerable challenge for caregivers, particularly in patients who are unable or unwilling to cooperate. Maintaining moisture and integrity of the gums and oral mucosa, however, will preserve optimal dental function, promote adequate nutritional intake, and optimize patient comfort. The need for frequent, vigorous mouth care cannot be overemphasized, particularly in patients who are "mouth breathers" or who have salivary gland dysfunction. Brushing the teeth twice daily, at a minimum, with ingestible toothpaste and moistening the buccal mucosa with artificial saliva between meals helps prevent tooth decay, gingivitis, and the emergence of oral ulcerations.

Regular bedside cleanings and scalings by the dental hygienist are an invaluable asset to the total health maintenance management of the Alzheimer dementia patient, provided these treatments do not serve as a substitute for routine, daily oral hygiene. In addition, periodic dental evaluations and consultation on an as-needed basis serve as an integral component of overall health care. The oral health care of the Alzheimer dementia patient is discussed in detail in Chapter 8.

Assessing Rest and Relaxation Needs

The activity, sleep, and rest requirements of the patient with advanced Alzheimer's disease are not known but do not appear to differ significantly from those of comparative age groups. Since patterns of rest and activity are highly variable, however, they must continually be assessed to ensure that adequate amounts of rest and high-quality sleep are attained. Sleep-wake cycle disturbances or day-night reversal with nocturnal wandering or excessive daytime sleeping are encountered in some patients, making it difficult to discern the amount of meaningful rest incurred.

The best indicator of adequate patient rest is patient behavior during the waking hours. A patient who is excessively irritable or agitated, for example, may be sleep deprived. A patient with altered spontaneity or flattened affect may, too, be fatigued. Caregiver understanding of patient rest parameters plays a vital role in managing sleep pattern disturbances. For example, the use of hypnotics or sedatives for quiet nocturnal wakefulness is contraindicated. Mild, transient nocturnal agitation, be it a latency difficulty or a problem with early morning awakening, however, can be initially treated symptomatically by minimizing stimulation during the night (e.g., noise, light) or by attempting to soothe the patient by touch, massage, or a warm drink. If these efforts are unsuccessful, pharmacologic agents may be indicated to promote rest, relaxation, and emotional comfort.

Managing Elimination Needs

Maintaining patterns of regular urinary and bowel elimination in the patient with little awareness of excretion needs are also vital components of the overall treatment plan. Although, owing to the absence of cortical control, incontinence is inevitable in advanced Alzheimer dementia, at its onset, evaluation of potentially reversible causes of incontinence is warranted.

With urinary incontinence, a thorough assessment of the patient's pharmacotherapeutic regimen is in order to ensure that medications used to manage behavioral or medical symptomatology are not interfering with urinary elimination. Anticholinergic agents, for instance, predispose the patient to urinary retention; some neuroleptic agents may alter mental alertness enough to impede normal micturition. Male patients are at risk for obstructive uropathy if benign prostatic hypertrophy is present. Frequency and urgency associated with urinary tract infection can result in incontinence. Once all correctable causes of incontinence have been excluded, techniques to effectively manage the incontinence can be devised on an individualized basis.

Incontinence is not an aesthetically pleasing phenomenon. Nevertheless, it is important for caregivers, both family and professional, to recognize and accept the fact that the issue is no longer one of the person forgetting how to locate the bathroom or being unable to communicate his or her need to void. Attempting to toilet the advanced Alzheimer dementia patient is unduly frustrating for both the patient and the caregiver. In addition, toileting or nagging the patient to go to the bathroom exacerbates the potential for catastrophic behavioral reactions and often results in the need to increase psychotropic medication. In the long run, denying the existence of incontinence and failing to acknowledge its presence and accept it as a permanent component of patient care is self-defeating and creates more physical work, emotional turmoil, and discomfort than it eliminates.

Options for the management of urinary incontinence include the use of disposable, adult-sized diapers designed to contain excretions while eliminating their contact with the patient's skin. They are advantageous in that they can be worn discreetly beneath clothing or bedding and are snug-fitting enough so that most patients are oblivious to their use. Currently, they are available in many commercial brands and are suitable for use in both male and female patients. Since urinary incontinence and diapering predisposes the patient to impairment of skin integrity and diaper rash, diapers must be checked at frequent, regular intervals for soiling and changed expeditiously.

Another option for urinary incontinence management in the male patient is the use of an external condom catheter that can be applied to the penis to contain urine as the patient voids. One disadvantage is that use of the catheter may predispose the patient to urethral stricture if it is applied too tightly and may place the incontinent patient at risk for penile skin breakdown. In some instances, the anatomy of the patient will preclude its use. However, the condom catheter will prevent contact of urine with the skin and in patients with sensitivity to contact with plastics such as polyvinyl chloride (found in many brands of adult diapers) will provide a satisfactory alternative for management of incontinence. Condom catheters are contraindicated in patients who are sensitive to their application and subsequently pull them off. A patient should never be mechanically or chemically restrained to prevent discontinuance of a condom catheter.

Indwelling Foley catheters provide another option, although their use is controversial. Generally, they are not tolerated well by patients with advanced Alzheimer dementia who tend to want to pull or tug at any foreign body within grasp. Thus, they predispose the patient to urinary tract trauma (urethral fracture) and to infection, which is potentially life threatening if urosepsis ensues. Most clinicians agree that because of the inherent risks involved, Foley catheters should not be employed for the sole purpose of managing urinary incontinence; rather, instrumentation of the bladder should be reserved for patients with physical or structural genitourinary abnormalities that prohibit normal bladder emptying. The use of a Foley catheter will also likely necessitate the use of patient hand restraints, which are not desirable in terms of promoting patient comfort and dignity.

A final alternative in the patient with obstructive uropathy is the suprapubic cystotomy catheter. This, however, presents an additional alteration in patient body image that many caregivers are reluctant to accept (unless it is absolutely necessary) and, in addition, subjects the patient to the trauma of an invasive surgical procedure, which the patient with advanced Alzheimer dementia, even under the most ideal of circumstances, may be unable to tolerate.

Effective monitoring of urinary elimination patterns includes evaluating and documenting clinical parameters such as variations in the intake and output of the patient, deviations in the color and concentration of the urine (observing for pyuria, hematuria or crystals), and unusual odor or excessive sediment. Providing meticulous peri-anal hygiene to ensure that the incontinence is not creating additional patient concerns, such as skin excoriations or patient restlessness and agitation secondary to the discomfort of being wet, is equally important. Sensitivity to the possible emergence of an actual or impending urinary tract infection, as evidenced by abdominal distention, suprapubic tenderness, or facial grimacing with the initiation of urination is vital to the implementation of prompt medical treatment.

With bowel elimination, efforts are directed at establishing some semblance of regular bowel evacuation. In advanced Alzheimer dementia the patient is prone to constipation because of physical immobility, impaired cortical control, variations in food and fluid intake, and the use of pharmacologic agents that contribute to constipation. Preventative measures include ensuring adequate oral fluid intake (a minimum of 1500 to 2000 ml/day unless contraindicated due to a co-existing cardiac condition), providing sufficient ingestion of dietary fiber, and administering small amounts of prune juice daily. Adding extra fiber in the form of unprocessed bran (usually 2 to 4 tablespoonfuls per day), which may be blended into cereal or juice in the morning, contributes to successful bowel elimination. The use of stool softeners is controversial yet is clearly beneficial in some patients. Cathartics should be avoided, if possible, because tolerance may develop. If absolutely necessary, 1 to 2 tablespoonfuls of a gentle laxative such as milk of magnesia provided every other evening may promote morning bowel movement. A glycerin or bisacodyl suppository administered every 3 days on an as-needed basis is also effective in stimulating bowel evacuation. If these interventions are not successful, a comprehensive assessment of the overall management of the patient must take place to determine the cause of abnormal bowel elimination. Enemas or harsher chemical cathartics are contraindicated except in the most extreme of cases since these serve only to further increase patient discomfort and cannot be administered safely in noncommunicative patients.

Meeting Comfort Needs

Of paramount importance in promoting quality of life is documentation of any physical discomforts the patient may be experiencing. For example, facial grimacing with joint motion during passive range of motion, which occurs during bathing and dressing activities, may not only signify a possible unwitnessed accident or injury to the patient but may also represent an impending flexion contracture, an arthritic event such as synovitis, effusion, or uric acid deposits, or a tactile agnosia that results in a hypersensitivity to touch. All of these discomforts are potentially amenable to symptomatic therapy.

Performing passive and, if possible, active range of motion of all joints during bathing, dressing, or grooming of the patient preserves mobility and delays the development of flexion contractures. The application of pillow splints to the upper and lower extremities is another intervention that may delay the development of contractures and promote patient comfort. Similar to pillow splinting is air-

Table 7-2 Comfort Checklist

Name: _____

S.S.#: _____

Date: _____

	None	Moderate	Severe
1. Vocalizations			
Verbalizes complaint	( )	( )	( )
Wailing	( )	( )	( )
Crying	( )	( )	( )
Moaning	( )	( )	( )
2. Motor Signs			
Restlessness	( )	( )	( )
Agitation	( )	( )	( )
Pacing	( )	( )	( )
Fidgeting	( )	( )	( )
Posture/Gait change	( )	( )	( )
Muscular rigidity	( )	( )	( )
Tense fingers	( )	( )	( )
Guarding	( )	( )	( )
3. Behaviors			
Anxiety	( )	( )	( )
Resistiveness	( )	( )	( )
Hypersensitivity to touch	( )	( )	( )
Signs of depressed mood	( )	( )	( )
Abnormal sleep pattern	( )	( )	( )
Poor Appetite	( )	( )	( )
Lacks animation/spontaneity	( )	( )	( )
Lethargy	( )	( )	( )
4. Facial			
Facial grimacing	( )	( )	( )
Wincing	( )	( )	( )
Wrinkled brow	( )	( )	( )
Frightened appearing	( )	( )	( )
Looks sad/worried	( )	( )	( )
5. Micellaneous			
Cautious breathing	( )	( )	( )
Shallow or rapid breathing	( )	( )	( )
Family/staff reports discomfort	( )	( )	( )

splinting, a treatment modality that emerged from an occupational therapy program originally designed for stroke patients.[20,21] Air splinting involves the application of inflatable plastic tubes to the patient's elbows, wrists, hands, and, occasionally, knees for brief, monitored periods of time on a daily basis. This intervention will decrease contractures already present or possibly eliminate or minimize the development of additional contractures, thereby making the patient more comfortable and facilitating provision of personal care by the nursing staff.

Although it is difficult to evaluate objectively the comfort level of a noncommunicative patient, observing for changes in patterns of nonverbal communication can lend the caregiver insight into the comfort status of the patient. For this reason, a comfort checklist (Table 7-2) was developed to facilitate systematic assessment of comfort parameters, including vocalizations, motor signs, behaviors possibly indicative of discomfort, and facial expressions. Treatment of discomfort is, in essence, always symptomatic; that is, attempts are made to identify its underlying cause and efforts are directed at alleviating its source.

Intercurrent illness should always be ruled out as an initial source of potential patient discomfort. Subtle behavioral changes such as lethargy, anxiety, or restlessness or more obvious physical signs such as pyrexia, tachypnea, or tachycardia may be the only indications of actual or impending episodic illness. Possible illnesses that must be empirically ruled out include gingivitis, dental abscesses, pharyngitis, otitis, bronchitis, pneumonitis, and cystitis. In addition, gastroenteritis (nausea, abdominal pain), constipation (fecal impaction, bowel cramps from cathartic administration, hemorrhoids), and dehydration (parched mucous membranes, thirst) may be the source of discomfort and place the already compromised patient at risk for further health status deterioration. The medical management of intercurrent illness is described in Chapter 9.

Assessing the patient's comfort level and evaluating for possible intercurrent illness is performed by obtaining vital signs and completing a physical assessment of the patient, if necessary, supplemented by laboratory testing. If physical examination and laboratory testing yield no source of illness, the caregiver proceeds further in attempting to identify the source of discomfort. For instance, if a patient exhibits wailing behavior, caregivers might attempt a position change in bed, provide some soft, soothing music, or simply offer some oral fluid or stay with the patient and hold his or her hand. The dichotomy of the use of touch is that while it sometimes calms the patient it also has the potential to excite.[22] Thus, patient response to touch must be carefully monitored to ensure therapeutic and not detrimental impact. If a patient exhibits facial grimacing or any deviance in baseline behavior that represents a change of concern to the caregiver, one might evaluate the patient by the same types of "process of elimination criteria." Although it is not the purpose of this text to imply that the care of the patient with advanced Alzheimer dementia is analogous to that of an infant, it is sometimes helpful to approach comfort assessment and management tactics in much the same way one would approach, for example, an infant who is crying. In rare instances, in which no obvious source of discomfort is identifiable and the patient remains considerably distressed, initiation of analgesics may be indicated on an empiric basis. If this treatment option is exercised, parameters by which the efficacy of such an intervention will be measured must be in place.

In many instances, lowering the demands or perceived demands placed on the patient will be conducive to promoting patient comfort. Although maintaining autonomy in any remaining function is a high priority, it may decrease the patient's anxiety or stress level to have things done for him or her at a certain point along the continuum of the illness. In addition, being sensitive to the pronounced startle reflex of the patient, potential hypersensitivity to touch, and some of the primitive, pathologic reflexes that emerge in advanced Alzheimer dementia will assist caregivers in symptomatically managing patient stress. Again, approaching the patient in a calm, confident, unhurried manner, maintaining a calm, quiet yet pleasant environment, avoiding unnecessary chatter around the patient and lowering vocal tone and rate when addressing the person, maintaining eye contact, and using touch judiciously will likely promote a sense of security conducive to patient relaxation and comfort.

In the interest of maintaining some semblance of self-identity of the patient with advanced Alzheimer dementia, it appears to be beneficial, whenever possible, to dress the patient in his or her own clothing, regardless of a bedfast or chair-bound state. Families appreciate seeing personalized efforts made to maintain the humanness of their loved ones. In dressing a patient, however, the emphasis must always be on patient comfort; so, if, for example, a patient with flexion contractures of the upper extremities would be subjected to undue suffering by having his or her deformed limbs manipulated into his or her own clothing, more comfortable hospital clothing or pajamas should be worn, or, in some cases absorbent, stretchy, cotton jerseys can be substituted.

Maintaining Safety in the Patient with Neurologic Manifestations

Approximately 10% of patients with advanced Alzheimer dementia will develop generalized seizures (clonic type with loss of consciousness).[6] Seldom are these seizures directly life threatening, although they do place the compromised patient at risk for airway obstruction and traumatic injury. Therefore, during a seizure episode, maintaining an airway free of obstruction from the tongue, secretions, or foreign body and protecting the patient from physical harm resulting from a fall or as a result of restrictive safety restraints that may be in place is paramount. Padding the side rails of bedbound Alzheimer dementia patients serves as a precautionary measure. Oral airways should be immediately accessible at the bedside with suctioning apparatus within reach. After the seizure the neurologic status of the patient warrants cautious monitoring for possible recurrent seizure activity or for evidence of increasing neurologic deficit. If no correctable metabolic abnormality is identified, conventional anticonvulsants are initiated and their serum levels monitored periodically. Medical management of seizure disorders is discussed in Chapter 9.

Myoclonus or myoclonic jerking (sudden, repeated retractions of the same muscle) is another common, clinically observable neurologic feature of advanced Alzheimer dementia. Myoclonus is neither life threatening to the patient nor indicative of impending generalized seizure. Treatment efforts focus on protecting the patient from physical injury that may result from myoclonus. If patterns of myoclonic activity are monitored, direct care provision can be provided when the frequency of myoclonic jerking is minimal. There is no known effective pharmacotherapeutic treatment of this phenomenon.

Primitive or pathologic reflexes that emerge in some advanced Alzheimer dementia patients may either impede or facilitate certain aspects of direct nursing care. For example, an exaggerated grasp response, in which the patient will firmly grasp onto any object within reach (including the caregiver), may make it difficult to bathe the patient, trim or clean his or her fingernails, or dress the patient. Sometimes, however, the grasp response is strong enough to raise the victim comfortably from the lying position with a gentle pulling motion. On the other hand, it may be dangerous if the patient grasps onto caregiver fingers, wrists, or hair and is unable to let go. A patient may also "grasp" another patient, provoking a catastrophic behavioral reaction.

Although the snout reflex may prohibit patients from opening their mouths to accept oral nourishment, a vigorous sucking response may promote acceptance and consumption of oral hydration and nutrition in the form of high-protein, calorie-packed eggnogs and milkshakes. There are no "norms" by which to evaluate the predominance of pathologic reflexes and how they will, if at all, impact on patient care.

Promoting Quality of Life

Quality of life is an ethical consideration for all people and poses a particular challenge to caregivers of institutionalized Alzheimer patients. Having a purpose for living and deriving enjoyment from life are both components of quality of life. Therapeutic recreation is one modality for enhancing the quality of life of the institutionalized Alzheimer patient.

The therapeutic recreation profession is concerned with individuals and how they cope with, adjust to, or compensate for illness or injury. Facilitating the expression of an appropriate leisure life-style as the goal of therapy goes beyond the disabling condition and seeks to assist the patient in establishing a meaningful and satisfying existence within the constraints of the illness. As a treatment modality, therapeutic recreation treats the functional deficiency or limitation imposed by the pathologic process, rather than the condition itself, in most cases.[23] It seeks to lessen the barriers imposed on the patient by both the disease and the institutional environment by using a variety of leisure modalities. The primary purpose of treatment is to maximize functional abilities and, in turn, to enhance the quality of life.

Because some of the functional losses of patients with Alzheimer dementia are possibly due to neglect and depression rather than to cognitive loss,[24] a structured, normalized environment is believed to be conducive to maximizing quality of life. The application of this, and other therapeutic recreation principles, to the care of the institutionalized patient with Alzheimer's disease has been described in the literature.[25] These principles include maintaining a daily exercise regimen, providing cognitive stimulation, providing regular social interaction, maintaining a structured milieu, and paying particular attention to the use of verbal and nonverbal communication techniques. Program implications for therapeutic recreation in the care of the Alzheimer dementia patient are described in Chapter 12.

The occupational therapy professional is also concerned with maximizing the functional ability of the advanced Alzheimer dementia patient. The main focus of intervention is to keep the body functioning at an optimal level physically (i.e., coordination, dexterity, and physical fitness) while monitoring for perceptual, environmental, and adaptive equipment needs. A secondary focus is to facilitate and support socialization. Specific occupational therapy interventions that contribute to the quality of life are discussed in Chapter 12.

Promoting quality of life in the person with advanced Alzheimer's disease requires special insight and unique human needs sensitivity on the part of the caregiver. Efforts must be continually directed at providing for physical comfort and emotional security. Each person with Alzheimer's disease, despite intellectual, behavioral, and functional deficits, which may in some respects "dehumanize" the person, must be recognized as an individual with intensive physical and emotional needs. Consequently, maintaining the dignity of the patient requires centering care around the unique and often fluctuating needs of each patient. Internalizing the philosophy that care is neither custodial nor performed in assembly-line fashion assists caregivers in identifying and meeting the emotional needs of the patient. Facilitating nonverbal communication during care, focusing on appropriate patient behaviors, reducing provocative stimuli, and exhibiting sensitivity to individuality are examples of interventions that promote inherent emotional security of the Alzheimer patient.

Interdisciplinary Management of Challenging Behaviors

Since the emotional responses of the patient with advanced Alzheimer dementia are unpredictable, at best, efforts must be directed at preventing overreaction to minor stressors or to stimulation that is not appealing to the patient, including occurrences such as physical aggression, verbal aggression, combativeness, or assaultiveness. The following interventions serve as guidelines inherent to minimizing the emergence of undesirable behaviors:

1. Simplify the environment.
2. Attempt to identify a pattern to the reactions (e.g., when and where they tend to occur).
3. Decrease the number of items placed in front of a patient during an activity such as at meal time.
4. Inform family of what to expect.
5. Avoid undue stress or confusion.
6. Search for underlying medical problems that may be precipitating abnormal behavior in the patient.
7. Ensure patient safety and feelings of security.
8. Avoid sensory deprivation or social isolation.
9. Avoid overstimulation.
10. Avoid clutter in the environment.
11. Promote patient comfort through personal elaboration (i.e., scrapbooks, photographs, personal items)
12. Avoid constant reality orientation questions since patients tend to get irritated when asked the same question over and over again.

Facilitating Communication

Because patients with advanced Alzheimer dementia are often verbally noncommunicative, it is unfair to assume that they are unable to nonverbally communicate or interact with their environment at all. Promoting sensory stimulation will, in some circumstances, improve patient quality of life and overall demeanor. The patient, when addressed, should be spoken to in vocal tones that are neither infantilizing nor condescending. If possible, eye contact should be made to engage the patient in the interaction at hand.

Issues of Institutional Care

In much the same way that family members of Alzheimer dementia patients require ongoing support, education, and ventilation of feelings, professional and nonprofessional health care providers have similar requirements. The direct care staff on an Alzheimer dementia specialty unit, for example, are affected in much the same way that the family has been. It is not uncommon for staff members to be plagued by feelings of helplessness over not being able to halt the disease process, guilt over whether they are doing everything possible to promote patient comfort and quality of life, and grief over the loss of the person's personhood.

Caring for advanced Alzheimer dementia patients who are unable to demonstrate or express their gratitude for the labor-intense efforts of the staff members requires a unique skill for caring. Staff members need a great deal of positive feedback, reinforcement, and support in terms of knowing that what they are doing for these patients is actually making life, as it is, as comfortable as possible for the patient and as tolerable as possible for the family.

The physical and emotional strain felt by caregivers justifies provision of adequate staffing patterns to assist in meeting the intensive needs of these patients. Part of the solution to preventing staff burnout includes having adequate personnel to care for these patients holistically and effectively.

A source of staff conflict involves the feelings that health care professionals have with respect to their own ambiguity and uncertainty about being in the health care profession and the recognition and acknowledgment of their own feelings about aging and dying. Support groups for staff members to afford the opportunity to ventilate feelings and verbalize concerns about the issues of aging and dying are therapeutic in alleviating this conflict.

Conclusions

Caring for the patient with advanced Alzheimer dementia is an intricate challenge for health care professionals. Requirements for effective, comprehensive caring include an interdisciplinary team, coordination of teamwork and service care delivery, an inherent philosophy of care, and continuous collaboration based on ongoing assessment, planning, intervention, and evaluation. Because of the intensive and complex needs of the patient, this care translates into considerable time, energy, perseverance, patience, and health care dollars. Minimizing the inevitable human suffering and loss associated with this tragic illness is the overall goal of treatment, keeping in mind that the illness, itself, is not treatable, but the patient is. Health care professionals, regardless of their area of specialization, may be confronted with caring for a patient with advanced Alzheimer dementia at any time. Thus, a greater understanding of the intricacies of the care required for this patient is imperative.

REFERENCES

1. McHugh PR: Alzheimer's disease, in Wyngaarden JB, Smith LH (eds): *Cecil's Textbook of Medicine*, ed 16. Philadelphia, WB Saunders, 1982.

2. Office of Technology Assessment: *Losing A Million Minds: Confronting the Tragedy of Alzheimer's Disease and Other Dementias*, OTA-BA-323. Washington, D.C., U.S. Government Printing Office, 1987.

3. Kelly CH: Anniversaries and Alzheimers, editorial. *Geriatr Nur* 1985;10:135.

4. Volicer L, Rheaume Y, Brown J, et al: Hospice approach to the treatment of patients with advanced dementia of the Alzheimer type. *JAMA* 1986; 256:2210-2213.

5. Liston EH: The clinical phenomenology of presenile dementia: A critical review of the literature. *J Nerv Ment Dis* 1979;167:329-336.

6. Seltzer B, Sherwin I: A comparison of clinical features in early and late-onset primary degenerative dementia—one entity or two. *Arch Neurol* 1983;40:143-146.

7. Mayeux R, Stern Y, Spanton S: Heterogeneity in dementia of the Alzheimer type: Evidence of subgroups. *Neurology* 1985;35:453-461.

8. Whitney FW: Alzheimer's disease: Toward understanding and management. *Nurse Practitioner* 1985;10:25-36.

9. Williams L: Alzheimer's: The need for caring. *J Gerontol Nurs* 1986;12:21-28.

10. Hayter J: Patients who have Alzheimer's disease. *Am J Nurs* 1984;74:1460-1463.

11. Pluckman ML: Alzheimer's disease—helping the patient's family. *Nurs '86* 1986;16:62-64.

12. Charles R, Truesdell ML, Wood E: Alzheimer's disease: Pathology, progression and nursing process. *J Gerontol Nurs* 1982;8:69-72.

13. Fabiszewski KJ: Caring for the patient with Alzheimer's disease. *Gerontology* 1987 (in press).

14. Phipps M: Staging care for pressure sores. *Am J Nurs* 1984;74:999-1003.

15. Volicer L, Seltzer B, Rheaume Y, et al: Progression of Alzheimer-type dementia in institutionalized patients: A cross-sectional study. *J Applied Gerontol* 1987;6:125-128.

16. Volicer L, Seltzer B, Karner J, et al: Feeding difficulties in patients with dementia of the Alzheimer type. (in preparation)

17. Norberg A, Norberg B, Gippert H: Ethical conflicts in long-term care of the aged: Nutritional problems and the patient-care worker relationship. *Br Med J* 1980;280:377.

18. Warden V: The special adult pureed diet: Addressing feeding problems in advanced Alzheimer's disease. (in preparation)

19. *Cincinnati Diet Manual*, ed 3. Greater Cincinnati Dietetics Association, 1983.

20. Johnstone M: *The Stroke Patient—Principles of Rehabilitation*, ed 2. New York, Churchill Livingston, 1982.

21. Johnstone M: Restoration of Motor Function in the Stroke Patient. New York, Churchill Livingston, 1978.

22. Dietsche LM, Pollman JN: Alzheimer's disease: Advances in Clinical Nursing. *J Gerontol Nurs* 1984;8:97-100.

23. Peterson C, Gunn S: *Therapeutic Recreation Program Design*. Englewood Cliffs, N.J., Prentice-Hall, 1984.

24. Fisk A: Management of Alzheimer's disease. *Postgrad Med* 1983:237-241.

25. Burnside I: Alzheimer's disease: An overview. *J Gerontol Nurs* 1979;5:14-20.

CHAPTER 8

Oral Health Care for Patients with Alzheimer's Disease

Judith A. Jones, Linda C. Niessen, Melody J. Hobbins, and Mario C. Zocchi

Good oral health is achievable and contributes significantly to optimum health, comfort, and sociability of demented patients. When a person is diagnosed as having Alzheimer's disease, he or she should be referred to a dentist for evaluation, a long-term oral health care plan developed, and dental treatment initiated as soon as possible. Oral health goals include freedom from pain and infection, prevention of new disease, appropriate treatment of existing disease, improvement and maintenance of facial aesthetics, and restoration or maintenance of function for as long as possible.

The purpose of this chapter is to assist health professionals (and family caregivers) in meeting the oral health needs of patients with Alzheimer's disease. In the first section, oral health problems and their risk factors are discussed. In the second section, details are provided regarding ways in which personal preventive care can be integrated into the long-term care for these patients. Oral care of Alzheimer patients from the point of view of the dental professionals is also addressed.

Oral Problems and Their Risk Factors

National epidemiologic data on the incidence and prevalence of oral diseases in demented patients are not available. Nevertheless, several studies indicate trends in disease patterns in patients who are institutionalized compared with those living in the community. Coupled with what is known about the etiology of oral diseases, five oral health problems and their risk factors in demented patients will be presented: (1) oral cancer, (2) xerostomia and salivary gland dysfunction, (3) dental caries, (4) periodontal disease, and (5) tooth loss.

Note: The authors wish to thank Jonathan Director and Marge Grant for their editorial assistance.

Oral Cancer

Nearly 75% of all oral cancer occurs in people over age 60.[1] The American Cancer Society estimated that in 1987 there were 30,000 new cases of buccal cavity and pharyngeal cancers (3% of all cancers).[2] Deaths due to oral cancer involved 9,400 persons (2% of all cancer deaths in the United States).[2] The average annual crude age-specific incidence rates of oral cancers increase dramatically with advancing age (Figure 8-1).[3] In women, they increase linearly from age 40 to 60, then plateau until age 80. In men, the increase continues from age 40 to 80, after which it appears to decline. Thus, oral cancer is most likely to occur in the same age groups in which there is increased frequency of dementia.

Significant reductions in mortality and morbidity are linked to early detection of oral cancers. Five-year survival rates are four times better in patients with local rather than metastatic disease (Figure 8-2).[4] These data support the need for health care providers to perform regular oral cancer screening in these patients.

Heavy tobacco and alcohol use have been shown to be risk factors for oral cancer.[5] Chewing tobacco and snuff habits are likewise associated with an increase in risk.[5] A health care professional should be especially thorough when examining the mouth and throat of a demented person who has used smokeless or regular tobacco and/or been a heavy alcohol user.

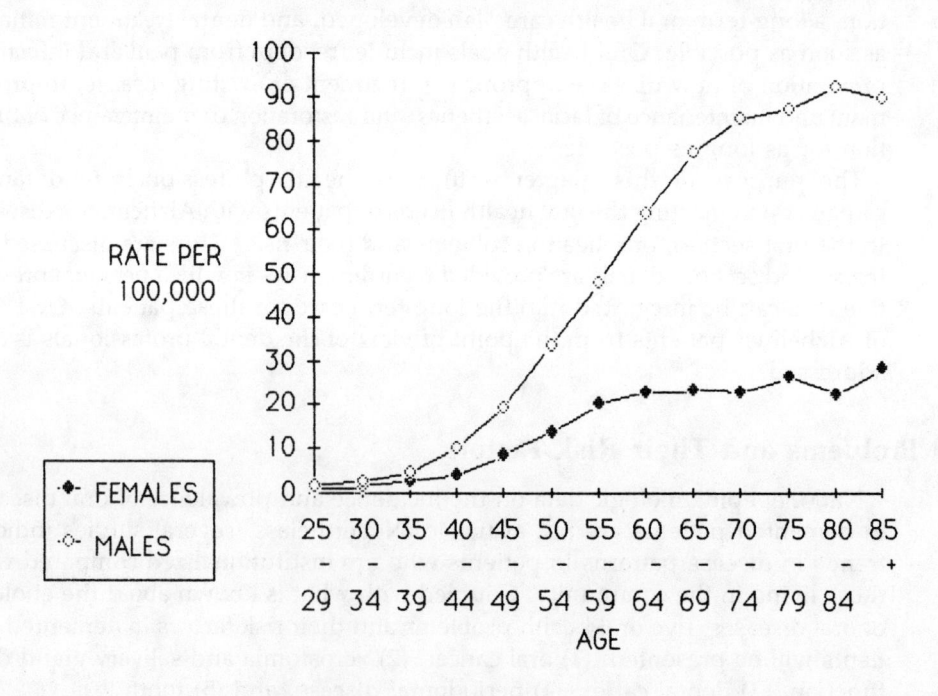

Figure 8-1 Average annual crude age-specific incidence rates per 100,000 U.S. population for cancers of the buccal cavity and pharynx, 1973-1977. *Source:* National Cancer Institute Monograph No 57 (pp 74-76), Public Health Service, No 81-2330, 1981.

Oral Health Care 113

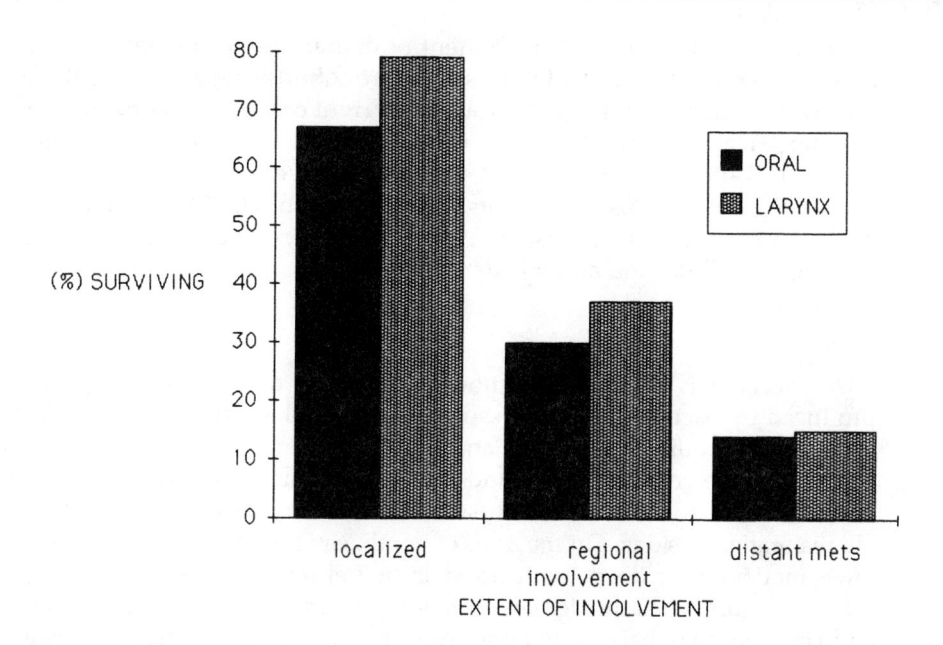

Figure 8-2 Five-year oral and laryngeal cancer survival rates, United States, 1973-1977. *Source: Cancer Facts and Figures: 1981* (p 7) by National Cancer Institute, Biometry Branch, American Cancer Society, © 1980.

Xerostomia and Salivary Gland Dysfunction

Saliva helps to maintain oral health by lubricating the oral mucosa, buffering acids produced by oral bacteria, mediating taste acuity, remineralizing teeth, and by its mechanical cleansing and antibacterial activities.[6] Salivary flow is clinically considered normal if the mouth is moist and the parotid and submandibular glands can be milked by digital pressure. Subjective complaints of mouth dryness are termed *xerostomia*, while an objective determination of this condition is referred to as salivary gland dysfunction.[7] As the dementia progresses, a patient's ability to discern and report dryness will diminish, making the clinical evaluation of salivary gland function by a caregiver more important.

Medications are the most common cause of salivary gland dysfunction in patients with dementia. Over 250 pharmacologic agents, particularly sympathetic and parasympathetic agonists and antagonists, may be associated with glandular hyposecretion.[8-11] Dehydration, diabetes mellitus, adrenal insufficiencies, hypothyroid states, and radiation therapy may also adversely affect salivary flow.[6] In patients with severe dryness, particularly mouth breathers, heavy deposits of mucus accumulate on the palate, tongue, and alveolar ridges, decreasing patient comfort and increasing the risk of aspirating dried mucus. This dryness should be alleviated if possible. Care of patients with diminished salivary flow will be discussed in the section on preventive care.

Tooth Loss

Because of the general improvement of dental care in the entire population, and the decreasing rate of edentulism, future cohorts of Alzheimer's disease victims will likely have more teeth than the current cohorts. National data indicate that the percentage of 65- to 74-year-old people who are edentulous declined from 55% in 1957-1958 to 45% in 1971-1974.[12] State surveys suggest that this trend is continuing in the 1980s. In patients missing some or all of their teeth, their ability to care for their prostheses, report mucosal irritations, and adapt to new prostheses will decline as their dementia progresses.

Dental Caries

Dental caries is a chronic infectious process that occurs when the acid wastes produced by bacterial plaque dissolve the mineral substance of the tooth. It is classified depending on location and severity. By location, caries is divided into coronal (on the crown portion) and root. Caries can be subdivided into primary (on an unaffected or sound tooth surface) and secondary (adjacent to/under an old restoration) lesions. On the basis of depth, caries is classified as incipient (shallow), moderate, or deep (with possible pulpal involvement).

Caries occurs when the demineralization process exceeds remineralization (similar in concept to imbalance of bone resorption and bone formation in osteoporosis). Incipient lesions may remineralize if saliva contains sufficient minerals, a process aided by the presence or application of topical fluorides.

The risk of caries apparently increases with the deterioration of functional capacity. Small studies have been conducted on institutionalized patients (medical diagnoses unreported) in Sweden, Canada, and Finland.[13-15] The trends reported in institutionalized patients suggest that dentate patients with dementia have significant caries experience. Diminished capacity for maintaining personal oral hygiene combined with decreased salivary flow and diminished cleansing capacity of the tongue are thought to contribute to this increase in caries.

Periodontal Disease

Periodontal disease (pyorrhea) is a chronic infection of the structures that support the teeth—the gums, periodontal ligament, and bone. National and state data indicate that although the proportion of adults with periodontal pockets increases with advancing age,[16,17] tooth loss due to periodontal disease in old age is not inevitable.[18] Oral hygiene is considered to be the key to tooth retention. Across all age groups, people with the greatest number of natural teeth consistently had the cleanest teeth.[18] Maintaining oral hygiene is most difficult in demented patients. The review of the Swedish literature reported that over two thirds of the institutionalized patients examined had unsatisfactory oral hygiene.[13]

Predicting periodontal disease in patients with Alzheimer's disease and other dementias would be difficult. These patients present with a complex of factors that affect present periodontal status, including socioeconomic status, past and present oral hygiene levels, and use of dental services. Once a person becomes demented, he or she is at increased risk for periodontal disease by virtue of his or her inability to maintain oral hygiene. Thus, personal preventive care is the key to good oral health during the inevitable cognitive and functional decline that accompanies the dementia.

Oral Health Care

Preventive Care

Grooming, such as shaving or hair combing, may more overtly enhance the patient's appearance, but care of the mouth is essential for good health. All people require oral hygiene care, even if there are no teeth present. Good oral hygiene enhances sociability by promoting attractive smiles and prevention of bad breath

Table 8-1 Caregiver–Patient Interchange

Caregiver:	"R, it is time to brush your teeth. Come with me to the bathroom."	Use of short words Use of simple sentences
R:	Nodded.	Nonverbal acceptance
Caregiver:	I put my arm around him. (He went to the bathroom with me.)	Nonverbal close contact
Caregiver:	I took out his toothbrush, put toothpaste on it and handed it to him. "R, brush your teeth now."	Use of objects to identify activity Use of simple sentences
R:	Looked at the toothbrush as if he had never seen it before.	Perception and analysis difficulty
Caregiver:	"R, brush your teeth now." I pointed to the toothbrush and his mouth.	Use of verbal repetition Use of supplemental gestures
R:	Looked at me quizzically, "You mean me?"	Partial analysis and synthesis
Caregiver:	"Yes," nodding.	
R:	Nodded his head, raised the toothbrush to the top of his head and began to very methodically brush his bald head.	
Caregiver:	"R," (pause) touched his hand, and maintained direct eye contact. "Brush your teeth." I pointed to my mouth and demonstrated with a toothbrush.	Moved slowly; use touch to gain attention and direct eye contact Verbal repetition, exact Use of demonstration and gesture
R:	"Oh, yeah." R raised the toothbrush to his closed lips and began to brush back and forth.	Association and synthesis Continuing not complete
Caregiver:	I nodded, "almost, R." I put my hand on his, pointed to my open mouth. "Open your mouth."	Positively reinforce partially correct response Touch to gain attention, coupled with gesture Breaking the task down to even simpler steps
R:	Looked at me blankly, raised the toothbrush to his mouth, slowly opened his mouth, and put the toothbrush in. Eyes directed toward the nurse.	Memory of familiar act stimulated
Caregiver:	I nodded vigorously, "Yes."	Positive reinforcement and nonverbal affirmation of correct response
R:	Began to brush slowly. Brushing became more vigorous.	Memory, analysis, synthesis completed Response activated

Source: Adapted with permission from *Journal of Gerontological Nursing* (1979;5:21-31), Copyright © 1979, Charles B Slack Inc.

(halitosis), improves comfort by reducing bad tastes and debris on teeth, and prevents oral diseases (caries and periodontal disease).

Good oral hygiene may prevent acute dental problems, such as pain and/or infection. It will also enhance taste and may improve the individual's nutrition. In addition, removal of debris and mucus on a regular basis may prevent aspiration of such debris.

As the dementia progresses, activities of daily living, including bathing and grooming, become the caregiver's responsibility. Caregiving and effective hygiene involve a delicate balance of the maintenance of patient autonomy with the objective of the emotional well-being of the caregiver. The incapacity of the impaired person to perform activities of daily living may be related both to problems of memory of what he or she is supposed to do and to apraxia,[19] the inability to perform purposeful movements.[20] During early stages of the illness, reminders may be sufficient. These reminders may need to be broken down to each step of the task,[19] while instruction and demonstration for each step may have to be repeated (Table 8-1).[21] Eventually the dementia will progress to the point that the responsibility of oral hygiene care must be totally assumed by the caregiver.

Personal Oral Hygiene

The primary objective of oral hygiene is the removal of bacterial plaque. Plaque is a densely populated mass of bacteria and debris that forms a coating on natural and artificial teeth. It is a sticky material that cannot be soaked or rinsed off; it must be mechanically removed. The bacteria present are responsible for most dental infections including decay and periodontal disease, as well as bad breath and inflammation or infection of gum tissue under dentures.

Bleeding gums often discourage people from brushing. Gum tissue that is inflamed or infected bleeds easily. Bleeding gums are a sign that an area needs a more thorough and frequent cleaning. Just as a wound needs cleansing, brushing into the gumline area removes bacteria and debris, permitting the "wounded" gums to heal. With continued brushing, bleeding should decrease soon thereafter.

The most versatile and effective tools for oral hygiene are a soft nylon toothbrush with two to four rows of bristles and any commercially available dentifrice containing fluoride. Used appropriately, this regimen will efficiently remove bacterial plaque and debris from gums, tongue, palate, dentures, partial dentures, and natural tooth surfaces. The surfaces adjacent to another tooth (proximal) are best cleaned with dental floss or a small conical brush where larger spaces are present. However, for the impaired person the use of floss to clean the bacterial plaque from the proximal surfaces, although important, may not be feasible.[22]

Fluoride

Fluoride is effective in preventing dental caries and periodontal disease. Fluoride has three mechanisms of action: (1) fluoride makes the tooth enamel more resistant to the decay process[23-25]; (2) the fluoride and stannous ions have some bactericidal properties[26]; and (3) fluoride promotes the remineralization of the tooth surfaces.[27] In addition to using a fluoride dentifrice, people at high risk of caries and/or periodontal disease should use a topical fluoride rinse or gel (Appendix 8-A). Both forms are safe and effective for use at home and in long-term care facilities.[28]

Fluoride rinses are probably the easiest product to use when a demented patient can still rinse for a specified period of time and expectorate. Two effective rinses are 0.05% NaF solutions (Fluorigard and ACT). Both are available without a prescription in supermarkets and pharmacies and should be used as directed. After use, the person should not rinse, drink, or eat for 30 minutes.

Fluoride gels, available by prescription only, should be used twice daily in patients who are unable to rinse and expectorate. Both 0.4% SnF_2 (Gel Kam) and 1.1% NaF (Prevident, Theraflur) are available for home use in either customized mouthguard trays or on a toothbrush instead of toothpaste. Like the fluoride rinses and fluoride treatments given in a dental office, when used as prescribed, one should not rinse, drink, or eat for 30 minutes after applying these fluoride preparations to the teeth.

Daily Hygiene Regimens

Although brushing teeth after meals and before bed is preferable, a thorough toothbrushing once a day may be the most a caregiver can manage. More frequent brushing is necessary if the person has a high decay rate, an oral infection, a diet high in sugars or fermentable carbohydrates (this includes many nutritional supplements), a dry mouth or is taking certain medications such as phenytoin. If the toothbrushing is to be done once a day, the most beneficial time is between the last food ingestion and bed time.

The tongue harbors numerous bacteria, which can be greatly reduced in numbers by brushing the tongue. After rinsing the brush with water, the bristles are placed on the backmost part of the tongue and the brush dragged forward. Three or four strokes should clean the tongue (Figure 8-3).

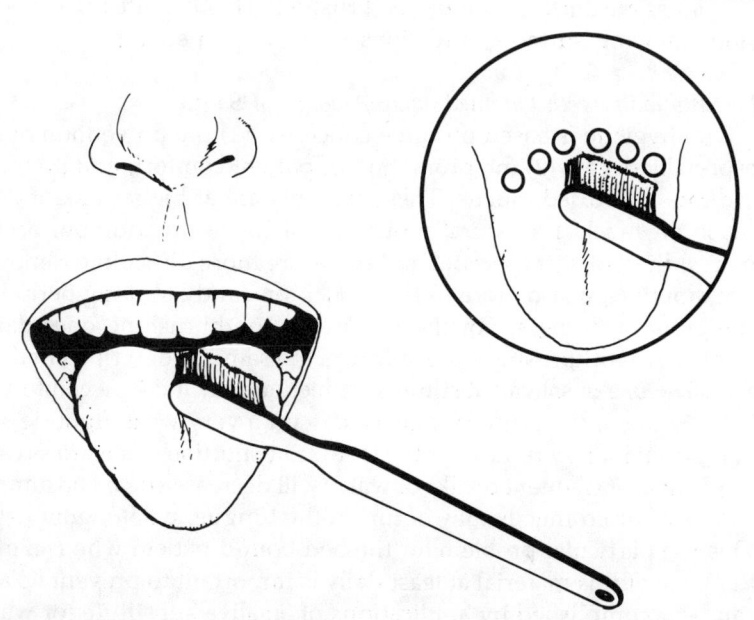

Figure 8-3 Toothbrush bristles are placed on backmost part of tongue and dragged forward. Three or four strokes should clean the tongue.

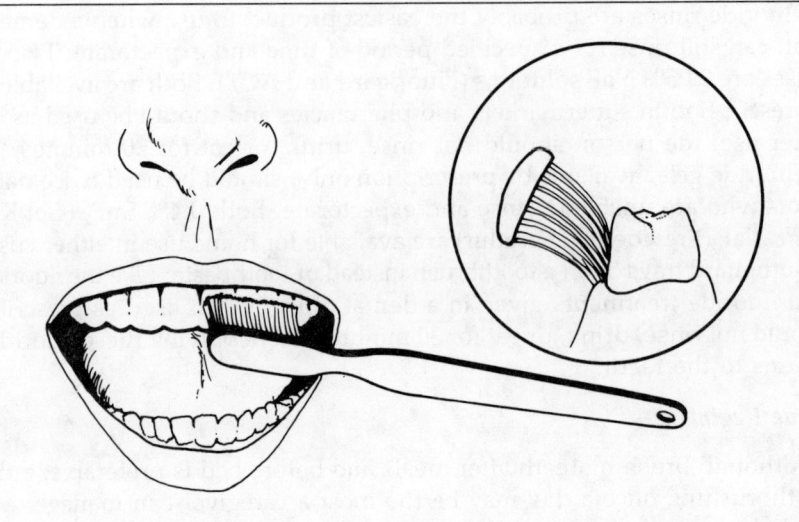

Figure 8-4 Place the toothbrush at a 45° angle with the bristles directed into the junction of the tooth and gum tissue.

Patients with Teeth and Adequate Salivary Flow

A ¾-inch of fluoride dentifrice or gel is applied onto the toothbrush. The brush is placed at approximately a 45° angle with the bristles directed into the junction of the tooth and gum tissue (Figure 8-4). Two to three teeth are brushed at a time, paying special attention to the gumline area. Either a small circular or a slight back-and-forth motion is effective and should be continued even if the gums bleed. All accessible surfaces should be brushed. This includes the cheek side, tongue side, chewing surfaces, and sides next to open spaces.

Patients with Teeth but Inadequate Amount of Saliva

Oral hygiene is based on three concerns: (1) the prevention of dental disease, especially decay; (2) the promotion of patient comfort; and (3) the prevention of aspiration of dried mucus. These patients are at higher risk of dental decay because they lack the natural protection of saliva. In addition, bacterial plaque is more adherent as it dries out and therefore more difficult to remove. People with dry mouths are also more likely to suck on candy for long periods to relieve the symptom of dryness. For these reasons, toothbrushing once daily is not sufficient. The toothbrushing procedure is the same as described in the previous section. The use of saliva substitutes as needed may increase comfort (see Appendix 8-A). Some of the artificial salivas contain a very weak fluoride solution to provide additional protection for the teeth. Substitution of sugarless candies for sugar candy and/or frequent drinks of water will decrease sugar consumption. Accumulations of dried mucus may occur on the tongue, palate, gum tissue, or cheeks. This is a particular problem for the bed-bound patient who is a mouth breather. Removal of this material at least daily is important to prevent its aspiration. This can be accomplished by applications of a saliva substitute (or water) to a toothbrush or a gauze-wrapped tongue blade and gently dislodging the hardened mucus. Moi-stir swabs are effective in prevention of mucus build-up.

Patients without Teeth but with Adequate Saliva

The goal of oral care for these patients is to keep the mouth clean and moist. Gums and the tongue are gently cleaned daily with a soft toothbrush moistened with water or mouthwash. The mouthwash will leave the mouth tasting fresh and clean. A piece of moistened gauze or disposable toothbrush may also be used to wipe the gum tissue.

Patients without Teeth and without Adequate Saliva

Very gentle cleaning is required. Dry mucous membranes are more tender and easily abraded. A soft toothbrush or piece of gauze moistened with a saliva substitute or water may be used to gently wipe the gum tissues. Dried mucus generally requires softening before it will dislodge. A toothbrush or gauze-wrapped tongue blade soaked with a saliva substitute can be used. Thorough removal of the material may take several attempts and is easier if done two to three times daily. The use of a saliva substitute to keep the mouth moist may increase the person's comfort.

Dentures and Partial Dentures

Dentures and partial dentures should be removed from the mouth and brushed thoroughly at least once per day to prevent the buildup of bacterial plaque, calculus (tartar), and debris. If teeth are present, they should be cleaned after the partial dentures are removed. Brushes designed especially for cleaning oral prostheses are available. These brushes cleanse all areas, including the gum tissue side, teeth, clasps (wires), and metal framework of dentures and partial dentures. However, thoroughly scrubbing all areas with a soft toothbrush and hand soap or liquid dish detergent is just as effective. Brush and rinse dentures over a sink partially filled with water or with a washcloth or towel in the basin to prevent breakage if the denture is dropped. Dentures should be removed for several hours during each day or night. When not in the mouth, dentures and partial dentures should be stored in cool water. Storage in liquid prevents warpage of the dentures. If denture cleaners are used, it is always necessary to thoroughly brush and rinse the dentures before placing them in the cleaning solution.

Uncooperative Patients

Three points are especially important with patients who resist the efforts of others to provide daily oral hygiene care: (1) never stick your fingers between their teeth, (2) get assistance to help hold the patient's head and hands, and (3) be persistent. The patient may be more cooperative at another time. Actively grabbing hands, a pathologic reflex rather than the patient's efforts to consciously resist care, may be temporarily occupied by the placement of a soft object, such as a rolled washcloth, into each hand. However, the personal safety of the caregiver mandates assistance in holding the hands of a combative patient.

If the patient will not open his or her mouth, an index finger can be placed in the groove between the cheeks or lips and jaw and pressure applied firmly but gently against the jaw. This may compel the patient to open his or her mouth. If the patient still will not open, the caregiver can usually wedge four or more tongue blades, fastened together, between the teeth. The blades are wrapped with adhesive tape, a 4 × 4-inch piece of gauze, or an elastic band. If the patient clamps down on the toothbrush or tongue blades, the caregiver can press an index finger between the lips or cheek and jaw and remove the object. If the patient persists in being uncooperative, accessible areas are brushed and cleaning of other areas is done at another time.

Toothbrush/Denture Identification

In the long-term care setting, keeping track of the demented patient's personal supplies and belongings is a challenge. Labeling toothbrush handles works in some environments. This can be easily done with a fine-tipped permanent marker and a coat of clear nail polish to render the marking more durable. All dentures should be labeled with the person's name. If the dentures have no name, they should be taken to a dentist for addition of an identifying label. This is particularly important if the patient requires long-term care in a nursing home where dentures are easily mixed up if the names are not on them.

Professional Dental Care

The goals of dental care for the patient with Alzheimer's disease are (1) to treat existing oral disease, (2) to maintain oral health, and (3) to prevent further oral diseases. Since Alzheimer's disease has a degenerative course, the first dental visit for a patient with this disorder may represent the patient's best cognitive functioning level. For this reason, the dental treatment plan should aim to restore oral function quickly and to institute an intensive preventive program. Complex oral restoration and rehabilitation have a better chance for success if done in the early stages of the disease. As cognitive function decreases, the patient's ability to adjust to prostheses diminishes along with his or her ability to cooperate during dental treatment.

Medical History and Dental History

The dental management of the patient with Alzheimer's disease will vary, depending on the level of the disease.[29] As usual, the dental evaluation begins with a thorough medical history. In this case, the medical history must be obtained from family members, the physician, or medical records. In addition to Alzheimer's disease, a patient may have other systemic diseases that may affect dental care. It is crucial that the dentist obtain a careful medication history. Of particular concern to the dentist are neuroleptic drugs and the tardive dyskinesias these drugs may induce, as well as phenytoin (Dilantin) and nifedipine and the gingival hyperplasia that they induce. Any question concerning the patient's medical history should be verified with the physician.

A dental history must be obtained from a caregiver or family member. What is the reason for the visit? Has the patient been experiencing dental pain? If so, how often? Does the patient demonstrate any abnormal grinding (bruxism), chewing, or swallowing habits? Are the family/caregiver's expectations of the dental care realistic? Although cosmetic interventions may help the family, they may not always be in the best interest of the patient. For example, dentures may not be indicated for an edentulous patient who has reached the point in the illness when he or she "forgets" how to chew food.

Examination

Dental visits should be scheduled with an awareness of the patient's best time of day. Does the person experience disorientation, confusion, and agitation at specific times in the day? Dental appointments should be as brief as possible, and the presence of a familiar caregiver in the operatory may allay the patient's fears.

The dental examination is the same as for all patients, but it must be done more quickly. Obtaining full-mouth radiographs may not be possible in one sitting. Instead, the dental team may need to expose a few radiographs at each visit if the dentist believes that a current full mouth series is indicated.

Treatment Planning

The goal of treatment planning should be to maintain oral health and function. Treatment planning should concentrate on preventing and controlling oral diseases. Without an aggressive approach to prevention, the dentulous patient will be susceptible to periodontal disease and dental caries.

Appropriate treatment planning for the patient with Alzheimer's disease is crucial to the success of any dental intervention. The elements of the dental treatment plan are presented in Table 8-2.[30] The dental treatment plan must first clearly delineate the role of the caregiver in the maintenance of daily oral hygiene. Second, the treatment plan must be realistic for the patient's medical and physical condition, as well as his or her oral health. Ettinger and Beck describe this as the rational treatment plan.[31,32] Third, the plan should be dynamic, including aggressive prevention to avert the decline in oral health function and should avoid the need for extensive restorative treatment at a time when the person is unable to cooperate for dental care. The fourth goal should be to minimize the stress of the dental visit. This can be accomplished by effective patient management techniques and both verbal and nonverbal communication skills.[19,21,33] Finally, both patient and caregiver will appreciate any positive reinforcement provided by the dental team. In the face of long-term deterioration, the caregiver may welcome short-term improvements in maintaining oral health.

Table 8-2 Goals of the Dental Treatment Plan

Dental Treatment Plan

1. Delineates role of caregivers/family members in maintenance and care of oral health
2. Is realistic
3. Is dynamic: it anticipates the decline in the treatment plan and requires aggressive prevention to prevent decline in oral health status
4. Minimizes stress of dental visit: keep appointments short; use good communication; use antianxiety agents
5. Emphasizes hopefulness in maintainance of oral health function

Source: Adapted with permission from *Special Care in Dentistry* (1986;6:6-12), Copyright © 1986, American Dental Association.

Many patients with Alzheimer's disease take medications with anticholinergic effects that dry the mouth. Without the protective effects of the saliva and in the absence of good oral hygiene, there is a greater risk of dental caries and periodontal disease. Fluoride in various forms, as mentioned previously, will help prevent both caries and periodontal disease.[23-25] More frequent recall visits may be necessary, at least initially, to assess the patient's and caregiver's ability to comply with the daily oral hygiene and prevention regimen. This is particularly important for patients who are taking phenytoin and nifedipine, both of which stimulate hyperplastic overgrowth of gingival tissue if oral hygiene is inadequate.

The treatment planning approach for various stages of Alzheimer's disease is outlined in Table 8-3. In the case of mild disease, the progressive nature of this dementia and dental diseases should be acknowledged and the patient should be quickly restored to good oral health. Subsequent care will concentrate on preventing dental disease as the course of the Alzheimer's disease progresses. Patients with moderate Alzheimer's disease may not be as amenable to dental treatment as patients in the early stages of the disease. For them, dental treatment consists of maintaining dental status and minimizing any deterioration. For instance, relining existing prostheses may be preferable to making new ones.

Patients with severe Alzheimer's disease often may be anxious, hostile, and uncooperative in a dental office. Dental treatment will be more difficult and the patient may require sedation to reduce his or her anxiety prior to the dental visit.

If the patient has a high caries rate or moderate periodontal disease and the caregiver is unable to perform adequate oral hygiene, more frequent professional dental prophylaxis is warranted. Traditionally, dentists recommend cleaning once

Table 8-3 Dental Treatment Considerations

Treatment Planning Approach	Mild Disease	Moderate Disease	Severe Disease
General Considerations	Minimal changes in dental practice	Sedation may be necessary; short appointments; more frequent recall visits	Sedation may be necessary; short appointments; more frequent recall visits
Specific Considerations	Aggressive prevention; use of topical fluorides; daily oral hygiene; oral health education of caregivers; design treatment plan anticipating decline	Aggressive prevention; use of topical fluorides; daily oral hygiene; oral health education of caregivers; design treatment plan with minimal changes (reline dentures rather than remake if possible)	Aggressive prevention; use of topical fluorides; daily oral hygiene; oral health education of caregivers; maintenance of dentition
	Restore to function as quickly as possible		Emergency care

Source: Adapted with permission from *Journal of American Dental Association* (1985;110:207-209), Copyright © 1985, American Dental Association.

every 6 months. However, for patients with more severe dental disease, prophylaxis every 2 to 4 months may be necessary. This decision should be made jointly by the caregiver and dentist. In long-term care institutions, an oral hygiene team can visit patients more regularly on the ward for preventive care.

As Alzheimer's disease progresses, patients are usually less able to tolerate long dental appointments. Later, as they progress beyond a hyperactive stage, the same person may again be able to tolerate longer visits. Thus, at various times in the progression of Alzheimer's disease, shorter and more frequent dental appointments may be necessary. Some patients may have difficulty tolerating even short appointments for therapeutic interventions. For these patients, sedation prior to dental treatment may be necessary even for simple procedures such as restorations, cleanings, or extractions. The choice of a sedative medication should be made in consultation with the physician. Chloral hydrate (500 mg) or oxazepam (10 mg) orally 1 to 2 hours before the appointment has been used with some success. More extensive dental treatment, such as multiple or difficult extractions, can be performed under general anesthesia if the swallowing reflex is intact. Alzheimer's disease in and of itself does not contraindicate general anesthesia; rather, coexisting systemic disease will affect the risk.

Conclusions

The goal of oral health care is to prevent loss of oral health and function as cognitive abilities decline. Patients with Alzheimer's disease are at increased risk for oral diseases because of their inability to maintain oral hygiene and the use of medications that decrease salivary flow and cause gingival overgrowth. Although dental professionals will design the prevention plan, caregivers are responsible for implementing it. The dental professional must assist and support the caregiver by identifying creative approaches for successfully conducting the daily oral hygiene regimen. Optimum oral health in a patient with Alzheimer's disease can only be accomplished by teamwork. The caregivers and dental professionals are the essential members of the team.

REFERENCES

1. Batsakis JG: *Tumors of the Head and Neck,* ed 2. Baltimore, Williams & Wilkins, 1979.

2. American Cancer Society: *Cancer Facts and Figures: 1987.* New York, American Cancer Society, 1987.

3. Young JL, Percy CL, Asire AJ, et al: *Cancer Incidence and Mortality in the United States, 1973-77.* SEER-NIH publication No. 81 (2330). National Cancer Institute Monograph No. 57. Bethesda, Md, Public Health Service, 1981.

4. National Cancer Institute, Biometry Branch: *Cancer Facts and Figures: 1981.* New York, American Cancer Society, 1980.

5. Douglass CW, Gammon MD, Horgan WJ: Epidemiology of oral cancer, in Shklar G (ed): *Oral Cancer* Philadelphia, WB Saunders Co, 1984.

6. Baum BJ: Alterations in oral function, in Andres R (ed): *Principles of Geriatric Medicine.* New York, McGraw-Hill, 1985.

7. Baum BJ: Evaluation of stimulated parotid flow rate in different age groups. *J Dent Res* 1981;60:1292-1296.

8. Baum BJ, Bodner L, Fox P, et al: Therapy induced dysfunction of salivary glands: Implications for oral health. *Spec Care Dent* 1985;5:274-277.

9. Brightman V, Felix D, Goldrich S: Drug induced xerostomia and dysguesia. *J Dent Res* 1979;58A:326 (abstract No. 936).

10. Bohen SL: Drug-related dental destruction. *Oral Surg Oral Med Oral Path* 1972;33:49-54.

11. Glass B, van Dis M, Languis R, et al: Xerostomia: Diagnosis and treatment planning consideration. *Oral Surg Oral Med Oral Path* 1984;58:248-252.

12. Weintraub J, Burt B: Tooth loss in the United States. *J Dent Educ* 1985;49:368-376.

13. Nordenram G, Böhlin E: Dental status of the elderly: A review of the Swedish literature. *Gerodontology* 1985;4:3-24.

14. Banting DW, Ellen RP, Filler ED: Prevalence of root surface caries among institutionalized older persons. *Commun Dent Oral Epidemiol* 1980;8:84-88.

15. Ekelund R: The dental treatment and oral condition and the need for treatment among residents of municipal old people's homes in Finland. *Proc Finn Dent Soc* 1984;80:43-52.

16. Douglass CW, Gillings DB, Sollecito W, et al: National trends in the prevalence and severity of periodontal disease. *J Am Dent Assoc* 1983;107:403-412.

17. Hughes JT, Rozier RG, Ramsey D: *Natural History of Dental Diseases in North Carolina*. Durham, NC, Carolina Academic Press, 1982.

18. Burt BA, Ismail AI, Eklund SA: Periodontal disease, tooth loss and oral hygiene among older Americans. *Commun Dent Oral Epidemiol* 1985;13:93-96.

19. Mace NL, Rabins PV: *The 36-Hour Day: A Family Guide to Caring for Persons with Alzheimer's Disease, Related Dementing Illnesses, and Memory Loss in Later Life*. Baltimore, MD, Johns Hopkins University Press, 1981.

20. Thomas CL (ed): *Taber's Cyclopedic Medical Dictionary*, ed 14. Philadelphia, FA Davis Co, 1981.

21. Bartol MA: Nonverbal communication in persons with Alzheimer's disease. *J Gerontol Nurs* 1979;5:21-31.

22. Mulligan R: Preventive care for the geriatric dental patient. *Calif Dent J* 1984;12:21-32.

23. Levine RS: The action of fluoride in caries prevention: A review of current concepts. *Br Dent J* 1976;140:9-14.

24. Shannon IL: Fluoride treatment programs for high-caries-risk patients. *Clin Prev Dent* 1982;4:11-20.

25. Striffler DF, Young WO, Burt BA: *Dentistry, Dental Practice, and the Community*, ed 3. Philadelphia, WB Saunders Co, 1983.

26. Tinanoff N, Weeks DB: Current status of SnF_2 as an antiplaque agent. *Pediatr Dent* 1979;1:199-204.

27. Newbrun E: *Cariology*. Baltimore, Williams & Wilkins, 1978.

28. Bayless MJ, Tinanoff N: Diagnosis and treatment of acute fluoride toxicity. *J Am Dent Assoc* 1985;110:209-211.

29. Niessen LC, Jones JA, Zocchi M, et al: Dental care for the Alzheimer's patient. *J Am Dent Assoc* 1985;110:207-209.

30. Niessen LC, Jones JA: Alzheimer's disease: A guide for dental professionals. *Spec Care Dent* 1986;6:6-12.

31. Ettinger R, Beck J: Medical and psychosocial risk factors in the dental treatment of the elderly. *Int Dent J* 1983;33:292-300.

32. Ettinger R, Beck J: Geriatric dental curriculum and the needs of the elderly. *Spec Care Dent* 1984;4:207-213.

33. Ruesch J, Kees W: *Non-verbal Communication*. Berkeley, University of California Press, 1956.

Appendix 8-A

Fluoride and Saliva Substitutes

A partial listing of fluoride and saliva substitutes is listed below by manufacturer.

Fluorides

0.4% SnF$_2$ Gels
- Veterans Administration Oral Disease Research Laboratory, Houston, Texas:
  Tin-Gel
- Scherer Laboratories:
  Gel Kam

1.1% NaF Gels
- Colgate-Hoyt:
  Prevident
  Thera-flur

0.05% NaF Rinses
- Colgate Palmolive:
  Fluorigard
- Johnson & Johnson:
  ACT

Saliva Substitutes

- Veterans Administration Oral Disease Research Laboratory, Houston, Texas:
  Oralube
  Oralube II (with 1000 ppm fluoride)
- Westport Pharmaceuticals:
  Salivart
- Ing's Dental Specialties, Fort Wayne, Indiana:
  Orex
- Remeda Pharmaceutical Co., Finland:
  Salisynt
- Kingswood Canada, Inc.:
  Moi-stir

- Richmond Pharmaceutical, Ontario:
  Saliment
- Scherer Labs, Dallas, Texas:
  Xerolube
    Fluoride Dentifrices (Approved by ADA Council on Dental Therapeutics)
- Colgate
- Crest
- Aquafresh
- Aim

CHAPTER 9

Management of Intercurrent Illnesses in Institutionalized Patients with Alzheimer Dementia

Kathy J. Fabiszewski, Rita A. Shapiro, and Donald C. Kern

Alzheimer dementia results in loss of intellectual, functional, and behavioral ability. These losses are progressive and irreversible. Ultimately, even the Alzheimer patient who premorbidly was the epitome of health and wellness will develop pathologic symptoms. These symptoms arise either as a result of co-existing illness or as a complication of the Alzheimer dementia. Thus, as the Alzheimer dementia advances, the health care of the afflicted person becomes increasingly intricate, intensive, complicated, and strenuous. The clinical management of the patient with total cognitive dependence brings with it the realization that almost all such patients will require institutional care at some time.[1]

If the current intensive search for drugs that reverse the cognitive losses in patients with Alzheimer's disease is successful, the clinical management of the disease may change radically.[2] The fact remains that, at present, there is no proven therapy that will reverse or arrest the progression of the disease. Enormous physical, emotional, and financial burden is created for family caregivers of the profoundly impaired Alzheimer dementia patient for whom there is no realistic hope for either recovery or improvement in function. For the health care professional, orchestrating an interdisciplinary treatment effort for the institutionalized Alzheimer patient is equally difficult. To some, these patients are simply neither challenging nor interesting; to others, their complex care needs are overwhelming. Subsequently, the temptation to abandon the patient or forego optimal health care provision by neglect may arise. Some patients with Alzheimer dementia may have co-existing medical or psychiatric conditions contributing to their dementia or causing superimposed acute confusional states that may be reversible. Acknowledging that optimal medical management of both co-existing disease and intercurrent illness in the institutionalized Alzheimer dementia patient can improve overall well-being, enhance quality of life, and promote comfort is a basic premise to caring for these unfortunate yet deserving patients.

The management of two categories of intercurrent illness common to the institutionalized Alzheimer dementia patient will be addressed in this chapter. These are stable, co-existing, chronic disease and intercurrent, episodic illness. Emphasis will be given to those aspects of care that differ from traditional models of intercurrent illness management seen in other institutionalized populations.

Assessing and managing health and intercurrent illness in the institutionalized patient with Alzheimer dementia differs from that of other middle-aged and elderly adults for a number of reasons. First and foremost is the fact that it is difficult to obtain a good history from the demented, noncommunicative patient. At the time of diagnosis, second-hand information may be obtained from family caregivers. Yet once the Alzheimer patient requires institutionalization, increased emphasis must be placed on objective data obtained from physical examination, nonverbal behaviors, and selective laboratory and roentgenographic studies. Such objective data must always be carefully correlated with the clinical picture. Patient evaluation with these methodologies is often impeded by the inability of Alzheimer patients to understand the rationale for the studies and subsequent inability to cooperate with the examination or with diagnostic studies.

Second, intercurrent illness in advanced Alzheimer dementia tends to present much differently than it does in other adults. Cognitive deficits impede symptom reporting and thus delay illness detection. Symptomatology tends to be very nonspecific. A minor behavioral change such as irritability or increased confusion, for example, may be the only sign of superimposed illness or drug toxicity. Unexpected complications may appear because the course of the illness is so difficult to monitor. Clinical courses of certain illnesses may be unpredictably peculiar. The physician is often forced to rely exclusively on empiric treatment that, in itself, may create additional diagnostic and therapeutic dilemmas.

Third, institutionalization, itself, may precipitate intercurrent illness and decrement in function in the intellectually impaired, physically debilitated patient. One such example might be the risk of contracting nosocomial infection; another might be the indiscriminate use of sedatives or restraint in bed for prolonged periods of time due to staffing constraints in the long-term care facility.

Finally, comes the issue of compliance. Any demented patient is unable to cooperate with the diagnostic and therapeutic interventions of medical, nursing, and other professional caregivers. Seldom will a patient with advanced Alzheimer dementia be able to cough and breathe deeply on command or bear down for fecal disimpaction. Many Alzheimer patients become assaultive during phlebotomy, become hyperactive during roentgenography, or spit out essential pills and elixirs that are not palatable to them. And because of the usual profound intellectual impairment seen in these patients by the time institutionalization is indicated, the majority are not "teachable" and are unable to participate meaningfully in their own care and health maintenance management.

Interdisciplinary Teamwork

It has been stated that the major role of the physician in the clinical management of the patient with Alzheimer dementia is that of a counselor who assists in the conservative treatment of the patient.[3] Winograd and Jarvik[4] have proposed the framework of the "seven I's" (intellectual failure, immobility, instability, incontinence, insomnia, iatrogenic conditions, and involvement of families) to assist physicians in addressing certain key problems that confront patients and caregivers.[4]

In the long-term care setting, managing the Alzheimer dementia patient is a formidable challenge that necessitates interdisciplinary teamwork. When treating the institutionalized Alzheimer patient, it is useful to keep in mind that a patient's ability to function depends on a combination of characteristics of the individual and the setting in which he or she is expected to function. The physician's first responsibility is to treat the patient to remedy the remediable by searching for and dealing with those conditions that are treatable.[5] After having improved the Alzheimer patient's ability (physiologically and psychologically) as much as possible, the physician's next task is to collaborate with other caregivers to structure an environment that will facilitate the patient's functioning with maximal autonomy. This latter mandate rests not on the physician alone but on the team of health care professionals and paraprofessionals who use the "therapeutic milieu" as the supportive environment in which the patient is to be cared for and nurtured.

Many institutionalized Alzheimer patients, given their debilitation and subsequent vulnerability to intercurrent illness, require frequent attention, but not necessarily the elaborate, direct care of a physician. Using the gerontological nurse practitioner as one mechanism by which to ensure that the complex, changing needs of the institutionalized Alzheimer dementia patient are met serves the purpose of relieving the physician of some traditional medical functions, and blends the traditional practice of medicine (concerned with curing) with the practice of nursing (concerned with caring). The gerontological nurse practitioner's contributions toward meeting the health care needs of this segment of the aging population can have a favorable impact on the quality of care and on the economics of health care delivery in terms of efficiency, productivity, volume, and cost-effectiveness. This, in turn, leads to enhanced physician productivity and efficiency and increased time available for other professional activities in the arenas of academia and research.

The role of the nurse practitioner was initially conceived in the mid 1960s when alleged unmet health needs of certain populations surfaced, necessitating the emergence of physician extenders. Nurses, by virtue of their "roots" in the tradition of health care, were not satisfied by this concept, and, as nursing's expanded role evolved, the professional identities of nurse practitioners were nurtured, along with the realization that the uniqueness of their role did not come from serving as a physician substitute but in the opportunity for independent, autonomous patient contact, allowing the consumer direct accessibility to nurses for health care services.[6] Gerontological nurse practitioners emerged in the early 1970s. Several studies demonstrated their efficacy as co-providers of health care for the elderly.[7,8]

In managing intercurrent illness in institutionalized Alzheimer patients, the attending physician and the nurse practitioner function in a collaborative, joint practice. The practice may be based on an inherent philosophy of care, on verbal agreements with respect to roles and responsibilities, and, in some cases, on written management guidelines (see Appendix 9-A).[9-11] Such guidelines serve to expedite and facilitate the diagnosis and treatment of commonly occurring episodic illnesses seen in institutionalized Alzheimer patients based on predetermined discussion between the physician and nurse practitioner. They should be designed to facilitate an initiation of diagnostic evaluation and intervention prior to collaboration with or referral to the attending physician and promote prompt revision of therapeutic regimens when the desired outcome is not satisfactorily attained by treatment modalities previously in place. Management guidelines provide a framework for joint clinical practice; they should not be misconstrued as rigid protocols. They result from acknowledgment that episodic health problems and intercurrent illnesses will be encountered numerous times in the long-term management of the institutionalized patient with Alzheimer's disease. Management guidelines outline predetermined, jointly agreed upon, problem-oriented approaches to deal with the often complex differential analysis of symptoms of an illness and decide on a plan of care. They should be individualized to optimally meet the needs of patients within the joint practice, while attempting to clarify the appropriate degree of involvement of both the nurse practitioner and the physician. State regulatory statutes for prescriptive authority for nurses functioning in expanded role practice and credentialing committees in long-term care facilities may require written management guidelines. Therefore, these guidelines are countersigned by the physician and the nurse practitioner to signify clear understanding of roles, responsibilities, and practice limitations with respect to delegated medical functions. They should serve as a model for efficacious provision of ongoing health care to institutionalized Alzheimer patients.

The physician–nurse practitioner partnership alone does not ensure optimal management of the day-to-day health and illness needs of the institutionalized Alzheimer patient. An integrated, dynamic, interdisciplinary treatment effort, based on a comprehensive understanding of the physiological, functional, emotional, and psychosocial needs of the Alzheimer patient and his or her family is required. Other team members might include the dietitian, who monitors the nutritional status of the patient and provides input regarding dietary adjustments necessary to maintain adequate nutrition; rehabilitation specialists (physical therapist, occupational therapist, corrective therapist, and recreational therapist), who evaluate mobility, safety, and stimulation needs of the patient and integrate appropriate therapeutic modalities into individual treatment plans; and the social worker or psychologist, who assess the well-being of both family and professional caregivers and assist in providing supportive and educational services.

Of paramount importance is the professional nurse and the nursing assistant who spend the greatest amount of time in direct contact with the patient and who often serve as the "eyes" of the physician in observing and reporting pertinent positive findings noted during daily personal care provision. Patient assessment by nursing staff members is an invaluable asset to the overall treatment effort. Nursing staff members, by virtue of their close and cautious proximity to the patient, are often first to become cognizant of subtle, yet potentially significant changes in such parameters as body temperature, blood pressure, oral intake (both hydration and nourishment), sleep patterns, bowel and bladder elimination patterns, and skin integrity. Undoubtedly, the integrated roles of all treatment team members are valuable assets to patient care, and the attending physician should acknowledge and value the assessments, interventions, and contributions of each team member in total patient care.

Determining the Extent of Appropriate Medical Care

Most long-term care facilities are limited in the extent of aggressive medical treatment that they can provide without relocating the Alzheimer patient to an acute care facility. Relocation can be traumatic to the patient who is disoriented and fails to comprehend the events precipitating such a transfer. Subsequently, since

Alzheimer dementia is incurable, treatment efforts are generally directed at alleviating distressing or uncomfortable symptoms of the illness, such as depression, agitation, insomnia, and wailing vocalization. Such symptoms can often be managed with supportive measures by first attempting to determine their underlying etiology. Then, efforts may be directed at alleviating their cause. If nonpharmacologic interventions are impractical or unsuccessful, then pharmacologic intervention is indicated. The pharmacologic management of such symptomatology is discussed in Chapter 11.

As the patient deteriorates mentally, there will be physical complications of Alzheimer dementia that will arise. For example, a gait disorder may become apparent on any given day, secondary to underlying neurologic degeneration. This disorder, however, is not truly benign because it predisposes the cognitively impaired patient to premature immobility if the patient were to fall and sustain traumatic injury (e.g., laceration or fracture). If rendered immobile for even the briefest period of time, the Alzheimer patient is likely to become chairfast or bedfast, further predisposing the patient to another series of intercurrent illnesses, including pneumonia, phlebitis, decubitus ulceration, and possibly failure to thrive syndrome. In summary, intellectual impairment leads to functional impairment, which leads to physical impairment, which leads to intercurrent illness. Intercurrent illness is thus an extension of the Alzheimer dementia progression and cannot be viewed as a separate entity.

In managing intercurrent illness in the institutionalized Alzheimer patient, acknowledging that chronic disability differs from acute illness and must be treated as such is imperative. Each patient must be evaluated systematically and comprehensively if optimal medical care is to be provided. On the opposite end of the spectrum is the notion that diagnostic and therapeutic procedures in the frail elderly carry with them a high risk of iatrogenic complications.[4] For example, some procedures that require patient sedation or anesthesia for completion may, in the long run, only serve to exacerbate patient confusion. Bowel preparation for certain diagnostic procedures may further debilitate the patient. The value and quality of diagnostic information to be obtained must always be weighed against the risks and difficulties of the procedure performance[4] as well as with the degree of patent discomfort inflicted. The premise that the overall condition of the patient is unlikely to improve (because of the underlying Alzheimer dementia pathology) must always be kept in mind.

A major question thus becomes whether the patient with advanced Alzheimer dementia should be relocated to an acute care facility in the event of development of intercurrent illness or whether conservative treatment efforts should be initiated without costly and often traumatic (for the patient) transfer to an unfamiliar environment. It is difficult to determine which modality is truly in the patient's best interest and, at present, there is a lack of knowledge about the optimal medical treatment of intercurrent illness in patients in nursing homes in general. A detailed discussion of ethical issues in the treatment of advanced Alzheimer dementia can be found in Chapter 10.

The Therapeutic Plan

The therapeutic plan for the institutionalized patient with Alzheimer dementia should be based on certain premises. The first is that the plan is directed primarily by two foci: (1) the specific extent of aggressive medical care desired by the family and (2) the overall treatment goals established on behalf of the patient. The second premise is that the plan is individualized and based on the assessments and diagnoses of all involved interdisciplinary team members. Third, the plan is interdisciplinary in focus, given the complex nature of the illness. In addition, family members should always be included in care planning if, in fact, they desire to be included.

It is most beneficial to be sensible and realistic in establishing a treatment plan. Preventing excess disability and promoting quality of life can be attained by periodic monitoring for decline in function, intellect, behavior, or overall health status or comfort level. In a long-term care facility, round-the-clock "surveillance" exists; having a gerontological nurse practitioner may increase the quality of such surveillance by facilitating systematic monitoring of all parameters and by vigorously following up on all suspicious findings and on the effectiveness of defined interventions.

Major Areas of Clinical Concern

A victim of Alzheimer dementia often requires intermittent medical care for other illnesses. Because dementia is most prevalent among the very old and because the very old are at risk of multiple medical disabilities, it is common for those with dementia to require attention for cardiac, pulmonary, and/or renal disease.[12] The majority of chronic diseases commonly encountered by the institutionalized Alzheimer dementia population can be managed according to currently established directives of care found in internal medicine or geriatric medicine textbooks and handbooks. The following discussion will focus on aspects of assessment and management that may differ in caring for an institutionalized Alzheimer dementia patient.

Infectious Disease (Fever)

Most Alzheimer patients ultimately die of an infective process manifested by fever, such as pneumonia, urinary tract infection, or septicemia. The significance of fever as a prognostic indicator cannot be overemphasized. Although fever may, in some instances, represent a benign, self-limiting condition such as dehydration, constipation, or a minor viral illness, if it persists for more than 24 hours, if the temperature is unusually elevated, or if the patient exhibits signs of clinical decompensation, complete investigation is warranted. It is unnecessary to treat uncomplicated febrile illnesses for the first day or so since this form of fever may be beneficial and protective.[13] Yet, because of the wide spectrum of prognostic implications, fever creates a great sense of urgency in both family members and in health care providers.[14] For the clinician, fever, although not a new or uncommon problem, assumes increasing importance in this type of patient because of the availability of new therapeutic approaches.[15]

Because of the noncommunicative nature of many institutionalized Alzheimer dementia patients, the approach to fever evaluation differs from that of a mentally intact patient. Initially, a fever evaluation of an institutionalized Alzheimer patient should include a review of past medical illnesses that might predispose the patient to fever. For example, the patient with benign prostatic hypertrophy or urinary incontinence is predisposed to urinary retention and urinary tract infection, which may be identified as the fever source. Or the patient with a history of diverticulosis is at risk for the development of diverticulitis and perforation if bowel elimination patterns are not cautiously monitored.

Second, a careful review of the patient's medication regimen is indicated at the onset of fever to rule out the possibility of a malignant neuroleptic syndrome or to ascertain that the recent addition of a sedative did not, for example, lead to lethargy with a subsequent reduction in oral fluid intake or to dysphagia with resulting aspiration pneumonitis. In addition, many neuroleptic medications predispose the patient to constipation, which, in itself, may lead to unforeseen temperature elevation.

Third, the staff caring for the patient should be interviewed for elicitation of any recent changes in patient functional or behavioral patterns. Note should be made of the patient's most recent voiding, bowel movement, and oral intake and also of any incidental findings, such as a recent episode of vomiting, a seizure, or a productive cough. It is also helpful to make note of any recent viral or bacterial illnesses of patients housed in close geographical proximity to the patient who develops fever.

Next, the patient should be systematically examined for any pertinent positive physical signs such as decreased skin turgor, tachypnea, adventitious breath sounds, abdominal distention or tenderness, or nuchal rigidity. In addition, cautious assessment should be made of the patient's mental status and level of consciousness and documentation made of any deviation from baseline mental status.

The standard recommended protocol for workup of fever in the noncommunicative patient consists minimally of a complete blood cell count (including white blood cell count and differential), erythrocyte sedimentation rate, electrolyte determinations, renal function studies, three sets of blood cultures, a urinalysis with culture and sensitivity, a sputum Gram stain with culture and sensitivity and a chest roentgenogram. Other studies such as throat culture, wound culture (e.g., from a decubitus ulceration), lumbar puncture, or a flat plate roentgenogram of the abdomen may be indicated, depending on the clinical presentation.

After a diagnostic fever evaluation is completed, empiric antibiotic coverage may be initiated, or if the patient appears comfortable and does not appear to be decompensating, initiation of antibiotics may be delayed or postponed until the results of cultures and other diagnostic tests are available. In the interim, antipyretics such as acetaminophen or acetylsalicylic acid may be administered.[13] Whenever possible, a conservative approach to fever management, awaiting culture results prior to initiating antibiotic therapy, should be employed since many pathogens common to the institutionalized population tend to be resistant to all but potent antibiotics such as the aminoglycosides or third-generation cephalosporins. The use of these agents in an elderly or debilitated patient predisposes that person to iatrogenic renal failure and ototoxicity, which are adverse reactions that are difficult to assess for and gauge in the marginally communicative patient. If these agents are used, serum peak and trough levels along with renal function studies should be monitored at frequent, regular intervals during the course of such antibiotic administration and adequate hydration must be ensured, using intravenous fluid administration if necessary.

Ideally, all episodes of fever treated with antibiotics should be comprehensively reevaluated after completion of their course; otherwise, it is not possible to ascertain whether the infectious source of the fever has been appropriately eradicated. Inadequate treatment of bacterial infection is a common cause of fever, and prior antibiotic treatment may only temporarily inhibit bacteremia.

Nutritional and Feeding Difficulties

Because of the variable ability of the Alzheimer dementia patient to consume adequate amounts of food and volumes of fluids, these victims easily fall prey to dehydration and malnutrition. Thus, alterations in nutritional status and in fluid and electrolyte balance are commonly encountered phenomena in institutionalized Alzheimer dementia patients. The nourishment and hydration of the noncommunicative patient who is totally dependent on others for feeding needs is further complicated by the availability and perseverance of qualified caregivers to provide necessary food and fluid.

Although obesity seems to be much less common than problems with weight loss and malnutrition, some Alzheimer dementia patients seem to especially enjoy eating. For these patients, consuming several thousand calories per day is not problematic per se; professional and family caregivers appear to derive a tremendous amount of pleasure and satisfaction from nurturing the patient who enjoys eating. However, in the patient with impaired physical mobility, particularly the bedfast or chair-bound patient, an excessive caloric intake not balanced by appropriate energy expenditure can result in obesity. Obesity, in turn, predisposes the patient to type II diabetes, hypertension, heart disease, and pressure ulcerations of the skin. In addition, overweight patients create an additional burden for caregivers who must struggle to lift, turn, and move the patient in bed and provide personal care. For these patients a weight-reduction diet (usually an initial caloric reduction to 1800 kcal/day, then, if necessary, serial caloric restrictions to 1500 kcal/day or, in some cases, 1200 kcal/day) is indicated with dietary consultation to ensure that high volumes of non-calorie-dense foods are provided. This allows the patient to receive larger portions of food with fewer calories. A small number of patients may exhibit behavior analogous to the Kluver-Bucy syndrome. They may inappropriately and rapidly engulf all mouthable objects in their vicinity. Since they may lack the capacity to distinguish edible from inedible objects, they require cautious supervision to safeguard them from aspiration.

On the opposite end of the spectrum is the patient who presents a feeding problem due to lack of appetite, the inability to recognize food (or to differentiate edibles from inedibles), the inability to derive pleasure from eating, or difficulty in swallowing. Malnutrition predisposes the patient to weight loss, reduced immunity to infections, and skin breakdown and further disturbs the body image of the patient.

Approaches to the management of feeding difficulties in Alzheimer dementia patients are discussed in Chapter 7. Since weight loss tends to accompany progression of Alzheimer dementia into the middle and later stages of the disease, the benefits of extensive gastrointestinal workup for the symptom of weight loss alone in the debilitated patient (who may not be a surgical candidate) must always be balanced with the possible costs (discomfort) to the patient. The administration of prophylactic multivitamins in any patient with a feeding disorder may serve as a comfort measure because it prevents possible symptoms of vitamin deficiency. Providing high-protein, high-caloric nutritional supplements such as Sustacal, Ensure Plus, and milkshakes at frequent intervals may prove beneficial. Monitoring oral intake via calorie counting and following serial patient weights provide the physician with parameters by which to assess the nutritional status of the patient over time. In addition, some practitioners find it useful to monitor serum total protein, albumin–globulin ratios, and total iron binding capacity as indicators of patient nutritional status, although the efficacy of these procedures is not known.

Bowel Elimination Disorders

Because of the variable intake of nourishment and hydration, impaired physical mobility (inactivity), and, perhaps, the inability of the patient with Alzheimer's disease to defecate frequently enough or in sufficient volume, institutionalized Alzheimer patients are at risk for the development of constipation and fecal incontinence.

Constipation may be defined as infrequent defecation, insufficient defecation, feeling of incomplete evacuation, or increased hardness of stools.[16] The prevalence of constipation increases with age alone.[17] It is imperative that constipation not be confused with what may be a preconceived idea of irregular bowel elimination on the part of caregivers. For example, the failure of the patient to have a daily bowel movement or even a twice weekly bowel evacuation may not exemplify constipation but may, in fact, represent a normal bowel elimination pattern for that particular patient.

A sudden, dramatic reduction in the frequency of bowel elimination or significant change in the character of stools, however, may signify a serious pathologic condition, such as carcinoma or diverticular disease, and when the patient is acutely ill and viewed as an appropriate surgical candidate, gastrointestinal or surgical consultation and evaluation may be warranted. If not evaluated and treated properly, constipation may lead to fecal impaction, mechanical bowel obstruction, volvulus, or perforation with resultant acute abdomen.

The Alzheimer patient with constipation of more insidious onset should be evaluated for the presence of etiologic factors that may contribute to or cause constipation. Examples may include physical inactivity, inadequate dietary fiber, insufficient fluid intake, poor muscle tone, pharmacologic agents (e.g., anticholinergics or neuroleptics), toxic causes, or laxative abuse. Dementia, itself, has been identified as a factor provoking constipation.[17]

The treatment of constipation should be aimed primarily at preventing its occurrence and, in instances when it does occur, should be aimed at attempting to alleviate its underlying cause. Examples of such treatment might include a bowel management regimen of encouraging appropriate fluid intake, ensuring adequate dietary fiber, administering stool softeners and, if necessary, using bulk laxatives or rectal suppositories for periodic planned bowel evacuation. Whenever feasible, medications that predispose the patient to constipation should be eliminated from the treatment regimen. Pharmacologic agents used in the management of bowel elimination pattern disturbances are discussed in Chapter 11.

Fecal incontinence is inevitable in advanced Alzheimer dementia because of profound cognitive impairment that interferes with the patient's ability to recognize, acknowledge, and communicate the urge to defecate. Although a distressing, socially isolating problem that generally does not receive much physician interest, premature fecal incontinence may be eliminated by avoiding the use of pharmacologic agents that cloud sensorium or may be minimized with a low-residue diet and periodic planned bowel evacuation stimulated by the postprandial gastrocolic reflux and a glycerin or bisacodyl rectal suppository. Bowel retraining and behavior modification modalities have not proven therapeutic to the severely demented patient who is unable to cooperate with such a program nor to the caregiver, who becomes frustrated by the exacerbation of aberrant behaviors by the patient as a result of the stress invoked by "involuntary" participation in such a program.

Urinary Elimination Disorders

Because the majority of institutionalized Alzheimer patients will ultimately be rendered incontinent of urine, there exists substantial potential for the development of genitourinary tract complications of Alzheimer's disease. At the onset of incontinence, therefore, it is advisable to seek urologic consultation to rule out structural abnormality or localized disease of the genitourinary tract. Male patients with Alzheimer dementia are often in the age group with a high prevalence of benign prostatic hypertrophy and may suffer from obstructive uropathy. Atrophic vaginitis in female patients may produce symptoms contributing to urinary incontinence. In addition, possible functional and iatrogenic causes of premature incontinence should be evaluated. These might include, but are not limited to effects of medications (particularly the anticholinergics, diuretics, and neuroleptics), impaired physical mobility (inability to get to the bathroom in time), and fecal impaction. The real issue becomes making the distinction between potentially correctable causes of incontinence or reversible urologic pathology and impairment of inhibition of elimination associated with the cognitive deficits of Alzheimer dementia itself that results in an uninhibited neurogenic bladder.

Urinary incontinence may not be curable in most patients with advanced Alzheimer dementia. Yet, managing urinary incontinence with caution is essential in maintaining patient well-being for a number of reasons. First is that, if successfully managed, the patient will be rendered comfortable, socially active, and dignified in spite of the condition. Second, the risk of urinary tract infection with urosepsis may be reduced. Third, physical complications of incontinence such as impaired skin integrity and decubitus ulcer formation and infection may be eliminated. Finally, consideration must be given to making life easier for caregivers and for minimizing the costs of caring for this condition and its complications.

The use of indwelling Foley catheters in this patient population is controversial at best. Clearly, the patient who does not understand the need for such a device is at risk for self-discontinuance and subsequent trauma to lower genitourinary tract tissues. In addition, a long-term urethral Foley catheterization predisposes the patient to symptomatic urinary tract infection, which is the most common cause of nosocomial Gram-negative bacteremia. Prior to resorting to indwelling Foley catheter drainage, urologic consultation should be sought; Foley catheters are probably not an appropriate treatment modality for the management of incontinence alone but may be indicated in some patients with detrusor instability, bladder outlet obstruction (and subsequent overflow incontinence), or neurogenic bladder. Urinary tract prophylaxis by acidification (ascorbic acid) and urinary antiseptic agents may be of benefit in delaying infection but does not prevent infection in the long-term management of the patient for whom there is no alternative but use of the Foley catheter. The primary goal in managing the Alzheimer patient who requires an indwelling Foley catheter is to prevent bacteremia; asymptomatic bacteriuria need not be treated.

For males without significant obstructive pathology, external collection devices are, therefore, preferable. They have a lower incidence of bacteriuria but do have potential side effects, including urethral and penile skin bacterial colonization, bacteriuria and urinary tract infections, and local complications such as balanitis or ulceration of penile skin. When the condom catheter is applied too tightly, urethral diverticulae fistulae or penile gangrene may occur. These problems can be avoided or treated early by proper application of the condom, prevention of kinking of the collection tube, and cleaning and drying the penis every 24 hours during daily condom changes, with removal if signs of inflammation develop. Patients with Alzheimer's disease often do not cooperate with optimal catheter care, frequently refusing care, manipulating the drainage system, and pulling off the condom. Therefore, it is often easier to rely on adult diapers, particularly for ambulatory patients, utilizing collection systems if decubiti develop.[18]

Mobility Problems

Because impaired cognition may result in apraxia, agnosia, and fear of falling, patients with Alzheimer dementia will experience deterioration in their ability to ambulate independently. Impaired physical mobility leads to increased overall dependence. Gait disturbances such as leaning, shuffling, scissoring, ataxia, and balance and coordination deficits lead to falls and traumatic injuries such as fractures. Although most of these falls are not associated with significant morbidity, increasing age and debility are associated with a marked increase in the risk of damage from falls.[17]

Treating the underlying cause of instability or a gait or balance disturbance is the rule of thumb in Alzheimer dementia. For example, if there is co-existing Parkinson's disease, manifested by bradykinesia and tremor, then initiation of antiparkinsonian therapy may be indicated. Treatment with carbidopa/levodopa, however, should be reserved for only those patients with the co-morbidity of Parkinson's disease and not for those patients with extrapyramidal side effects of neuroleptics. Orthostatic hypotension may be treated by reevaluating the patient's medication regimen and by more cautious monitoring of fluid balance. Visual impairment may be minimized with appropriate corrective lenses and routine, periodic optometric evaluations. In some instances, the patient may experience perceptual deficits that impede judgment for which there is no known effective medical treatment. However, the importance of optimizing environmental management using shock-absorptive, slip-resistant flooring, well-padded clothing, adequate lighting, grab-bars in bathrooms, and well-demarcated stairs cannot be overemphasized.[19] In cases of perceptual deficit, treatment involves referral to a physical therapist or corrective therapist for supervised ambulation and gait maintenance. Concurrent muscle strengthening and evaluation of the need for assistive devices, such as a cane or walker, are important interventions employed in the management of mobility difficulties. Seldom is gait retraining successful once the ability to ambulate is lost. Therefore, free ambulation is encouraged for as long as possible and Posey restraints should be avoided unless absolutely necessary for safety. Restraints are potentially counterproductive as inactivity may accentuate other risk factors for falls such as muscle weakness and poor balance.[19] Emphasizing strategies that prevent toxic reactions to medications such as sedatives, hypnotics, antihypertensives, and major tranquilizers, and control wandering behavior may also prevent falls and fractures.[19] Thus, the overall goal of therapy is to prevent unnecessary trauma and injury and to avoid further contributing to the debility of the impaired patient.

Regular prophylactic podiatric care is an important preventative measure for patients who tend to be hyperactive and prone to pacing. Podiatric problems such as bunions, callouses, and paronychia may cause pain and reluctance or inability to walk, leading to premature immobility. The need for properly fitted footwear cannot be overemphasized. Ambulatory patients with peripheral vascular disease, such as arterial or venous insufficiency, are at risk for retarded mobility due to pain (if claudication is present) and altered sensation. They should be monitored carefully for the development of blisters, ulcerations, and injuries to the lower extremities.

Degenerative joint disease is common with aging. The treatment of rheumatologic problems is difficult and, although it does not in essence differ from the treatment of arthritic conditions in any older adult, the effectiveness and the possible adverse reactions of salicylates or nonsteroidal anti-inflammatory agents are very difficult to evaluate in the noncommunicative patient. Prior to initiation of treatment with anti-inflammatory agents in the Alzheimer patient, it is recommended that mechanisms be in place to assess for conditions such as asymptomatic gastrointestinal bleeding and dyspepsia. In terms of monitoring patient response to therapy some clinicians find it beneficial to follow serial erythrocyte sedimentation rates in the patient with stiffness, joint pain and discomfort, erythema, swelling, or limitation in mobility resulting from co-existing rheumatologic disease. Goniometric evaluations may help to evaluate the efficacy of pharmacologic intervention on joint mobility and overall patient function. It should be noted that salicylate and indomethacin toxicity may cause central nervous system impairments, and reversible cognitive dysfunction has even been reported with naproxen and ibuprofen.[20]

Cardiovascular Disease

It is often difficult to differentiate clinically whether a dementia is pure Alzheimer's type dementia or whether it may be a combined Alzheimer/multi-infarct dementia. For this reason, it is important that any patient with dementia be evaluated for the presence of co-existing cardiovascular disease, particularly asymptomatic hypertension, congestive heart failure, and cardiac dysrhythmias. Controlling hypertension and other cardiovascular disease may prevent small strokes (lacunar infarcts), which can cause further deterioration of cognitive function. Hypertension should be treated aggressively yet cautiously in patients with dementia.

Guidelines for the management of hypertension are well-described in other texts. In the treatment of the institutionalized patient with this disorder caution must be exercised in the selection both of therapeutic agents and of ideal dosage. Diuretics remain one of the primary therapies for hypertension. Complications of diuretic administration in this patient population include dehydration/volume depletion, electrolyte imbalance, and glucose intolerance, all of which can cause serious symptomatology in the intellectually impaired, frail dementia patient. In addition, attention must be paid to ensuring blood pressure high enough to maintain adequate cerebral perfusion. Serial orthostatic apical pulses and blood pressures should be monitored by nursing staff; "cutoffs" for withholding doses should be provided. Attention must be paid to other factors that will effect blood pressure readings over time, such as weight loss, reduced dietary sodium intake, and the sometimes erratic oral fluid intakes of patients with Alzheimer's disease. Renal function must also be periodically evaluated. Patients on thiazide diuretics and psychotropic medications are at risk for postural hypotension. Any patient on a non-potassium-sparing diuretic should be fully supplemented with potassium; it cannot be assumed that dietary maintenance of potassium will be effective in patients whose dietary intake may vary. Other antihypertensive agents such as methyldopa, propranolol, and reserpine may have reversible adverse cognitive effects.[21]

Congestive heart failure in the Alzheimer patient can be managed largely based on patient symptomatology. Since many patients in the advanced stages of Alzheimer dementia become less physically active and increasingly immobile, dyspnea on exertion is no longer a problem. If orthopnea, paroxysmal nocturnal dyspnea, or pedal edema are present or if cardiac dysrhythmias occur, a sodium-restricted diet, oral fluid restriction, or diuretic therapy may be indicated. If diuretics are ineffective in alleviating uncomfortable symptomatology, digitalis therapy may be indicated. If digitalis therapy is initiated, provision should be made for periodic monitoring of serum digoxin levels, electrolytes, uric acid levels, and blood urea nitrogen/creatinine since the risk of toxicity in this patient population demands special attention, as does correction of underlying hypoxia, if possible. Digoxin toxicity tends to have an insidious onset and is a lethal complication of the management of congestive heart failure. The need for continuance of digoxin therapy should be reevaluated at periodic intervals.

Pulmonary Conditions

Co-existing chronic obstructive pulmonary disease in the institutionalized Alzheimer patient is best managed conservatively, with efforts directed at minimizing any respiratory distress without subjecting the patient to adverse behavioral effects of bronchodilators (e.g., excitability, nervousness). The mainstay of treatment for chronic obstructive pulmonary disease should be focused on elimination of smoking and other respiratory irritants, attention to adequate hydration, and secretion management. Low-flow oxygen therapy may be indicated in hypoxia that is not compensated; yet periodic arterial blood gas analysis is a painful procedure for the profoundly impaired Alzheimer dementia patient. It is also recommended that periodic serum theophylline levels be monitored in patients receiving theophylline-type preparations.

Because of the hypoactive or ineffective gag reflex seen in patients with advanced Alzheimer dementia (the etiology of which is not clear), the aspiration of oral secretions such as saliva or food and fluid into the lungs is a major problem, which leads to potentially life-threatening conditions such as pneumonia and atelectasis. Since insertion of a nasogastric tube or permanent feeding gastrostomy tube into the stomach may actually destroy normal protective mechanisms against aspiration by, for example, contributing to esophageal sphincter incompetence or high gastric residual volumes and subsequent regurgitation, these measures should not be viewed as the ultimate solution to the problem. A swallowing disorder in any patient warrants evaluation to search for potentially reversible causes such as oversedation, inappropriate consistency of foods or feeding techniques, or occult dental problems that may impair the patient's ability to masticate properly. Although the best treatment for aspiration is prevention, supportive measures such as oxygen, pulmonary toilet, bronchodilators, and antimicrobial agents may be indicated.

Endocrine Disease

The prevalence of symptomatic and asymptomatic diabetes mellitus increases with age as does glucose intolerance.[17] Symptoms such as polyuria and excessive thirst are difficult to discern in incontinent and noncommunicative patients. Although insulin-dependent diabetes has seldom been seen as a co-existing illness with Alzheimer dementia,[22] hyperglycemia of the less severe type or chemical diabetes, also known as impaired glucose tolerance, has been noted. Attempting optimal control of hyperglycemia with weight control and dietary management is the first step; if this is ineffective, oral antidiabetic agents, particularly the second-generation sulfonylureas, are well-tolerated even though they are more potent than chlorpropamide; they are less likely to interact with other drugs because of binding properties and have dual excretion via bile and kidney. Hypoglycemia is uncommon with these agents and can be avoided if they are used correctly and if appropriate dietary precautions are employed.

Co-Existing Neurological Disorders

In addition to its devastating effects on cognition, behavior, and function, Alzheimer's disease is associated with other neurological signs and symptoms, most notably seizures and disorders of movement and gait. Patients with Alzheimer's disease may also have unrelated co-existing neurological disorders. Since the prevalence of Alzheimer's disease increases with age, it is also more likely to co-exist with other age-related conditions such as cervical and lumbar spondylosis, brain infarctions and transient ischemic attacks, and Parkinson's disease.

Although it is commonly assumed that seizures occur only rarely and late in the course of Alzheimer's disease, approximately 10% of institutionalized Alzheimer disease patients suffer new-onset, unprovoked, generalized seizures.[23] Most seizures are tonic-clonic type without associated status epilepticus. There appears to be no significant difference in seizure incidence related to age of onset of dementia nor duration of illness. Seizures occur an average of 6.5 years after dementia onset but may range from 2 to 15 years after symptom onset.

At the onset of seizure activity, a precipitating, reversible metabolic, infectious, or toxic (drug-induced) cause must be ruled out by prompt blood screening consisting minimally of a complete blood count, serum glucose, electrolytes, blood urea nitrogen, calcium and magnesium. In addition, the recent hospital course and medication regimen must be reviewed, a thorough physical and neurological examination performed, and an electroencephalogram obtained. Rarely is a precipitating factor uncovered in the Alzheimer disease patient population. Interictal electroencephalogram will usually show no change or diffuse slowing; epileptiform discharges are rarely seen. Treatment usually consists of anticonvulsant monotherapy, e.g., phenytoin, although given the fact that seizure recurrences may be infrequent, the efficacy of anticonvulsant therapy in this patient population is not known. Similarly, approximately 10% of institutionalized Alzheimer dementia patients experience myoclonus, an irregular, shock-like jerking of a muscle or muscle group.[23] There is no known connection between the presence of myoclonus and seizures.

In a prospective, longitudinal study of 121 patients with Alzheimer's disease, Mayeux et al.[24] found that 11 (9.9%) showed myoclonus on initial neurological assessment, with 8 others developing myoclonus during four-year follow-up examinations. They described symptom heterogeneity in Alzheimer's disease and proposed four subtypes: extrapyramidal, myoclonic, benign, and typical. No significant difference was found in symptom duration in the myoclonic subgroup; however, the onset of dementia was at an earlier age and more rapid deterioration was measured on the Mini-Mental State examination.[24]

The myoclonic jerks in Alzheimer's disease appear to primarily affect individual limbs, especially distally. Infrequently, they may be associated with generalized body jerks as well as generalized seizures. In jerk locked electroencephalogram averaging analysis focal contralateral negative cerebral potentials may precede the myoclonic jerks. The cortical and electrophysiological data in one group of patients with Alzheimer's disease formed a distinct entity, dissimilar from the type seen in patients with Jacob-Creudtzfeldt disease (subacute spongiform encephalopathy).[25]

Myoclonus appears to be more prevalent in patients with longer duration and more severe dementia. Reversible causes of myoclonus, e.g., toxic and metabolic encephalopathies, should always be ruled out. Nursing and family caregivers should be educated about the association of myoclonus and Alzheimer's disease. Only when myoclonus is severely disturbing to the caregivers or interfering with voluntary functional activities should any attempt at pharmacological treatment be initiated. There is no specific treatment for myoclonus in Alzheimer dementia, but administration of benzodiazepines is sometimes useful.

Alzheimer's disease patients with co-existing cerebral infarctions (the so-called mixed dementia) or Parkinson's disease may benefit from neurological consultation for evaluation and treatment of these conditions. Recurrent brain infarction may be prevented by influencing stroke risk factors by blood pressure control, optimization of cardiac status, dietary lipid modification, cigarette cessation, and the addition of anti-platelet agents such as aspirin. For the small subgroup of stroke or transient ischemia attack patients with concomitant Alzheimer's disease on chronic anticoagulation with warfarin, frequent reassessment of the risk-benefit ratio of anticoagulation, with attention to the patient's mobility safety (gait stability, tendency to wander, or self-injury risk) and compliance with medication, and regular prothrombin tests are imperative.

Proper diagnosis is important for the small group of patients with presumed mixed Alzheimer's disease patients for two primary reasons. First, extrapyramidal signs have been reported to occur frequently in Alzheimer patients, both independent of and associated with neuroleptic use.[24,26] Secondly, patients with Parkinson's disease may develop dementia which, at autopsy, may be pathologically associated with Alzheimer changes. Although the true prevalence of the co-existence of these two disorders is not known, recent data suggest that the majority of Alzheimer patients with extrapyramidal signs, particularly rigidity, show post-mortem changes of Parkinson's disease as well as Alzheimer's disease.[27,28] The effectiveness of antiparkinsonism medication in these patients is not known. Potential adverse reactions of antiparkinsonism medication include cognitive worsening, hallucinations, or frank confusional states, frequently manifesting as a toxic psychosis. Additionally, pedal edema, orthostatic hypotension, gastrointestinal disturbances, and drug-induced dyskinesia or dystonia may occur.

Since they are at increased risk for the development of adverse cognitive behavioral side effects of common antiparkinsonism agents, patients with Parkinson's disease who become demented are difficult to treat. Neurological consultation is recommended for diagnostic distinction of co-existing Parkinson's disease from other para-Parkinson states as well as for guidance for anticipated trials of antiparkinsonism therapy.

As mentioned earlier, most patients with Alzheimer dementia eventually develop impaired ambulation secondary to reluctance to walk, apraxia, or extrapyramidal features. Once patients develop a severe gait disorder, therapeutic attempts for gait retraining are rarely successful. Unfortunately, physical immobility may lead to sensory deprivation, social isolation, and possibly, a more rapid cognitive and behavioral decline. Gastrointestinal dysfunction with increased slowing of bowel transit time contributing to constipation and fecal impaction, worsened swallowing reflexes, disruption of sleep-wake cycles, venous stasis with thrombosis, and contractures may also occur in the mobility compromised patient.

Decubitus Ulcerations

Immobility is a major contributor to decubitus ulcer formation. Decubiti may be a source of pain, provide culture media promoting growth of resistant microorganisms, and are major consumer of nursing time and health care cost. Patients with Alzheimer's disease become particularly prone to develop decubiti when risk factors such as protein and/or calorie malnutrition, sphincteric incontinence, and physical immobility are present. In addition, the diminution of skin thickness, elasticity, and subcutaneous fat that occurs with normal aging may promote their development.

Decubiti are much easier to control than they are to treat. They can be prevented by modifying risk factors, cushioning bony prominences, changing positioning frequently, and observing religiously for early local erythema or tenderness. Four basic therapeutic principles for the treatment of pressure sores include elimination of local pressure, cleansing and debridement of necrotic tissue, promoting new tissue growth, and treating any factors retarding healing.[29] Povidone-iodine, hydrogen peroxide, and sodium hypochlorite have been used to cleanse and retard bacterial growth. However, they may retard healing more than plain normal saline. Enzyme products and surgical debridement may be necessary to remove purulent and necrotic material. Systemic antibiotics are usually reserved for coexisting osteomyelitis. A positive nutritional balance and urinary and fecal continence via the temporary use of catheters or rectal tubes may be necessary for decubitus ulceration healing. On rare occasions, surgical grafting may be required.

REFERENCES

1. Kvale JN: Alzheimer's disease. *Am Fam Physician* 1986;34:103-110.

2. Katzman R: Alzheimer's disease. *N Eng J Med* 1986;314:964-973.

3. McKhann G, Drachman D, Folstein M, et al: Clinical diagnosis of Alzheimer's disease: Report of the NINCSD-ADRDA work group under the auspices of Department of Health and Human Services task force on Alzheimer's disease. *Neurology* 1984;34:939-944.

4. Winograd CH, Jarvik LF: Physician management of the demented patient. *J Am Geriatr Soc* 1986;34:295-308.

5. Kane RL, Ouslander JG, Abrass IB: *Essentials of Clinical Geriatrics.* New York, McGraw-Hill Book Co, 1984.

6. Mahoney D: The role of the gerontological nurse practitioner. *Massachusetts Nurse* 1983;11:8-17.

7. Schultz PR, McGlone FB: Primary health care provided for the elderly by nurse practitioner/physician team: Analysis of cost-effectiveness. *J Am Geriatr Soc* 1977;25:443-446.

8. Simborg DW, Starfield BH, Horn SD: Physicians and non-physician health practitioners: The characteristics of their practices and their relationships. *Am J Public Health* 1978;68(11):44-48.

9. Hudak CM, Redstone PM, Hokanson NL, et al: *Clinical Protocols: A Guide For Physicians and Nurses.* Philadelphia, JB Lippincott, 1976.

10. Hoole AJ, Greenberg RA, Pickard CG: *Patient Care Guidelines for Nurse Practitioners,* ed 2. Boston, Little, Brown & Co, 1982.

11. Futrell MF, Brovender S, McKinnon-Mullett, et al: *Primary Health Care of the Older Adult.* North Scituate, Mass, Duxbury Press, 1980.

12. Office of Technology Assessment: *Losing a Million Minds: Confronting the Tragedy of Alzheimer's Disease and Other Dementias,* OTA-BA-323. Washington, D.C., U.S. Government Printing Office, 1987.

13. Gray JD, Blaschke TF: Fever: To treat or not to treat. *Rational Drug Ther* 1985;19(12):1-6.

14. Sheon RP, Van Ommen RA: Fever of obscure origin: Diagnosis and treatment bases on a series of sixty cases. *Am J Med* 1963;34:486-499.

15. Jacoby GA, Swartz MN: Fever of undetermined origin. *N Eng J Med* 1977;289:21-25.

16. Chopra S, Curtis RL: Constipation, in Walshe TM (ed): *Management of Clinical Problems in Geriatric Medicine.* Boston, Little, Brown & Co, 1985.

17. Rowe JW, Besdine RW (eds): *Health and Disease in Old Age.* Boston, Little, Brown & Co, 1982.

18. Warren JW: Catheters and catheter care. *Clinics in Geriatric Medicine* 1986;2(4):857-72.

19. Buchner DM, Larson EB: Falls and fractures in patients with Alzheimer type dementia. *JAMA* 1987;257(11):1492-1495.

20. Goodwin JS, Regan M: Cognitive dysfunction associated with naproxen and ibuprofen in the elderly. *Arthr and Rheum* 1982;25(8):1013-1015.

21. Larson EB et al: Adverse drug reactions associated with global cognitive impairment in elderly persons. *Ann Int Med* 1987;107:169-173.

22. Volicer L, Bird ED, Fabiszewski KJ: Diabetes mellitus with dementia of the Alzheimer type. (submitted for publication)

23. Hauser, WA et al: Seizures and myoclonus in patients with Alzheimer's disease. *Neurology* 1986;36:1226-30.

24. Mayeux R, Stem Y, Spanton S: Heterogeneity in dementia of the Alzheimer type: evidence of subgroups. *Neurology* 1985;35(4):453-461.

25. Wilkins D (Hallett et al): Physiologic analysis of the myoclonus of Alzheimer's disease. *Neurology* 1984;34(7):898-903.

26. Molsa PK, Marttila RJ, Rinne UK: Extrapyramidal signs in Alzheimer's disease. *Neurology* 1984;34:1114-6.

27. Leverenz J, Suni M: Parkinson's disease in patients with Alzheimer's disease. *Arch Neuro* 1987;43:662-4.

28. Ditter SM, Mirra SS. Neuropathologic and clinical features of Parkinson's disease in AD patients. *Neurology* 1987;37:754-760.

29. Levercnz (Longe): Pressure sores: Prevention and treatment. *Senior Medical Review* 1987;1(4):1-8.

Appendix 9-A

Management Guidelines

1. Format for Consolidation of Monthly Orders:

Allergies:

Diet:
    a. Double portions
    b. Force fluids or restrict fluids
    c. Nutritional supplements (e.g., Ensure, Sustacal)

Activity:
    a. With or without supervision
    b. With or without posey restraint; hand mitts as needed
    c. Privileges to leave ward on pass with relatives

Nursing:
    a. Monitoring vital signs and other parameters
    b. Dressings
    c. Treatments (e.g., chest physiotherapy)
    d. Intake and output
    e. Precautions (e.g., seizure, wound)
    f. Oral care is not a treatment (e.g., Tin-Gel) and does not require an order.
    g. Urine fractionals

Medications:
    a. Routine
    b. As needed
    c. Vitamins per recommendation of dietitian
    d. Medications per recommendation of consulting physician

Laboratory Studies:
    a. Admission profile
    b. Routine blood glucose tests
    c. Serial levels of anticonvulsants, cardiac agents, and so on

Miscellaneous:
    a. Consultations
    b. Tuberculosis testing (Mantoux skin tests)

2. All patients, unless otherwise specified, may have orders for the following medications and treatments:
    a. Minimum fluid intake of 2400 mL/24 hr
    b. Unprocessed bran, 2 to 4 tablespoonfuls daily (individualized)
    c. Metamucil, 1 to 2 tablespoonfuls orally twice daily
    d. Surfak, 240 mg orally daily, or Colace, 100 to 300 mg orally daily
    e. Milk of magnesia, 30 mL orally at bedtime, as needed
    f. Senokot, 1 tablet orally daily; may advance to twice daily as needed
    g. Perdiem granules, 1 to 2 teaspoonfuls orally daily
    h. Glycerin suppository, rectally as needed
    i. Dulcolax suppository, rectally as needed
    j. Fleet enema as needed
    k. Tylenol, 650 mg orally or rectally every 4 to 6 hours as needed for discomfort
    l. Chloral hydrate, 500 mg orally at bedtime as needed; SOS x 1 as needed or Restoril 15 mg orally at bedtime as needed: SOS x 1 as needed
3. Physiologic bowel action is preferable to use of cathartics. When appropriate, activity, a high fiber diet (unprocessed bran), proper fluid intake, gastrocolic-reflex stimulants (e.g., coffee, warm water), and establishment of a proper "habit time" should be employed.
4. All Foley catheters will be changed once a month.
5. Nasogastric and gastrostomy tubes will not be changed routinely, only when they are running sluggishly.
6. Routine vital signs are obtained once per month, unless otherwise indicated. All patients are to be weighed monthly unless otherwise indicated.
7. With regards to psychotropic/neuroleptic medications, therapy is initiated at the lowest possible dosage and then increased gradually.
8. All orders written by the nurse practitioner according to management guidelines will be countersigned by the physician within 72 hours.

SIGNATURES: _____ M.D. _____ R.N.

DATE: _____

Fever

Definition: Temperature in excess of 102°F for 24 hours or longer or septic-appearing patient who may be hypothermic or unable to mount febrile response

Parameters To Assess and Monitor:

Subjective:
1. Pain
2. Malaise
3. Fatigue
4. Duration of temperature elevation
5. Pattern of fever
6. Shaking/chills
7. Weight change
8. Night sweats
9. Stiff neck
10. Headache
11. Earache
13. Chest pain
14. Cough
15. Sputum production
16. Dyspnea
17. Abdominal pain
18. Urinary frequency
19. Dysuria
20. Foul/dark urine
21. Bone or joint pain
22. Rashes/pustules
23. Vomiting/diarrhea

Objective:
1. General
2. Integument (color, turgor, integrity)
3. Vital signs (check temperature rectally; check pulse, respirations, and blood pressure)
4. Skin: rash, wounds, petechiae, pustules/abscesses
5. Head: sinus tenderness
6. Ears: tympanic membrane inflammation, bulging, loss of landmarks
7. Throat: pharyngeal inflammation, exudate
8. Neck: stiffness
9. Nodes: lymphadenopathy, tenderness
10. Chest: rales or localized rhonchi and wheezes
11. Heart: measurement of size, auscultation for murmur or rub
12. Abdomen: tenderness, costovertebral angle tenderness, splenectomy
13. Extremities: swelling, erythema, tenderness of legs
14. Neurologic: change in mental status, focal abnormalities
15. Musculoskeletal: rule out septic joint

Assessment: Fever: Temperature elevation in excess of 102°F

Plan:
1. Attempt to determine and alleviate the underlying cause as rapidly as possible.
2. All patients may have a standing order for Tylenol 650 mg orally or rectally every 4 to 6 hours as needed for temperature in excess of 102°.
3. Force fluids; monitor intake and output until fever is reduced to 101°F for 24 hours.
4. Monitor vital signs every 4 hours and as needed monitor neurologic signs if indicated.
5. Obtain urinalysis, urine culture and sensitivity before Tylenol is administered.

6. If temperature is in excess of 103°F for 24 hours, obtain a complete blood cell count with differential, blood cultures, and chest film, if preliminary urine culture and sensitivity shows no growth.
7. Throat culture, for pertinent positive subjective and objective findings
8. Wound culture, as needed
9. Sputum for Gram stain and culture as needed for pulmonary symptomatology or abnormal chest film.
10. Rule out drug fever.
11. Comfort measures including tepid sponge baths, and so on

SIGNATURES: _____ M.D. _____ R.N.

DATE: _____

Patient Fall/Trauma

Definition: An unexpected event in which injury or potential injury occurs

Parameters To Assess and Monitor:

Subjective:
1. Pain/discomfort/swelling/erythema/bleeding
2. Loss of consciousness
3. Alteration in baseline sensorium
4. Nausea, vomiting
5. Headache

Objective:
1. General appearance (including color, evidence of laceration, abrasion)
2. Vital signs, postural blood pressure
3. Neurologic exam: include level of consciousness, pupillary reaction, funduscopic examination, motor assessment, cranial nerve check, sensory examination, reflexes, coordination, gait, and station.
4. Musculoskeletal exam: include range of motion (of affected body part) and check for evidence of deformity (including palpable defects).
5. Head, eye, ear, nose, throat exam: ear discharge, nasal discharge or bleeding behind tympanic membrane

Assessment: Fall/trauma

Plan: *Emergency Measures*:
1. Immediately call physician for patient who has hemorrhage (severe), is in shock, is unconscious, and has suspected spinal trauma.
2. Immobilize suspected fractures or patients with suspected spinal trauma.

Routine Measures:
1. Obtain roentgenogram of any obvious or suspected deformity to rule out fracture.
2. Cleanse, debride, and suture uncomplicated superficial lacerations as indicated.
3. Tetanus toxoid, 0.5 mL IM for dirty open wounds (if no booster in 5 years).
4. Obtain urinalysis and complete blood cell count, as needed.
5. Observe carefully including neurologic check and vital sign check every 4 hours for 24 hours.
6. Obtain consultation/referral to appropriate specialty in suspicious cases.

SIGNATURES: _____ M.D. _____ R.N.

DATE: _____

Rashes

1. Atopic Dermatitis

Definition: Dry thickened skin with accentuation of normal lines and folds; sometimes hyperpigmentation with chronic inflammation

Parameters To Assess and Monitor:

Subjective:
   a. Pruritus
   b. Pain/discomfort

Objective:
   a. Skin turgor
   b. Dryness
   c. Thickening/texture
   d. Hyperpigmentation
   e. Location (flexor areas of extremities, eyelids, back of the neck, and dorsum of hands and feet)
   f. Signs of second-degree bacterial infection

Assessment: Atopic Dermatitis

Plan:
   a. Prevention of further skin drying by minimizing baths and limiting use of soap to Lowila; tub bath with Alveeno or Alpha Keri as needed.
   b. Apply Eucerin cream topically to affected areas on every shift.
   c. Apply hydrocortisone 1% topically to affected areas on every shift as needed.
   d. If necessary for pruritus, an antihistamine may be administered:
     • Benadryl, 25 mg orally every 6 hours as needed
     • Atarax, 25 mg orally every 6 hours as needed
   e. Failure to respond to treatment in 2 weeks warrants consideration of dermatology consultation.

2. Seborrheic Dermatitis

Definition: An oily, scaly condition of the skin affecting areas with large numbers of sebaceous glands

Parameters To Assess and Monitor:

Subjective:
   a. Eruption (symmetrical, scaling)
   b. Point of eruption initiation (scalp, eyebrows, eyelids, nasolabial and postauricular folds, external auditory canal, presternal area, axillae, groin)
   c. Oily skin
   d. Acne

Assessment: Seborrheic dermatitis

Plan:
   a. Sebulex shampoo twice weekly
   b. 2% sulfur and 2% acid cream on skin every shift
   c. In severe cases, apply hydrocortisone 1% cream topically to affected areas every shift for 7 days; if not effective, consider a trial of fluorinated steroid preparation every 7 days.

d. Failure to respond to treatment in 2 weeks warrants consideration of dermatology consultation.

3. **Candidiasis**

    Definition: An erythematous, macular rash caused by the fungus *Candida albicans*

    Parameters To Assess and Monitor:

    Subjective:
    a. Pruritus
    b. Erythema
    c. Burning sensation/burning pain
    d. History of diabetes mellitus

    Objective:
    a. Erythema
    b. Macular rash with well-defined red, eroded patches with scaling and pustulovesicular borders
    c. Location (usually involves intertriginous areas of vulva)
    d. Whitish exudate may be present in intertriginous areas.

    Laboratory studies: Check urine for glycosuria or serum glucose if patient is diabetic.

    Assessment: Candidiasis

    Plan:
    a. In a diabetic patient treatment must begin with controlling diabetes; a physician is consulted for management after evaluation is completed.
    b. Mycostatin cream is applied to affected areas every shift for 1 week.
    c. If not effective, apply a trial of Lotrimin or Monistat cream every shift for 1 week.
    d. Failure to respond to treatment in 2 weeks warrants consideration of dermatology consultation.

4. **Scabies**

    Definition: An intensely pruritic rash caused by the mite *Sarcoptes scabiei*

    Parameters To Assess and Monitor:

    Subjective: a. Pruritus (usually more severe at night)

    Objective:
    b. Location of lesions:
    Men—interdigital folds, wrists, elbows, genitalia, ankles, feet
    Women—palms, nipples, interdigital folds, wrists, elbows, genitalia, ankles, feet
    c. Secondary lesions: excoriation, pustules and crusts of secondary bacterial infection, eczema with weeping or scaling or both

    Laboratory studies: Skin scraping for verification

    Assessment: Scabies

    Plan:
    a. Apply Kwell 1% lotion (1 ounce is sufficient) to *entire* body from neck down with special attention to hands, feet, and

intertriginous areas. Avoid contact with eyes or mucous membranes. (Precede application with warm bath using a soft brush, leave medication on for 24 hours; remove medication in a bath similar to the first.)
b. Hygiene (patient, laundry, linen)
c. Treat staff, families, other patients; consult with infection control nurse.
d. Give Benadryl, 25 mg orally every 6 hours as needed for pruritus
e. Failure to respond to treatment warrants dermatology consultation.

5. **Tinea Corporis (Ringworm)**

    Definition: Superficial fungal infection involving the trunk or limbs

    Parameters To Assess and Monitor:

    Subjective:
    a. Asymptomatic, usually
    b. Mild pruritus

    Objective:
    a. Erythematous, scaling patches (usually one or two) are round or oval.
    b. Patches start small then expand outward with clearing of eruption in the center of the patch and activity restricted to the border of the lesion.
    c. Border of the lesion is usually raised and scaly.
    d. Location: usually face and arms but can be anywhere

    Assessment: Tinea corporis

    Plan:
    a. Apply Tinactin 1% cream or solution topically every shift for 2 to 3 weeks.
    b. If no improvement, apply Lotrimin 1% cream or solution topically every shift for 2 weeks.
    c. All scalp fungal infections are to be referred for dermatology consultation.

6. **Tinea Pedis (athlete's foot)**

    Definition: A pruritic, cracking and peeling eruption of the feet, especially the toe webs

    Parameters To Assess and Monitor:

    Subjective: a. Intense pruritus of affected areas

    Objective:
    a. Cracking, peeling eruptions between the toes and occasionally with spreading to the soles and sides and tops of feet
    b. Vesicles may or may not be present
    c. Toenails thickened
    d. Fungal infection of hands and/or dry skin

    Assessment: Tinea pedis

    Plan:
    a. Hygiene (thorough washing and drying, application of absorbent cotton socks)

b. Apply Burow's solution soaks twice daily for 20 to 30 minutes if vesicles present.
   c. Use Tinactin powder or cream topically every shift for 2 weeks.
   d. Apply Mycostatin cream topically every shift for 2 weeks if Tinactin is ineffective
   e. Failure to respond to treatment warrants consideration of dermatology consultation.

7. **Eczematous Dermatitis**

   Definition: A chronic skin condition characterized by erythematous, papular, or vesicular lesions

   Parameters To Assess and Monitor:

   Subjective:
   a. Pruritus
   b. Local edema
   c. Vesiculation may or may not be present
   d. Scaling/crushing
   e. Weeping
   f. Fissuring
   g. Skin thickening may occur

   Assessment: Eczematous dermatitis

   Plan:
   a. Remove the allergen or primary irritant if condition is exogenous.
   b. Apply Hydrocortisone 1%, Valisone 0.1%, Synalar 0.01%, or Kenalog 0.25% topically every shift to affected areas for 10 days.
   c. Failure to respond to treatment warrants consideration of dermatology consultation.

SIGNATURES: _____ M.D. _____ R.N.

DATE: _____

Herpes Zoster (Shingles)

Definition: An acute vesicular eruption, distributed along the dermatones of infected nerve roots, usually localized to the face or trunk (unilaterally), and caused by reactivation of a latent viral infection.

Parameters To Assess and Monitor:

Subjective: 1. Pain usually precedes eruption of lesions by 48 hours and may be quite severe.

Objective:
1. Fever
2. Integument: eruption begins with red macules and progresses sequentially to papules, vesicles, pustules and crusts, usually resolving in 1 to 2 weeks; it follows a dermatomic pattern and usually affects thoracic and cervical nerve roots.
3. Regional lymph glands may be enlarged with tenderness.
4. Ensure no ocular involvement.

Assessment: Herpes Zoster

Plan:
1. Consult with physician on need for serum antibody level or hyperimmune studies.
2. Apply calamine lotion topically to rash every shift or Burow's solution soaks to vesicles or crusts for 30 minutes every 4 hours.
3. Give Tylenol 650 mg orally or rectally every 4 hours as needed for discomfort or temperature greater than 102°F.

SIGNATURES: _____ M.D. _____ R.N.

DATE: _____

Constipation

Definition: Excessive hardness of stool that may result in a decrease in frequency from the patient's usual elimination routine.

Parameters To Assess and Monitor:

Subjective:
1. Hard stools
2. Difficulty in moving bowels; pain on defecation
3. Decreased frequency of bowel movements
4. Abdominal distention
5. The absence of abdominal pain, nausea, vomiting, or history of blood in stools

Objective:
1. Check skin turgor and mucous membranes for dehydration.
2. Abdominal exam:
   - *inspection*
   - *palpation*: no abdominal tenderness should be present
   - *percussion*
   - *auscultation*: bowel sounds should be present without hyperactive rushes or tinkles
3. Rectal exam: check for fecal impaction; order stool guaiac test.

Assessment: Constipation

Plan:
1. Attempt to determine the underlying cause and alleviate it (e.g., discontinue opiates, hydration, increase activity level if feasible).
2. Obtain nutrition consultation for high-fiber diet.
3. Give unprocessed bran, 2 to 4 tablespoonfuls orally every morning (individualized).
4. Give milk of magnesia, 30 mL orally at bedtime as needed.
5. Give Dulcolax suppository rectally every 3 days as needed.
6. Remainder of bowel regimen is per management guidelines/ward policy.
7. Sigmoidoscopy per ward physician is ordered in unusual/extreme cases of failure to respond to conservative treatment.
8. Surgical consultation is needed after three reports of guaiac-positive stools or any suspicion of an acute abdominal condition.
9. If problem persists for unexplained reasons, order electrolytes, calcium, and/or thyroid studies.

SIGNATURES: _____ M.D. _____ R.N.

DATE: _____

Abdominal Pain/Distention

Definition: Subjective or objective discomfort or distress localized to the abdominal area

Parameters To Assess and Monitor:

Subjective:
1. Pain:
   - location, radiation, if any
   - character
   - onset
   - course
   - duration of each episode
   - precipitating, ameliorating, aggravating factors
   - relationship to activity, position, meals, defecation
2. Abnormal distention
3. Eructation or passage of flatus
4. Use of gastrointestinal irritants (caffeine, alcohol, medications)
5. Appetite
6. Nausea, vomiting
7. Change in bowel habits
8. Urinary symptomatology

Objective:
1. Anxiety, nervousness, depression
2. Weight loss
3. Fever
4. Cardiac exam
5. Abdominal exam: *inspection*: symmetry
   palpation: tenderness; mass; rigidity; guarding; costovertebral angle tenderness
   percussion: check for shifting dullness, distended bladder, fluid wave
   auscultation: presence and quality of bowel sounds
6. Rectal exam: check for fecal impaction, rectal mass, tenderness; check stool guaiac
7. Laboratory studies: stool guaiac test, complete blood cell count with differential, electrolytes, blood urea nitrogen, creatinine with fever; may obtain urinalysis, urine culture and sensitivity

Assessment: Abdominal pain/distention

Plan:
1. Goal is to determine the underlying cause and alleviate it.
2. If fever is present, obtain complete blood cell count with differential, electrolytes, blood urea nitrogen, creatinine, urinalysis and urine for culture and sensitivity; consider obtaining liver function tests, serum amylase, and kidney/ureter/bladder film.
3. If aerophagia is suspected, consider trial of simethicone (Mylicon), 50 mg orally three times a day with meals and/or rectal tube as needed.

4. If gastritis is suggested, consider trial of antacid 30 mL orally after meals and at bedtime; if persistent and patient is not acutely ill, obtain upper gastrointestinal film and/or barium enema study.
5. If acute abdomen is suspected, give patient nothing by mouth and obtain surgical consultation stat.
6. If cardiac etiology is suspected, obtain electrocardiogram with rhythm strip and contact physician.
7. Give mild nonnarcotic analgesics (e.g., Tylenol 650 mg orally or rectally every 4 to 6 hours as needed).
8. Review medication list (e.g., nonsteroidal anti-inflammatory drugs).

SIGNATURES: _____ M.D. _____ R.N.

DATE: _____

Diarrhea

Definition: Frequent passage of watery bowel movements that are in variation from usual bowel pattern

Parameters To Assess and Monitor:

Subjective:
1. Abdominal pain
2. Cramping
3. Nausea/vomiting
4. Anorexia
5. Food intolerance
6. Recent dietary changes
7. Duration of symptoms
8. Character and frequency of stools (include presence of blood, pus, or mucus)
9. Usual bowel habit
10. Use of cathartics or antibiotics
11. Pain on defecation

Objective:
1. Temperature, pulse, respiration, blood pressure
2. Skin turgor
3. Mucous membrane inspection
4. Abdominal exam: note distention, tenderness (diffuse, localized, and/or rebound), the presence of hyperactive bowel sounds (as opposed to high-pitched rushes or tinkles)
5. Rectal exam: rule out fecal impaction; order guaiac stool test.

Assessment: Diarrhea

Plan:
1. Goal is to determine cause and alleviate it; treatment is symptomatic.
2. Give clear liquid diet until 24 hours without diarrhea (resting gastrointestinal tract).
3. Monitor intake and output to ensure sufficient hydration.
4. Hold antacids, laxatives, if patient is on any; reassess need for antibiotic continuance if patient is receiving any.
5. If diarrhea persists for more than 24 hours or if patient has more than four stools in one day, administer Kaopectate 60 mL after each loose stool (not to exceed six times/day).
6. If Kaopectate is ineffective, administer Lomotil 1 tablet orally four times a day until diarrhea stops.
7. If Kaopectate is ineffective, administer Paregoric 1 teaspoonful orally every 4 hours (not to exceed 4 teaspoonfuls/day); may substitute deodorized tincture of opium (D.T.O.), 6 drops orally every 6 hours as needed for Paregoric.
8. If patient is on tube feeding or nutritional supplements, consult with dietitian as needed and reduce osmolality of fluids being administered.
9. If diarrhea persists for more than 36 hours or if patient demonstrates symptoms of dehydration, obtain electrolytes, complete blood cell count with differential, and stool specimens

for culture and sensitivity, fecal leukocytes, *Clostridium difficile*, and ova and parasites. In addition, an intravenous line of $D_5 1/2NS$ with 40 mEq KCl/L at 100 mL/hr will be initiated. The need for a kidney/ureter/bladder film or plain film of the abdomen will be addressed.
10. Order proctoscopy on ward by attending physician as needed.
11. Surgical consultation will be sought for persistent bloody stools, rebound tenderness, or diarrhea persisting for more than 72 hours.

SIGNATURES: _____ M.D. _____ R.N.

DATE: _____

Urinary Tract Infection

Definition: A bacterial infection of the kidneys, collecting system of the kidneys, or bladder, or a combination of these

Parameters To Assess and Monitor:

Subjective:
1. Dysuria
2. Frequency
3. Urgency
4. Incontinence (sudden onset)
5. Flank and/or suprapubic pain
6. Fever/chills

Objective:
1. Fever in excess of 101.5°F for 24 hours (unexplained)
2. Lethargy/irritability/anorexia
3. Lower abdominal tenderness
4. Costovertebral angle tenderness
5. Hematuria, pyuria

Laboratory:
1. Urine for routine analysis (check white and red blood cell counts and/or bacteria)
2. Urine (clean voided specimen) for culture and sensitivity (check colony count)

Assessment: Urinary tract infection

Plan:
1. Only symptomatic infections will be treated (recurrent infections tend to be refractory to treatment).
2. Force fluids, as tolerated, to induce diuresis and flush out urinary tract.
3. Allergies will be checked and documented.
4. Pending sensitivity validation:
   a. Oral antibiotics that the organism is sensitive to will always be used initially.
   b. Sulfonamides are the drug of choice: give Bactrim, 2 tablets orally twice daily for 10 days.
   c. Cephalosporins are the second drug of choice: give Keflex, 500 mg orally four times a day for 10 days (or Keflin, 500 mg IV every 6 hours for 10 days).
   d. Broad-spectrum antibiotics are third choice: give ampicillin, 500 mg orally four times a day for 10 days, or tetracycline, 500 mg orally four times a day for 10 days.
   e. Physician consultation will be sought prior to initiation of therapy with an aminoglycoside.
   Specific dosage will vary depending on appearance of patient; usually 1 g/day is sufficient if only lower urinary tract is involved.
5. Urinalysis and urine culture and sensitivity will be obtained 48 hours after initiation of antibiotic therapy and 48 hours after discontinuance of antibiotics.
6. Urologic consultation will be sought in the event of recurrent urinary tract infections with particular reference to prophylaxis

(Mandelamine, Hiprex, ascorbic acid) and the indication for further diagnostic testing (intravenous pyelography, cystometrograms, cystourethroscopy).
7. Patients on aminoglycosides should have the following laboratory studies monitored: serial blood urea nitrogen, creatinine, and peak and trough serum levels 24 hours after therapy initiation, or before and after third dose, whichever comes first, then every 72 hours for duration of therapy.

SIGNATURES: _____ M.D. _____ R.N.

DATE: _____

Conjunctivitis

Definition: Inflammation of the eyelid or bulbar conjunctiva, or both

Parameters To Assess and Monitor:

Subjective:
1. Eye pain
2. Irritation
3. Mild photophobia
4. Excessive lacrimation
5. Unilateral or bilateral

Objective:
1. Integument (e.g., seborrheic dermatitis)
2. Eye examination: injected conjunctiva; presence of hordeolum
   a. Discharge:
      - purulent in bacterial infection
      - mucopurulent in viral infection
      - mucoid and stringy or watery in allergic reaction
   b. Conjunctival edema
   c. Clear cornea
   d. Normal pupillary size and reaction to light
3. Laboratory studies: culture and sensitivity of discharge

Assessment: Conjunctivitis

Plan:
1. If conjunctivitis is caused by allergy, attempt to eliminate exposure to allergic elements; apply cool compresses every 4 hours to minimize discomfort.
2. If conjunctivitis is mild and associated with upper respiratory tract infection, no specific treatment is indicated.
3. If hordeolum or chalazion is concurrently present, apply warm compresses for 20 minutes four times a day.
4. Obtain culture and sensitivity of discharge if condition is not responsive to treatment in 48 hours.
5. Apply Ilotycin ophthalmic ointment to affected eye(s) twice daily for 10 days; check sensitivities when available.
6. If patient is able to watch television, use sodium sulfacetamide 10% (Sulamyd) 2 drops to affected eyes every 4 hours with Ilotycin at bedtime.
7. Neosporin or garamycin may be substituted for Ilotycin or Sulamyd as needed for specific symptomatology or sensitivities. If drops, apply every 2 to 4 hours; if ointment, twice daily application is sufficient.
8. Perform lid hygiene with baby shampoo twice daily for 10 days and as needed.
9. Ophthalmologic consultation will be ordered if symptoms fail to respond to treatment.

SIGNATURES: _____ M.D. _____ R.N.

DATE: _____

Nausea/Vomiting

Definition: Inclination of or actual ejection through the mouth of gastric contents

Parameters To Assess and Monitor:

Subjective:
1. Onset of symptoms (relationship to meals, position change, medication administration)
2. Duration of symptoms
3. Associated abdominal pain or discomfort (location of pain)
4. Anorexia (or change in appetite)
5. Constipation (or recent change in bowel habit)
6. Diarrhea
7. Fever
8. Headache
9. Hematuria
10. Chest pain

Objective:
1. Vital signs
2. Skin turgor
3. Mucous membrane inspection
4. Abdominal exam: check for distention, firmness, organomegaly, tenderness, the presence of bowel sounds in all four quadrants, masses, pain, rebound tenderness, and shifting dullness.
5. Rectal exam: rule out impaction, mass. Obtain guaiac stool test.
6. Describe vomitus (amount, color, consistency, duration of vomiting, odor, projectile, guaiac).

Assessment: Nausea/vomiting

Plan:
1. Goal is to determine underlying cause and alleviate it; treatment is symptomatic.
2. If viral in etiology, usually symptoms improve spontaneously within 24 to 48 hours.
3. Restrict dietary intake to clear liquids as tolerated for duration of symptoms.
4. Give compazine, 25 mg orally, rectally, or intramuscularly every 6 hours as needed, or Vistaril, 25 mg orally or intramuscularly every 6 hours as needed, or Benadryl, 25 mg orally every 4 to 6 hours as needed for patient distress.
5. With symptoms of dehydration in a patient with nausea and vomiting of 12 hours duration, the patient will be kept NPO, a nasogastric tube will be passed and attached to low intermittent suction for decompression, and an IV of $D_5 1/2NS$ with 20 mEq KCl/L at 100 mL/hr will be initiated.
6. Intake and output will be monitored.
7. Failure of symptoms to improve after 24 hours warrants kidney/ureter/bladder film or plain film of the abdomen, electrolytes, and complete blood cell count.

8. If acute abdomen is suspected or evident, or with frank hematemesis, surgical consultation will be ordered.
9. Review medication list (e.g., nonsteroidal anti-inflammatory drugs).

SIGNATURES: _____ M.D. _____ R.N.

DATE: _____

Seizure/Seizure Disorder

Definition: Clonic or tonic muscular contractions, or both, usually associated with unconsciousness, sometimes accompanied by salivation and followed by incontinence

Parameters To Assess and Monitor:

Subjective: 1. May or may not have classic cry at seizure onset

Objective:
1. Description from aura to postictal phenomenon: headache, drowsiness, confusion, sore tongue, motor activity, focal neurologic abnormalities, disturbance of thought, repetitive behavior, unconsciousness, incontinence
2. Predisposing factors:
   a. Hyperpyrexia
   b. Subtherapeutic anticonvulsant level
   c. Abrupt change in metabolic products
   d. Brain tumor or injury
   e. Cardiac arrhythmia
   f. Cerebral infarct
   g. Infective process
   h. Recent head injury
   i. Malignancy
3. Vital signs
4. Eyes: extraocular muscles and funduscopic exam
5. Mouth: trauma
6. Ears: discharge
7. Neck: jugular venous pressure, carotid bruits, nuchal rigidity
8. Cardiac exam: inspection, palpation, percussion, auscultation
9. Pulmonary exam: inspection, palpation, percussion, auscultation
10. Neurologic exam: cranial nerves, motor, sensory, reflexes, level of consciousness
11. Laboratory studies: check SMA-18 (particularly glucose, calcium, sodium) and magnesium and obtain complete blood cell count with differential; check serum anticonvulsant level.

Assessment: Seizure/seizure disorder

Plan:
1. Laboratory studies: check glucose, calcium, sodium, magnesium, and serum anticonvulsant level (if on anticonvulsants); also, complete blood cell count with differential.
2. If initial seizure, obtain electrocardiogram, electroencephalogram, and computerized axial tomogram (individualized if recent testing has been completed).
3. Consider neurologic consultation; question need for lumbar puncture, further diagnostic workup.
4. For seizure in progress:
   a. Do not restrain, maintain airway; suction as needed.
   b. Pad surrounding area to prevent injury.
   c. Use soft mouth gag if jaw is open.

d. For seizure activity (tonic-clonic) more than 3 minutes in duration, initiate IV of normal saline and administer 1 ampule of 50% dextrose.
　　　e. For seizure activity more than 5 minutes in duration, administer Valium 1 mg/min IV push until seizure stops and page physician stat.
　　　f. Administer oxygen at 3 L via nasal cannula if seizure persists for more than 5 minutes.
　5. Post seizure:
　　　a. Maintain at bed rest for 4 hours.
　　　b. Order seizure precautions.
　　　c. Check vital signs and neurologic signs every hour for four times.
　　　d. Give nothing by mouth until responsive.
　6. Notify physician if anticonvulsant levels are outside of therapeutic range for medication adjustment.
　7. Status epilecticus: stat neurologic consult and start initial IV of normal saline at KVO rate.
　8. Follow-up: individualized per attending physician

SIGNATURES: _____ M.D. _____ R.N.

DATE: _____

CHAPTER 10

Ethical Issues in the Treatment of Advanced Alzheimer Dementia: Hospice Approach

Ladislav Volicer, Yvette L. Rheaume, June Brown, Kathy J. Fabiszewski, and Roger J. Brady

Much attention has been focused recently on the plight of terminally ill patients. It is recognized that it is increasingly difficult to achieve "death with dignity" if modern medical technology is used indiscriminately.[1] Furthermore, there is concern that the cost of intensive medical care for terminally ill patients may divert funds from more fruitful medical or public health interventions.[2] Thus the use of medical technology in the care of terminally ill patients creates a problem that combines both ethical and economic issues.

Alzheimer's Disease As a Terminal Illness

Dementia of the Alzheimer type is a progressive degenerative disorder. There is no treatment to stop or reverse progression of the disease. Therefore, the disease could be considered a terminal illness in the same way as is an incurable cancer. However, although Alzheimer dementia destroys higher brain functions, it affects the function of other organs much less. Many patients survive into a stage in which they lose their independence, ability to walk, and finally even responsiveness to any sensory stimuli. Some patients even lose the ability to swallow food and liquids and are fed by a nasogastric or a gastrostomy tube. To describe complete loss of higher brain functions in advanced dementia of Alzheimer type, the term "mentally dead" is used[3]; this condition is also called a "persistent vegetative state."[4,5]

Despite this vegetative condition, patients may survive for years if intensive medical care is provided. Intensive medical care also includes careful monitoring for the first sign of possible infection and vigorous treatment, using the most potent parenteral antibiotics if necessary.

Treatment of an infection requires a multitude of diagnostic procedures, which include chest roentgenograms; sputum, blood, and urine cultures; and arterial blood gas analysis. These procedures are often uncomfortable or painful, especially if a confused patient has to be restrained in order to obtain a blood or sputum sample. The treatment itself may lead to discomfort if it requires restraining the patients to prevent their removal of intravenous lines or if painful intramuscular injections are required.

In addition, even routine nursing care inflicts discomfort for these patients, requiring moving contracted limbs for bathing, forcing the patients to open their mouth and swallow for hydration and nutrition, inserting catheters for urinary elimination, and so on. Therefore, the following question is often posed by those who provide the care for the patient: Are these diagnostic procedures and treatments prolonging life or merely prolonging dying?

The optimal medical care for patients suffering from advanced dementia of the Alzheimer type should balance the benefits of care against the suffering caused by the treatment. If the treatment merely prolongs the patient's suffering, without any hope for improvement in his or her condition, then prolongation of life may not be in the patient's best interest. A hospice approach that concentrates on measures that are necessary to keep a patient comfortable, without striving for maximal survival time, without hastening death, but allowing its natural process, may be more appropriate for patients with advanced Alzheimer dementia.[6]

Decisions To Limit the Scope of Medical Care

Until relatively recently physicians were expected to make all decisions regarding the extent of medical care. Very often patients were not even informed about the nature of their disease. However, this paternalistic attitude was discredited when courts established that a competent person has a right to refuse medical treatment if he or she considers it useless or if it involves too great a burden.[7] The hospice movement is using this approach in the care of terminally ill patients. Unfortunately, the use of hospices for the treatment of incompetent patients is hindered by legal considerations. However, these considerations should not limit a person's right not to be exposed to treatment that does not lead to meaningful improvement or that involves a great burden.

The main unresolved question is how to make a decision limiting the medical care of an incompetent patient. There are three possible ways to arrive at such a decision. The first is the extension of the old paternalistic medical model that presumes that a physician is able to decide impartially and compassionately which course of action to take in an individual case. The second lets the courts decide the course of action, and yet another method is to use the wishes of the patient that were expressed before he or she became incompetent. This approach uses either "living will" documents or reports of family members about the person's wishes expressed verbally.

The decision making by a physician is not a satisfactory alternative. The training of physicians is more and more oriented toward technical aspects of medical care. Modern medical care is often fragmented because it is provided by several physicians with different specialties. It also involves many other professionals such as nurses and social workers who might have differing opinions about what constitutes optimal medical care for an individual patient. Even if a physician could decide such a course of action it might not be desirable. The danger exists that the physician would take into consideration his or her perception of the quality of life of a patient. Quality of life is an elusive concept that is extremely subjective and could be easily misinterpreted. As stated by Hufeland more than 150 years ago, "If a physician presumes to take into consideration in his work whether a life has value or not, the consequences are boundless and the physician becomes the most dangerous man in the state."[8]

The decision making by a physician is influenced by fear of malpractice suits. This fear leads to a legalistic approach to medical care decisions that is based on the principle that only a court proceeding can satisfy requirements of a proper process.[9] However, there are several arguments against asking courts to make medical decisions for incompetent patients. The court proceedings are expensive and usually time consuming. Medical decisions often have to be made very rapidly when the patient's condition changes. It is also possible to argue that a judge is not competent to make medical decisions and that the government should not be asked to decide how an incompetent person should die.[10]

Limiting the extent of medical care in incompetent patients relies on explicit or implied wishes the person expressed before he or she became incompetent. These wishes might be in the form of a "living will," oral directions to a family member about what should be done if the person becomes mentally debilitated, or informal discussion with a family member about the plight of debilitated people in general. Although making decisions about one's own life, which would apply when one is unable to make a decision, is an appealing idea, it has some disadvantages. It is impossible to predict ahead of time all the various situations and options that might apply, or to describe precisely when a decision (e.g., withdrawal of a treatment) should be executed. The "living will" could be, of course, worded in general terms, but then it provides little guidance in a specific situation. In addition, the legal status of "living wills" is at present unclear in some states. Same lawyers recommend that instead of making a "living will" a person should give a durable power of attorney to a trusted relative or friend who would make the necessary decisions if the person is incapacitated.

Most Alzheimer patients do not have a living will and many also did not discuss treatment options and limitations with their family members prior to onset of symptoms. In that situation it is possible to rely on the substituted judgment expressed by a family member or a court-appointed guardian.[9] However, it would be a mistake to ask for a decision without providing guidance. The family members and guardians have often limited background and understanding of medical problems that have to be resolved. Furthermore, asking a family member to make a decision may place too great a burden on him or her. It is very difficult to be in a position in which one feels that he or she has to decide about the life and death of a loved one. In addition, family members might have differing opinions and a disagreement might split the families.

The optimal way of making a decision about medical care for an incompetent patient should include participation of staff members involved in the direct care and as many family members as possible. The goal is to establish a "moral community" that can work together in harmony.[11] This does not preclude disagreement because all possible inputs and solutions should be considered. However, a process has to be established by which these disagreements are resolved and by which a consensus is achieved.

Description of a Formal Hospice Approach Program

The need for close interaction between the staff at the Geriatric Research Education Clinical Center of E.N. Rogers Memorial Veterans Hospital and the families of patients was recognized from the beginning of the Alzheimer program in 1978. Periodic meetings between an interdisciplinary team and family members were instituted to discuss questions regarding optimal medical management, use of tube feeding in patients with swallowing difficulties, and autopsy permission in the event of a patient's death.[12] An urgent need for ethical considerations in the management of patients was also recognized and a symposium discussing these problems was organized.[13] In spite of these efforts, the management of individual patients was still inconsistent, and patients with intercurrent illnesses were often transferred to an acute medical unit for aggressive treatment not available on the ward. This was partly due to the delayed recognition of the legality of "Do Not Resuscitate" orders by the Veterans Administration (in 1983) and partly due to the lack of explicit philosophy underlying the approach to the management of patients with advanced Alzheimer dementia.

This philosophy was formulated in the spring of 1985. We began with the premise that because we are unable to improve or cure the dementia, it is possible to consider it a terminal disease similar to incurable cancer. Many patients with incurable cancer choose hospice treatment over aggressive chemotherapy, irradiation, or surgery because they prefer increased comfort over maximal survival time. We believed that a similar approach was appropriate also for patients with advanced Alzheimer dementia,[6] and instituted a formal hospice approach program.

The first step included the designation of specific levels of care. This avoided uncertainty about the extent of appropriate medical care, which is especially stressful for nurses who were left to make the minute-by-minute decisions about the management strategy, in the absence of an attending physician. The first four levels were similar to those described by Besdine,[14] and the fifth was added to specify handling of feeding difficulties. These levels of care are as follows[15]:

1. The patient receives an aggressive diagnostic workup, treatment of coexisting medical conditions, and transfer to an acute-care unit if necessary. In the event of a cardiopulmonary arrest, resuscitation is attempted. Tube feeding is used if normal food intake is not possible.
2. The patient receives complete care as defined above but resuscitation is not attempted in the event of cardiac or respiratory arrest ("do not resuscitate" [DNR]).
3. This level involves DNR and no transfer to an acute-care unit for medical management of intercurrent life-threatening illnesses. This eliminates use of respirators, cardiovascular support, and so on, which are available only in an acute medical setting.
4. This care level includes DNR, no transfer to acute-care unit, and no workup and antibiotic treatment of life-threatening infections (pneumonia, urinary tract infection). Only antipyretics and analgesics are used to ensure patient comfort. Partial isolation techniques are used for staff protection.
5. Supportive care is given as defined above but eliminating tube feeding by a nasogastric tube or gastrostomy when normal food intake is not possible. Fluids necessary for hydration are provided orally only if the patient is not comatose.

Assignment of Optimal Care Levels

Assignment of an optimal care level to an individual patient involves a several step procedure. The patient is initially observed for a 3- to 4-month period to determine his or her level of cognitive and functional abilities. Variables observed include the degree of patient's contact or interaction with the environment, coexisting medical conditions that increase the patient's discomfort (e.g., contractures, decubitus ulcers), and expressions of discomfort exhibited by the patient (grimacing, vocalization). On the basis of this observation, the nursing staff and the attending physician develop a consensus regarding an optimal care level for this particular patient. This consensus is used as a guideline for discussion with the patient's family, which takes place when the family meets with the interdisciplinary team. The team includes the head nurse and/or other nurses from the unit, a social worker, a nurse practitioner, the attending physician, and a chaplain. The importance of involvement of a social worker and a chaplain in the meeting with the patient's family is described in separate sections later in this chapter.

The meeting is usually started by the social worker, who knows the family members best. Many family members of our patients participate in support groups for spouses or adult children of Alzheimer patients (see Chapter 3). The social worker introduces the purpose of the meeting and asks the family members if they have any questions that they would like to present. The head nurse and nurse practitioner describe their perception of the patient's condition and the behavior of the patient when the family is not visiting. After the questions are answered the attending physician explains the hospice approach to care of Alzheimer patients. The physician states that the main goal of the treatment is to keep patients comfortable because nothing can be done to stop or reverse Alzheimer dementia. He or she explains that this approach is not consistent with aggressive medical procedures that increase discomfort of the patients. The physician then asks if the patient, before he or she became demented, expressed any wishes regarding survival in a debilitated state or with the help of machines. The staff recommendation is then presented in terms of decisions regarding resuscitation, use of respirators and other machines for support of failing physiological functions, use of antibiotics, and use of artificial feeding.

The staff explains that aggressive medical measures are very stressful for confused patients, who do not understand the need for a respirator, intravenous lines, and feeding tubes. The patients often try to remove these devices and have to be prevented from doing so by being restrained in a bed or a gerichair or by being medicated. The physical restraint is especially stressful for patients who are still able to walk by themselves. The staff explains that in the late stages of Alzheimer dementia even antibiotic therapy can produce unjustifiable discomfort. Optimal antibiotic therapy requires blood drawing, sputum suctioning, and sometimes intravenous drug administration. In contrast, comfort measures, which include drugs to prevent pain and fever, provide immediate relief of symptoms. Osler's statement that "pneumonia is the friend of the aged"[16] is quoted to support the suggestion that in some cases it is better to "let nature take its course." The issue of feeding by a nasogastric tube, if a patient develops swallowing difficulties, is also discussed. It is stressed that limited care does not mean abandoning patient's needs and that feeding of a patient with swallowing difficulties is continued even if a decision not to use a nasogastric tube is reached.

The presentation and discussion is modified according to the optimal level of care staff recommended and according to the previous wishes of the patient. If the recommendation is for level 3 and the patient has no swallowing difficulties, levels 4 and 5 are not discussed. However, in some cases the family members mention spontaneously that they do not want tubes used for feeding. Thus some patients are assigned to level 3 care and would receive antibiotics for infections but would not receive food and liquids by a nasogastric tube.

The team participants in the conference make suggestions to the family regarding optimal level of care. These suggestions attempt to shift the burden of initiative away from the family members without exerting a pressure to accept these recommendations. We attempt to create an atmosphere of mutual empowerment in which the staff defers to family member(s) for the final decision, which then provide the staff with the authority for patient management in an acute situation. The presence of a hospital chaplain is invaluable in providing spiritual support and answering ethical concerns. It is stressed during the discussion that a decision reached at the conference can be changed at any time if the family requests it. The family members present at the conference are also encouraged to discuss the conference and the decisions with other family members who were unable to attend.

After the family conference, a written summary of the discussion is prepared, signed by all participants, and sent to the family members who attended the conference. In a cover letter, each family member is asked to review the summary and either to sign it if he or she agrees with it or to ask for modifications. Another copy of the summary, marked "interim report," is included in the front of the patient's hospital chart and explicit limitations of medical care are specified on the order sheet (e.g., "Do not transfer to an acute medical unit."). When the original summary is signed by the family members it is substituted for the interim report. The level of care assignment is reviewed every month and the conference is repeated if the patient's condition changes significantly.

Role of the Social Worker in the Hospice Approach

To suppose that making the decision that would limit medical care is a simple process is to deny the variables of being human. It would be arrogant to suggest that there is only one correct decision. Although the treatment team may be fully in accord in proposing to limit medical care, the attempt to persuade an uncertain spouse or reluctant children may impose severe emotional distress, and may be an abuse of power.

All concerned family members are encouraged to participate in the family conference when treatment recommendations are presented. Often, in a supportive arena, where the educational process encourages questions and allows for the differing perspectives of spouse, children, and siblings, family members are able to develop a consensus for their decisions. They are then better able to support and comfort one another through the course of the patient's illness. The social worker, as facilitator for the family conference, must represent the families as he or she would the patient, if the patient were able to verbalize his or her wishes. The social worker must be "in tune" with family members lest their sometimes small voice be lost amid those of the "giants" wielding the power and mystique of the medical profession.

Many mourning spouses can speak well and confidently for themselves, either concurring with the team recommendations or opposing them. However, there are others who need help to hear what is difficult to hear because of the painful nature of content and to say or do what they want but fear. Often they need help to put the issues into a framework they understand or to help the team to understand them.

For example, an elderly woman, hearing the recommendation to not prolong the dying process may hear only that she is being asked to stop caring for her husband. For some, the "do not resuscitate" order may seem to be a betrayal of the marriage vow, a violation of a most sacred oath. The social worker must be alert to the needs of a spouse who may be unable to express his or her feelings. Without the explanation that is needed for the specific situation and needs, the spouse may reject a plan that most clearly represents his or her standards for care. Or the spouse may, with an inability to resist the perceived authority represented, agree to a plan, only to go home and revise the decision, feeling ashamed and alienated. If the courage to change his or her mind does not come, the spouse may live with a sense of guilt for "abandoning" the patient.

A spouse who is comfortable with the decision for limited medical care can meet unexpected resistance from children. The social worker can be alert to this possibility, to the reality that supporting this decision is for some children (no matter what age) the ultimate disobedience against the ill parent. This may be too frightening a decision to bear. At other times, when the children are placed in a role reversal, they need the assistance in making a decision that the grieving spouse of a patient is unable to do. Resistance to limited medical care is sometimes based on a lack of understanding. When a loving adult child asks, "If I say 'yes', is this murdering my father?" the team may feel outraged or painfully uncomfortable. However, to flee from this directness of thought and feeling is insensitive and irresponsible.

There are many variables in the family life that contribute to the decision-making process of family members. The social worker may be aware of some of them and must always attempt to accommodate any of them. Religious and cultural traditions can be immutable guidelines. What outsiders might think can be a fearful pressure to one uncertain or unable to express how he or she thinks. The family member can be helped with fuller explanations and by guidance toward articulating his or her own thoughts and wishes.

Through the lonely vigil, the dying of a beloved family member is incredibly sad. At times the overwhelming feelings create for the families an unremitting wish for death to end the hurting for both the patient and themselves. Families can be helped to know that the wish for death is not the acceptance of an act of murder. The suffering family members must be helped to avoid making decisions from only despair or rage. The social worker can help them support what is most noble in themselves so that they gain comfort and pride in their acts. We must respect the spouse who can only cling to the remaining spark of life and love that was. To fight long after the battle is lost may not be a measure of the life that is left in the victim but the spouse's fear of the void that comes after the patient's death.

Spiritual Care of the Alzheimer Patient and Family

There is a crucial need to minister to the family of the Alzheimer patient. Long before the patient is hospitalized it is the family, and in particular the spouse, who is the principal caregiver. The marriage commitment "in sickness and in health" is viewed most seriously by the spouse who believes that it is his or her responsibility to care for the patient until he or she is physically unable to do so.

A patient's spouse can become angry: angry with God, with children, and with others. He or she may even question the existence of a Merciful God who would allow such human suffering. The spouse needs someone to listen to him or her. There is the need to articulate the feelings of anger and resentment that surface even while trying to provide loving care to a spouse who does not respond.

The chaplain and the pastoral care team allow the spouse to vent his or her feelings about the real issues troubling him or her once the patient is admitted to the hospital. The pastoral caregiver with good listening skills will always provide enough time to permit the spouse to talk freely, and needs to affirm the spouse's devotion, compassion, and dedication.

On admission, every patient is visited by a chaplain. This gives us an opportunity to evaluate the patient to determine how we can best meet his or her religious needs. These needs differ according to each patient's religion. Most of our patients are of the Catholic faith. There is a small number of these patients who receive communion regularly. Those who cannot receive it are given a blessing when a member of the pastoral care team makes ward rounds. Once the death appears imminent, the chaplain is called to administer the "Sacrament of the Sick and/or Prayers for the Gravely Ill." It is comforting and reassuring to the family to know that the patient's spiritual needs are being met even though the needs may be limited.

A number of patients attend chapel services from time to time, accompanied by a staff member or family member. One patient attends mass every Sunday with his wife and two sons. After mass they have breakfast together off the hospital grounds. It is interesting to note that this patient acts appropriately and even joins in the prayers in a devout manner during the celebration of mass.

The presence of the chaplain at the family meetings, at which questions are discussed regarding optimal medical management with the staff, is both supportive and valued. Such meetings with clergy present "give permission" for family members to ask questions that deal directly with ethical and moral questions regarding life and death. It can also be a learning experience for families who need to know more about advanced Alzheimer dementia. The chaplain as a teacher explains the Judeo-Christian tradition that holds that all human life is a gift of God and needs to be protected and fostered. The chaplain as ethicist points out the values and norms to be appropriated when trying to make a practical decision in particular cases.

Finally, pastoral care needs to embrace and affirm the hospital caregivers in their difficult task of treating the Alzheimer patient. The heroic efforts of the physicians and nursing staff in maintaining the patient's comfort and quality of life are extraordinary. The kindness and sensitivity demonstrated by a treatment team that genuinely cares about each patient have a rippling effect within the hospital community. A healthy attitude that is shared by such a team can transform a hospital ward into a sanctuary of hope and healing.

Results of Experience with the Hospice Approach

The introduction of the hospice approach to management of patients with advanced dementia of the Alzheimer type was well accepted by the nursing staff. Only 2 nurses of 31 requested reassignment to a different unit, and 1 of these requested to be transferred back a year later. Physicians and members of the nursing staff recommended similar optimal care levels for individual patients, and these recommendations were related to the severity of Alzheimer dementia; however, they were frequently not followed during the family conference. Some families decided that an optimal level of care higher than that recommended by the staff was appropriate and some families decided that a lower care level was optimal.

Forty patients, who were initially included in the hospice approach, were analyzed in detail regarding decision making and an outcome during the first year of this program.[15] None of these patients was assigned to level 1, one was assigned to level 2, 14 to level 3, 6 to level 4, and 19 to level 5. We have found that family members were more likely to agree to level 4 or 5 care if they had some evidence that the patient would want to limit his or her treatment. Evidence for this belief varied from direct statements made by the patient before dementia occurred, to the patient's decisions about another family member in a similar situation. Thirteen of these patients died during the first year of this program; one in level 2, 3 in level 3, one in level 4, and 8 in level 5. The duration of stay in the hospital was similar for level 2 and 3 patients and for level 5 patients (43 months). The duration of hospitalization was also not significantly different from duration of stay of 23 Alzheimer patients who died in the same hospital before initiation of the hospice approach.[15]

These results indicate that a hospice approach to Alzheimer dementia is quite acceptable for both patients' families and the staff. Some limitation of aggressive interventions was agreed on for all patients and unquestionably resulted in a decrease of patients' discomfort. At the same time the mortality rate was not changed significantly. This is because in many cases demented patients undergo diagnostic testing and are treated aggressively for infection every time they develop a fever. However, in evaluating 63 episodes of fever that occurred in 40 patients with advanced Alzheimer dementia over an 18-month period we have found that approximately one third of all fever episodes may not be clinically significant.

Of the 32 episodes of fever that occurred in 21 patients whose family members requested vigorous workup and treatment of all possible infections with antibiotics, 4 patients died, while in 28 episodes, response to aggressive medical treatment was favorable. In the 19 patients in whom fevers were treated with comfort measures only, there were 31 episodes of fever. In 21 cases, the patient's response to symptomatic treatment without diagnostic workup or antibiotic administration was favorable. Ten patients treated with comfort measures only died, but usually not during their first encounter with an infection. There has been no significant difference in the lethality of infections in patients treated with antibiotics and those treated for comfort only.

These results indicate that fever may represent only benign, self-limiting conditions, such as mild dehydration or viral syndromes, in patients with advanced Alzheimer dementia. Because of the noncommunicative nature of the patients and often the absence of recognizable physical signs of intercurrent illness in Alzheimer patients, the options of the physician include either immediately performing diagnostic tests and treating the patient with antibiotics, or treating the patient symptomatically with antipyretics, analgesics, oxygen, oral hydration, and pulmonary toilet if necessary. We believe that treatment of infections with antibiotics by itself does not increase patient's comfort but it may actually inflict discomfort. Therefore, we propose that the routine use of antibiotics as a treatment modality for fever in this patient population is not indicated.

Legal Basis of the Hospice Approach

In general, no consensus has been reached regarding the most appropriate procedure for obtaining approval of decisions to limit treatment of incompetent patients. Some authors and courts believe that such a decision should be made only by courts. Baron[9] suggests that courts are the most appropriate authority because the decision process should have four process elements that are inherent to the judicial system. These process elements are (1) principled decision, (2) impartial decision, (3) adversary quality, and (4) public nature of the process.

We believe that the procedure by which the level of optimal care is assigned to our patients contains all the necessary elements of the proper process listed above. Excellent correlation of staff recommendations with the severity of this incurable disease indicates that these recommendations are based on an objective evaluation of the patient condition.[15] Of course, the final assignment of care level does not always correspond with the staff recommendation. This is due to modification of this recommendation by family members during the family conference. Such a modification is very appropriate because the family provides the best information about the most likely wishes of the patient. Thus, we believe that the process of reaching a final decision can be rationally explained and, therefore, can be considered principled.

The second and third element of the process, impartiality and an adversary nature of the proceedings, are satisfied by the inclusion of a wide range of health professionals, and often also of several family members, in various stages of the decision. The meeting of direct care providers prior to a family conference provides input from nurses and nursing assistants, as well as medical input from the ward physician. Diverse opinions are actively sought and openly discussed. All staff members are encouraged to make their own recommendations about the optimal care for the individual patient. The same open atmosphere is fostered at the family conference. Input from family members is sought and reconciled with staff recommendations. The presence of a social worker and a chaplain provides an additional point of view for discussion about social and ethical problems.

The final element, a public nature of the proceedings, is satisfied at several levels. All staff are notified of patients to be discussed and when. The summary of the family conference is included in front of the patient's chart where all staff members can read it. The hospice approach to Alzheimer dementia was presented to the hospital ethics committee for comments and recommendations and to the professional staff of the hospital. The hospital ethics committee concluded that "this procedure seems to comply with the principles of autonomy in its modified form for the incompetent patient. A discussion of the therapy is done with concern for the principles of beneficence and nonmaleficence." Finally, the program was widely publicized in medical literature[15] and was described in the lay press.

We believe that consideration of ethical principles is more important than legal considerations. These principles include respect for patient's autonomy, avoidance of harm and suffering (nonmaleficence), and providing beneficial care (beneficence). It is possible to argue that nonmaleficence is more important than beneficence, if beneficial care results in too great a burden to the patient.[17] This is a situation of many Alzheimer patients, who suffer from a terminal disease in which aggressive medical care results mainly in extension of the dying process at a cost of increased confusion and suffering. By proper communication between staff caregivers and family members of Alzheimer patients it is possible to determine the optimal care for an individual patient that takes into consideration not only his or her real or implied wishes but also the family's religious and cultural traditions and the severity of the disease. It is hoped that this approach can avoid disagreements and involvement of courts in medical decision making. As stated in one of the reactions to presentation of this program: "When physician, nurse, social worker, administrator, and family all stand together on this, outsiders trying to dictate another course will be seen as misguided and perhaps a bit silly."[18]

Hospice Approach and Quality of Life

The main goal of the hospice approach is prevention of patients' discomfort. The hospice approach substitutes aggressive measures aimed at maintaining patient's comfort and quality of life for aggressive medical treatments. These measures include recreational and occupational therapies (see Chapter 12), which attempt to maintain and use remaining functional abilities, and intensive nursing care. Nursing diagnoses used for determination of the nursing care plan are included in Appendix 10-A.

Management of Respiratory Distress

Patients need special supportive measures when death is imminent, in terms of both physical and emotional care. When a patient develops a life-threatening condition and the decision to treat with comfort measures only has been instituted, the goal of treatment is to ease the distressing symptoms and provide for a peaceful death. In a hospice approach, there is no need for extensive medical technology. However, oxygen delivery systems are necessary to ease respiratory distress. Suctioning is also a supportive measure, if used judiciously. Caring for patients experiencing acute respiratory distress in the long-term institutional environment is possible. Patients are moved to a single room for privacy and infection control and to provide more space for comfort measures. With shortness of breath, there is an increased need for oxygen. However, patients are unable to recognize this need and to ask for assistance. Careful nursing assessment is necessary to identify the symptoms of respiratory distress in a mute patient who develops behavioral changes such as restlessness and alterations in respiratory rate and depth. Low flow oxygen delivered by nasal cannula or mask seems comfortable and easily tolerated by most patients.

A nasal cannula does not interfere with eating but is easily dislodged in a restless patient. A face mask may be used in a restless patient but it may be hot and confining and may irritate the skin. The use of humidification is recommended with either device to increase a patient's comfort and to prevent drying of oral and nasal mucous membranes of the nose and mouth. Additional comfort measures for nasal cannula include the following:

1. Moistening of lips and nares with water-soluble lubricating jelly every 4 hours
2. Applying gauze padding under nose and over ears to protect pressure areas from tubing
3. Removing cannula, cleaning it, and reapplying it every 4 hours
4. Providing meticulous oral hygiene every 4 hours

Additional comfort measures for face mask include the following:

1. Placing gauze pads between mask and bony facial prominences
2. Massaging face with fingertips every 2 hours
3. Adjusting straps loosely
4. Removing the mask every 2 hours, washing the patient's face, and drying it thoroughly.

In patients suffering from pneumonia the increased production of mucus and thickened pulmonary secretions might increase respiratory discomfort. A modified form of postural drainage is recommended to clear the airway of excessive secretions. To institute this measure the bed is placed in a Trendelenburg position (head lower than the rest of the body), the patient is turned from side to side, and the amount of secretions that drain by gravity from the patient's mouth is monitored. Postural drainage is performed before giving food or liquid, and a staff member stays in the room with the patient at all times. A suction machine is kept available for use if the patient is unable to handle the volume of secretions or is unable to effectively cough.

If suctioning is necessary, two nurses should perform this procedure. One nurse should assist by gently opening the patient's mouth and keeping it open with a padded tongue blade. The other nurse should gently suction and remove excessive secretions. If secretions are copious, it is preferable to control this symptom by administering atropine because suctioning may create anxiety and discomfort in the terminally ill patient who is aware.

Management of Feeding Difficulties

In the terminal phase of Alzheimer dementia severe feeding difficulties are common. Many patients lose their appetites and are unwilling or unable to open their mouths when being spoon fed. Others are completely unaware of their environment and sleep during feeding. Some hold food in their mouths and forget to swallow, while others scowl and seem distressed while being spoon fed. In addition, many patients in the terminal stage of Alzheimer's disease have difficulty swallowing, resulting in severe coughing and choking spells when being fed. The family decision not to use feeding tubes in patients who have severe feeding difficulties creates a major challenge for care providers. Modified diet textures (pureed diet), nutritionally complete liquids (e.g., Sustacal) and, most importantly, gentle spoon feeding techniques are used. With supportive nutritional therapy, the staff strives to provide comfort measures for the patient who is experiencing feeding difficulties.

For the patients who have lost the ability to chew food pureed food is provided. For patients who, in addition to losing the ability to chew are also difficult to feed, a special low-volume high-caloric-density pureed diet was developed by a team of nurses and dietitians.[20] This special adult pureed diet provides adequate nutrition and hydration, decreases the danger of choking and aspiration, and decreases the time needed to feed Alzheimer patients. The food is served lukewarm because hot liquids or cold foods seem to stimulate the coughing reflex. Pleasant tasting and sweet supplements such as yogurts and puddings are used to obtain the low volume and provide necessary calories and protein. Eggnog and high-protein high-caloric-density liquids (Ensure Plus) are offered with the evening meal. Nourishments are well tolerated if given slowly, in small amounts, and at frequent intervals during the day and evening hours.

When a patient refuses to open his or her mouth, sleeps while being fed, or holds pureed food in his or her cheeks, it is necessary to reassess the feeding strategy. In some patients who refuse to open their mouths, low doses of anti-anxiety medications (diazepam [Valium] or oxazepam [Serax]), given an hour before meals, are sometimes effective in improving feeding. At this stage liquids are swallowed easier than pureed food. Consequently, pureed meals are replaced by nutritionally complete liquids such as Sustacal and Ensure Plus. The appropriate selection of liquids is made by a clinical dietitian who calculates the energy requirements of the bedfast patient and individualizes the nutritional care plan. The liquid nourishment is offered to sip through a straw for those patients who are still able to do it. Sipping liquids seems to reduce choking because intake volume is regulated by the patient. To prevent gastric dilatation, fluids are offered on an hourly basis. When too much liquid is ingested at one time patients are predisposed to gastric overload, which may result in vomiting and possible aspiration. When a patient is sustained only on a liquid diet the following comfort measures are recommended:

1. Feeding with the head of the bed elevated at a 45° angle
2. Feeding very slowly, only a sip at a time by cup or straw
3. Assessing that liquids are swallowed and not held in the mouth
4. Evaluating any facial expression that may indicate distress
5. Offering tepid liquids to prevent any mouth or lip discomfort
6. Keeping the patient in a side-lying position with head elevated at a 45° angle during daytime hours. This position seems to prevent inadvertent regurgitation and possible aspiration.

Pureed and liquid modified diets will sustain a terminally ill Alzheimer patient for varying lengths of time. Swallowing problems will recur in cycles and in increasing severity. Because of the cyclic nature of feeding difficulties, pureed foods are reintroduced when patients stop choking. In patients who experience persistent feeding problems, weight loss with drastic change in physical appearance occurs. To provide additional calories and to increase the caloric density of foods, carbohydrate supplements, such as glucose polymers (Polycose), are added to either the liquid or pureed diets. This addition may prevent further weight loss but weight gain is unlikely because the patients are not able to ingest the amount of calories necessary to gain weight. As the swallowing reflex becomes more impaired, coughing and choking spells increase in frequency and severity. At this stage of the terminal illness emphasis is placed on sustaining the patient at the most comfortable care level while attempting to meet his or her nutritional needs.

In a patient who is terminally ill, nutritional status and oral hygiene are closely related. A combination of decreased intake, loss of appetite, and dryness of mouth results in decreased saliva production. In addition, halitosis, thickened saliva, and crusted saliva deposits detract from the patient's general appearance. Dryness of the mouth is particularly distressful but easily treated with frequent mouth care. Mouth dryness can be managed by using half-strength hydrogen peroxide for debridement of crust formation and Tin-Gel, a water-free 0.4% sodium fluoride, as a preventive measure against crust development. (A discussion of oral care for the Alzheimer patient is presented in Chapter 8.) Frequent sips of refreshing beverages appear to keep the mucosa moist. The room air moisture content is increased with the use of a bedside vaporizer or by a room humidifier. If necessary oral hygiene is provided every 2 hours and the use of irritants, including lemon glycerine preparations, hot food or beverages, and poorly fitting dentures, is avoided. Alzheimer patients also suffer from dry, cracked lips. Frequent application of lanolin or petroleum jelly is soothing and effective.

Management of Discomfort

Any behavioral changes in a mute and semicomatose patient should alert the nurse to possible discomfort and distress. Behavioral clues such as increased restlessness, sounds that resemble moaning and groaning, as well as facial expression such as frowning and scowling may be the only indication of distress. To decrease restlessness and promote comfort, administration of oral morphine sulfate is effective. Quite small doses (5 to 10 mg every 4 to 6 hours) decrease restlessness in a terminal Alzheimer patient. A loud vocalization (yelling) occurs in some Alzheimer patients and is a difficult phenomenon to manage. It is important to exclude any possible physical cause of the patient's discomfort that may be the reason for vocalization. If none is identified, antianxiety agents (e.g., oxazepam [Serax]), or neuroleptics (e.g., thioridazine [Mellaril]) are sometimes tried empirically. However, at this stage, when patients are speechless and their only response is yelling, most medications are usually ineffective. Staff members and especially families have a great difficulty in accepting the patient who is unresponsive to quieting medications. It helps somewhat if the yelling patient, unresponding to medications, is placed in a private room away from bedfast patients and their visiting families.

Family and Staff Response to the Dying Alzheimer Patient

As patients experience drastic weight loss and changes in physical appearance, families often express helplessness. They sometimes voice their ambivalence over decisions to limit the extent and scope of medical interventions, especially over the decision not to institute artificial tube feedings. They wish that the patient's suffering would end as soon as possible through death; yet they admit that they cannot "let go." Some families fear that their relative may starve to death without the tube feeding; some grieve the loss of the familiar physical appearance of their loved one. A combination of extensive weight loss, absence of dentures, and absence of eye glasses causes drastic changes in a patient's image.

In many cases these strong feelings probably motivate the families to visit more frequently and intensify their direct caregiving at the bedside. Some spouses visit daily and spend hours force feeding the patient because of their concern over "inadequate" nurturing. When feeding problems persist, the emotional strain for the family intensifies. Individual counseling is highly recommended and is provided for them by social service and psychiatry. The adaptive and maladaptive responses of families are discussed in Chapter 3.

Managing and coping with feeding difficulties is a major challenge to nurse caregivers in long-term facilities. Since Alzheimer patients are completely mute in the terminal phase, communication skills are necessary for the interpretation of patients' feeding behaviors. For example, there are bewildering remnants of facial expressions that need interpretation for signs of discomfort and distress. Most patients keep eye contact in varying degrees of expressions; some look at caregivers with a piercing gaze, others only glance. Other facial expressions consist of inappropriate smiles, laughter, and puzzling frowns and scowls. A solemn, yet scowling face conjures up feelings of ambivalence in a staff member who needs to decide if feeding should be continued. In contrast, it is clear to everyone that a patient who incessantly coughs while being fed is best left to rest and recuperate from the spell.

It is evident that providing care in an atmosphere of frequent death is emotionally stressful, especially for nursing staff. Because of the crisis and trauma associated with dying, people who care for the dying patients are seen as being at high risk to experience crisis and trauma themselves.[19] Caring for terminally ill Alzheimer patients is especially traumatic and stressful for staff because these patients are totally unaware and incapable of knowing that they are dying. In particular, the effects of the disease render the patient incapable of the intimate process of dialogue and interaction with the caring staff. In addition, the concept of terminal care for an Alzheimer patient is markedly different from terminal care for patients whose death is near and expected within weeks, days, or hours. Terminal care for the Alzheimer patient begins when the decision is made to limit the extent of medical care. Death, at that point, is not usually imminent but is anticipated to occur within a wide range of months to several years.

For some nurses, psychological strain emerges from the continuous exposure to this "lingering" nature of dying. Other nurses become distraught by the atmosphere of helplessness and hopelessness conveyed by so many families. Faced with caring for only Alzheimer patients, even the most experienced nurses may find themselves, at times, withdrawing from bedside care during the patient's last moment of life. Consequently, staff reactions and emotional responses regarding patient death need to be identified and discussed. A weekly structured support group for the staff led by a psychiatrist who is familiar with hospice principles is beneficial. In the spirit of open communication, discussion topics vary from coping with stresses to patient care assessments. This peer support group is also used for ongoing staff development in caring for the terminal patients and their families and for the identification and treatment of staff burnout issues.

REFERENCES

1. Stollerman GH: Lovable decisions: Rehumanizing dying. *J Am Geriatr Soc* 1986;34:172-174.

2. Angell M: Cost containment and the physician. JAMA 1985;254:1203-1207.

3. Volicer L, Hermann H, Rheaume Y: Allowing the debilitated to die. *N Engl J Med* 1984;310:530.

4. Cranford RE: Termination of treatment in the persistent vegetative state. *Semin Neurol* 1984;4:36-44.

5. Walshe TM, Leonard C: Persistent vegetative state: Extension of the syndrome to include chronic disorders. *Arch Neurol* 1985;42:1045-1047.

6. Volicer L: Need for hospice approach to treatment of patients with advanced progressive dementia. *J Am Geriatr Soc* 1986;34:655-658.

7. Veatch RM: An ethical framework for terminal care decisions: A new classification of patients. *J Am Geriatr Soc* 1984;32:665-669.

8. Wertham F: The geranium in the window: The "euthanasia" murders, in Horan DJ, Mall D (eds): *Death, Dying and Euthanasia*. Frederick, Md, Aletheia Books, University Publications of America, 1980.

9. Baron C: Law and public policy: The case for the courts. *J Am Geriatr Soc* 1984;32:734-738.

10. Mariner WK: Decision making in the care of terminally ill incompetent persons: Concerns about the role of the courts. *J Am Geriatr Soc* 1984;32:739-746.

11. Cassell EJ: Life as a work of art. *Hastings Center Rep* 1984;14:35-37.

12. Howell M, Fabiszewski K: A model for family meetings in the long-term care of Alzheimer's disease. *J Gerontol Social Work* 1986;9:113-117.

13. Hermann HT: Ethical dilemmas intrinsic to the care of the elderly demented patient. *J Am Geriatr Soc* 1984;32:655-656.

14. Besdine RW: Decisions to withhold treatment from nursing home residents. *J Am Geriatr Soc* 1983;31:602-606.

15. Volicer L, Rheaume Y, Brown J, et al: Hospice approach to the treatment of patients with advanced dementia of the Alzheimer type. *JAMA* 1986;256:2210-2213.

16. Ungar BL, Barlett JG: Nosocomial pneumonia, in Gleckman RA, Gantz NM (eds): *Infections in the Elderly*. Boston, Little, Brown & Co, 1983.

17. Beauchamp TL, Childress JF: *Principles of Biomedical Ethics*, ed 2. Oxford, Oxford University Press, 1983.

18. Campion EW: Caring for the patient with Alzheimer's disease. *JAMA* 1987;257:1051.

19. Koff TH: *Hospice: A Caring Community*. Cambridge, Mass, Winthrop Publishers, 1980.

20. Warden VJ: Special adult pureed diet: Addressing feeding problems in advanced Alzheimer's disease. *Geriatr Nurs* 1988 (in press).

Appendix 10-A

Hospice Care Plan

Nursing Diagnosis	Outcome	Nursing Intervention
Alteration in comfort	Patient will experience maximal comfort, as evidenced by relaxed facial appearance, decrease in moaning and thrashing, increase in daytime sleep.	1. Use prescribed analgesics, such as liquid morphine, for pain as ordered. 2. Perform frequent mouth care using Oralube rather than mouthwash or lemon-glycerine. 3. Suction only when removal of secretions is necessary for patient comfort. 4. Turn frequently to relieve pressure areas; special skin care. 5. Use air mattress on bed. 6. Use loose, nonrestrictive clothing. 7. Place patient in a room with a fan or air conditioner in warm weather. 8. Administer antipyretics for fever reduction with a temperature 101°F or higher. 9. Administer food and fluids only as tolerated by mouth. 10. Change frequently for incontinence.
Ineffective airway clearance	Patient will have respirations of adequate depth and rate. Will breathe comfortably.	1. Encourage postural drainage by putting bed in Trendelenburg position and placing patient on his or her side.

Source: Courtesy of Patricia Wilbur, RN, AD.

Nursing Diagnosis	Outcome	Nursing Intervention
		2. Encourage patient to expectorate whenever possible.
3. Perform pharyngeal suctioning only when absolutely necessary.
4. Perform frequent mouth care with Oralube.
5. Suggest use of atropine sulfate to reduce respiratory secretions.
Coping, Family, Potential for Growth	Family members will anticipate death, go through the grieving process, and continue with their own lives after patient's death.	1. Prior to and during terminal stage, educate family regarding the course and stages of the disease in order for them to know what they may expect.
2. Be completely honest with family about patient's condition, giving as much information as possible.
3. Have patient placed on seriously ill list when death is imminent to make family members realize seriousness of the condition.
Feeding difficulties resulting in:
1. Potential for aspiration
2. Alteration in nutrition, less than body requirements
3. Fluid volume deficit	Patient will eat or drink enough calories to sustain weight as long as possible without complications	1. When patient has reached the stage of refusing to open mouth, modify diet to provide high-calorie liquid sustenance. Do the same for patient who chokes on pureed foods or sleeps while being fed.
2. When patient is at a stage where he or she chokes or coughs with liquids, give pureed consistency foods. Mix liquids in with pureed food to provide some hydration. Use ice cream and yogurt as liquids.
3. Elevate head of bed 45° at meals and for 1/2 hour after.
4. Never force feed.

CHAPTER 11

Drugs Used in the Treatment of Alzheimer Dementia

Ladislav Volicer

Despite recent advances in our knowledge about Alzheimer dementia, there is still no treatment available that can stop or reverse the progression of the disease. There are, however, many drugs that are useful for the management of symptoms commonly exhibited by Alzheimer patients. In this chapter the beneficial and adverse effects of these medications will be described as well as their mechanisms of action. Since different symptoms appear at different stages in the course of Alzheimer's disease (see Chapter 2), different drugs are indicated at each stage. Therefore, the drugs will be described according to the stage of the disease in which they are used most commonly. There is considerable overlap of symptoms in different stages, so that most of the drugs discussed can be used in more than one stage of the disease.

Drugs Used in the Early Stage of Alzheimer Dementia

The first manifestation of Alzheimer dementia is often memory disturbance. Therefore, attempts to treat the early stages of this disease are frequently directed at the improvement of memory function and other cognitive deficits. In addition to cognitive problems, many patients also exhibit mood and personality changes in the early stages of the illness (see Chapter 2). Drugs affecting mood (antidepressants) are frequently employed in the early stages of Alzheimer dementia, although they do not directly affect the dementing process.

Ergoloid Mesylates

A mixture of ergoloid mesylates (Hydergine, Niloric) is the only drug preparation that has been shown to be effective in improving the cognitive performance of patients with early-stage dementia and that is available for this use in the United States. Ergoloid mesylates are extracted from ergot. Their chemical structure is quite complex and includes a tryptamine-like portion that is similar to the neurotransmitter serotonin. Ergoloid mesylates affect several neurotransmitter systems in the brain. In animal experiments, they have been shown to act as norepinephrine antagonists and to decrease production of cyclic adenosine monophosphate and of sodium-potassium-dependent adenosine triphosphatase activity. Ergoloid mesylates also block the effects of dopamine and serotonin and increase choline acetyltransferase activity in the brains of aged animals.[1] In humans, ergoloid mesylates increase fast electroencephalographic activity without any significant effect on the cerebral blood flow. It is not clear which of these mechanisms is responsible for the beneficial effects of ergoloid mesylates observed in patients with dementia.

In controlled clinical trials, ergoloid mesylates were found to improve some symptoms of dementia in elderly patients, including decreased alertness, confusion, emotional lability, and bothersomeness. However, in most of these studies different types of dementia were not differentiated,[2] so it is not certain that these effects would occur in Alzheimer patients. Ergoloid mesylates have been approved by the Food and Drug Administration (FDA) for use in idiopathic decline of mental capacity but not for a specific disease. One of the few studies of ergoloid mesylates specifically directed to patients with Alzheimer dementia was conducted in several Veterans Administration medical centers. In this study the effect of ergoloid mesylates on intellectual and emotional functioning in mildly demented patients was compared with desipramine, thiothixene, and placebo using several standardized rating scales. The only significant difference between ergoloid mesylates and placebo was on the *Pervasive Affective Disturbance Scale* of the *Zung Symptom Checklist* in which patients receiving ergoloid mesylates performed worse than patients receiving placebo. On other scales, patients on ergoloid mesylates were rated better than patients on the other two medications, but there was no significant difference from the placebo. On the *History of Psychic and Somatic Complaints in Elderly Scale* patients on ergoloid mesylates were rated worse than patients on desipramine or thiothixene. Thus, it is possible that ergoloid mesylates do improve cognitive performance of Alzheimer patients somewhat but, at the same time, increase their complaints.

Treatment with the mixture of ergoloid mesylates is relatively safe. The most significant adverse effect is an orthostatic hypotension, which might lead to dizziness, fainting spells, and falls. With sublingual administration of ergoloid mesylates some irritation of the mouth, transient nausea, and gastric disturbances have also been reported. Since the mixture of ergoloid mesylates is the only medication currently available for the treatment of cognitive symptoms in Alzheimer dementia and because it is relatively safe, many physicians routinely use it in early stage dementia. It has also been reported that ergoloid mesylates inhibit platelet aggregation.[3] This could decrease the progression of multi-infarct dementia, which sometimes coexists with Alzheimer dementia and may be difficult to distinguish from it.

Vasodilators

The earliest approach to the drug treatment of dementia was based on the hypothesis that dementia occurs in older people because the blood supply to the brain is compromised by aging-induced "hardening of the arteries." In 1780, the American physician Dr. Benjamin Rush used a rotating chair in which elderly demented patients were strapped and spun around. He reasoned that the centrifugal force would increase blood flow to the brain and improve brain function. A similar hypothesis, but with a somewhat more modern technology, was the basis of a therapy introduced in the 1920s. Patients with dementia were placed in a hyperbaric chamber in an attempt to increase oxygen supply to the brain and improve cognitive function. Needless to say, neither the rotating chair nor the hyperbaric chamber is effective in the treatment of dementia.

Based on the vascular hypothesis, a whole class of drugs was developed and tested for the treatment of dementia. These drugs, vasodilators, were supposed to dilate brain blood vessels and thus increase the oxygen supply to the brain. The vasodilator drugs include papaverine (Pavabid, Cerespan), cyclandalate (Cyclospasmol), isoxsuprine, nylidrin, niacin derivatives, and some other agents that are not available in the United States. When studied by rigorous double-blind techniques, however, most of these drugs were found to be ineffective in improving the symptoms of dementia. An exception is nafronyl, which was found to be somewhat effective in improving cognitive function and is used abroad in patients with Alzheimer dementia.[4] Its effectiveness is similar to that of the ergoloid mesylate mixture, which was also originally developed as a vasodilator. Neither nafronyl nor ergoloid mesylates, however, improve dementia symptoms by producing vasodilation. According to our current understanding, the blood supply to the brain in Alzheimer patients is intact. Although oxygen consumption in the brain is lower in Alzheimer patients than in controls, this decrease is a consequence of brain cell death and brain atrophy rather than a cause for degeneration of the brain.

Multi-infarct dementia, on the other hand, is believed to be a consequence of cerebrovascular disease. Even in this form of dementia, however, vasodilation would not be beneficial for the regions of the brain supplied by pathologically constricted blood vessels. Vasodilators do not increase blood flow in a blood vessel that is narrowed by an atherosclerotic process, because such a vessel is rigid and cannot be dilated effectively. In fact, since it is the normal vessel that will dilate after administration of vasodilators, the blood is siphoned off through dilated normal blood vessels away from the cerebral regions that are supplied by pathologically constricted blood vessels (so-called steal effect). Therefore, vasodilation may actually worsen symptoms in some patients with cerebral atherosclerosis.

Blood flow measurements indicate that nafronyl actually does not increase blood flow to the brain. It may produce its beneficial effect by directly influencing cerebral metabolism because it increases the pyruvate/lactate ratio in cerebrospinal fluid and fast electroencephalographic activity.[4] However, its exact mechanism of action is unknown.

Cholinergic Drugs

Several lines of evidence indicate that the cholinergic system in the brain is abnormal in Alzheimer dementia.[5] This system, whose neurotransmitter is acetylcholine, regulates a variety of brain functions, including memory processes. Activity of the enzyme choline acetyltransferase, which synthesizes acetylcholine from choline and acetate, is markedly decreased in postmortem brain tissue or biopsy specimens taken from Alzheimer patients. Postmortem investigation also shows that the number of cholinergic nerve cells in the basal forebrain of Alzheimer patients is markedly smaller than in nondemented people of the same age.[5] This is true especially in patients with onset of dementia before the age of 65. In addition, drugs that impede the cholinergic activity by blocking cholinergic receptors produce temporary memory disorders in normal people. It is not clear, however, that the memory disturbance induced by these drugs is the same as that observed in Alzheimer dementia.

Considering this information, it might be predicted that increasing central cholinergic activity would be beneficial in Alzheimer's disease. There are three strategies that could be used in an attempt to increase cholinergic activity. These include administration of acetylcholine precursors, the use of drugs that stimulate acetylcholine receptors, and administration of drugs that inhibit acetylcholine metabolism.

Acetylcholine Precursors

Animal experiments have shown that oral or parenteral administration of choline increases acetylcholine levels in the brain.[6] Based on this information, many investigators have attempted to improve cognitive function in Alzheimer patients by oral administration of choline-containing lecithin. This strategy is similar to that used in treatment of Parkinson's disease, a condition in which a biochemical deficit of the neurotransmitter dopamine can be corrected by the administration of the dopamine precursor levodopa.

Although different doses of lecithin have been investigated in the treatment of Alzheimer dementia and, in some cases, the trials were continued for a long time period, no significant effects of acetylcholine precursors on memory processes have been observed.[7] It is possible that although the administration of lecithin does increase acetylcholine synthesis, it does not increase the physiologic release of acetylcholine from cholinergic nerve endings. In contrast to the dopaminergic system, which provides tonic inhibition to the basal ganglia, the cholinergic system provides selective stimulation of distinct brain areas. Therefore, a general increase in acetylcholine levels might not improve selective acetylcholine release. Alternatively, since acetylcholine is only one of several neurotransmitters affected by the Alzheimer dementia, an isolated improvement of the cholinergic function might not lead to significant clinical improvement.

Cholinergic stimulants

Central cholinergic activity could also be influenced by the administration of drugs that directly stimulate cholinergic receptors. Again, this strategy is similar to one form of treatment of Parkinson's disease in which dopaminergic agonists (e.g., bromocriptine) are quite effective. Systemic administration of cholinergic agonists, however, leads to cholinergic stimulation of peripheral organs and to undesirable side effects such as diarrhea, abdominal cramping, and bradycardia. The direct administration of cholinergic agonists into the brain appears to be more promising because it would lead to fewer side effects.

Harbaugh and co-workers[8] implanted a pump that injected a cholinergic agonist, bethanechol, directly into the cerebral ventricles of Alzheimer patients. They reported some improvement in some patients with minimal side effects. However, the patients were evaluated only subjectively and no objective ratings were performed. The value of this method for treatment of Alzheimer dementia will have to be evaluated on larger numbers of patients using objective rating scales.

Acetylcholine Esterase Inhibitors

Acetylcholine esterase is an enzyme that terminates the action of acetylcholine released from nerve endings by breaking it down into choline and acetate. The first acetylcholine esterase inhibitor to be investigated in Alzheimer dementia was physostigmine (Antilirium). Intravenous administration of this drug improved memory in normal volunteers and also in some Alzheimer patients. However, intravenous administration is not practical for long-term management. Treatment with oral physostigmine improved cognitive function in some Alzheimer patients but even in those individuals the effect of physostigmine was quite small and only temporary.[7] The use of physostigmine has two major disadvantages. The drug has a short duration of action and has to be administered every 2 to 4 hours to produce sustained inhibition of acetylcholine esterase. In addition, physostigmine potentiates cholinergic activity not only in the brain but also in peripheral organs and this results in a high incidence of side effects, such as diarrhea, abdominal cramps, and bradycardia.

An effort has been made to develop and test other acetylcholine esterase inhibitors that might be more selective for the brain acetylcholine esterase. A pronounced improvement of cognitive function in Alzheimer patients who received tetrahydroaminoacridine (THA) has been reported.[9] This inhibitor caused relatively few side effects and was most effective in early stage Alzheimer patients. Unfortunately, limited long-term follow-up indicated that the effectiveness was not sustained with time. Such a result might be predicted since inhibition of cholinesterase activity does not affect the basic degenerative process of Alzheimer dementia leading to progressive loss of cholinergic neurons. Since inhibition of cholinesterase merely potentiates existing cholinergic activity, its effectiveness will be lost when cholinergic neurons disappear. Recently, a large-scale trial of THA had to be terminated because the drug caused liver damage.

Antidepressants

The incidence of depression in patients with dementia of Alzheimer type is not clear. It is difficult to diagnose depression in a demented patient because many symptoms of major depressive disorders are similar to those of Alzheimer's disease (e.g., sleep disturbance, fatigue, psychomotor agitation or retardation, loss of interest in usual activities, and diminished ability to think or concentrate). The major criterion, depressed mood, may be difficult to assess by subjective report because of poor motivation to report, loss of affect recognition, or aphasic difficulties.

Estimates of coexistent depression in dementia vary widely, from 15% to 57%.[10] Since many authors do not mention how they resolved the diagnostic dilemma, it is difficult to interpret these reports. Another issue concerns whether dementia can be caused by depression. Some authors refer to a "pseudodementia," as a main symptom of depression in older people. However, even in elderly patients who improve following antidepressant treatment, the follow-up indicates that many of them later develop a classic picture of progressive Alzheimer dementia.[11]

There is no agreement concerning the use of antidepressants in the treatment of Alzheimer dementia. Reisberg[12] mentions "mourning" following insight into the illness and "blunting" of the emotions but does not recommend treatment. On the other hand, Reifler and co-workers,[11] who found depression in 31% of their patients, report that treatment led to improvement in mood, vegetative signs, and activities of daily living in 85% of these patients. The potential benefits of antidepressant therapy have to be balanced with the possibility of side effects induced by antidepressants, which include life-threatening cardiovascular complications. Since the prognosis of Alzheimer dementia is unfortunately poor, however, it may be reasonable to risk possible side effects of antidepressant treatment in order to exclude treatable depression as a possible underlying cause of the disturbed mental state.

Many drugs exhibit antidepressant activity. According to their mechanism of action, they can be divided into inhibitors of monoamine oxidase (e.g., tranylcypromine [Parnate]) and inhibitors of norepinephrine and/or serotonin reuptake (e.g., imipramine [Tofranil], amitriptyline [Elavil], doxepin [Sinequan], nortriptyline [Pamelor], amoxapine [Asendin], nomifensine [Merital]). Both classes act by potentiating the effect of norepinephrine or serotonin, either by blocking their metabolism (inhibitors of monoamine oxidase) or by prolonging their action on the receptors (inhibitors of reuptake). Most inhibitors of reuptake block the reuptake of both serotonin and norepinephrine, but to a different degree. These agents also affect other receptors, mainly muscarinic and histamine receptors. This leads to two most common side effects: anticholinergic effects and sedation. Anticholinergic effects include blurred vision, dry mouth, sinus tachycardia, constipation, urinary retention, increased intraocular pressure, and worsening of memory function. One classic and two newer antidepressants will be described in more detail.

Desipramine

Desipramine (Norpramin) is a representative of the most commonly used "tricyclic" antidepressants, named according to their chemical structure. Desipramine predominantly blocks norepinephrine reuptake and has a much smaller effect on serotonin reuptake. Desipramine does not have a strong anticholinergic activity and produces less sedation than other antidepressants. It is metabolized by hydroxylation in the liver, and this process is decreased by cimetidine (Tagamet) but not by aging.[13]

Administration of desipramine poses a risk to patients with cardiovascular or thyroid disease because of the possibility of an arrhythmia or acute myocardial infarction (although this risk is lower than with other tricyclic antidepressants). It also poses a problem for patients with a history of urinary retention or glaucoma, because of the anticholinergic activity, and for patients with a history of seizure disorder, because desipramine lowers the seizure threshold. Patients should be warned that while taking desipramine they might be more sensitive to the effects of alcoholic beverages. The therapeutic effect of desipramine may be seen after 2 to 5 days, but full effect usually requires continuation of treatment for 2 to 3 weeks.

Maprotiline

Maprotiline (Ludiomil) has a four-ring chemical structure instead of the three-ring structure characteristic of most other antidepressants. It also preferentially inhibits the reuptake of norepinephrine, and its metabolism is inhibited by cimetidine (Tagamet). Maprotiline has fewer anticholinergic side effects than other antidepressants, and it has been used successfully in patients who developed acute urinary retention during treatment with other antidepressants. It is also effective in decreasing anxiety but produces more sedation than desipramine.

Maprotiline should be also given with caution to patients with cardiovascular or thyroid disease, because of the possibility of arrhythmias and acute myocardial infarction, and to patients with history of seizures, because it lowers seizure threshold. The development of seizures is more likely if the patient is being treated simultaneously with a neuroleptic drug (e.g., haloperidol [Haldol]), or if benzodiazepine therapy has been recently discontinued. Reports that maprotiline has an earlier therapeutic effect than other antidepressants have not been confirmed by subsequent studies.[14]

Trazodone

Trazodone (Desyrel) is a triazolopyridine derivative unrelated to the other antidepressants. Its main action is on the serotoninergic system. It blocks both serotonin reuptake and serotonin receptors. Trazodone is metabolized by hydroxylation in the liver, and this process is inhibited by cimetidine (Tagamet). It does not have any anticholinergic activity but produces sedation, dizziness, hypotension, and cardiac arrhythmias with a frequency similar to that of the other antidepressants. One of its more serious side effects, discovered after it was used for several years, is the development of priapism, a prolonged, painful penile erection that, in some cases, requires surgical treatment and may lead to permanent impotence.

Trazodone has been reported to improve assaultive behavior in patients with organic brain syndrome, including Alzheimer dementia.[15] In the four patients described, the clinical presentation did not suggest a primary depressive illness and neuroleptics were ineffective in controlling the symptoms. Trazodone is effective in decreasing aggressive behavior in some animal models, and it is possible that its effect on the serotoninergic system mediates this activity.

Aspirin

The diagnosis of Alzheimer dementia is made by exclusion of other causes of dementia (see Chapter 2). However, distinguishing the clinical features of other causes of dementia from those of Alzheimer dementia may be difficult. This is especially true for multi-infarct dementia, which is caused by repeated occlusions of small blood vessels in the brain.[16] Furthermore, Alzheimer dementia and multi-infarct dementia are often combined, and in one third of demented patients both infarcts and Alzheimer changes were found at autopsy.[16] It is unclear which of these changes are more important for the clinical syndrome of dementia.

Therefore, it is important to consider the possibility that a patient diagnosed as having Alzheimer dementia may also have multi-infarct dementia. Drugs that inhibit platelet aggregation, (e.g., aspirin) may prevent further occlusion of cerebral vessels. Small doses of aspirin are optimal for inhibition of production of thromboxane, which promotes platelet aggregation, without decreasing the production of prostacyclin, which inhibits platelet aggregation and dilates blood vessels. Thus, either one children's aspirin (65 mg) every day or a regular aspirin (325 mg) every other day might be beneficial in patients with dementia by decreasing the probability of further infarcts.

Drugs Used in the Middle Stage of Alzheimer Dementia

Behavioral problems are the hallmark of this stage of the disease. These include hyperactivity and restlessness, sleep disturbances, resistiveness, and assaultiveness. Many of these problems can be symptomatically managed by modification of the patient's environment, gentle persuasion, and exercise (see Chapter 7), but in most cases, sooner or later, the patient requires a psychotropic medication. Initially, drugs with fewer side effects, mainly hypnotics are used, and only if these drugs are not effective, are neuroleptics used. The effectiveness of β-adrenergic blocking agents, another class of drugs, in the treatment of behavioral problems of Alzheimer patients needs to be further investigated.

Hypnotics

The hypnotics include drugs with mainly hypnotic effect (e.g., diphenhydramine and chloral hydrate) and the benzodiazepines, which in addition to the hypnotic effect also have antianxiety and anticonvulsant effects. The contribution of anxiety to a patient's restlessness is difficult to determine. In some cases hospitalized patients become more restless after a visit of a family member and appear to be anxious. However, benzodiazepines do not appear to be significantly more effective than diphenhydramine in the treatment of these patients. All drugs from this group, however, are useful for treatment of disturbances of the sleep–wake cycle, which are quite common in this stage of Alzheimer dementia.

Dipenhydramine

Originally developed as an antihistamine, diphenhydramine (Benadryl) has a pronounced sedative effect. It is a common ingredient of nonprescription sleeping pills. In addition to its antihistamine effect, it also has anticholinergic activity. However, with doses used clinically the incidence of anticholinergic side effects is quite low. The maximum activity of diphenhydramine occurs approximately 1 hour after administration and lasts 4 to 6 hours.

Diphenhydramine should be given with caution to patients with a history of bronchial asthma or increased intraocular pressure (glaucoma). Monoamine oxidase inhibitors potentiate the anticholinergic effects of diphenhydramine. The sedative effect of diphenhydramine is not very strong. In a study of elderly women, a 50 mg/70 kg dose of diphenhydramine did not produce significant sedation.[17] However, in Alzheimer patients diphenhydramine is quite effective both as a daytime sedative and as an evening hypnotic in doses of 25 to 50 mg.

Benzodiazepines

All benzodiazepines have hypnotic, antianxiety, and anticonvulsant effects. They are not selective for one or the other effect, although some are marketed as hypnotics (e.g., flurazepam [Dalmane], triazolam [Halcion]), some as antianxiety agents (e.g., lorazepam [Ativan], prazepam [Centrax], chlordiazepoxide [Librium], halazepam [Paxipam], clorazepate [Tranxene], alprazolam [Xanax]), and others as anticonvulsants (e.g., clonazepam [Clonopin], diazepam [Valium]). All act by potentiating the effect of the main endogenous inhibitory neurotransmitter, γ-aminobutyric acid (GABA). GABA increases permeability of nerve membranes for chloride ions that results in hyperpolarization. Benzodiazepines differ in their time of onset and duration of action.

Oxazepam. Oxazepam (Serax) is a short-acting benzodiazepine with a relatively slow onset of action. The maximal effect appears approximately 2 hours after oral administration and is maintained for 8 to 12 hours. Oxazepam is inactivated by conjugation with glucuronic acid in the liver and other tissues. Since this process is not limited to hepatic microsomes, oxazepam is safer than other benzodiazepines in patients with liver disease and in elderly patients. The main disadvantage of oxazepam is the occurrence of paradoxical stimulation in some patients.[18] This stimulation, which is similar to alcoholic intoxication, occurs about 1 hour after oxazepam administration and lasts 30 to 60 minutes. In some patients, oxazepam loses its effectiveness after being used for several weeks. It is not clear if this is due to the progression of the disease or to development of tolerance. Oxazepam, like other benzodiazepines, should be discontinued gradually to prevent a withdrawal state that could precipitate convulsions.

Diazepam. The onset of action of diazepam (Valium) is very rapid and the action is prolonged. Diazepam has a long biological half-life (1½ days) and is metabolized in the liver into an active metabolite that has an even longer biological half-life. Therefore, prolonged diazepam administration can lead to accumulation of diazepam and its metabolite and to a gradual increase in sedation. In elderly patients low doses of diazepam should be used (2 to 5 mg) because its metabolism is decreased with age. Diazepam has strong muscle relaxant activity and it has been found to be useful in some patients who develop muscle rigidity.

Temazepam. Temazepam (Restoril) is marketed as a hypnotic. It has a slow onset of action and its effect lasts about 8 hours. Thus it is useful in patients who have little difficulty falling asleep but tend to wake up during the night. Development of tolerance is a major problem when temazepam is used on a regular basis. Therefore, diphenhydramine is used for initial treatment of sleep disturbances, and temazepam is not used in patients who are receiving other benzodiazepines during the day. In patients who have difficulties falling asleep but sleep well after they do fall asleep, triazolam (Halcion) might be a better choice because of its fast onset of action. However, its therapeutic effect lasts only about 6 hours and a rebound anxiety during the next day has been described.[19]

Chloral Hydrate

Chloral hydrate decreases sleep latency and the number of nocturnal awakenings and has very little effect on rapid eye movement (REM) sleep. The mechanism of action of chloral hydrate is not well understood. The hypnotic effect appears to be mediated by its metabolite trichloroethanol, which has a biological half-life of 8 to 10 hours. The adverse effects of chloral hydrate include gastrointestinal irritation and rare allergic reaction. Although its metabolism is not affected by aging of the individual, chloral hydrate does influence the metabolism of several drugs. This effect is mediated by either inhibition of their liver metabolism or by displacement of these drugs from protein binding by one of the chloral hydrate metabolites, trichloracetic acid. Chloral hydrate should not be given to patients with significant liver or kidney impairment. It is useful in patients receiving benzodiazepines during the day whose sleeping disturbances do not respond to diphenhydramine.

β-Adrenergic Receptor Antagonists

β-Adrenergic receptors are present in the heart, blood vessels, bronchial and other smooth muscle, fat tissue, brain, and other organs. There are two types of β-adrenergic receptors: $β_1$, located in the heart, and $β_2$, located in smooth muscles. β-Adrenergic receptors mediate stimulation of heart rate and contractility, vasodilation, bronchodilatation, and some metabolic processes. β-Adrenergic receptor antagonists are used mainly in the treatment of cardiovascular diseases, including hypertension, coronary artery disease, cardiac arrhythmias, and migraine headache. However, they also have some effects on the brain and have been found to prevent anxiety states (stage fright) and to produce depression as a side effect when used for the treatment of cardiovascular diseases.

Several β-adrenergic receptor antagonists are available for clinical use. The oldest drug in common use is propranolol (Inderal), which blocks both types of β-adrenergic receptors. Other β-blockers (e.g., metoprolol [Lopressor]) are selective for $β_1$-receptors or block β-receptors only partially (e.g., pindolol [Visken]). Propranolol has been reported to decrease the occurrence of rage and violent behavior in patients with brain damage due to a trauma, infection, alcohol abuse, or anoxia.[20] The same effect has been reported for pindolol,[21] which has the added advantage that it does not decrease the heart rate as much as propranolol and, therefore, it does not have to be discontinued because of bradycardia.

Evidence for the effectiveness of β-adrenergic blocking agents in treatment of Alzheimer dementia is much weaker. Petrie and Ban[22] described three patients with the clinical diagnosis of Alzheimer dementia whose agitation was improved by propranolol treatment. A decrease in patients' pacing behavior after propranolol administration has also been observed, but often the pacing was replaced by a bizarre behavior (e.g., rearranging of furniture, removing railing) that was more disruptive than pacing.

β-Adrenergic blocking agents should not be administered to patients suffering from bronchial asthma because they could precipitate an asthmatic attack. In this respect selective $β_1$-blockers are safer than nonselective ones. β-Blockers also should not be administered to patients with sinus bradycardia and cardiac block or to patients with marginal cardiac function because they could precipitate congestive heart failure. β-Blockers should be given with caution to patients with diabetes mellitus, because they block tachycardia induced by hypoglycemia, and to patients with hyperthyroidism, because they mask some symptoms of this disease. The dosage of β-blockers should be decreased gradually to prevent rebound coronary ischemia and hyperthyroidism.

Neuroleptics

Despite the effectiveness of drugs mentioned in the previous sections, most Alzheimer patients sooner or later require treatment with neuroleptics, which are more effective for treatment of behavioral problems than benzodiazepines.[23]

These drugs were developed for the treatment of psychotic disorders. The antipsychotic effect is presumably generated by the blockade of dopaminergic receptors in the brain. It is not clear if this is also the mechanism of their action in Alzheimer patients. Although "psychotic symptoms" (e.g., hallucinations and delusions) occur in some Alzheimer patients, they are relatively uncommon and may not be directly related to behavioral problems seen in most Alzheimer patients. In addition to the effect on dopaminergic receptors, neuroleptics also affect α-adrenergic, histamine, and serotonin receptors. It is possible, therefore, that the beneficial effect of neuroleptics in Alzheimer dementia has a different mechanism of action than the antipsychotic effect.

Unfortunately, all neuroleptics often produce undesirable effects. The most common of these are extrapyramidal effects, anticholinergic effects, and postural hypotension. The most common extrapyramidal effects are muscle rigidity and tremor at rest. Other extrapyramidal effects include acute dystonia (spasm of muscles of tongue, face, neck, or back) and akathisia (motor restlessness), which may occur soon after initiation of neuroleptic therapy, and tardive dyskinesia (involuntary movements of face and other muscles), which may occur when neuroleptics are used chronically. Anticholinergic effects include dry mouth, blurred vision, constipation, and urinary retention.

According to the incidence of undesirable effects, it is possible to distinguish two groups of neuroleptics. Drugs from one group (e.g., haloperidol [Haldol], thiothixene [Navane]) produce more extrapyramidal effects but have little anticholinergic activity. Drugs from the second group (e.g., chlorpromazine [Thorazine], fluphenazine [Prolixin, Permitil]) produce more anticholinergic side effects but less extrapyramidal effects. Both of these groups seem to be equally effective in treatment of behavioral problems in Alzheimer patients.[24] Therefore, the choice of an agent depends on the patient's condition and the probability and danger of these two kinds of undesirable effects. It is more important to avoid anticholinergic effects in a patient with prostatic hypertrophy, or who still has some preserved memory function, than in a patient who is in a more advanced stage of dementia and has some signs of muscle rigidity.

In addition to the three main adverse effects described above, neuroleptics may also produce sedation. Hypersensitivity to neuroleptics may also occur and lead to rash, dermatitis, or jaundice. To prevent neuroleptic side effects it is important to use the lowest effective dose and to reevaluate the need for treatment periodically. Very commonly with progression of Alzheimer dementia, the need for neuroleptic medication decreases and only a few patients in the late and terminal stages of Alzheimer's disease require neuroleptic medication.

Haloperidol

The main advantage of haloperidol (Haldol) is the lack of anticholinergic activity. Haloperidol is effective in low doses (0.5 to 1 mg twice or three times a day) in controlling behavioral problems of Alzheimer patients.[25] However, the incidence of extrapyramidal effects is rather high. A cholinergic receptor antagonist (e.g., benztropine [Cogentin], trihexyphenidyl [Artane]) has sometimes been added to haloperidol treatment to prevent or to decrease extrapyramidal effects. However, this approach negates the advantage of haloperidol over neuroleptics with anticholinergic activity. If extrapyramidal effects pose a problem, it may be better to switch from haloperidol to another neuroleptic with lower incidence of extrapyramidal effects.

Thioridazine

Thioridazine (Mellaril) is another neuroleptic that has been consistently found to be effective in the treatment of behavioral problems in Alzheimer patients.[24] It is metabolized into an active metabolite mesoridazine (Serentil), which is itself also used as a neuroleptic. Thioridazine produces fewer extrapyramidal symptoms than haloperidol but is more likely to cause anticholinergic effects and postural hypotension. Low doses are again effective, ranging from 10 mg twice a day to 25 mg three times a day.

Loxapine

Loxapine (Loxitane) is a neuroleptic that has been found to be as effective as thioridazine in the treatment of behavioral problems in Alzheimer patients.[26] The incidence of orthostatic hypotension in patients treated with loxapine is lower than in patients treated with thioridazine. The dose of loxapine is 2.5 to 5 mg twice or three times daily.

Drugs Used in the Late Stage of Alzheimer Dementia

With the progression of Alzheimer dementia, hyperactivity and behavioral problems decrease and other symptoms start posing a problem. Patients in this stage often are no longer able to walk by themselves, either because they are at risk of injury from not recognizing obstacles and walking into walls and furniture or because they develop motor incoordination, lean to one side, and are at risk of falling. The two most bothersome symptoms occurring at this stage are seizures and constipation.

Anticonvulsants

Convulsions are not very common but are an alarming occurrence in 10% to 20% of Alzheimer patients. The seizures are usually easily controlled by anticonvulsants. The most commonly used anticonvulsant is phenytoin (Dilantin). In addition to its anticonvulsant activity, phenytoin is described as having other effects that might be beneficial in Alzheimer patients (e.g., improvement in cognitive function [27] and reduction in irritability and anxiety[28]). However, it is not known whether phenytoin has these effects in Alzheimer patients.

Phenytoin is a relatively toxic drug that has to be administered with caution. Toxic effects include neurologic features (nystagmus, ataxia, diplopia, and vertigo), behavioral features (hyperactivity, confusion, drowsiness, and hallucinations), gingival hyperplasia, and gastrointestinal features (nausea, vomiting, anorexia, epigastric pain). The toxic effects can be prevented by maintaining phenytoin plasma concentrations within the therapeutic range (10 to 20 µg/mL). The metabolism of phenytoin decreases with increased plasma concentration; therefore, the dose has to be increased very slowly. After the therapeutic concentration is reached, phenytoin can be administered in a single daily dose.

Laxatives

Constipation occurs frequently in patients with late-stage Alzheimer dementia, and almost all patients require some treatment. There are several factors that predispose these patients to constipation. Drugs with anticholinergic activity and other drugs (opiates, analgesics, antacids, clonidine, monoamine oxidase inhibitors, verapamil) decrease intestinal motility. Decreased food and liquid intake decreases the stool volume and softness, and a lack of motor activity could be also a predisposing factor. In addition, it is possible that the disease process itself leads to discoordination of processes needed for normal bowel movements. There are several drugs that may be used in the treatment of constipation in Alzheimer patients.

Bulk-Forming Laxatives

The most satisfactory treatment for functional constipation is an increase in dietary fiber. This can be provided by a diet rich in whole grains, bran, vegetables, and fruit. Bran can be added to some foods by nursing staff at the bedside. Other preparations include psyllium (Metamucil, Konsyl), methylcellulose (Cologel), and polycarbophil (Mitrolan).

Dietary fiber acts as a laxative by binding water and ions in the intestinal lumen. This effect increases softness of the feces and increases bulk. Some components of dietary fiber (e.g., pectin) are metabolized by bacteria to osmotically active products that further increase softness and bulk of the feces. The main danger of bulk-forming laxatives is intestinal obstruction and impaction. It is important to exclude impaction as a cause of constipation before administering bulk-forming laxatives.

Osmotic Laxatives

Osmotic laxatives are various salts of magnesium and phosphate salts of sodium, which are poorly absorbed and therefore bind water in the intestinal lumen. In addition, magnesium salts increase secretion of cholecystokinin, which stimulates intestinal fluid secretion and motility. The most commonly used agent is milk of magnesia, which is an aqueous suspension of magnesium hydroxide. It is usually given in the evening (30 mL) to promote morning bowel evacuation.

Although magnesium salts are poorly absorbed, some absorption does occur. This can lead to magnesium accumulation in patients with compromised kidney function and magnesium toxicity. Similarly, sodium phosphates (Phospho-Soda) should not be given to patients with congestive heart failure or hypertension, whose salt intake should be restricted. Hypertonic solutions of osmotic laxatives can produce significant dehydration and have to be administered with sufficient fluids to prevent fluid loss.

Stimulant Laxatives

Stimulant laxatives directly stimulate intestinal motility and also promote accumulation of water and electrolytes in the intestinal lumen. Some of this activity is due to increased synthesis of prostaglandins. Therefore, drugs that inhibit prostaglandin synthesis (aspirin and other nonsteroidal anti-inflammatory agents, (e.g., ibuprofen [Motrin], indomethacin [Indocin]) reduce the activity of stimulant laxatives. There are many agents in this group with different properties and uses, but only some of them are suitable for long-term management of constipation in Alzheimer patients.

Prune Juice. Administration of prune juice provides gentle stimulation of intestinal motility and promotes bowel evacuation. In a pilot study, administration of prune juice, 120 mL every morning, was found to be as effective as administration of docusates in promoting bowel evacuation in Alzheimer patients. Prune juice is well accepted by the patients and provides an additional source of fluid.

Docusates. Docusate sodium (Colace, Doxinate), docusate calcium (Surfak), and docusate potassium (Kasof) are surfactants used industrially as emulsifying, wetting, and dispersing agents. In clinically used doses they have minimal laxative effect and act mainly by keeping feces soft. Docusates increase absorption of other drugs, and this effect could precipitate drug toxicity. There is also a possibility that they potentiate hepatotoxic effects of some drugs (e.g., danthron [Modane]).

Bisacodyl. Bisacodyl (Dulcolax) is a derivative of phenolphthalein, which was originally used as a food additive. Bisacodyl is available in rectal suppositories and produces bowel evacuation in 15 to 60 minutes. It may be used when bowel evacuation does not occur for 3 consecutive days despite the use of other laxatives described previously. The main danger of bisacodyl is fluid and electrolyte deficit resulting from an excessive laxative effect. Bisacodyl suppositories may also produce a burning sensation in the rectum and mild proctitis. They should be used only as an agent of last resort, as rarely as possible. If a patient does not tolerate rectal suppositories, bisacodyl may be administered orally. Alternatively, a rectal enema may be used for bowel evacuation in a refractory patient.

Drugs Used in the Terminal Stage of Alzheimer Dementia

Alzheimer dementia is not lethal by itself because it mostly spares the autonomic nervous system. The patients therefore die of intercurrent illnesses, with pneumonia and urinary tract infection being the two most common processes. The terminal stage is often prolonged over several days or weeks. Maintenance of a patient's comfort during this period is a considerable challenge for staff members. It requires mainly intensive nursing techniques (see Chapter 10), but some drug treatment is also useful.

Morphine

During the terminal stage of the disease some Alzheimer patients develop hypersensitivity to touch. This could be related to the decreased endorphin concentration in the cerebrospinal fluid reported by some investigators.[29] Small doses of oral morphine solution (5 to 10 mg every 4 to 6 hours) appear to greatly increase the comfort of these patients during routine nursing procedures. Other patients develop restlessness, moving continually in the bed. The movements can lead to skin abrasion and pose a risk for development of decubitus ulcers. Small doses of morphine are also effective in decreasing this restlessness.

Used in these small doses morphine does not cause substantial respiratory depression or vomiting, and the main adverse effect is constipation. There is little development of tolerance, and the same doses are effective for several weeks. If a patient is unable to swallow an oral solution, 2 mg of morphine given subcutaneously is effective.

Atropine

The decreased ability to cough together with increased secretion due to an inflammatory process often leads to fluid accumulation in the bronchial tree of terminal Alzheimer patients. The fluid accumulation often requires frequent suctioning, which decreases comfort of the patient. Atropine may be administered to these patients to block cholinergic receptors and to decrease respiratory secretion and the need for frequent suctioning. Scopolamine has a similar effect and may have the added advantage of producing drowsiness and euphoria.

REFERENCES

1. Ermini M, Markstein R: Hydergine therapy: Mechanism of action. Br J Clin Pract 1982;36:suppl 16.

2. Loew DM, Weil C: Hydergine in senile mental impairment. Gerontology 1982;28:54-74.

3. Sinzinger H: Double blind study of the influence of co-dergocrine on platelet parameters in healthy volunteers. Eur J Clin Pharmacol 1985;28:713-716.

4. Cook P, James I: Cerebral vasodilators. N Engl J Med 1981;305:1508-1513,1560-1564.

5. Coyle JT, Price DL, DeLong MR: Alzheimer's disease: A disorder of cortical cholinergic innervation. Science 1983;219:1184-1190.

6. Bartus RT, Dean RL III, Beer B, et al: The cholinergic hypothesis of geriatric memory dysfunction. Science 1982;217:408-414.

7. Brinkman SD, Gershon S: Measurements of cholinergic drug effects on memory in Alzheimer's disease. Neurobiol Aging 1983;4:139-145.

8. Harbaugh RE: Intracranial drug administration in Alzheimer's disease. Psychopharmacol Bull 1986;22:106-109.

9. Summers WK, Majovski LV, Marsh GM, et al: Oral tetrahydroaminoacridine in long-term treatment of senile dementia, Alzheimer type. N Engl J Med 1986;315:1241-1245.

10. Lazarus LW, Newton N, Cohler B, et al: Frequency and presentation of depressive symptoms in patients with primary degenerative dementia. Am J Psychiatry 1987;144:41-45.

11. Reifler BV, Larson E, Teri L, et al: Dementia of the Alzheimer's type and depression. J Am Geriatr Soc 1986;34:855-859.

12. Reisberg B: Clinical presentation, diagnosis, and symptomatology of age-associated cognitive decline and Alzheimer's disease, in Reisberg B (eds): Alzheimer's Disease. New York, Free Press, 1983.

13. Abernethy DR, Greenblatt DJ, Shader RI: Imipramine and desipramine disposition in the elderly. J Pharmacol Exp Ther 1985;232:183-188.

14. Coccaro EF, Siever LJ: Second generation antidepressants: A comparative review. J Clin Pharmacol 1985;25:241-260.

15. Simpson DM, Foster D: Improvement in organically disturbed behavior with trazodone treatment. J Clin Psychiatry 1986;47:191-193.

16. Liston EH, La Rue A: Clinical differentiation of primary degenerative and multi-infarct dementia: A critical review of the evidence: II: Pathological studies. Biol Psychiatry 1983;18:1451-1484.

17. Berlinger WG, Goldberg MJ, Spector R, et al: Diphenhydramine: Kinetics and psychomotor effects in elderly women. Clin Pharmacol Ther 1982;32:387-391.

18. Lion JR, Azcarate CL, Koepke HH: "Paradoxical rage reactions" during psychotropic medications. Dis Nerv Syst 1975;36:557-558.

19. Kales A, Soldatos CR, Bixler EO, et al: Early morning insomnia with rapidly eliminated benzodiazepines. Science 1983;220:95-97.

20. Yudofsky S, Williams D, Gorman J: Propranolol in the treatment of rage and violent behavior in patients with chronic brain syndromes. Am J Psychiatry 1981;138:218-219.

21. Greendyke RM, Kanter DR: Therapeutic effects of pindolol on behavioral disturbances associated with organic brain disease: A double blind study. J Clin Psychiatry 1986;47:423-426.

22. Petrie WM, Ban TA: Propranolol in organic agitation. Lancet 1981;1:324.

23. Kirven LE, Montero EF: Comparison of thioridazine and diazepam in the control of nonpsychotic symptoms associated with senility: Double-blind study. J Am Geriatr Soc 1973;21:546-551.

24. Helms PM: Efficacy of antipsychotics in the treatment of the behavioral complications of dementia: Review of the literature. J Am Geriatr Soc 1985;33:206-209.

25. Steinhart MJ: The use of haloperidol in geriatric patients with organic mental disorder. Curr Ther Res 1983;33:132-143.

26. Barnes R, Veith R, Okimoto J, et al: Efficacy of antipsychotic medications in behaviorally disturbed dementia patients. Am J Psychiatry 1982;139:1170-1174.

27. Smith WL, Lowrey JB: Effects of diphenylhydantoin on mental abilities in the elderly. J Am Geriatr Soc 1975;23:207-211.

28. Stephens JH, Shaffer JW: A controlled replication of the effectiveness of diphenylhydantoin in reducing irritability and anxiety in selected neurotic outpatients. *J Clin Pharmacol* 1973;13:351-356.

29. Kaiya H, Tanaka T, Takeuchi K, et al: Decreased level of beta-endorphin-like immunoreactivity in cerebrospinal fluid of patients with senile dementia of Alzheimer type. *Life Sci* 1983;33:1039-1043.

CHAPTER 12

Education and Training of Interdisciplinary Team Members Caring for Alzheimer Patients

Yvette L. Rheaume, Kathy J. Fabiszewski, June Brown, Phyllis Innis, Mary Glennon, Deborah Berkley, Susan Shea, and Ladislav Volicer

As increasing numbers of patients with Alzheimer's disease require continuous long-term care, there is a corresponding need for high-quality services provided by a staff expert in care and research in this area. To provide a range of long-term services, certain requirements are essential to ensure specialized care in meeting the intensive physical, emotional, and psychosocial needs of patients with Alzheimer's disease. Because of the intensity of care and the duration of long-term care, provisions for the education and training of staff and the development of interdisciplinary planning teams are crucial components in providing comprehensive care. Finally, an essential component in ensuring high quality care is a consistent conceptual framework of patient care, supported by administration and adhered to by all staff.

Most people caring for victims of Alzheimer dementia have not received any training specifically oriented toward care of these patients. Until relatively recently, Alzheimer dementia was not generally recognized as a specific and common disease. Most Alzheimer patients were considered to have "organic brain syndrome," a diagnosis that did not differentiate between various causes of dementia. Consequently, care of Alzheimer patients in nursing homes and other chronic care facilities was provided without any consideration for their special needs.

A similar situation existed in the E.N. Rogers Memorial Veterans Hospital 10 years ago when the Geriatric Research Education Clinical Center (GRECC) was formed and assumed responsibility for three inpatient units. Because the hospital was a neuropsychiatric facility, the patient population on these intermediate medical wards consisted of patients with various chronic neurologic diseases (multiple sclerosis, Huntington's disease, Korsakoff psychosis, Alzheimer dementia) combined with patients suffering from chronic mental diseases. Investigation of Alzheimer dementia has been the main research focus of GRECC since its inception. GRECC investigators differentiated Alzheimer dementia and organic brain syndrome from other causes of dementia in patients hospitalized in various units of the hospital.[1] Additional patients suffering from Alzheimer dementia were accepted for outpatient studies, and many of them were later admitted to GRECC wards. This work led to a larger proportion of Alzheimer patients hospitalized on GRECC units and to further clinical and research programs.

Early in the program, it was recognized that Alzheimer dementia affects not only the victim but his or her entire family. To relieve stress and strain on family caregivers, supportive services including individual counseling and support groups for spouses and adult children of Alzheimer patients were conducted by a psychiatrist, psychologist, and social worker. Additional support for family caregivers included short-term admission of Alzheimer outpatients to provide respite from the continuous care they required and home visits to patient's families. The home visits by nursing and social services were later discontinued because of lack of administration support as well as lack of personnel resources. The respite admissions developed into a formal program (see Chapter 6).

As the number of Alzheimer patients increased it became clear that they have special needs. In response to that, several programs were instituted, some more successful than others. One of the unsuccessful programs was stratification of the units. One of the 25-bed units was designated to contain 2 respite beds, into which patients were admitted for 2 weeks each, and the initial place for any Alzheimer patient admitted for long-term care. When these patients' physical function deteriorated and skilled care was needed, they were transferred to one of the other two units for long-term care. This arrangement was not successful for several reasons:

1. Transferring patients to an unfamiliar clinical unit generated stress for both patients and their families. Both patients and their family members get to know staff on a unit and have difficulties developing new relationships. In addition, deterioration of the patient's physical functions sometimes coincided with the transfer to the new unit. As a consequence, families blamed ("scapegoated") the new staff for the change in patient function, even though patient function declines in the natural progression of the illness even in the absence of a transfer.
2. Grouping together on one clinical unit only ambulatory patients suffering from the middle stages of Alzheimer's disease caused problems in daily interactions of these patients. A higher patient-to-staff ratio is necessary to supervise and care for restless and disoriented ambulatory patients. The incidence of patients experiencing aggressive and catastrophic reactions increased and contributed to staff burnout.
3. Staff morale was affected on the other two clinical units where patients were transferred for long-term care and terminal care. Nursing staff on these units suffered from the stress of caring for only terminally ill patients. Nursing staff felt deprived of the human contact of the less regressed patients with Alzheimer's disease.

Successful clinical programs included strengthening interdisciplinary staff meetings to plan for the multiple needs of these patients, the initiation of family conferences in planning levels of medical care, and the institution of formalized staff support groups led by psychiatry and social service. The function and impact of interdisciplinary staff meetings are discussed later in this chapter. Family meetings were initiated because there was a need to include family members in planning continuing care for the institutionalized patient with Alzheimer's disease. Since patients are unable to make choices regarding treatment, help was sought from patients' families. As a result of family involvement, the hospice approach was developed (See Chapter 10).

In this chapter an experiential orientation and training program for professional and nonprofessional nursing staff is described. Certain sections in this chapter focus on criteria for staff selection and incentives for retention, an orientation and training program, and staff support programs and the advantages of continuing education for staff development. Special emphasis is placed on the need for a humanistic approach as the philosophical basis of patient care management. Each patient is recognized and accepted as a unique person, with his or her own special needs. Consequently, the approach and management of the patient is personalized. Each person is cared for, during his or her shortened life span, with respect and regard for his or her worth. This is perceived as an inalienable patient's right to comprehensive care directed by the expertise of interdisciplinary services. The presence of a clearly stated humanistic philosophy of care, supported by administration and implemented by a sensitive and compassionate staff, is the crucial component for ensuring high quality care and for contributing to peak performance and high staff morale. This humanistic approach as the conceptual framework strengthens interdisciplinary planning and comprehensive patient care throughout the respite program, long-term care, and, finally, the hospice program.

Need for a Specialty Care Unit

Increased attention is focused on the need for specialty care units to provide patients and their families with comprehensive care and interdisciplinary planning. To best provide continuous high-quality services, a special care unit based on the principles of homogeneous grouping is recommended along with a humanistic care approach as the most beneficial and protective living arrangement for patients institutionalized with Alzheimer dementia. By tradition, homogeneous grouping is a concept based on the belief that when the largest number of patients suffering from the same illness are grouped together in one designated area, patients will derive the greatest amount of benefits such as the provision of interdisciplinary services, activities, and specialty trained staff.[2]

Based on clinical experience, when patients with Alzheimer dementia reside together in one unit, there is a heightened awareness of the impact of patient behaviors, and the need for a protective environment, as well as a sensitivity to dilemmas in patient care. In addition, there is a recognition that most institutionalized patients with Alzheimer's disease suffer from similar neurologic symptoms that endanger their physical safety. These behaviors include the following:

1. Agnosias, visual and tactile: the inability to recognize or understand the significance of objects in the environment, thereby making the patients prone to injuries and falls (see Chapter 7).
2. Hyperorality, the tendency of the patients to touch environmental objects with their hands or their mouths. In response to that, a protective environment was developed (see Chapter 6).

3. The loss of the ability to react appropriately when injured. Therefore, staff members skilled in physical assessment are necessary.
4. Patients can accidentally inflict injury on other patients. Therefore, patients with impaired physical mobility need special protection.

Advantages of homogeneous grouping are as follows:

1. The greatest number of patients will benefit from protective environments to meet their need for physical and emotional security.
2. Activities are delivered on the unit so that the greatest number of patients will have access.
3. An interdisciplinary team plans, directs, and evaluates patient care modalities.
4. Staff support is available to develop coping strategies.
5. Family needs are recognized in structured support groups.
6. Staff are trained in interactive communication skills when managing patients.
7. Patients exhibiting certain behaviors (e.g., pacing) can share their activities and interact on a level that is comfortable to them.
8. Terminally ill patients can be afforded privacy and dignity.

Criteria for Staff Selection

Staff expectations and development begin during the employment interview. During the initial interview, the applicants' communication abilities are assessed. The applicants should be questioned about their professional motives for seeking employment in an Alzheimer special care unit. The professionals should be able to identify their feelings about caring for memory-impaired patients, perceptions about patients with limited life spans, and personal sensitivity in coping with stress as well as their willingness to interact with teams and support groups. At the time of interview, expectations about a helping relationship in patient care, the philosophical framework, and peer expectations are openly discussed. Personal and professional qualities of a hospice nurse are highly suitable characteristics needed in the care of the patient with Alzheimer's disease. A compassionate nature is not readily observed during interviews; however, during a 6-month orientation and training program, levels of sensitivity, human competence, and interpersonal skill may be developed in motivated employees. Employees are encouraged to explore and learn interactive skills and in turn be evaluated for their interest and capacity to care for patients and their families afflicted by Alzheimer's disease.

Nurses are the backbone of long-term care; yet long-term care is a low-prestige and low-paying specialty.[3] Attracting and retaining knowledgeable, skilled, enthusiastic, and empathic professionals to direct and coordinate the care of Alzheimer dementia patients requires ingenuity, perseverance, and willingness of nursing administrators to invest considerable time and energy in recruiting and then educating and providing specialized training to nursing personnel.

Seldom do nurses with prior training in caring for dementia victims apply for a position in the GRECC's 75-bed inpatient specialty program for Alzheimer dementia care. In recent years, however, more and more nurses with geriatric or long-term care experience have become attracted to these special care units. These nurses recognize the opportunity to integrate direct patient care and the role of clinical research and intramural and extramural (community) education. Some nurses from other departments within our large medical center are attracted to the GRECC unit and have requested assignment there. For the most part, motivated professionals whose willingness to learn and participate in interdisciplinary planning is combined with the personal attribute of patience are highly suitable for practice on a specialty unit.

Another group from which to draw is that of new graduate nurses. Since they receive only limited clinical experience (both acute and chronic) during generic nursing education, they sometimes request consideration for employment because of the limited use of medical technology on these units. For these new graduates, the Alzheimer specialty unit provides a supportive atmosphere for beginning assessment skills, documentation skills, and for team problem solving.

Nursing professionals who previously practiced in acute care settings such as intensive care units are also a valuable group of nurses from which to draw. These nurses generally possess clinical confidence and expertise in physical assessment. In an acute care setting, however, nursing assessments tend to be less valued because of the acuity of the patient illnesses and the urgency with which care is often delivered, "competition" with medical residents and consultant physicians, and the need to focus their nursing energies on managing high-technology machinery such as Swan-Ganz catheters and ventilators rather than on the patients themselves. For these experienced professionals, caring for patients in an Alzheimer unit provides them with a unique opportunity for autonomous and collaborative practice.

A number of critical variables must be entertained in selecting nursing staff, both professional and nonprofessional, to care for the patient with Alzheimer's disease. Although the ingredients that comprise the "ideal" Alzheimer caregiver are endless, examples of desirable characteristics include maturity, patience, demonstrated ability to work well with others, flexibility, and compassion. Although experience in caring for the elderly is desirable, many people with little or no long-term care experience repeatedly demonstrate the potential to grow and have, in fact, grown to become true assets to the GRECC program. The desire to learn is important. The ability to function as a team member is a necessity. Willingness to accept the fact that the patient with Alzheimer's disease cannot be cured of this illness is essential.

Orientation and Training

An adjustment period of at least 6 months is necessary for the nurse caregiver to learn communication skills for the optimal management of patients' behaviors and to learn interdisciplinary interactive skills for planning patient and family care. New nurse employees frequently question their competence and their tolerance during the orientation and training period. All new employees experience an adaptive process before becoming comfortable with patients and their families (Figure 12-1). Faced with seemingly overwhelming tasks in caring for patients who need constant care and supervision, compounded by the expectations to interact with skilled team members, some employees experience a type of "reality shock."[4] This reaction is partly caused by the impact of the illness and the shock of not being prepared to care for this type of patient. Most nurses were not pre-

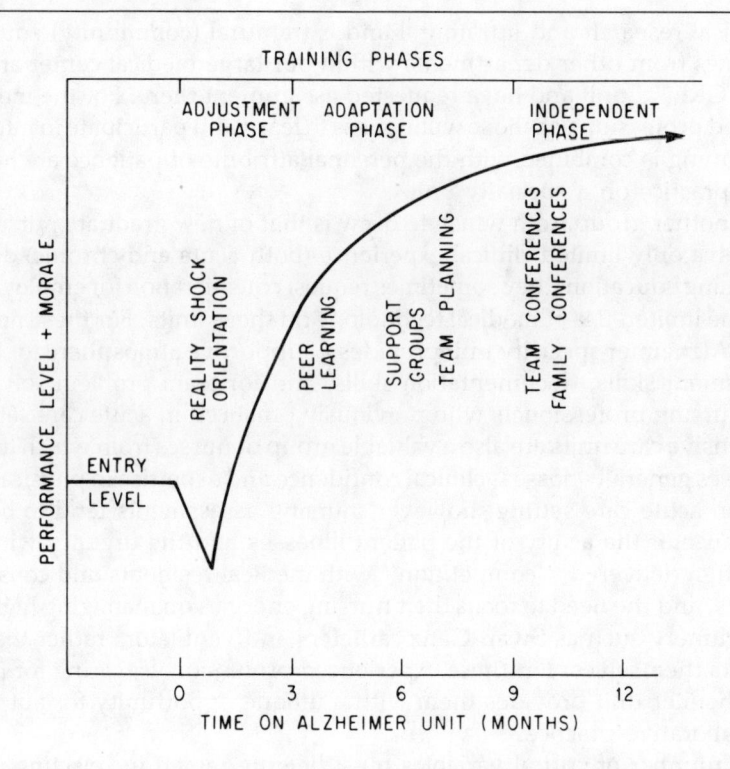

Figure 12-1 Performance curve and training phases of nursing staff caring for Alzheimer patient on a special unit.

pared in nursing schools to cope with memory-impaired patients and to cope with their stressed families or to cope with the frequent exposure to the death of the patient with advanced Alzheimer's disease. Because of these stresses, some employees request a different assignment and leave the unit, although most adjust with the helping attitude of a supportive staff. In the 10 years of clinical experience at our GRECC, we have found that peer teaching/peer mentorship are the best training programs for nurse and nursing assistants.

Peer Teaching

Peer teaching/learning is an educational model that was designed for undergraduate student nurses and is also advocated for introducing student nurses to the real-life situation of independent practice and review. To deliver high quality care, a peer teaching/learning model is an effective method for orienting and training new employees to understand and deliver comprehensive care to patients with Alzheimer's disease. The major advantage of this model is that experienced and dedicated professionals, who were involved in the development of the GRECC unit, become strong advocates in teaching and maintaining the treatment philosophy, patient care patterns, interdisciplinary team planning, and empathic attitudes. Criteria for responsible and consistent peer teacher behavior include the following:

1. Sensitivity to the anxiety level of the learner
2. Empathic attitude toward learner's ability to adapt
3. Patience in teaching patient communication skills
4. Willingness to guide learner in caring for patients
5. Responsiveness to learner's needs
6. Consistency in giving positive feedback/constructive criticism

Nurse peer teachers in the GRECC have reported positive feedback similar to recent viewpoints in the literature. For example, it has been described that, in general, students who teach other students frequently learn as much or more than the student they teach.[5]

Each new hired individual professional as well as nursing assistants are assigned to an individual peer nurse teacher who functions in the dual capacity of a teacher and supervisor. As a consequence, there is continuous interaction and feedback between the learner and the peer teacher during patient encounters. This model provides new nurses with opportunities to assume responsibility for learning at their own pace, to practice direct patient care under an experienced peer, and to better accept guidance as well as constructive criticism from their peer teacher. In addition, this teaching method fosters a mutual respect and an informal support network between the peer teacher and learner.

Staff morale and clinical functioning, during the orientation period, is considerably influenced by the organizational climate, and especially by the attitudes and behaviors of the nursing staff. Proper motivation should be provided for the new staff early in this orientation. Consequently, focus is placed on staff development that begins during orientation/training and is ongoing to provide staff with opportunities for achievement and responsibility in excellence in patient care, personal growth through participation in support networks, professional advancement, and recognition. The following objectives for the training program are interrelated with our treatment aims. Each staff member should

1. Understand the humanistic philosophy of caring for patients with Alzheimer's disease.
2. Learn about the impact of the progressive nature of the illness on the patient and the family.
3. Learn about the dynamics of a helping/responding relationship toward patients and their families.
4. Learn about the standards of care for patients' special needs.
5. Understand the importance and application of communication skills.
6. Become aware of personal feelings about the illness and its impact on families.
7. Learn about support networks for nursing staff, other interdisciplinary staff and families.
8. Learn about the necessity for interdisciplinary team functioning for patient care planning.
9. Learn about the concepts of loss, prolonged grieving, and mourning experienced by families while patients are in long-term care.
10. Understand the functions of the respite program and his or her role in care of the patient.
11. Understand the need for research programs and his or her active participation in collecting and analyzing data.

A curriculum sample is included in Appendix 12-A. Feedback is a crucial element in the helping/responding relationship between the peer teacher and learner. Less anxiety and frustration and improved adaptive skills have resulted from this type of orientation. Employees seem to make an easier transition from orientation to training and seem to cope in a mature and independent way with problems elicited by patient behaviors and their responses to care. During the first 6 months of employment, individuals become adjusted to staff expectations, interdisciplinary interactions, and support systems. Some nurses perceive their training phase as a preparation for improved cooperation and collaboration among interdisciplinary team members. Within a year, most nurses are prepared to become role models and for the additional responsibilities for peer supervision and review.

Peer Mentoring

Most of the powerful executives have been taught by mentors in their employment settings and attribute much of their success to these supportive relationships.[6] In recent years, mentoring, as an important career advancement strategy, has played an increasingly significant role in the upward mobility of nursing professionals. Training nurses to assume major clinical, administrative, educational, and research roles in Alzheimer dementia care can and should involve a peer mentoring relationship.

In Alzheimer dementia care, nurses, as mentors, can provide career advice, education, and social support.[7] This type of assistance allows the newly graduated new employee opportunities to gain appropriate skills and take professional risks,[8] both of which can greatly accelerate career growth.

Ongoing Staff Education

Continuing education is as important for permanent staff members as orientation is to the new employee. The staff member must be made to realize that he or she is doing an important job and encouraged to make that effort as self-satisfying as possible. To foster group harmony and maintain cohesion, there must be continuous communication among the staff and the nursing unit administrator.

Daily discussions between staff members are conducted, preferably at the start of each tour of duty. The goals of these discussions are to share a wide range of nursing perspectives and feelings and the difficulties involved in delivering direct patient care. Consistent oral care, incontinence, and maintenance of skin integrity are also discussed. Staff members, who have been caring for the Alzheimer patients for a long period of time, need to reinforce to new employees the importance of a calm, quiet approach with this type of patient.

Developing morale is a group responsibility, even an expectation of all staff members. Tension and conflict are unavoidable in interpersonal relationships and is an expected occurrence in the intensive environment of caring for patients with Alzheimer's disease. As a consequence, each staff member, especially the nurse unit administrator, should be sensitive to evidence of staff frustrations including hostility and anger, as well as withdrawal and loss of concern and feeling for patients. These symptoms have been defined as ''staff burnout,''[9] a phenomenon of emotional and physical exhaustion. In general, burnout seems to occur in work situations when the patient–staff ratio is so high that the staff feels overwhelmed and unable to relate comfortably with patients and their families. For example, frustrations may intensify from time to time; at this point, staff members and the nurse administrator should sit down to calmly discuss the negative impact on the patient and the staff person when and if frustration takes over. Staff is reminded that the Alzheimer patient seems to mirror or mimic a frustrated caregiver's facial expressions and body movements. As a consequence a soft touch and a smile may change a hostile patient into a patient who is exhibiting more quiet and cooperative behavior.

When staffing is low, some staff members have the tendency to rush the feeding of patients. To prevent this behavior and attitude the importance of feeding patients the right diet, slowly to prevent choking and aspiration is stressed frequently through staff education.

There must be a good rapport between the staff members and the unit administrator. The unit administrator may set behavioral patterns of staff members that promote a calm environment. One stressed staff person can disrupt the whole unit, causing chaos and disruptive behavior in patients. It is also important to discuss grievances of the staff in an amicable way. Requests for time off should be honored when possible. If a staff member has a problem with a certain patient, his or her assignment should be changed if possible. Once a week, a staff support group led by a psychiatrist is held so that staff may vent their problems and frustrations. These meetings help the staff to realize that someone cares how they feel about their difficult work. Meetings of the staff are conducted as often as possible, at least two to three times weekly, to reduce tension and to foster participation in the decision making on the unit. Decisions are made about frequency of rest periods for ambulatory patients, how to dress ambulatory patients comfortably, and how often to get patients in the last stages of the disease out of bed.

In-service education on the unit, given by the nurse practitioner or the ward physician, is usually held on a weekly basis. At this time, the staff has the opportunity to choose the topic of their interest, one week in advance. The topic may be an illness secondary to the Alzheimer dementia or an unrelated illness. The important aspect is to keep the staff interested in caring and involvement with this type of patient.

Each staff member in turn, if he or she so desires, is encouraged to read the history of a patient of his or her choosing and discuss the patient's needs and their assessment at an informal staff meeting. The staff members are usually proud of this and place the history they have written and summary of feedback they received in the patient's record.

All outside workshops are discussed with the staff. Each staff member in turn is encouraged to attend a workshop, from time to time, away from the hospital. These workshops may be on Alzheimer's disease or other related illnesses. The staff is encouraged to share their information from these workshops with others. One or two staff members may attend and participate in teaching activities in nursing homes, day care centers, universities, and other hospitals seeking knowledge in caring for Alzheimer patients. The unit should keep current with new movies and other information on Alzheimer's disease. These movies are shown to the staff on the unit as well as families, if they happen to be present.

As part of the continuing education on the unit, a discussion group has been formed with the spouses of the patients for the purpose of building good rapport between the staff and families. This is not a support group, but it gives families the opportunity to ask questions regarding a patient's condition and current treatments. This provides the staff an hour once a month to relax and talk with the families in an informal way.

Staff Support

The unusual nature of concentrated and intensive care provided to institutionalized patients suffering from Alzheimer's disease requires continuous staff support. It is crucial for the morale and performance of staff members that each person be understood, supported, and recognized in a positive way for their efforts. Nursing staff, especially, need a support group led by a skilled counselor to help them identify and cope with ambivalent feelings regarding the patients and to guide them in assessing and resolving these difficult emotional issues. Staff stress can be minimized by the use of weekly support groups led by professionally trained personnel such as a psychiatrist, social worker, or a psychiatric clinical nurse specialist. Within the protective climate of a support group, staff become more sensitive to one another's needs.

Caregiving Dilemmas

A patient in the advanced stages of Alzheimer's disease with whom there is no mental contact may be an overpowering presence, a mute symbol of failure to help, to the sensitive caregiver. Nursing staff are subject to severe emotional distress when caring for patients in the advanced stages of Alzheimer dementia who are suffering from feeding difficulties.[10]

Specifically, when the decision not to use tube feeding for a patient has been previously endorsed by his or her family through the interdisciplinary team conference, it is the nursing staff who must provide the patient care. The experience of feeding a patient who may accept food only to spit it out or to choke, or who may even with clenched jaws refuse to eat, fosters frustration, anger, and often a sense of failure in the caregiver. The immobile, contracted, and mute patient may maintain eye contact and follow the caregiver with an unremitting stare that feels either like a plea for help or seems accusatory. A grimace, a snarl, or a fleeting facial contortion that looks like sorrow or pain seems a message to the most dispassionate observer. To force feed creates in the caregiver a sense of inducing pain or discomfort. Ironically, not feeding does not always give the caregiver a sense of relief. If the patient continues to stare or to display what seems to be a variety of emotions, the caregiver may be subject to emotions in response to the patient's behavior. It is not unusual for the caregiver to perceive the patient as frightened, sad, angry, or feeling helpless and unconsciously to replicate that feeling.

As a consequence, the dilemma between force feeding or allowing the patient to become malnourished because of persistent feeding problems becomes a perplexing predicament. Whatever the action taken, the patient's responses, real, reflex, or imagined, impose powerful emotional responses in the caregiver. Added to this dilemma is the anxiety within the caregiver to respect and acknowledge the patient that was and to assure himself or herself that he or she is not uncaring and unfeeling toward the patient. At this point, to define a patient as being in a vegetative state threatens the caregiver's own identity and self-respect. The need to validate his or her own worth leaves the caregiver open to the possibility that he or she may be ignoring the spark of humanity that might be remaining in the patient. Consequently, he or she may interpret the patient's refusal to eat as a wish to die, or a snout reflex that looks like a kiss as a will to live. Thus, while serving the philosophy of allowing the patient to die because of advanced dementia,[11] the caregiver is giving himself or herself and others the message that the patient is perhaps capable of conscious action.

To cope with the emotional stress and the guilt or frustration, the staff member may use defense mechanisms such as flight or scapegoating. The "flight" may be evidenced by reduction in caregiving, avoiding patient contact as much as possible. This can be a forerunner of guilty feelings within the caregiver, and a sense of failure in meeting personal standards of care. Flight from other staff members and the patient's family may result in further isolation. When the burden becomes too overwhelming, the defense of scapegoating may relieve internal tensions. By finding fault with other staff members, or the patients, self-blame may be eliminated. Unfortunately, this may result in still further isolation, poor or abusive treatment for the patient, and faulty or unfair judgments of other staff members or the patient's family. As the patient must be protected from neglect or abuse, so must staff members be protected from their own action of flight or scapegoating to prevent emotional burnout. The destructive elements of ambivalence may be strongly defended against, leaving the caregiver unaware of feelings of self-doubt or self-hate. The scapegoating that is a defense mechanism against these feelings may be directed at the treatment team, the patient, and/or the family. The family is often engaged in the same maladaptive coping process. Whether fleeing from the patient and one another, or scapegoating, all the caregivers may be depriving themselves of the capacity to comfort and be comforted. Compassion for one another is essential to reduce the stress. The nursing staff needs leadership and a forum to support them, to recognize and analyze the symptoms of ambivalent feelings toward patients, and to help them reaffirm the treatment philosophy and goals of concern and tender care for patients.[12]

Avoiding Depersonalization

Empathic understanding and responses are expected staff attitudes and behavior toward the patient with Alzheimer's disease. However, the continuous stress induced by the very nature of concentrated long-term care may generate feelings of detached concern for the patient. For example, a disconcerting aspect of institutionalization is the potential to sometimes depersonalize the patient. This is especially true of the patient with advanced Alzheimer dementia who is already deeply regressed because of the effects of the disease. An institution with its inherent need to structure and make aspects of care routine may be less concerned with the impact of depersonalization on a patient who is demented than a patient who is competent, alert, and oriented. Consequently, a heightened awareness on the part of the nursing staff is required to avoid inadvertent acts of depersonalization. In staff support groups, emphasis is placed on protecting the identity of the patient from the introduction of new "pet" names, from infantalization, or from mispronunciation of names. Although this does not always have a direct impact on the patient, the family may be distressed, yet hesitant to protest, and the staff then enters into an unconscious conspiracy to separate the patient from his or her past identity.

An exaggerated example of a kind of depersonalization came to us when a patient's name was seriously misspelled on his clothing, as well as on his room label. The error was discovered by accident and was corrected. The grateful wife said that she had not complained because she feared sounding critical. This behavior is not hard to understand in the light of the spouse's battered ego structure (see Chapter 3) of one who has a perceived loss to the concept of the right to claim respect. Staff are reminded to be meticulous in the spelling and pronunciation of the patient's name and to be equally cautious about conferring nicknames.

Understanding the Stress of Visiting Families

The professionally trained leader of the staff support group should foster adaptive capacities in the nursing staff to help them interact with stressed families who visit the patients in the long-term care setting. Relatives of the institutionalized Alzheimer patient bring their confusion, grief, anger, and guilt with them when they visit the patient and thus often add to the stress of the nursing staff. There are some ways in which the staff may be helped to understand why a family member behaves in this manner, perhaps then easing the burden of tolerating and accepting that behavior. The social worker as a team member provides elements of the family history and dynamics that may explain the actions of a difficult, often demanding visitor.

A spouse visiting a patient who no longer recognizes or is indifferent to his or her presence often displaces the hurt and anger onto the staff rather than direct them to the ill patient. If a staff member understands why he or she is the "target," of these feelings, the spouse's anger may not be taken personally. A spouse who demands endless information from the nursing staff may be considered disturbing and disruptive. The social worker can help the staff understand that questions asked of them are used as screens to disguise those questions that have no answer ("How long will this go on?") or answers that no one wants to hear ("Has he forgotten me?"). The staff who understands and accepts the source of families' stress learns to feel less frustrated when answering repetitive questions or deferring their answers.

The staff's capacity to understand and cope with a visitor's seemingly outrageous demands can lessen their sense of humiliation and anger, especially when unjustly criticized. Knowing that a wife may feel jealous of a female nurse who becomes the new caregiver can help that nurse feel less defensive about the hug she has just given the patient to calm him. To know that this simple caring gesture may symbolize to the wife the unbridgeable gap between her and her husband-patient helps the nurse tolerate any stressful behavior that the wife might exhibit toward her. Nursing staff can be helped to refer families to other team members for assistance. Not all in the series of difficult behaviors of visitors can be addressed or understood, but it can be useful for other disciplines to assist with difficult situations and to help keep communications open.

The social worker should convey praise to the nursing staff from the family who may not think to be as direct with compliments as with criticism and should help extricate the staff from a family who tries to absorb them in a personal relationship that may be burdensome. Since the relationship between staff and patient's families may extend over several years, staff members need the opportunity to acknowledge their feelings over the issues that may arise. Just as all patients are not lovable, neither are all families. The treatment team should maintain and foster an atmosphere of open communication to lessen the tensions in the long-term setting where many feelings and impulses must be contained. As a result it is advisable for the staff to have a forum such as formal staff support groups in which the members can express their feelings about the emotional demands created by caring for patients for whom rehabilitation and cure are not possible. It is unconscionable to overlook the stress of caring for patients whose dying process seems endless. When the disease has claimed the essence of the patient's identity as a person,[13] what remains may be only fleeting glimpses of what used to be. The pull to reclaim that human contact, or to retreat from it, may seem relentless. The social worker can help staff members to accept their feelings, to laugh, to be angry, and to mourn. Working with a patient population that exemplifies isolation and withdrawal requires the efforts of every team member to teach, learn, and support one another. Psychiatric consultation on an ongoing basis is especially useful to the staff in helping them to identify and accept their ambivalent feelings and to cope with the continual stress of caring for patients with Alzheimer's disease.

Retention Incentives

With respect to the nursing profession, formal collegiate education has only recently begun to direct initiatives toward motivating and preparing nursing professionals for roles in long-term care. Previously, it was thought that promotion into administrative positions or turning to academia were the only opportunities for gaining recognition or reward in the health care system. Now the specialty of gerontology is a highly visible and acclaimed field in nursing that offers endless opportunity for specialization.

Developing expertise in clinical, administrative, educational, or research roles in Alzheimer care provides unique opportunities for personal and professional achievement as well as innovative career positions. Many challenging and rewarding positions do exist and continue to emerge for nursing professionals in the field of Alzheimer care such as nursing unit administrators, inservice educators, clinical nurse specialists and nurse practitioners. These positions are highly competitive for individuals who are highly motivated, self-directed, conscientious, and inquisitive. Nursing professionals are continually striving to improve the quality of care and methods of care delivery, to upgrade standards of care, and to improve the education of Alzheimer caregivers and the support systems for family members. Professional nursing roles in Alzheimer care that contribute to retention of qualified professionals are summarized in Table 12-1.

Team Approach to Care of Alzheimer Patients

Involvement of a team of caregivers from different disciplines is crucial in providing optimal care for an Alzheimer patient. This is due to several factors:

Table 12-1 Professional Nursing Roles in Alzheimer Care

Professional Nursing Roles	Alzheimer Care Requirements

Clinical	• Provide direct patient care
	  —Assess cognitive and functional changes
	  —Perform nursing assessments
	  —Formulate nursing diagnoses
	  —Provide helping interventions
	  —Evaluate patients responses
	• Participate in interdisciplinary team planning
	• Coordinate out-patient and in-patient service needs
	• Establish an interdisciplinary allegiance with all members of the health care team
	• Participate in treatment decision-making
	• Support families/significant others in care and treatment issues
	• Facilitate communication between patient and family

Administrative	• Establish patient/staff ratios • Facilitate program development and implementation • Provide leadership • Coordinate staff development through eduction • Develop patient care standards • Ensure quality assurance

Educational	• Educate professional and nonprofessional caregivers
	  —Perform orientation and training programs
	  —Participate in ongoing inservice education
	  —Participate in staff development programs
	  —Attend continuing education workshops developed by staff
	  —Participate in nursing grand rounds

Research	• Test behavioral interventions • Develop innovative models for patient management • Participate in clinical drug studies • Collect data for longitudinal studies • Publish clinical research findings

1. Most Alzheimer patients suffer from few, if any, physical ailments apart from the dementing process. Many are physically fit and able to engage even in strenuous physical activity if it does not require cognitive skills. Opportunity for such an activity could improve their quality of life and might even delay physical deterioration. Involvement of occupational, recreational, and physical therapists in care of Alzheimer patients provides expertise and resources for involvement of patients in these activities.
2. Alzheimer dementia is a disease that affects not only the patient but also the family. The impact of the disease on the family is strong when the patient is still being cared for at home (see Chapter 2) and continues even after the patient is institutionalized. The patient's deterioration is reflected within the family as feelings of grief and loss, often combined with guilt feelings for abandoning the patient to institutional care. Participation in treatment deci-

sions for an incompetent patient can increase the feelings of grief and guilt. The staff in recognizing that family members need support can refer them to a social worker, a member of clergy, or psychiatric staff.
3. Management of an Alzheimer patient does not require high level, technology intensive, medical care. Very often most of the medical care can be provided by a nurse practitioner or a physician assistant. Involvement of a nurse practitioner is especially beneficial because members of the nursing staff are often more comfortable approaching a nurse practitioner than a physician about relatively minor problems involving chronic care (e.g., skin care, management of catheters, minor changes in patient's behavior). The nurse practitioner can also be an important contact between the staff and patients' families, responding to their inquiries about patient's condition, changes in medications, and so on.

Involvement of professionals from several disciplines in the care of an Alzheimer patient promotes either multidisciplinary or interdisciplinary care. There is a difference between these two approaches.[14] Multidisciplinary care involves activities of individuals from different disciplines toward a common goal, who work independently of each other and use only their traditional strategies and skills. In contrast, interdisciplinary care involves individuals from different disciplines who have responsibilities beyond their traditional roles on behalf of the group effort. For example, a nurse may function in the role of a physical therapist when managing a patient's functional disability or a nurse may function in the role of a social worker when interacting with a patient's family. This broadening of a role is only possible when team members are flexible, can effectively communicate with each other, and are able to accept constructive criticism and guidance from each other. Through communication, a team achieves a sense of cohesion and is able to achieve patient care that is better than what would be achieved if each individual provided patient care independently.

Team meetings are important opportunities for communication among team members. GRECC team meetings are scheduled every 1 or 2 weeks and are attended by the attending physician, nursing unit administrator and/or other nurses from the unit, nurse practitioner, social worker, clinical dietitian, recreational therapist, occupational therapist, and members of other disciplines. At each meeting the charts of three or four patients are presented and discussed. The current treatment plan is evaluated and changes are made. A patient's behavioral responses to on-ward and off-ward activities are described. Emphasis is placed on the discussion of the effects of medication(s) on a patient's behavior and function. Involvement of the patient's family is also noted and any problems are discussed. If necessary, it is decided that a family conference will be scheduled.

An important consideration is communication between staff members working evening and night shifts and attending physician, nurse practitioner, and other team members. This communication is facilitated on one of the units by use of message books into which the staff writes comments and questions. These are either acted on by the attending physician and other staff members or an explanation of why they were not acted on is provided.

The impact of interdisciplinary planning and evaluation of care results in a collegial staff relationship that generates open communication and constructive criticisms as well as mutual support in promoting high-quality patient care and continued development of the team members.[15] In addition, interdisciplinary team members have an increased sense of competence and consider the team development and interdisciplinary team support as effective coping strategies that help them manage stresses of caring for Alzheimer victims.

Program Implications for Therapeutic Recreation

The multiple skills and mutual support that are inherent in interdisciplinary teamwork can favorably influence the overall management of patients with Alzheimer's disease. Meaningful social and recreational activities provided through the expertise of a recreational and occupational therapist are essential for improving the physical and social function of these patients.

Facilitating socialization and providing for gross motor activity are two areas of therapeutic recreation highly suited to the needs of the Alzheimer patient. The key to effective programming is to simplify the activity in an attempt to reduce the number of signals that the impaired brain must sort out. As a result, program planning must be designed to meet individual needs and assessed frequently since patient symptomatology tends to vary from day to day.

When provided outlets for physical and emotive energies, Alzheimer patients appear more relaxed and less physically hyperactive. Motor skills seem to be retained longer if used regularly. For example, exercise is a particularly effective way in which to keep the impaired person involved in activities since it may be easier for the patient to use his or her body rather than to think and remember.[16] In addition, sufficient exercise appears to help patients sleep better at night.

Examples of specific exercise programs used with success in this population include bowling, dance, calisthenics, exercise from a chair, and bicycling on a stationary bicycle. Other programs include movement to music, adapted parachute games, and beachball volleyball.

Lifelong habits and pursuits that were previously enjoyable to the Alzheimer patient appear to persist the longest. Thus, in developing the program, it is important to simplify the activity and involve the patient at whatever level he or she is comfortable. Since intellectual capacity is reduced, yet not totally eliminated, patients can usually respond at some level.

Recreational programs that offer opportunity for socialization, with human contact, conversation, and cognitive and environmental stimulation, also appear to be beneficial. For example, normalization, the total integration of the person into everyday life, is a crucial area of concern to the therapeutic recreation specialist when devising programs for the Alzheimer patient. Accessing the patient to consistent patterns and conditions of everyday life that are as close as possible to the norms and patterns of the mainstream of society is essential in reducing the barriers imposed by the disease and the institutional setting.[17] Pet therapy, theme parties, and introducing music and special foods into programs facilitate normalization and help orient the patient. Music is an excellent means of stimulating positive responses of enjoyment from Alzheimer patients since many advanced patients retain the ability to sing long after their speech has become impaired. Remote memory and rote memory are areas that can also be reached during therapy, such as reminiscence therapy, music therapy, and dance and movement therapy.

Keeping the patient as active as possible prevents patient apathy and listlessness.[16] When the environment becomes too complicated for the patient, he or she may cope by withdrawing. Caregiver insistence on patient cooperation during recreational activities may stress the patient and result in catastrophic behavioral reactions in the patient who has comprehension deficits. To avoid this, it is helpful to reinvolve the patient in an activity at a simpler level with lower patient expectations.

The most effective tool to facilitate positive behavioral responses and promote communication is touch through human contact. When words fail, as they so often do in the advanced Alzheimer patient, touch can sometimes get the message to the brain. For example, touching a patient's hand with a spoon is one way to get him or her to pick it up. Touch and affection, as well, are important elements in fostering emotional security, self-esteem, and feelings of contentment.

Therapeutic Recreation Goals and Objectives

Goals and operational objectives that may be used in planning therapeutic recreation activities for the advanced Alzheimer patient include the following:

1. *Address purpose for living needs*. Provide the patient with structured, consistent programming, the goals of which are to promote self-esteem and provide continuity in the patient's daily regimen. For effective intervention to take place it is important to establish a significant trusting relationship, if possible, and to use a warm, friendly approach.
2. *Increase opportunities for socialization*. These opportunities can be provided through programs such as socials, entertainment, sing-a-longs, pet therapy, and community trips.
3. *Stimulate cognitive functioning*. This can be accomplished through sensory stimulation techniques, including olfactory, gustatory, tactile, visual, and auditory stimulation.
4. *Enhance the quality of life*. Normalizing the environment (i.e., offering food-oriented programs, theme parties, pet therapy, and soft music and using posters and wall decorations to lessen the effects of institutionalization) addresses quality of life.
5. *Minimize anxiety and encourage appropriate behavior*. Use self-monitoring techniques with the patients, using one- and two-step commands, involving patients in large muscle activities such as walking groups, bowling, and rhythm band and exercise groups.
6. *Orient to environment*. Provide reality orientation and environmental orientation and offer memory aids when patients retain the ability to read.
7. *Access patient to intact strengths*. Offer programs within patient's leisure interest area.
8. *Stimulate vocalization and interaction skills and abilities*. Examples of ways to facilitate this goal would be to use object identification games, word games adapted to the patient's ability, and music therapy.
9. *Promote self-esteem*. This may be achieved through grooming programs, competition and mastery in recreational pursuits, the use of praise and compliment during an activity, and the use of extrinsic rewards.

10. *Increase opportunities for contentment and enjoyment.* Involve the patient in a relaxing, normalizing activity.

Each goal and objective must be adapted to the needs of each individual patient, with the ultimate goals of maximizing functional abilities at the patient's current level of function (Table 12-2).

Program Implications for Occupational Therapy

Given the intensive, emotional needs of the patient with advanced Alzheimer dementia, several members of the interdisciplinary treatment team must share responsibilities in the emotional care of the patient including nursing, therapeutic recreation, occupational therapy, and physical therapy.

Table 12-2 Recreational Therapy in Alzheimer's Disease

Stage	Activity	Avoid	Note	Goal
Early	Leisure education for families Educate families on how to provide in-house leisure program for patients	Giving false expectations of patient's performance ability or prognosis of the disease		To enable families to better cope with stress of managing family member, which may in turn impact on patient's ability to remain at home
Middle	Community trips Music therapy Exercise/adapted sports Socials Cognitive stimulation Reminiscence Environmental stimulation		Watch programmatical factors that best elicit positive behavorial responses.	To maximize the quality of patient's life. To promote fitness To increase/facilitate socialization and communication To promote adjustment to environment
Advanced	Music therapy Gross motor activities Socials Environmental stimulation Sensory stimulation	Overstimulating patient	Watch programmatical factors that best elicit more subtle responses such as affect and nonverbal communication.	To maximize the quality of life To promote socialization, to promote patient's awareness of self, others, and environment
Terminal	Touch Music, in close proximity to patient Environmental adaptations to ensure comfort and security		Patients who do not have the capacity to respond to simple intervention techniques may not be appropriate for treatment.	To make patient comfortable

Table 12-3 Occupational Therapy in Alzheimer's Disease

Stage	Activity	Avoid	Note	Goal
Early	Home visits—to help family adapt to environment			To keep patient functioning as independently as possible
Middle	Walking group Simple hobby groups—on and off the unit		Environmental factors may affect responses	To maintain overall fitness and promote adjustment to environment
Advanced	Walking group—with limits Feeding equipment	Stairs	Watch depth perception	To maintain overall fitness To promote socialization with other patients To provide increased sensory stimulation
Terminal	Air splinting Positioning in bed Feeding Equipment	Sharp adaptive feeding utensils Air splinting lower extremities due to blood pressure problems	Consider covering splints since patients may bite them.	To maintain or decrease contractures To make patient comfortable

The primary goal of occupational therapy in the management of the advanced Alzheimer patient is to maximize functional ability. The main focus of intervention is to keep the body functioning at an optimal level physically (i.e., coordination, dexterity and physical fitness) while monitoring for perceptual, environmental and adaptive equipment needs. A secondary focus is to facilitate and support socialization (see Table 12-3).

Maintaining physical fitness through the use of structured exercise, such as a patient walking group and other exercise groups on the Alzheimer specialty unit, can help to prevent excess disability and keep the patient as physically functional as possible. The purpose of a walking group, for example, is to maintain or increase the overall fitness of the patient by the use of structured exercise.

One such experience (Shea A, personal communication) involved a group of six to eight patients with Alzheimer's disease who had the physical capacity to participate in a walking group. Under the constant supervision of two occupational therapists, this group met two to three times a week for a one hour walk around the grounds of the facility. To provide sensory stimulation, the group was taken to such areas as the cafeteria and the greenhouse. To assess their perceptions, patients were closely observed in their responses to people encountered on their walks as well as their responses to the environment. Patients were selected for the group according to their level of physical ability (e.g., fast or slow pace) as well as according to perceptual ability (e.g., depth perception as related to stair climbing). Objectives of patient participation in this group included maintenance of physical fitness, increased socialization through contact with other residents and staff, improved endurance, and increased sensory stimulation through environmental variation.

The physical therapist is another necessary member for interdisciplinary team planning. The goal of the physical therapist is to help plan physical activity that will maximize the patient's diminishing functions. While loss of physical function along with independence is inevitable, it is critical to ensure that the patient does not lose more than that which is caused by the disease process. In advanced stages of Alzheimer's disease, immobility problems are common; therefore, the physical therapist should be actively involved in planning physical activity such as assisted ambulation as well as helping patients transfer from bed to chair.

Maintaining Patient Dignity

Each discipline contributes to fostering patient dignity in a variety of ways. Staff are encouraged to dress patients in their own clothes when attending occupational or recreational therapy programs either on or off their unit of residence. Introducing patients to one another and facilitating mastery of skills at the patient's competency level and other facets of the group process also help to foster patient dignity. Normalization of the environment provides a climate conducive to affirming the dignity of the individual.

Interdisciplinary Management of Challenging Behaviors

Since the emotional responses of the patient with advanced Alzheimer dementia are unpredictable, at best, efforts must be directed at preventing overreaction to minor stressors or to stimulation that is not appealing to the patient, including occurrences such as physical aggression, verbal aggression, combativeness, or assaultiveness. The following interventions serve as guidelines to minimize the possibility of undesirable behaviors:

1. Simplify the environment.
2. Attempt to identify a pattern to the reactions (e.g., when and where they tend to occur).
3. Decrease the number of items placed in front of a patient during an activity such as at meal time.
4. Inform family of what to expect.
5. Avoid undue stress or confusion.
6. Search for underlying medical problems that may be precipitating abnormal behavior in the patient.
7. Ensure patient safety and feelings of security.
8. Avoid sensory deprivation or social isolation.
9. Avoid overstimulation.
10. Avoid clutter in the environment.
11. Promote patient comfort through personal elaboration, (i.e., scrapbooks, photographs, personal items).
12. Avoid constant reality orientation questions since patients tend to get irritated when asked the same question over and over again.

Facilitating Communication

Because patients with advanced Alzheimer dementia are often verbally noncommunicative, it is unfair to assume that they are unable to nonverbally communicate or interact with their environment at all. Promoting sensory stimulation will, in some circumstances, improve patient quality of life and overall demeanor. The patient, when addressed, should be spoken to in vocal tones that are neither infantilizing nor condescending. If possible, eye contact should be made to engage the patient in the interaction at hand.

Both recreational and occupational therapy facilitate communication. Patients have been observed to become increasingly verbal in normalized settings as they feel more comfortable and they receive environmental, social, and behavioral cuing. Patients are asked lead-in type questions and are allowed to touch and be touched by others. Music is a dynamic intervention tool vital to the communication process because of the stimulation it provides of the rote memory aspect of the brain and its soothing, relaxing effect.

Educating Additional Support Personnel

Other support staff who must meet the needs of patients with Alzheimer's disease include the housekeeping team. Keeping the environment clean and pleasant may be an overwhelming task. Housekeeping staff also need education on how to manage and communicate with patients, especially those who constantly pace. Since patients have the tendency to pace, washing and waxing floors are problematic. To facilitate housekeeping, floors are cleaned only during mealtimes when patients are seated for the maximum amount of time. To minimize odors from incontinence, trash receptacles are emptied frequently and light disinfectants are used for cleaning purposes. Environmental cleanliness is crucial in maintaining an esthetic atmosphere for the Alzheimer patient.

REFERENCES

1. Seltzer B, Sherwin I: "Organic brain syndromes": An empirical study and critical review. *Am Psychiatry* 1978;135:13-21.

2. Weisberg J: A success story: Grouping the alert with the mentally impaired. *Geriatr Nurs* 1984 (September/October):312-316.

3. Office of Technology Assessment: *Losing a Million Minds: Confronting the Tragedy of Alzheimer's Disease and other Dementias*, OTA-BA-323. Washington, D.C., U. S. Government Printing Office, 1987.

4. Kramer M: *Reality Shock: Why Nurses Leave Nursing*. St. Louis, CV Mosby, 1974, pp 27-66.

5. Clark CC: *Classroom Skills for Nurse Educators*. New York, Springer, 1978.

6. Hunt DM, Michael C: Mentorship: A career training with development tool. *Acad Manag Rev* 1983;8:475-485.

7. Rogers JC: Sponsorship: Developing leaders for occupational therapy. *Occup Ther* 1982;36:309-313.

8. Cambell-Heider N: Do nurses need mentors? *Image* 1986;18:110-113.

9. Tines A, Meslack C: Characteristics of staff burnout in mental health settings. *Hosp Comm Psychiatry* 1973;29:233-237.

10. Norberg A, Norberg B, Bone G: Ethical problems in feeding patients with advanced dementia. *Br Med J* 1980;281:848-849.

11. Volicer L: Need for hospice approach to treatment of patients with advanced progressive dementia. *J Am Geriatr Soc* 1985;34:655-658.

12. Charatan FB, Foley CJ, Libow LS: The team approach to geriatric medicine. *Geriatr Med* 171.

13. Shrade D: On dying more than one death. *Hastings Center Rep* 1986;16:12-16.

14. Melvin JL: Interdisciplinary and multidisciplinary activities and the ACRM. *Arch Phys Med Rehab* 1980; 61:379-380.

15. Petrosino B: Nursing in hospice and terminal care research and practice. *Hospice J* 1986;2:63-79.

16. Mace NL, Rabins PV: *The 36-Hour Day*. Baltimore, Johns Hopkins University Press, 1981.

17. Peterson C, Gum S: *Therapeutic Recreation Program Design*. Englewood Cliffs, NJ, Prentice-Hall, 1984.

Appendix 12-A

Curriculum for Orientation of Professional Nurses to Alzheimer Dementia Caregiving in the Long-term Care Facility

I. Overview of the Nature of the Disease
   A. Pathology
   B. Causes—theories
   C. Symptoms
   D. Diagnosis
   E. Treatment
II. Stages of the Disease
   A. Course of Alzheimer dementia
   B. Staging instruments
   C. Disease progression
III. Principles of Institutional Care
   A. Unit philosophy
      1. Standards of care
   B. Unit routines
   C. Unit environment
      1. Safety
      2. Security
   D. Unit programs
      1. Clinical
         a. Respite care
         b. Hospice care
      2. Educational
         a. Grand rounds
         b. Informal
      3. Research
         a. Longitudinal study
         b. Respite study
IV. Principles of Patient Care
   A. Challenging behaviors
      1. Mood—depression

    2. Restlessness
    3. Anxiety
    4. Agitation
    5. Assaultiveness
    6. Aggression
    7. Catastrophic reactions
    8. Sundowning
    9. Wandering
    10. Perseveration
    11. Hallucinations
  B. Self-care deficits—Activities of daily living
    1. Feeding difficulties
    2. Incontinence management
    3. Dressing and grooming
  C. Communication
  D. Apraxia
  E. Agnosia
  F. Comfort
V. Interdisciplinary Teamwork
  A. Team members
  B. Roles, responsibilities, and interface
VI. Nursing Process in the Care of the Alzheimer Dementia Patient
  A. Assessment of the noncommunicative patient
  B. Nursing diagnosis
  C. Nursing care planning
    1. Respite patients
    2. Ambulatory patients
    3. Hospice patients
  D. Designing appropriate interventions
  E. Evaluating effectiveness of interventions
VII. Hospice Care
  A. Alzheimer dementia as a terminal disease
  B. Principles of decision-making
  C. Nursing ethics
VIII. The Alzheimer Dementia Family
  A. Spouses
  B. Siblings
  C. Adult children
  D. Visiting
  E. Family involvement in direct caregiving
IX. Quality Assurance

Glossary

Acetylcholine. A neurotransmitter involved in memory processes.

Acetylcholine Esterase Inhibitors. Chemicals that decrease acetylcholine metabolism.

Acetylcholine Precursors. Chemicals (e.g., lecithin) from which acetylcholine is made in the body.

Activities of Daily Living. Normal, routine functions of self-care performed from day to day such as personal hygiene, eating, dressing, grooming, using the toilet, etc.

Acute Care. Short-term medical and nursing care and restorative services provided in a hospital setting in response to a medical crisis.

Adult Day Care. The provision of a range of mental health and social services for physically, cognitively, or emotionally impaired and socially isolated individuals. Generally, funds for adult day care, where provided, are state funds. Adult day care programs for dementia victims will often include reality orientation and socialization.

Adversary Quality. Involvement of two or more parties who try to win the other to their point of view.

Agnosia. Inability to recognize objects or sounds despite preserved sensory function.

Alzheimer Dementia. See Alzheimer's disease.

Alzheimer's Disease. A type of dementia of unknown cause but characteristic pathology, in which the symptoms show a gradual but relentless onset. It involves loss of intellectual ability of sufficient severity to interfere with social or occupational functioning, memory loss, possible personality change, and impairment of abstract thinking, judgment, spatial orientation, and/or language in an individual with a clear state of consciousness.

Alzheimer's Disease and Related Disorders Association. The national voluntary health agency dedicated to research for the prevention and treatment of Alzheimer's disease and related disorders, and to providing assistance to patients and their families. The toll free telephone number is 1-800-621-0379.

Aminoglycosides. Potent parenterally-administered antibiotics, often required to eradicate nosocomial infections in patients residing in long-term care facilities.

Anticonvulsants. Drugs used in treatment of seizures.

Antidepressants. Drugs used in treatment of depressive disorders.

Aphasia. Inability to speak.

Apraxia. Inability to carry out purposeful movement despite intact comprehension and preserved motor function.

Artificial Feeding. Any form of nourishment or hydration by other than the oral route. Examples of artificial feeding include intravenous feeding, hyperalimentation, nasogastric tube feeding and gastrostomy tube feeding.

Aspiration. Accidental inhalation of particles of food or fluid into the lungs, usually occurring in individuals who lack the ability to feed themselves or to swallow effectively.

Ataxia. Incoordination; impaired gait.

Autonomy. Freedom to make decisions.

Biomedical Research. Research involving biology, medicine, and physical science that seeks to identify causes and treatments of certain health care problems.

Beneficence. Duty to help others.

Bradykinesia. Extreme slowness of movement.

Care Levels. The extent of medical care provided for a patient.

Catastrophic Reaction. A sudden, often unpredictable, and seemingly unprovoked outburst of physical or verbal aggression displayed by individuals with Alzheimer's disease in reaction to a stimulus.

Cephalosporins. A class of broad-spectrum antibiotics useful in treating some community-acquired and nosocomial infections.

Cholinergic Agents. Chemicals that mimic the effects of acetylcholine.

Cholinergic Stimulants. Chemicals that mimic the effects of acetylcholine by stimulating acetylcholine receptors.

Chronic Care. See long-term care.

Chronic Illness. A disease that is usually incurable and is characterized by long duration and/or frequent recurrence.

Community Care. Medical and/or personal care services provided in the community including services such as adult day care, home health care, homemaker services, companions, respite programs, case management services, and habilitation services. Medicaid will provide for these services only if they are provided within a "medical model" of care. These services can be costly if recipients pay out of pocket.

Competence. Ability to make an informed and rational decision.

Constipation. Infrequent defecation, insufficient defecation, feeling of incomplete evacuation or increased hardness of stools.

Contractures (muscular). Fixity of joints due to muscle imbalance.

Decubitus Ulceration. An impairment of skin integrity such as a bedsore caused by prolonged physical immobility and malnutrition, and aggravated by sheering force or pressure.

Delirium. A temporary state of decreased mental ability accompanied by a clouding of consciousness.

Dementia. Any state of decreased mental ability of long duration (months to years) in an alert individual.

Dementia of the Alzheimer Type. See Alzheimer's disease.

Dental Caries. Disease of the hard structures of the teeth, characterized by demineralization of the inorganic structures (enamel) and breakdown of the organic structures (dentin).

Depersonalization. Dealing with patients as if they were not real persons, but only objects. Failure to recognize the individuality of patients.

Diagnosis Related Group (DRG). A classification scheme, recently implemented by Medicare, placing hospitalized patients into 468 groups based on medical condition and other easily measured variables. Hospitals are paid a fixed price for care based on each patient's DRG.

Disorientation. Inability to indicate knowledge of time, place, person, or circumstances.

Do Not Resuscitate (DNR). A physician's order not to initiate procedures (cardiac compressions and artificial respiration) aimed at reviving a patient whose heart or breathing stopped.

Dopamine. A neurotransmitter involved in regulation of movements and in schizophrenia.

Dysphagia. Difficulty to initiate swallowing.

Epidemiology. The science concerned with studying the distribution and determinants of disease in populations.

Ergoloid Mesylates. Substances extracted from ergot used to treat behavioral and cognitive deficiencies in elderly individuals.

Ethics Committee. A group of professionals providing advice to medical staff in situations involving ethical dilemmas.

Ethical Dilemma. A situation in which two or more ethical principles are involved in a contradictory fashion.

Executor. A person who acts as personal representative of the estate of one deceased and who administers the will.

Food Refusal. The active rejection of food by either ceasing to feed oneself or by refusing to open one's mouth when spoon-fed.

Force Feeding. Feeding a patient against his/her wishes by either natural or artificial means.

Gastrostomy Tube. A tube inserted surgically into the stomach of individuals who are unable to consume hydration and nutrition in the normal way for a prolonged period of time.

Geriatrics. The medical specialty dealing with providing care for elderly individuals.

Gerontology. Scientific investigation of the aging process.

Guardianship/Conservatorship. A guardian or conservator is a person or institution appointed by the court having jurisdiction over such matters and who is judiciously charged with the duty of caring for the property and/or the person of one who is judged incapable. Such a person is often called a ward or an incompetent.

Habilitation. Therapy aimed at maintenance of existing function rather than at restoration of lost abilities.

Halitosis. Offensive breath odor.

Hallucinations. The subjective perception of an object or event that does not objectively exist.

Holistic Health Care. Health care that attends to the "whole" patient as a person, with physical, emotional, psychosocial, and spiritual needs.

Home Health Care. The provision of medical and personal care services in the home by outside organizations.

Homogeneous Grouping. A concept based upon the belief that when the largest number of patients suffering from the same illness are grouped together in one designated area, patients will receive the greatest amount of benefits such as the provisions of interdisciplinary services, activities, and specially trained staff.

Hospice Approach. Care aimed at providing maximal comfort not maximal survival time.

Hospice Care. A comprehensive program of care with emphasis on care rather than cure, and comfort rather than rehabilitation.

Huntington's Disease. A hereditary, degenerative disease of the brain that is characterized by abnormal choreiform movements.

Hyperactivity. Excessive or continuous motor activity or movement.

Hyperoralia. An apparent compulsion for oral stimulation manifested by exploration of objects in the environment by placing them in the mouth.

Hypermetamorphosis. The subconscious, compulsive exploration of objects in the environment by touching them with the hands.

Hypnotics. Drugs used to treat sleep disturbances.

Iatrogenic Illness. An abnormal mental or physical condition resulting from medical intervention. Such illnesses can be avoided by proper and judicious care by physicians.

Impartial Decision. Decision made without prejudice.

Incidence. The rate at which new cases of a disease occur.

Institutional Care. Medical, personal and/or custodial care provided in formal settings. Such services may be provided for in nursing homes, board and care facilities, and mental health facilities.

Intercurrent Illness. A secondary or concurrent illness that occurs or co-exists in a hospitalized individual with a separate, usually unrelated, primary medical condition.

Interdisciplinary. A model-of-care delivery that stresses collaboration among the wide array of health care providers involved in the management of a patient with a complex illness.

Interdisciplinary Team. A group of health care and social service providers who work together in a collaborative fashion to provide the most comprehensive care possible to individuals and families with complex illnesses.

Intermediate Medical Care. Medical care for patients, usually with chronic illnesses, who are expected to stay in the hospital longer than in an acute care situation. Often, these individuals are too ill to reside at home or in a nursing home, yet are stable enough not to require acute or intensive care.

Intervivos Estate or Financial Plan. A plan that involves the creation of an estate, its maintenance and conservation, together with its utilization to provide support and security for an individual or family.

Intervivos Trust. A trust created during the lifetime of the patient (intervivos) that is an agreement whereby the patient formally transfers assets and/or property to a trustee who agrees to hold and manage the property on behalf of the patient (and sometimes for members of the patient's family—the beneficiaries as well—for some particular period of time.

Joint Tenancies. Forms of joint ownership established, for example, when one individual places funds in a deposit type account or purchases other types of assets such as securities or real property in his or her name and that of another person.

Kluver-Bucy Syndrome. A group of symptoms first described in monkeys with bilateral temporal lobe ablation, but also found, in part, in some human conditions. Symptoms include emotional placidity, visual agnosia, hypersexuality, and a compulsive exploration of objects in the environment by placing them in the mouth.

Korsakoff's Psychosis. Memory deficit induced by vitamin B_1 deficiency most commonly occurring in patients with alcoholism.

Laxatives. Drugs used in treatment of constipation.

Lecithin. A chemical from which acetylcholine is made in the brain.

Living Will. The written instructions of an individual about limitations of medical care desired in the event of certain medical events or illnesses.

Long-Term Care. A continuum of medical and personal care services provided to incapacitated individuals in formal (institutional) or informal (home) settings. Services may be provided continuously or intermittently, and others are delivered indefinitely.

Malignant Neuroleptic Syndrome. A collection of symptoms, usually including fever, indicating a potentially fatal reaction to neuroleptic medication administration.

Medicaid. A joint federal/state medical welfare program with a strict means test for eligibility. It provides medical and health related services to low-income individuals. Eligibility requirements and benefit packages vary from state to state. Generally, Medicaid will pay for nursing home and home health care for those who meet the eligibility requirements. Some state plans do pay for adult day care; very few cover the cost of respite care.

Medical Model of Care. Diagnostic and treatment services that emphasize the role of the physician over that of other health and social service professionals.

Medical Technology. Machines and chemicals (drugs) used in treatment of diseases.

Medicare. The federal insurance program initiated in 1965 that provides medical care for those 65 or older and the disabled. Medicare provides reimbursement for hospital and physician expenses and limited benefits for skilled nursing home care, home health care, and hospice care. Because it does not cover protracted long-term care, its use to dementia victims is limited to diagnostic and treatment costs.

Mentor. A professional sponsor who assists an individual to advance within a given system or area of expertise. Someone who provides career advice, education, and social support.

Mind Reading. The assumption that a caregiver knows what the Alzheimer patient is thinking, often based on personal experience. Also a practice that presumes the patient has greater mental capacity than may be possible.

Moral Community. A group of people acting according to the same moral principles.

Multi-Infarct Dementia. Dementia caused by patchy deterioration with evidence of cerebral and/or systemic vascular disease.

Multiple Sclerosis. A degenerative brain disease affecting the brain's white matter.

Multidisciplinary Care. A model of care that emphasizes utilization of a wide range of health care professionals appropriate to a specific care situation.

Myoclonus. Irregular jerks of a muscle or group of muscles.

Neuroleptic Agent. A pharmacologic agent (usually an anti-psychotic) used in the management of psychotic or other disturbing behaviors that produce symptoms resembling nervous system disease.

Neurotransmitter. A chemical used by nerve cells to communicate with each other.

Nonmaleficence. Duty not to harm others.

Norepinephrine. A neurotransmitter involved in regulation of mood, appetite, blood pressure, and other functions.

Nosocomial Infection. A hospital-acquired infection.

Nursing Home. A facility that provides 24-hour supervision, skilled nursing services, and personal care to incapacitated individuals. An estimated 50% of nursing home residents are cognitively impaired.

Nursing Home Cap Program. Provides nursing home care and other medical care coverage to residents of nursing homes with incomes less than $1,000 (1986 requirement).

Nutritional Compromise. Occurs when body nutritional requirements are less than or inadequately met. Nutritional compromise predisposes an individual to malnutrition.

Optimal Medical Care. Interventions provided in the best interests of the patient.

Oral Disease. Any disease of the structures of or involving the mouth.

Orthopnea. Difficulty breathing, usually associated with a change in body position from erect sitting or standing to lying down.

Ototoxicity. Toxic to the ears; resulting in hearing loss and/or tinnitus.

Outright and Complete Transfer. Involves the legal transfer of an asset by the patient to another person. Unlike the transfer with the retained interest, this transfer involves no retained legal rights.

Pacing. A pattern of movement described as constant, purposeless walking observed in some moderately demented individuals.

Palliative Care. Care delivered for the purpose of palliation or relief of discomforting symptomatology, usually as a result of a terminal illness.

Parkinson's Disease. A neurological disorder characterized by hypokinesia, tremor, and muscular rigidity.

Paroxysmal Nocturnal Dyspnea. Difficulty breathing that occurs during the night, whereby, generally, the affected individual is awakened with shortness of breath or air hunger. It is caused by shifting of the interstitial and intravascular fluid volume of the body into the position of most dependency.

Paternalism. Making decisions for the patient without involving him or her in the process.

Pathological Reflex. An abnormal reflex indicating an abnormal or diseased state such as advanced dementia. Examples of pathological or primitive reflexes include the sucking reflex, the snout reflex, the grasp reflex, or the palmomental reflex.

Pathological Bonding. An overly intense and self destructive maladjustment in the spouse's attachment to the Alzheimer patient when the marital bond becomes a more maternal bond accompanied in some cases by sexual role change brought by the patient's regression to more childlike behaviors. This bonding often results in slavelike caregiving arising from spouse's confusion about the changed roles.

Periodontal Disease. Inflammatory condition of the gingiva and underlying structures of the teeth.

Perseveration. The repetition of seemingly meaningless words or actions whereby the individual appears to "gets stuck" on one particular activity without the ability to stop it.

Persistent Vegetative State. The retention of spontaneous respiration, sleep-wake cycle, and some reflex activity without awareness and interaction with the environment.

Philosophy of Care. The underlying principles that govern the delivery of care in a specific setting.

Pick Disease. Primary degenerative dementia characterized by a specific pattern of brain atrophy and presence of Pick bodies in the brain.

Plaque. A densely populated mass of bacteria and debris that forms a coating on natural and artificial teeth.

Power of Attorney. An agency agreement (principal/agent) wherein the patient appoints another individual as his or her agent for the purpose of transacting a variety of matters on his or her behalf. It indicates that another person is qualified to make decisions for a patient if he or she becomes incompetent. A durable power of attorney survives the incompetence of the principal.

Preceptor. A staff member who takes the responsibility to orient and train another staff member to job expectations and requirements of a position.

Prevalence. The amount of disease found in a population at a point in time.

Preventive Medicine. A medical specialty that concerns itself with activities that help avoid the development or exacerbation of physical, emotional, or mental disease or injury.

Primary Degenerative Dementia. A dementia for which no specific cause can be found on clinical examination.

Primary Health Care Team. A group of health care professionals who provide comprehensive diagnostic and evaluative services and continuing care to a discrete population of patients.

Primary Prevention. The form of prevention that attempts to intervene before a disease process begins.

Principled Decision. Decision made according to a stated principle.

Quality of Life. Having a purpose for living and deriving enjoyment from life. The practice of medicine and health care aspires to improve the quality of life of patients by maintaining health, relieving pain and other distressing symptoms, and supporting compromised functions.

Rehabilitation. Restoration of lost function or ability. Examples include physical therapy, occupational therapy, corrective therapy, and recreational therapy.

Respite Care. Any formal support service or treatment intervention aimed primarily at providing temporary physical and emotional relief to the family caregiver of a frail elderly or demented individual.

Risk Factors. Those determinants of a disease that are associated with statistically increased likelihood of acquiring or exacerbating disease.

Salivary Gland Dysfunction. Inadequate functioning of the salivary glands due to disease, radiation, or medication.

Secondary Dementia. Disease process that has dementia as one of several consequences.

Secondary Prevention. The form of prevention that involves early detection of a disease process with intervention to either block or at least retard the development of clinical sequelae.

Sedatives. Drugs used to treat behavioral problems due to hyperactivity.

Sensory Deprivation. Lack of appropriate levels of sensory stimulation necessary for maintaining normal contact with the environment often manifested by blunting of affect, reduced spontaneity, apathy, or cognitive impairment.

Sensory Overload. More sensory stimulation than an individual is able to effectively cope with, often manifested by anxiety, restlessness, agitation, or, in some cases, by catastrophic behavioral reactions.

Septicemia. Bacteria or pathogens in the bloodstream. It is a morbid condition because bacteria may readily multiply in the bloodstream.

Serotonin. A neurotransmitter involved in regulation of sleep, appetite, mood, and other functions.

Shadowing. An inappropriate behavior characterized by the continual, purposeless following of a caregiver by a patient. It is a form of motor hyperactivity.

Skilled Nursing Facility. Nursing homes certified to provide Medicare and/or Medicaid skilled nursing care. In 1982, there were 7,000 skilled nursing home facilities in the United States. These facilities must provide 24-hour services by licensed practical nurses and employ at least one registered nurse on the day shift, 7 days a week.

Special Care Unit. A formalized area where patients with Alzheimer's disease are cared for under special guidelines, treatment philosophies, and interventions. Staff are specially trained and the environment is adaptive to their needs.

Staff Burnout. A phenomenon of emotional and physical exhaustion that occurs in work situations when the patient/staff ratio is so high that the staff feels overwhelmed and unable to relate comfortably with patients and other staff.

Staging of the Disease. Attempt to define discrete progressive phases of Alzheimer's disease.

Sundowning. A syndrome characterized by restlessness, excitement, increased confusion, hallucinations, and agitation seen in the late afternoon or early evening in patients in the middle and, sometimes, later stage of Alzheimer's disease.

Supportive Care. Care delivered for the purpose of preserving remaining function and promoting comfort in an individual for whom there is no reasonable hope for complete recovery.

Supplemental Security Income (SSI). A federal income support program for aged, disabled, and blind individuals with incomes below a minimum level.

Symptom Heterogeneity. The wide array of varying symptoms which can be manifest at different stages of an illness, such as is seen in persons with Alzheimer's disease.

Terminal Illness. Irreversible disease leading to death.

Terminal Care. Care for a dying patient.

Tertiary Prevention. The form of prevention that attempts to avoid complications and premature deterioration in an established disease condition.

Testamentary Substitute. An instrument that serves to transfer property interests upon the death of an individual instead of a will. Property held jointly with rights of survivorship such as a joint bank account may, for example, be a testamentary substitute.

Therapeutic Lying. A practice that may substitute "lies" for absolute truths that are distressing to the Alzheimer patient, based on the premise that complex truthful statements may confuse and agitate him or her.

Therapeutic Milieu. An environment designed to promote comfort during or recovery from an illness.

Traditional Estate Plan. A so-called post mortem estate plan provides for the distribution of the estate thus created, utilized, and preserved upon the death of an individual.

Transfers with Retained Interest. Involves the legal transfer of an asset by the patient to another while reserving to the transferor (the patient) certain legal rights to enjoy that property for some period of time, most commonly, for the rest of the patient's life.

Uncoordinated Swallowing. The inability to properly chew and swallow food placed in the mouth when spoon-fed.

Urosepsis. A urinary tract infection that spreads into the bloodstream.

Vascular Dementia. See Multi-Infarct Dementia.

Vasodilators. Drugs promoting blood flow by enlarging the lumen or blood vessels.

Veterans Administration (VA). A federal government agency that provides health care and long-term care services on a priority basis to veterans with service-connected disabilities. The VA plays an important role in Alzheimer's disease research, education, and long-term care.

Walkers Heel. A group of heel problems that include bone bruises and heel spurs usually caused by wearing poorly designed shoes or walking for long hours on hard surfaces.

Will. A person's post-mortem declaration of intention with respect to the distribution of his or her property and other matters.

Xerostomia. Dryness of the mouth.

Index

A

Abdominal pain, management of, 155-56
Acetylcholine, 225
Acetylcholine esterase inhibitors, 189
Acetylcholine precursors, 188
ACT (*0.05% NaF rinse*), 117
Activities of daily living, 225
   evaluation of, 17-18, 24-25
Acute care, 225
B-Adrenergic receptor antagonists, 194
Adult day care, 48
Adversary quality, 225
Age, as primary risk factor, 5-6
Aggression, 89. *See also* Behavior, undesirable
Agnosia, 95
Alcohol, use of and cancer, 112
Alprazolam (Xanax), 192
Aluminum exposure, as risk factor, 7
Alzheimer dementia. *See* Alzheimer's disease
Alzheimer patient. *See also* Alzheimer's disease; Dying Alzheimer patient
   aggression in, 89
   agnosia in, 95
   apraxia in, 95
   assessment of, *16*
   assistance, need for, 18
   care of, 108
      areas of concern in, 10
      philosophy of, 91
      team approach in, 90-91
   categories of need in, 79
   clinical management of, 70-73
   cognitive functions in, 16-17, 20
   comfort of, 93, 102-05, *103*
   definition of, 2
   dental management of, 120-23
   disability in, 92
   eating problems in, 25
   elimination needs in, 100-02
   evaluation of
      follow-up, 20-27
      initial, 14-16
   feeding problems in, 96-99, *96*
   fever evaluation in, 132-33
   health status of, 92
   hyperoralia in, 89, 95
   incontinence in, 24-25
   institutionalization of, 90
   intercurrent illnesses in, 127-43
   legal management for, 57
   maintaining dignity of, 220
   medication, administration of, 25
   medication regimen, review of, 133
   neurologic functions in, 17, 23-24
   with neurologic manifestations, 105-06
   noncognitive functions in, 17, 21-23
   normalcy in, episodes of, 30
   nutritional needs in, 25, 95-99
   oral health care for, 99-100, 111-23. *See also* Oral hygiene
   physical needs of, 94
   problems in, diagnosis of, 93-94
   psychosocial functions in, 18-19, 26-27
   relaxation needs of, 100

Note: Page numbers in *Italic* indicate material occurs in a figure or table.

relocation of, 131
respite care of, 75-85
responses in, 92
rest needs of, 100
safety of, 92
security of, 92
sexuality and, 37-38
skin integrity of, 94-95
team approach to care of, 213-16
uncooperative, 119-20
Alzheimer's disease, 226. *See also* Alzheimer patient(s)
  advanced stage of, 89-90
    drugs used in treatment of, 196-98
    ethical issues in treatment of, 167-81
    management of, 87-108
  age and, 5
  aluminum and, 7
  antecedent thyroid disease and, 7
  antipsychotics, use of in, 22-23
  behavioral symptoms in, 22-23. *See also* Behavior
  clinical features of, 1
  depression in, 21
  drugs used in treatment of, 185-99
  early stage of, 88-89
    drugs used in treatment of, 185-92
  early symptoms of, 29-30
  economic considerations in, 43-52. *See also* Financing of medical care
  epidemiology of, 3-5
  features of, 13
  genetics and, 6
  geographic location and, 6
  head trauma and, 6-7
  incontinence in, 24-25
  late stage of, 89-90
    drugs used in treatment of, 196-98
  legal and epidemiology of, 3-5
  features of, 13
  genetics and, 6
  geographic location and, 6
  head trauma and, 6-7
  incontinence in, 24-25
  late stage of, 89-90
    drugs used in treatment of, 196-98
  legal considerations in, 53-73. *See also* Legal considerations
  management of, 93-106
    assessment, 93
    interventions, 94
    maintaining skin integrity, 94-95
    meeting physical needs, 94
  maternal age and, 7
  medications used in, 22-23, 25
  middle stage of, 89
    drugs used in treatment of, 192-96
  mood disturbance in, 21
  occupational therapy in, *219*
  outpatient with, management of, 13-27
  personal costs of, 43-45
    management of, 50-52
  personality change in, 21
  prevention of, 5-10
    ethics of, 10-11
    primary, 5-7
    secondary, 7-9
    tertiary, 9-10
  race and, 6
  recreational therapy in, *218*
  sedatives, use of in, 22-23
  sleep disturbance in, 23
  societal costs of, 43-45
  socioeconomic status and, 7
  stages of, *15*, 88-90
  as terminal illness, 167-68
  terminal stage of, 90
    drugs used in treatment of, 198-99
  treatment goals, 92-93
Alzheimer's Disease and Related Disorders Association, 48, 226
Aminoglycosides, 226
Amitriptyline (Elavil), 190
Amoxapine (Asendin), 190
Antecedent thyroid disease, as risk factor, 7
Antibiotic therapy, in late stage, 171
Anticonvulsants, 196
Antidepressants, 189-91
Antilirium (physostigmine), 189
Aphasia, 226
Appetite, lack of, 134
Apraxia, 95
Artane (trihexyphenidyl), 195
Artificial feeding, 97-98. *See also* Feeding problems
Ascorbic acid, urinary incontinence and, 137
Asendin (amoxapine), 190
Aspiration, 99
Aspirin, 191-92
Assessment
  continual, 93
  of nutritional status, 95-99
  of rest and relaxation needs, 100
Assets. *See* Legal considerations

Ataxia, 226
Athlete's foot, management of, 151-52
Ativan (lorazepam), 192
Atopic dermatitis, management of, 149
Atropine, 199
Attributable risk, 3
Autonomy, 226

B

Balance disturbance. *See* Mobility problems
Bedsore. *See* Decubitus ulcerations
Behavior, 22-23
   inconsistent, 30
   undesirable, 107
      drugs used in treatment of, 192-96
      guidelines to minimize possibility of, 220
      interdisciplinary management of, 220
      intervention guidelines to minimize, 107
      management of, 107
   unsafe, 203-04
Benadryl (diphenhydramine), 22, 23, 81, 192
Beneficence, 226
Benzodiazepines, 22, 23, 192-93
Benztropine (Cogentin), 195
Biomedical research, 226
Bisacodyl (Dulcolax), 198
Bleeding gums, 116
Bowel elimination, 102
   disorders, 135-36
Bradykinesia, 226

C

Cancer, oral, 112-13
Candidiasis, management of, 150
Carbidopa and levodopa (Sinemet), 24, 137
Cardiovascular disease, 138-39
Caregivers, strain felt by, 108. *See also* Family caregivers; Nursing staff
Care levels, 170-72
Caries. *See* Dental caries
Catastrophic reaction, 226
Catheter(s)
   external condom, 101
   indwelling, 101, 136-37
   suprapubic cystotomy, 101
Centrax (prazepam), 192
Cephalosporins, 227
Cerespan (papaverine), 187
Chaplain. *See* Hospital chaplain
Chloral hydrate, 123, 193-94

Chlordiazepoxide (Librium), 192
Chlorpromazine (Thorazine), 195
Choking risks, 99
Cholinergic drugs, 187-89
Cholinergic stimulants, 188-89
Chronic care. *See* Long-term care
Chronic illness, 227
Cimetidine (Tagamet), 9, 190, 191
Clinical management, 70-73
Clinical programs
   successful, 202-03
   unsuccessful, 202
Clonazepam (Clonopin), 193
Clonopin (clonazepam), 193
Clorazepate (Tranxene), 192
Cogentin (benztropine), 195
Cognitive functions
   evaluation of, 16-17
   follow-up evaluation of, 20
Colace (docusate sodium), 198
Cologel (methylcellulose), 197
Comfort of patient, 93, 102-05
   checklist, 103
Communication, 35-36, 107
   facilitation of, 221
Community care, 227
Competence, 227
Condom catheter, 101
Congestive heart failure, 139
Conjunctivitis, management of, 161
Conservatorship, 57-58, 70-72
Constipation, 135-136
   drugs used in treatment of, 197-98
   guidelines to management of, 154
Contractures (muscular), 227
Convulsions, drugs used in treatment of, 196
Cyclandalate (Cyclospasmol), 187
Cyclospasmol (cyclandalate), 187

D

Dalmane (flurazepam), 192
Danthron (Modane), 198
Death, impact of, 40
Death with dignity, 167
Decision-making
   authority, 70-73
   by court, 169
      process elements, 176
   ethical principles in, 177
   by family members, 169, 172-73
   impartial, 176

to institutionalize, 90
to limit medical care, 168-69
  by patient, 169
  by physician, 169
  principled, 176
  process, 176-77
Decubitus ulceration, 142-43
De facto management, 72-73
Degenerative joint disease, 138
Delirium, 227
Dementia, 227
  definition of, 2, 231
  misdiagnosis of, 7-9
  reversible, 8-9
Dementia of the Alzheimer type. *See*
  Alzheimer's disease
Dental care, 120-23. *See also* Oral hygiene
  dental history, obtaining, 120
  examination, 121
  goals of, 120
  medical history, obtaining, 120
  treatment planning, 121-23
    considerations in, *122*
    goals of, *121*
Dental caries, 114, 227
Dentures
  care of, 119
  identification of, 120
Depersonalization, 227
Depression
  drugs used in treatment of, 189-91
  reversible causes of dementia, 8-9
Dermatitis
  atopic, 149
  eczematous, 152
  seborrheic, 149-50
Desipramine (Norpramin), 190
Desyrel (trazodone), 191
Diabetes mellitus, 140
Diagnosis
  discussion of, with family, 19-20
  of problem, 93-94
Diagnosis Related Group (DRG), 227-28
Diarrhea, management of, 157-58
Diazepam (Valium), 23, 179, 193
Digitalis therapy, 139
Digoxin toxicity, 139
Dilantin (phenytoin), 23, 120, 196
Diphenhydramine (Benadryl), 22, 23, 81, 192
Disability, prevention of, 92
Discomfort, management of, 180
Disorientation, 228

Distention. *See* Abdominal pain
Diuretics, complications of, 139
Docusate calcium (Surfak), 198
Docusate potassium (Kasof), 198
Docusate sodium (Colace, Doxinate), 198
Do not resuscitate (DNR), 170
Dopamine, 228
Doxepin (Sinequan), 190
Doxinate (docusate sodium), 198
Driving, 33
Drug(s). *See also specific drugs*
  B-adrenergic receptor antagonists, 194
  antibiotics, 133
  anticonvulsants, 196
  antidepressants, 189-91
  antihypertensive, 139
  aspirin, 191-92
  atropine, 199
  benzodiazepines, 141
  cephalosporins, 133
  cholinergic, 187-89
  diuretics, 139
  effects on mentation, 8-9
  ergoloid mesylates, 185-86
  hypnotic, 9, 23, 100, 192-94
  laxatives, 197-98, 197-98
  morphine, 198
  neuroleptics, 194-96
  psychotropic, 10, 92
  sedative, 9, 22-23, 100, 123
  used in treatment of Alzheimer's disease,
    10, 185-99
    in early stage, 185-92
    in late stage, 196-98
    in middle stage, 192-96
    in terminal stage, 198-99
  vasodilators, 186-87
Dulcolax (bisacodyl), 198
Dying Alzheimer patient family response
  to, 180-81
  staff response to, 181
Dysphagia, 228

E

Eczematous dermatitis, management of, 152
Elavil (amitriptyline), 190
Elimination
  bowel, 102
  urinary, 100-02
Endocrine disease, 140
Ensure Plus, 179

Enternal nutrition, 98
Epidemiology, 2
Ergoloid mesylates (Hydergine, Niloric), 185-86
Estate planning, 63-64. *See also* Legal considerations, property
Ethical dilemma, 228
Ethics committee, 228
Executor, 228

F

Face mask, comfort measures for, 177-78
Facial expressions, interpretation of, 181
Fall. *See* Patient fall
Family. *See also* Family caregiver
  attitudes about respite care, 77-78
  discussion of diagnosis with, 19-20, 30
  early symptoms of Alzheimer dementia and, 29-30
  formation of rapport with, 19-20
  institutional care and, 38-40
  stress of, 212-13
Family caregiver
  caring for, 29-40
  counseling for, 36-37
  education of, 25-26, 31-32
  evaluation of, 31-32
  impact of death on, 40
  institutional care and, 38-40
  needs of, 25-26
  problems of, and intervention strategies for, 26-27, 32-36
  sexuality and, 37-38
  training of, 25
Fecal incontinence. *See* Bowel elimination
Feeding problems, 95-99, 134-35
  coping with, 181
  guidelines for improvement in, 99
  incidence of, 96
  management of, 178-80
Fever, management of, 132-34
  guidelines for, 146-47
Financial issues, 43-52
  personal, 43-44
  societal, 44-45
Financial planning, 64-69
  health care issues, 64-68
Financing of medical care. *See also specific agencies*
  community based resources, 47-48
  government involvement in, 45-47
  home based resources, 47-48
  mechanisms for, 45-47
  personal costs, 43-45
  proposals for, 49-50
  societal costs, 43-45
Floating-bed system, 75-76
Flouride dentifrices, 126
Flouride gels, 117
Fluoride(s), 116-17, 125
Fluorigard (0.05% NaF rinse), 117
Fluphenazine (Prolixin, Permitil), 195
Flurazepam (Dalmane), 192
Foley catheter, 101, 136-37
Food refusal, 228
Force feeding, 228

G

Gait disturbance. *See* Mobility problems
Gastrostomy tube, 228
Gel Kam (0.4% SnF_2 gel), 117
0.4% SnF_2 gels, 125
1.1% NaF gels, 125
Genetics, as risk factor, 6
Geographic location, as risk factor, 6
Geriatric diet, 98
Geriatric Research Education Clinical Center (GRECC), 201-02
Geriatrics, 228
Gerontological nurse practitioner, 129
Gerontology, 228
Glucose polymers (Polycose), 179-80
"Grasp" response, 105-06
Guardianship, 57-58, 70-72

H

Habilitation, 229
Halazepam (Paxipam), 192
Halcion (triazolam), 192, 193
Haldol (haloperidol), 22, 191, 195, 195-96
Halitosis, 229
Hallucinations, 229
Haloperidol (Haldol), 22, 191, 195, 195-96
Head trauma, as risk factor, 6-7
Health care issues, 64-68
  financial planning strategies, 67-68
  physical management requirements, 64-65
  public welfare availability, 66-67
  resource availability, 65-66
Health status, 92
Herpes zoster, management of, 153
Holistic health care, 229

Home assistance, 32-33
Home health care, 229
Homogeneous grouping, 229
Hospice approach, 229
  description of, 169-81
  legal basis of, 176-77
  levels of care in, 170
    assignment of, 171-72
  and quality of life, 177-80
  results of experience with, 175-76
Hospice care, 229
Hospice care plan, 183-84
Hospital chaplain, 172, 174
Huntington's disease, 229
Hydergine (ergoloid mesylates), 185
Hydration status, 99
Hydrogen peroxide, 143
Hyperactivity, 229
Hypercaloric diet, 82, *83*
Hyperglycemia, 140
Hypermetamorphosis, 229
Hyperoralia, 89, 95, 229
Hyperparathyroidism, as cause of reversible dementia, 9
Hypertension, 138-39
Hypnotic drugs, 192-94
Hypoglycemia, 140
  as cause of reversible dementia, 9
Hyponatremia, as cause of reversible dementia, 9
Hypothyroidism, as cause of reversible dementia, 8-9

I

Iatrogenic illness, 229
Ibuprofen (Motrin), 197
Ibuprofen toxicity, 138
Imipramine (Tofranil), 190
Impartial decision, 229
Incidence, 229
Inderal (propranolol), 194
Indocin (indomethacin), 197
Indomethacin (Indocin), 197
Indomethacin toxicity, 138
Infectious disease, management of, 132-34
Instability, 137-38. *See also* Mobility problems
Institutional care, 38-40, 230
  decision for, 90
  issues of, 108
Institutionalization. *See* Institutional care

Intercurrent illness(es). *See also specific illnesses*
  areas of concern in, 132-43
  assessment of, 128
  bowel elimination disorders in, 135-36
  cardiovascular disease in, 138-39
  co-existing neurological disorders in, 140-42
  determining medical care for, 130-31
  discomfort in, 104
  endocrine disease, 140
  examination of patient in, 133
  feeding difficulties in, 134-35
  fever evaluation in, 132-33
  management of, 127-43
    guidelines for, 144-65
  medication review in, 133
  medications, use of in, 133
  mobility problems in, 137-38
  nutritional difficulties in, 134-35
  pulmonary conditions in, 139-40
  staff interview in, 133
  therapeutic plan for, 131-32
  urinary elimination disorders in, 136-37
Interdisciplinary, 230
Interdisciplinary team, 90-91. *See also* Nursing staff
  approach to care, 213-16
  members, 130, 171
  ongoing staff education, 208-10
  orientation and training of, 205-08
  staff selection, criteria for, 204-05
  staff support, 210-13
  support personnel, 221
Interdisciplinary teamwork
  in advanced Alzheimer's dementia, 90-91
  in intercurrent illnesses, 128-30
Intermediate medical care, 230
Interventions, creative, 94
Intervivos estate, 230
Intervivos trust, 59-60
Isoxsuprine, 187

J

Joint tenancies, 60-61
Judicial determination, 70-72

K

Kasof (docusate potassium), 198
Kluver-Bucy syndrome, 25, 95, 134
Konsyl (psyllium), 197
Korsakoff's psychosis, 230

L

Laxatives, 197-98
  bisacodyl, 198
  bulk-forming, 197
  docusates, 198
  osmotic, 197
  prune juice, 198
  stimulant, 197-98
Lecithin, 188
Legal considerations, 53-73
  assets
    identification of, 55-57
    management of, 53-54
    security of, 56
  business issues, 56
  in caring for family caregivers, 34
  clinical management issues, 70-73
  conservatorship, 57-58
  decision-making authority, 70-73
  de facto management, 72-73
  employment issues, 56
  financial planning, 64-69
  guardianship, 70-72
  health care issues, 64-68
  intervivos trust, 59-60
  joint tenancies, 60-61
  judicial determination, 70-72
  liabilities, identification of, 55-57
  management devices available, 57
  mental capacity issues, 68-69
  outright and complete transfer, 61-62
  patient management, 70-73
  personal grant of decision-making authority, 72
  power of attorney, 58-59, 72
  property issues, 62-69
    conservation of, 62-69
    estate planning, 63-64
    management of, 54-62
    preservation of, 62-69
  transfers with retained interest, 61
Levodopa, 188
Levodopa and carbidopa (Sinemet), 24, 137
Liabilities. *See* Legal considerations
Librium (chlordiazepoxide), 192
Liquid diet, 179
Living will, 169
Long-term care, 231
Lopressor (metoprolol), 194
Lorazepam (Ativan), 192
Loxapine (Loxitane), 196
Loxitane (loxapine), 196

Ludiomil (maprotiline), 190-91
Lying. *See* Therapeutic lying

M

Malignant neuroleptic syndrome, 231
Malnutrition, 134
Maprotiline (Ludiomil), 190-91
Mass lesions, as cause of reversible dementia, 8-9
Maternal age, as risk factor, 7
Maternal pathologic bonding, 38
Medicaid, 46-48, 66-67
Medical care
  of alzheimer patient, 10
  decision to limit scope of, 168-69
Medical model of care, 231
Medical technology, 231
Medicare, 45-47, 48, 66
Medication(s). *See also* Drugs
  antiparkinsonism
    adverse reactions of, 142
    dental treatment and, 123
  regimen, review of
    in infectious disease, 133
    in neurological disorders, 141
  salivary gland dysfunction and, 113
Mellaril (thioridazine), 22, 180, 196
Mental capacity issues, 68-69
Mentally dead, 167
Mentor, 231
Merital (Nomifensine), 190
Mesoridazine (Serentil), 196
Metabolic abnormalities, as cause of reversible dementia, 8-9
Metamucil (psyllium), 197
Methylcellulose (Cologel), 197
Methyldopa, 139
Metoprolol (Lopressor), 194
Milk-based foods, monitoring of, 99
Mind reading, 231
Mineral supplementation, 99
Misdiagnosis, 7-9
Mitrolan (polycarbophil), 197
Mobility problems, 137-38
Modane (danthron), 198
Mood, 21
Moral community, 169
Morphine, 198
Motrin (Ibuprofen), 197
Mouth dryness, 113
  management of, 180

Multidisciplinary care, 213-15
Multi-infarct dementia, 231
Multiple sclerosis, 231
Music, effects of, 221
Myoclonic jerks. *See* Myoclonus
Myoclonus, 23, 105, 141

N

Nafronyl, 187
Naproxen toxicity, 138
Nasal cannula, comfort measures for, 177-78
Nausea, management of, 162-63
Navane (thiothixene), 195
Neuroleptics, 194-95
Neurological disorders, 140-42
Neurologic functions, evaluation of, 17, 23-24
Neurotransmitter, 232
Niacin derivatives, 187
Niloric (ergoloid mesylates), 185
Nomifensine (Merital), 190
Noncognitive functions, evaluation of, 17, 21-23
Nonmaleficence, 232
Nonverbal communication, 36
Norepinephrine, 232
Norpramin (desipramine), 190
Nortriptyline (Pamelor), 190
Nosocomial infection, 232
Nurse caregiver. *See* Nursing staff
Nurse practitioners. *See* Nursing staff
Nursing home, 232
Nursing Home Cap Program, 47
Nursing roles in Alzheimer care, *214*
Nursing staff. *See also* Interdisciplinary team
　avoiding depersonalization, 211-12
　behavior criteria for, 206-07
　burnout in, 208-09
　caregiving dilemmas, 210-11
　orientation of, 205-08
　　curriculum for, 223-24
　peer mentoring, 208
　peer teaching, 206-08
　retention incentives, 213
　scapegoating, 211
　selection of, 204-05
　support, 210-13
　training of, 205-08
　training phases of, *206*
　treatment aims of, 207
　understanding stress of families, 212-13
Nutritional compromise, 232
Nutritional difficulties, 134-35
Nutritional needs, 95-99
Nutritional supplementation, 99
Nylidrin, 187

O

Obesity, 134
Occupational therapy, 106, *219*
　program implications for, 218-20
Optimal medical care, 232
Oral cancer, 112,
　incidence rates of, *112*
　survival rates, *113*
Oral disease, 232
Oral health care. *See* Oral hygiene
Oral hygiene, 99-100, 111. *See also* Dental care
　caregiver-patient interchange in, *115*
　daily regimens, 117-119
　denture identification, 120
　dentures, 119
　goal of, 123
　objective of, 116
　personal, 116-20
　preventive care, 115-16
　problems, 111-14
　professional, 120-23
　saliva and, 118, 119
　teeth, *118*
　without teeth, 119
　tongue, cleaning of, 117, *117*
　tools for, 116
　toothbrush identification, 120
　uncooperative patients, 119-20
Oral intake of foods, 99
Orthopnea, 232
Orthostatic hypotension, 137
Ototoxicity, 232
Outpatient. *See also* Alzheimer patient
　management of, 13-27
Outright and complete transfer, 61-62
Oxazepam (Serax), 22, 81, 123, 179, 180, 193
Oxygen therapy, 139-40

P

Pacing, 138
Pain, abdominal, 155-56
Palliative care, 233
Pamelor (nortriptyline), 190
Papaverine (Pavabid, Cerespan), 187
Parkinson's disease, 24, 137-38, 141, 142
Parnate (tranylcypromine), 190

Paroxysmal nocturnal dyspnea, 233
Partial dentures. *See* Dentures
Paternalism, 233
Pathological bonding, 233
Pathological reflex, 233
Patient fall, 148
Pavabid (papaverine), 187
Paxipam (halazepam), 192
Pectin, 197
Periodontal disease, 114
Permitil (fluphenazine), 195
Perseveration, 233
Persistent vegetative state, 167
Personality change, 21
Personality disorders. *See* Behavior
Pharmacologic treatment, 10
Phenobarbital, 23
Phenytoin, 117
Phenytoin (Dilantin), 23, 120, 196
Philosophy of care, 233
Phospho-Soda (sodium phosphates), 197
Physical fitness, 219-20
Physical needs in patient with self-care deficit, 94
Physical therapist, 220
Physician-nurse practitioner partnership, 129-30
Physostigmine (Antilirium), 189
Pick disease, 233
Pindolol (Visken), 194
Plaque, 233
Podiatric problems, 138
Polycarbophil (Mitrolan), 197
Polycose (glucose polymers), 179-80
Posey restraints, 138
Postural drainage, 178
Potassium, hypertension and, 139
Povidone-iodine, 143
Power of attorney, 58-59, 72
Prazepam (Centrax), 192
Preceptor, 234
Prevalence, 234
Preventive medicine, 2-3
Prevident (*1.1% NaF gel*), 117
Primary degenerative dementia, 234. *See also* Alzheimer's disease
Primary health care team, 234
Primary prevention, 234
  of Alzheimer's disease, 5-7
  definition of, 2
Principled decision, 234
Prolixin (fluphenazine), 195

Property. *See* Legal considerations, property
Propranolol (Inderal), 139, 194
Prune juice, 198
Psychosocial functions, evaluation of, 18-19, 26-27
Psyllium (Metamucil, Konsyl), 197
Pulmonary conditions, 139-40
Pureed diet, 98, 179
Pyorrhea, 114

Q

Quality of life, 234
  concept of, 168-69
  hospice approach and, 177-80
  promotion of, 106-07

R

Race, as risk factor, 6
Rashes, management of, 149-52
Recreational therapy, 106, *218*
  goals and objectives of, 217-18
  program implications for, 216-17
Reflexes, pathologic, 105-06
Rehabilitation, 234
Relative risk
  definition of, 3
Relaxation needs, 100
Reserpine, 139
Respiratory distress, management of, 177-78
Respite care, 75-85
  admission, types of, 77
  communication in, 81-82
  crisis admission, 77
  definition of, 75
  description of, 75
  effects of, 84-85
  emotional security in, 80-81
  family attitudes about, 77-78
  inpatient program, 76-77
  institution-based, 75-85
  personal comfort in, 82-84
  physical security in, 80, *80*
  plan, 78-85, *79*
  regular admission, 77
  social interactions in, 81-82
  stabilization of dementia, 84-85
Respite care plan, 78-85, *79*
Respite patients. *See* Alzheimer patient(s)
Responses, positive, stimulation of, 92
Rest needs, 100

Restoril (temazepam), 193
Restraints, 138
Reversible dementia, 8-9
Rheumatologic problems, 138
Ringworm, management of, 151
0.05% NaF rinses, 125
Risk factors, 3

S

Safety of patient, 92, 105-06
Salicylate toxicity, 138
Salivary gland dysfunction, 113. *See also* Mouth dryness
Saliva substitutes, 125-26
Scabies, management of, 150-51
Seborrheic dermatitis, management of, 149-50
Secondary dementia, 234
Secondary prevention, 2
   of Alzheimer's disease, 7-9
Security of patient, 92
Sedatives, 235
Seizure(s), 105, 140-41
   drug-induced, 141
   management of, 164-65
Seizure disorder. *See* Seizure(s)
Sensory deprivation, 235
Sensory overload, 235
Septicemia, 235
Serax (oxazepam), 22, 81, 179, 180, 193
Serentil (mesoridazine), 196
Serotonin, 235
"Seven I's", 128
Sexuality, 37-38
Shadowing, 235
Shingles, management of, 153
Sinemet (carbidopa and levodopa), 24
Sinequan (Doxepin), 190
Skilled nursing facility, 235
Skin condition, 94-95
Sleep disturbance, 23
   drugs used in treatment of, 193-94
Social Security benefits, management of, 62
Social supports, 10
Social worker, 171-73
Socioeconomic status, low, as risk factor, 7
Sodium hypochlorite, 143
Sodium phosphates (Phospho-Soda), 197
Special care unit, 203-205
Spiritual care, 174
Spouse. *See* Family caregiver
SSI (Supplemental Security Income), 46-47

Staff. *See* Interdisciplinary team
Staff burnout, 208-09
Staging of the disease, 235
Suctioning, 178
Sundowning, 235
Supplemental Security Income (SSI), 46-47
Supportive care, 235
Suprapubic cystotomy catheter, 101
Surfak (docusate calcium), 198
Sustacal, 178, 179
Swallowing problems, 140, 179
Symptom heterogeneity, 235

T

Tagamet (cimetidine), 190, 191
Team approach to care, 90-91, 98. *See also* Interdisciplinary treatment team
Teeth, care of, 118-19. *See also* Oral hygiene
Temazepam (Restoril), 193
Terminal care, 236
Terminal illness, 236
Tertiary prevention, 9-10
   definition of, 2-3
Testamentary substitute, 236
Tetrahydroaminoacridine (THA), 189
THA (tetrahydroaminoacridine), 189
Theraflur (*1.1% NaF gel*), 117
Therapeutic lying, 34-35
Therapeutic milieu, 236
Therapeutic recreation. *See* Recreational therapy
Thioridazine (Mellaril), 22, 180, 196
Thiothixene (Navane), 195
Thorazine (chlorpromazine), 195
Tinea corporis, management of, 151
Tinea pedis, management of, 151-52
Tin-Gel, 180
Tobacco, use of and cancer, 112
Tofranil (imipramine), 190
Tongue, care of, 117, *117*. *See also* Oral hygiene
Toothbrush identification, 120
Tooth loss, 114
Traditional estate plan, 236
Transfers with retained interest, 61
Tranxene (clorazepate), 192
Tranylcypromine (Parnate), 190
Trauma, management of, 148
Trazodone (Desyrel), 191
Treatment goals, 92-93
Trendelenburg position, 178
Triazolam (Halcion), 192, 193
Trihexyphenidyl (Artane), 195

Index

U

Ulcerations. *See* Decubitus ulcerations
Uncoordinated swallowing, 236
Urinary elimination, 100-02
Urinary incontinence, 24-25, 136-37
   ascorbic acid and, 137
   management of, 100-02
Urinary tract infection, management of, 159-60
Urosepsis, 236

V

VA (Veterans Administration), 47
Valium (diazepam), 23, 179, 193, *193*
Vascular dementia. *See* Multi-infarct dementia
Vasodilation, 187
Vasodilator drugs, 186-87
Veterans Administration (VA), 47, 236
Violence, 34
Visken (pindolol), 194

Visual impairment, 137
Vitamin supplementation, 99, 134-35
Vocalization, loud, 180
Vomiting, management of, 162-63

W

Walkers heel, 236
Weight changes, 99
Weight loss, 134-35
Will, 237

X

Xanax (alprazolam), 192
Xerostomia, 113

Y

Yelling, 180

About the Editors

Ladislav Volicer, MD, PhD, received his medical degree in 1959 at the Charles University in Prague, Czechoslovakia, and doctorate in Pharmacology in 1964 from the Pharmacological Institute, Czechoslovak Academy of Science, Prague, Czechoslovakia. He has been a Visiting Associate at the National Heart Institute, National Institutes of Health, Bethesda, Maryland, Research Associate at the Institute of Pharmacology, Czechoslovak Academy of Science, and Research Assistant Professor at the Department of Pharmacology, University of Munich. In 1969, Dr. Volicer joined Boston University School of Medicine where he is currently a Professor of Pharmacology and Psychiatry, and Assistant Professor of Medicine. In 1978, Dr. Volicer joined the Geriatric Research Education Clinical Center at the E.N. Rogers Memorial Veterans Hospital. He served as an Acting Director in 1985-86, and is currently a Deputy Director of the Center.

Kathy J. Fabiszewski, RN, MS, serves as Gerontological Nurse Practitioner in the Dementia Study Unit of the E.N. Rogers Memorial Veterans Hospital in Bedford, Massachusetts. She received her Bachelor of Science degree in nursing from Salem State College and her Master of Science degree in Gerontological Nursing, with preparation as a Nurse Practitioner, from the University of Lowell, Lowell, Massachusetts. Currently, she serves as Instructor in the Department of Health, College of Health Professions at the University of Lowell and is also an adjunct clinical faculty member in the Graduate School of Nursing. She is a charter member of Sigma Theta Tau, Eta Tau Chapter and Eta Omega Chapter, recipient of the Outstanding Young Woman of American Award, and is active in a number of professional organizations including the American Nurses' Association, the Gerontolgical Society of America, and the Alzheimer's Disease and Related Disorders Association. In addition, she is an Officer in the United States Army Reserves, Army Nurse Corps, and has been awarded the Army Commendation Medal and the Army Achievement Medal.

Yvette L. Rheaume, RN, BSN, is a Nursing Unit Administrator for the Dementia Study Unit at the E.N. Rogers Memorial Veterans Hospital in Bedford, Massachusetts. She received her Bachelor of Science in Nursing degree from St. Anselm's College and is ANA certified in Gerontological Nursing. Currently, she is matriculating for a masters degree in Business Administration at the University of New Hampshire Graduate School of Business. She has co-authored several papers in the area of scientific research and management of the patient with Alzheimer's Disease.

Kathryn E. Lasch, MSW, PhD, holds a Bachelor of Arts degree in psychology and Masters of Science of Social Work (MSSW) from the University of Wisconsin. She received a Masters in sociology and a doctorate in sociology from the University of Michigan. She received a dissertation grant from the National Center for Health Services Research. Her thesis was entitled "The Political Culture of Medical Technology Assessment". She received a postdoctoral fellowship from the Institution of Social and Policy Studies, Yale University, and worked on an analysis of birth cohort effects in the rates of psychiatric disorder with the Depression Research Unit, Yale University. She currently is employed as a medical sociologist by the Veterans Hospital, Bedford, Massachusetts, and is a research associate in the University Professors Program at Boston University. In addition, she is a visiting lecturer in the Community Health Program, Tufts University.